KU-683-120

The Courage
Book of Sporting Heroes
1884–1984

THE COURAGE BOOK OF SPORTING HEROES 1884-1984

Compiled and edited by Chris Rhys

SELECTION PANEL
Bill Beaumont · Bobby Charlton · Denis Compton · Henry Cooper · David Hemery

Stanley Paul

London Melbourne Sydney Auckland Johannesburg

To Molopo

Stanley Paul & Co. Ltd

An imprint of the Hutchinson Publishing Group

17–21 Conway Street, London W1P 6JD

Hutchinson Publishing Group (Australia) Pty Ltd
16–22 Church Street, Hawthorn, Melbourne, Victoria 3122

Hutchinson Group (NZ) Ltd
32–34 View Road, PO Box 40–086, Glenfield, Auckland 10

Hutchinson Group (SA) Pty Ltd
PO Box 337, Bergvlei 2012, South Africa

First published 1984
© Chris Rhys 1984

Set in Monophoto Photina by Jolly & Barber Ltd, Rugby

Printed and bound in Great Britain by Butler & Tanner Ltd,
Frome and London

This book is sold subject to the condition that it shall not by way
of trade or otherwise be lent, resold, hired out or otherwise
circulated without the publisher's prior consent in any form of
binding other than that in which it is published and without a
similar condition including this condition being imposed on the
subsequent purchaser

Rhys, Chris
    Our greatest sporting heroes 1884–1984.
    1. Athletes – Biography   2. Games – Biography
    I. Title
    796′.092′2   GV697.A1

ISBN 0 09 153620 0

Contents

Preface

The association between Courage and the best of sporting achievements extends over many years through an active sponsorship programme. It is appropriate to build on this association with our support for a publication which celebrates 100 great sporting heroes of the past century.

Chris Rhys has compiled a book which not only informs and entertains, but also fuels debate and controversy. However, whilst there may be arguments about the relative merits of stars from the great variety of sports covered, all will agree that each and every sportsman and sportswoman chosen by the distinguished selection panel is a true 'sporting hero'.

Courage is proud to have its name coupled with a work which records so much outstanding endeavour. Those of us who play at less illustrious levels or merely applaud from the sidelines will find inspiration in this splendid catalogue of a century of sporting brilliance.

Mike Reynolds
Director of Publicity and Sponsorship
Courage Limited

Acknowledgements

In compiling *The Courage Book of Sporting Heroes* I have consulted various reference books too numerous to mention individually but to which I owe a great debt. Ian Morrison's ability to supplement my basic research with additional material has been invaluable.

My colleagues, Andy Smith and Ian Carnaby, at the BBC Sports Desk have been a great help, and thanks are also due to Roddy Bloomfield and Dominique Shead at Stanley Paul for their patience and guidance throughout the many revisions and updating of the information.

Photographic acknowledgements

For permission to reproduce copyright photographs, the publishers would like to thank Sport & General Press Agency, All-Sport Photographic, Colorsport, *Boxing News*, Associated Sports Photography, Peter Roberts, Gilbert Odd, Mike Patrick, Keystone Press Agency, Press Association, Le-Roye Productions Ltd, Patrick Eagar, Ken Kelly, E. D. Lacey and Syndication International.

Introduction

Selecting a hundred sporting heroes would, on the face of it, appear to be a fairly straightforward task. Two thirds of the entries virtually picked themselves. Then, as in arguments on the merits of our international cricket, rugby and football teams, or even of local darts sides, divergences occurred and matters became complicated.

We made our selection in the following way. To begin with we collected relevant information from the national sporting bodies on the number of people actively playing various games and the number of spectators. When those lists were collected, we next considered the worldwide appeal of each sport, whether it was thought of as a national sport in Britain, and the radio and television audience figures.

All this information was graded and fed into a small computer for analysis. The results were as follows:

1 Football, cricket, athletics
2 Racing, Rugby Union, boxing, tennis, motor racing, golf
3 Equestrian sports (apart from racing) and the growth sports of gymnastics, snooker, darts, skating and skiing
4 Speedway, Rugby League, weightlifting, cycling, squash, motor-cycling, bowls, swimming
5 Minor sports

Next the panel made its selection. John Goodbody, Reg Gutteridge and Reg Hayter added valued and constructive observations, two BBC sports commentators gave their opinions and finally five enthusiasts from a local quiz league made suggestions. On the basis of this, a list of 170 names was drawn up.

The panel was asked to bear in mind the following criteria when making its selection:

(a) whether the sportsman was an Olympic or world champion
(b) whether the sportsman was front-page news or charismatic
(c) whether he was a television personality
(d) that due credit be given to 'Old Time Greats'
(e) women in sport
(f) each panellist's choice in his own sport
(g) the popularity of a particular sport
(h) overseas stars

Marks out of 10 were then awarded in these categories and all the results were fed back into the computer. The result is *The Courage Book of Sporting Heroes*.

Then, just when the selection seemed watertight, along came John McEnroe, Viv Richards, Tessa Sanderson and others.

The debate continues. An uncontentious solution will never finally be found. Your views may not coincide completely with those of the panel, but we hope that the personalities included in this book represent the best in sporting achievement over the past hundred years.

Vassily Alexeev

In his prime, Vassily Alexeev, world super heavyweight weightlifting champion from 1970 to 1977, was the most decorated man in the Soviet Union. His optimum weight was around 23 st 5 lb. To maintain that bulk breakfast would be an omelette. It contained thirty-six eggs. His normal lunch was six steaks washed down with twenty pints of beer. After training, he would return home, and have the same again. The Russian Olympic handbook listed his hobby as cooking!

Vassily was born in the village of Pokrovo-Shishkino, in the Ryazan region of the Soviet Union, 150 miles southeast of Moscow. He preferred to remain in the locality, took up weightlifting as a hobby, coached himself, and also gained a degree in mining engineering at Trud College in Ryazan.

He first made the national squad in 1970. He was then twenty-eight years old (born 7 January 1942). A family man with two children, he enjoyed reading. In the same year he became national and world champion in the over-110-kg class, and began a domination of that division which was to last for seven years. His frame was as recognizable as Muhammad Ali's. He won two Olympic titles in 1972 and 1976, was world champion for eight years and was European champion from 1970 to 1978. Such was his domination that his victory in 1976 at the Montreal Olympics was by the staggering margin of 77 lb.

His training schedule was unique: he trained when he wanted to. Sometimes, he didn't train at all. The one rule he made was that whatever training he did, it was not repetition work.

His wife, Olympiada Ivanova, a qualified masseuse, was a constant help.

Vassily's finale was at the Moscow Olympics. No longer Soviet champion, he travelled the 150 miles to the Lenin Stadium and was given the honour of leading the host nation at the opening ceremony. He held the national flag aloft in his massive right fist without need for a support socket. But, in competition, going for a hat trick of Olympic gold medals and under pressure from the new discovery, Sultambai Rakhmanov, a schoolteacher from the Ukraine, Vassily slipped in an undignified heap during the clean and jerk routine and failed to record a lift. With uncharacteristic charity, his government upped his military rank to major and awarded him the title of honoured Master of Sport.

Although Vassily Alexeev's name has since been erased from the world record lists, he still holds one world record. His aim was to set 100 world records. Between 20 January 1970 and 1 November 1977 he set eighty. He is the most prolific world record breaker in the history of any sport.

Weightlifting Rules

Each competitor has three attempts at each weight, and must successfully execute two methods of lift – the 'snatch' and the 'jerk'. The jerk is a two-movement lift, from floor to shoulders, and then to the fully extended arm lift above the head. The snatch is a one-movement lift direct from the floor to outstretched arms above the head.

The totals of a competitor's best lift with each method are added together to give his aggregate lift, which counts towards his final score. He cannot proceed to a greater weight until he has successfully lifted the preceding weight, and he cannot attempt a weight lower than that previously lifted by another competitor.

FACTFILE

Born 7 January 1942, Pokrovo-Shishkino, Ryazan, USSR

European champion	World champion	Olympic champion
1970	1970	1972
1971	1971	1976 (440 kg)
1972	1972	
1973 (417.5 kg)	1973 (402.5 kg)	
1974 (422.5 kg)	1974 (425 kg)	
1975 (427.5 kg)	1975 (427.5 kg)	
1976 (Olympic champion)	1976 (Olympic champion)	
1977 (430 kg)	1977 (430 kg)	
1978 (415 kg)		

(Until 1972, overall champions were those with the best totals from three lifts – the snatch, the jerk and the clean and press. The latter lift was then dropped from the programme. The weights above are from the winning totals from 1973.)

*Alexeev could jerk over 550 lb (250 kg), which was nearly twice his own weight, but to give some idea of what 550 lb is like, here are some comparisons. It is the equivalent to three and a half 11-st men, 110 average house bricks, 250 bags of sugar, 585 soccer balls, 2933 medium-sized eggs

*Alexeev's dimensions were: weight 23 st 5 lb; chest 58 in; biceps 21 in; waist 48 in; thighs 34 in (more than an average man's waist)

The shapely Vassily Alexeev, the most prolific record-breaker in the history of international sport

Fred Archer

Fred Archer committed suicide at the age of twenty-nine. In a fit of delirium brought on by the constant battle to keep his riding weight down, and with the death of his young wife two years earlier still tormenting him, he took a gun from his bedside table and ended one of the most glittering careers British racing has ever known.

Archer died in 1886. He had just become champion jockey for the thirteenth consecutive season; in all he rode 2748 winners from 8084 mounts – a success ratio of better than one in three. Twenty-one Classics came his way, and in the year before his death he partnered the winners of 246 races – a record which stood until Gordon Richards broke it in 1933. He rode 200 or more winners in a season on eight occasions; even in these days of helicopter travel and night meetings, Lester Piggott's best total is 191.

To understand his meteoric rise, and the tragedy which ensued, it is necessary to know something of the racing world of a century ago. Archer was born in Cheltenham in 1857, the son of a steeple-

FACTFILE

Born 11 January 1857, Cheltenham, England
Died 8 November 1886, Newmarket, England

Champion jockey 1874, 1875, 1876, 1877, 1878, 1879, 1880, 1881, 1882, 1883, 1884, 1885, 1886
Most winners in one season 246 (in 1885)

*Archer was described as 'The Best Friend the Punter Ever Had' and this was certainly apt when one looks at the prices of his Classic winners: fifteen of the twenty-one at odds of 5–1 or less, and only two of them at 20–1 or more. The full list is as follows:

Price	Horse	Race	Year
1–7	Ormonde	St Leger	1886
1–3	Wheel of Fortune	Oaks	1879
1–3	Paradox	2000 Gns	1885
40–85	Ormonde	Derby	1886
8–15	Melton	St Leger	1885
40–75	Wheel of Fortune	1000 Gns	1879
5–4	Spinaway	Oaks	1875
65–40	Silvio	St Leger	1877
65–40	Jannette	Oaks	1878
15–8	Melton	Derby	1885
2–1	Bend Or	Derby	1880
2–1	Iroquois	St Leger	1881
85–40	Lonely	Oaks	1885
5–2	Jannette	St Leger	1878
9–2	Galliard	2000 Gns	1883
11–2	Iroquois	Derby	1881
10–1	Spinaway	1000 Gns	1875
10–1	Atlantic	2000 Gns	1874
100–9	Silvio	Derby	1877
25–1	Charibert	2000 Gns	1879
40–1	Dutch Oven	St Leger	1882

*Archer's father won the 1858 Grand National on Little Charlie
*Archer won the Caesarewitch in 1872, at the age of fifteen
*His first race in public (excluding pony races) was on 28 September 1870, when he rode Athol Daisy to victory in the Nursery Handicap at Chesterfield
*His last race was on 4 November 1886, when he rode Tommy Tittlemouse in the Castle Selling Plate at Lewes
*His younger brother, Charles Edward Archer (1858–1922), was a jockey until he developed weight problems, and then turned to training. He trained winners of the Manchester Cup, the Stewards' Cup, the Manchester November Handicap, and the Lincoln in 1893 and 1900. He was a heavy gambler, and there were many unproven rumours of him and Fred being in collusion
*Archer died on 8 November 1886 (his wife died on 7 November 1884) when, at 2.25 p.m., his sister, Mrs Colman, visited him on his sick bed, and in front of her he took a revolver and shot himself in the mouth. The incident took place at his home at Falmouth House, Newmarket. The jury at the inquest returned that he had 'committed suicide whilst temporarily insane'. He was buried at Newmarket Cemetery on Friday, 12 November 1885. His estate was £60,000
*Now, in the age of the train and with the advent of the private helicopter, top jockeys can easily travel from meeting to meeting, but a hundred years ago it was not so easy to get around the country.

Compare Fred Archer's riding programme for the first week in July 1882 with Lester Piggott's for the corresponding week exactly 100 years later:

Fred Archer (1882)

Monday, 3 July	No mounts	
Tuesday, 4 July	Newmarket	5 mounts (3 × 1st)
Wednesday, 5 July	Newmarket	5 mounts (2 × 1st, 2 × 2nd, 1 × 3rd)
Thursday, 6 July	Newmarket	5 mounts (4 × 1st, 1 × 2nd)
Friday, 7 July	Newmarket	4 mounts (1 × 1st, 3 × 2nd)
Saturday, 8 July	No mounts	

Lester Piggott (1982)

Monday, 5 July	Windsor	4 mounts (1 × 1st, 1 × 2nd, 1 × 3rd)
Tuesday, 6 July	Newmarket	5 mounts (2 × 1st, 1 × 2nd, 1 × 3rd)
Wednesday, 7 July	Newmarket	5 mounts (2 × 1st, 1 × 3rd)
Thursday, 8 July	Newmarket	6 mounts (no placings)
Friday, 9 July	York	5 mounts (2 × 1st, 2 × 3rd)
	Chester	5 mounts (3 × 1st)
Saturday, 10 July	York	5 mounts (1 × 1st, 1 × 2nd, 1 × 3rd)

	Archer	Piggott
Total meetings	4	7
Total courses	1	4
Total mounts	19	35
Firsts	10	11
Seconds	6	3
Thirds	1	6
Unplaced	2	15
Total winners that season	210	188

A painting of Fred Archer on the Triple Crown winner Ormonde in 1886

chase jockey, William Archer. He became apprenticed to trainer Matthew Dawson at Heath House, Newmarket, when he was only eleven and rode his first winner under Jockey Club Rules at thirteen. When he rode Lord Falmouth's Atlantic to victory in the 2000 Guineas in 1874 his position as stable jockey was assured; indeed he went on to ride the winners of eleven more Classics in the same colours.

Racing dominated the sporting scene. London cab drivers would hail each other with cries of 'Archer's up!' and the thousands who followed his mounts seldom experienced a lean run. He was utterly dedicated to passing the post first; meek and solemn he may have looked, but behind the sad brown eyes there burned a determination to succeed. He used his long legs to squeeze the last ounce out of his mounts; he was much freer with the whip than would be tolerated nowadays; and on one occasion he even put his brother Charles over the rails rather than let him sneak up on the inside. A reputation for meanness was justified, and indeed amused him, but he was never afraid to back his fancy, even if he then rode like a demon to beat the horse he'd supported. Like many great jockeys before and since, Archer made nothing from his betting exploits, and the scurrilous stories that occasionally circulated in the less reputable press were almost certainly without foundation. Yet as his popularity reached its height, few appreciated the immense physical toll his efforts were taking. Like Piggott, Archer stood 5 ft 10 inches, but he

had much greater difficulty in keeping his weight down and the necessary ruthless wasting both weakened and depressed him.

In 1880 he won the Derby by a head on Bend Or, despite having shed a stone the previous week. A vicious horse named Muley Edris had savaged him on the gallops and when he rode in the big race one arm was almost useless, strapped to a steel brace.

His iron determination overcame all discomfort, but then personal tragedy struck. He had married Matthew Dawson's niece, Helen Rose, but their first child, a son born in January 1884, lived only a few hours. Later the same year whilst riding at Liverpool, he was informed that his wife had given birth to a daughter. He hurried home full of joy, but it was his last happy moment for he arrived to find Helen Rose dying.

Archer never recovered, although it was typical of him that the following year he rode more winners than ever before. Shortly before his death he realized the need to take a long rest, but he had driven himself so mercilessly in the preceding weeks that the fever had too strong a hold. He died in his sister's arms.

Fred Archer's epitaph read: 'The backers have lost the best friend they ever had.' True as that undoubtedly was, some will prefer the perhaps apocryphal story of the young jockey, head in hands in the weighing room, shedding tears because he'd been unable to ride both winners in a dead heat.

Henry Armstrong

Henry Armstrong is the only boxer to have held three world boxing titles at the same time. In 1938 he was champion of the world in the featherweight, lightweight and welterweight divisions. But when you look at Armstrong's birthdate, something unusual can be sensed – he was born on 12.12.12 (12 December 1912).

Home was Columbus, Mississippi, not Columbus, Ohio, and he was christened Henry Jackson. He was brought up in St Louis, before moving to Los Angeles. There he met Al Jolson, who, hearing about his ability as an amateur boxer (fifty-eight wins in sixty-two contests), introduced him to manager Eddie Mead. Grateful for the

FACTFILE

Born 12 December 1912 (12.12.12), Columbus, Mississippi

First professional fight 27 July 1931, *v.* Al Iovino (ko by 3)
Total professional fights 175
    Wins 144
    Kos 97
    Draws 9
    Defeats 22
Last professional fight 14 February 1945, *v.* Chester Slider (l pts 10)
World title fights 26
    Wins 22

*Apart from Armstrong six men have held three different world titles:

Roberto Duran 1972 lightweight, 1980 WBC welterweight, 1983 WBA light middleweight
Alexis Arguello 1974 WBA featherweight, 1978 WBC junior lightweight, 1981 WBC lightweight
Bob Fitzsimmons 1891 middleweight, 1897 heavyweight, 1903 light heavyweight
Barney Ross 1933 lightweight, 1933 junior welterweight, 1934 welterweight
Wilfredo Benitez 1976 WBA light welterweight, 1979 WBC welterweight, 1981 WBC light middleweight
Tony Canzoneri 1928 featherweight, 1930 lightweight, 1931 junior welterweight

Armstrong's world title fights

	Featherweight	Lightweight	Welterweight	Middleweight
29.10.37	Pete Sarron w ko 6			
31. 5.38			Barney Ross w pts 15	
17. 8.38		Lou Ambers w pts 15		
9.38	Relinquished title			
25.11.38			Ceferino Garcia w pts 15	
5.12.38			Al Manfredo w ko 3	
10. 1.39			Baby Arizmendi w pts 10	
4. 3.39			Bobby Pacho w ko 4	
16. 3.39			Lew Feldman w ko 1	
31. 3.39			Davey Day w ko 2	
25. 5.39			Ernie Roderick w pts 15	
22. 8.39		Lou Ambers l pts 15		
9.10.39			Al Manfredo w ko 4	
13.10.39			Howard Scott w ko 2	
20.10.39			Ritchie Fontaine w ko 3	
24.10.39			Jimmy Garrison w pts 10	
30.10.39			Bobby Pacho w ko 4	
11.12.39			Jimmy Garrison w ko 7	
4. 1.40			Joe Ghounly w ko 5	
24. 1.40			Pedro Montanez w ko 9	
1. 3.40				Cerefino Garcia drew 10
26. 4.40			Paul Junior w ko 7	
24. 5.40			Ralph Zanelli w ko 5	
21. 6.40			Paul Junior w ko 3	
23. 9.40			Phil Furr w ko 4	
4.10.40			Fritzie Zivic l pts 15	
17. 1.41			Fritzie Zivic l rsf 12	

Professional defeats

1931	Al Iovino	ko by	3
1932	Eddie Trujillo	pts	4
	Al Greenfield	pts	4
	Baby Manuel	pts	6
1933	Baby Arizmendi	pts	10
1934	Baby Arizmendi	pts	12
	Baby Manuel	pts	10
1935	Davey Abad	pts	10
	Baby Arizmendi	pts	12
1936	Joe Conde	pts	10
	Ritchie Fontaine	pts	10
	Tony Chavaz	dis	8
1939	Lou Ambers (World lightweight title)	pts	15
1940	Fritzie Zivic (World welterweight title)	pts	15
1941	Fritzie Zivic (World welterweight title)	ko by	12
1942	Reuben Shank	pts	10
1943	Willie Joyce	pts	10
	Beau Jack	pts	10
	Ray Robinson	pts	10
1944	Willie Joyce	pts	10
	John Thomas	pts	10
1945	Chester Slider	pts	10

Henry Armstrong captures the first of his world titles, battering Pete Sarron into a sixth-round submission, to take the world featherweight championship in 1937

chance, he began his early career, not as Henry Jackson, but as 'Melody' Jackson. They played the wrong tune in his first professional fight: he was knocked out in three rounds by Al Iovino in Braddock, Pennsylvania, on 27 July 1931.

Six years later he was to fight for the world title. He had progressed through a crop of Young Joes, Babys and Kids to a shot at the world featherweight title held by Pete Sarron. Armstrong had already had no fewer than eighty-six fights and had lost twelve. Sarron was counted out in the sixth round, in New York.

Now fighting under the name Henry Armstrong and managed by Mead and Wirt Ross, he was in a remarkable groove. From January 1937 to August 1939 he won forty-six consecutive fights – thirty-nine inside the distance – and claimed three world titles.

On 31 May 1938 Armstrong outpointed the legendary Barney Ross to win the welterweight title. In his next fight he stepped down a division to outpoint Lou Ambers for the lightweight crown. That night, 17 August 1938, he was champion in three weight divisions at the same time.

The record lasted until September 1938. Now operating as a welterweight, he couldn't make the featherweight limit of 9 st. He was 10 st 5 lb and fit. He relinquished the title.

He contented himself with defending the welterweight title. Stepping down to the lightweights, he was outpointed by Ambers in August 1939. He couldn't make the lightweight limit either. The forty-six fight winning streak had gone.

Now based firmly in the welterweights, Armstrong tried for his fourth title. Having beaten Ceferino Garcia of Cuba in a welterweight

title defence a couple of years earlier, he was disappointed by a drawn match for the middleweight championship of the world in March 1940. Later that same year he lost the welterweight title on points to Fritzie Zivic. In January 1941, in an attempt to regain the title, Zivic knocked him out in twelve rounds. That was only his second knockout defeat in 126 fights; the first was by Iovino in his very first fight.

After losing the title, Armstrong had another forty-nine fights. He lost only seven. A win over Zivic was no consolation; Zivic had lost the title. He fought five world champions. Only three beat him. One was a young up-and-coming prospect – Sugar Ray Robinson.

Armstrong battled on until 1945. On St Valentine's Day he was outpointed over ten rounds by Chester Slider, whoever he was. That was it.

He had 175 fights, winning 144 and losing twenty-two. Only six boxers had a better record than Armstrong's ninety-seven knockouts. 'Homicide Hank', as he was known, had great stamina. He was fast, and had a reputation to the end of being an all-out attacking boxer. He was durable; only Iovino and Zivic knocked him out.

For five years after retirement Armstrong seemed bent on self-destruction. His business deals were mismanaged. Found drunk and penniless in a gutter, he was appalled by his own condition. He turned to the church for help.

In 1951 he became an ordained Baptist minister.

Severiano Ballesteros

Probably the best and certainly the most exciting golfer in the world today, Seve Ballesteros has destroyed the myth of American invincibility and the idea that to play at the highest possible level it is necessary to be a regular on the US Tour.

Ballesteros is rated by Jack Nicklaus as the longest hitter in the world with a 1 iron and he is capable of making the most impossible-looking shots feasible. Typically, in his match with Arnold Palmer in the 1983 World Matchplay Championship, Palmer had not had a bogey all day and approaching the seventeenth was 2 up. Ballesteros won the hole with a birdie, then levelled with a brilliant eagle on the last with a 50-yard chip. The game went into sudden death and it was Ballesteros who survived, winning at the twenty-first.

He first appeared in Europe in 1974 – largely unnoticed by the British press – and finished 118th in the order of merit. The Spanish press, preoccupied with football and cycling, also largely ignored him. But in 1976 in the Open at Royal Birkdale he led for the first three rounds and the question being asked was whether this unknown teenager (he was nineteen years three months old) could hold on against the big guns. The short answer was no; Johnny Miller overhauled him, and Ballesteros found himself joint second with Nicklaus. But at last Europe had discovered a new star.

By the end of 1978 he had won fifteen events, including his first on the US Tour – the Greater Greensboro' Open. He had only two wins in 1979, but one was at Lytham in the Open. He became the third youngest winner ever and the first continental European winner since Arnaud Massy in 1907.

The Americans remained unimpressed. They called him 'the car-park golfer' after a remarkable shot at the sixteenth on his final round in 1979 at Lytham – played out of the car park and onto the green to within 15 feet of the pin. The meticulous Hale Irwin, two ahead at the start of the day, watched aghast as Ballesteros blasted into, and out of, sand traps and rough to snatch the lead.

Ballesteros won on a course which the experts said was unsuited to his wild game. Accuracy was supposed to be required. Ballesteros hit only two fairways in the last two rounds and thrilled the fans as he launched into massive drives, then surged down the fairways after the ball. One American writer said, 'If Houdini could hit a 300-yard drive, he might have been Ballesteros.'

Less than a year later the Americans were starting to warm to the handsome young Spaniard. He won the Masters at Augusta. He shot 66, then 69 and 68, to go into the last round leading by 7 strokes. By the turn he was 10 ahead but then dropped 5 shots, found the water twice, before coming home to win – the youngest Masters winner ever.

In 1981 and 1982 he dispelled the thoughts of those who felt he would not make a good matchplay golfer. He beat Ben Crenshaw in the World Matchplay final at Wentworth in 1981 in a close contest and retained the title a year later when he birdied the first play-off hole in his match with Sandy Lyle, putting through a Red Sea parting of water on the green.

By the end of 1983 at the age of twenty-six he had won twelve more professional tournaments than Nicklaus at the same age, including his second Masters. He started his final round at Augusta in 1983 with an outward half of 31 and chipped audaciously at the last to win by 4 strokes.

'There are many judges,' says Michael Hobbs in his book 'Fifty Greatest Golfers', 'who would argue that no contemporary or indeed predecessor has been so outstanding for the contrasting talents of prodigious power and subtlety.'

After an uninspired start to the 1984 season – perhaps living in the USA did not help – Ballesteros returned to Europe and handsomely won his second British Open. Two European tournament winners, Vicente Fernandez and Jaime Gonzalez, both South Americans, advised some correction to Ballesteros's swing. A birdie on the seventy-second hole of the Open at St Andrews gave him a tournament statistic of 12 under par and a win by 2 strokes from defending champion Tom Watson and the West German Bernhard Langer.

Seve lives in his family's house at Santander in northern Spain, listens to tapes of his Barcelona psychiatrist when problems arise, and answers facile questions with a sharpness and wit sometimes disguised by his heavy accent. 'We understand you have four girl-friends.' 'Maybe more,' he replies, flashing his dazzling smile. 'It's very boring playing the same course every day.'

FACTFILE

Born 9 April 1957, Pedrena, Spain

'Big Four' wins 4
British Open 1979, 1984
US Masters 1981, 1983
Ryder Cup appearances 1979, 1981, 1983
World Cup
   Team 1976 (with M. Pinero), 1977 (with A. Garrido)
World Matchplay 1981 (beat B. Crenshaw), 1982 (beat S. Lyle)

*In 1974, his first year on the European Tour, Ballesteros finished with £2915 in prize money

*He celebrated his twentieth birthday whilst competing in the 1977 US Masters – the youngest competitor ever in the tournament
*After his British Open win in 1979, he was honoured by having a cask of Jerez sherry dedicated to him, one of only seven people to have had such an honour bestowed upon them –'Winston Churchill, Napoleon and the Beatles being the others
*By the end of 1983 he had won £487,744 in Europe – the largest sum won by any player on the European Tour
*He has chalked up victories on all five continents
*Has so far won the Opens of Britain, Holland, France, Switzerland, Germany, Japan, Spain and Ireland
*His brother, Manuel, is also a professional golfer
*Seve is attached to La Manga Golf Club in Spain

The feature of Ballesteros's game – recovery shots from the rough, bunkers, bushes and even car parks. Here he plays out of the sand in the 1983 Irish Open

Sir Roger Bannister

The 6th of May 1954 was one of those days in history when people remember where they were because something out of the ordinary happened. At 6.07 p.m., at the Iffley Road track, home of the Oxford University Athletics Club, Roger Bannister, running for the AAA, broke the four-minute barrier for the mile. It was like the first landing on the moon. The announcement was made, fittingly, by Norris McWhirter (later to find fame as editor and compiler of *The Guinness Book of Records*) over the PA system that Bannister had recorded a time of 3 minutes 59.4 seconds. Bannister collapsed into the arms of the Reverend Nicholas Stacey. The BBC thought the record so significant that they interrupted the news to make the announcement.

Ironically, Iffley Road was where athletics success first began for Roger Gilbert Bannister. In 1946, as an undergraduate, he won the Freshmen's Sports mile. His time was seven seconds under five minutes.

Bannister's international record was remarkably brief. He took the bronze medal in the 800 metres in the European Championships in 1950 before he had even won an AAA title. In 1951 he won the mile in the AAA Championships in 4 minutes 7.8 seconds, won the 880 yards the following year, and returned to miling to take the 1953 and 1954 championships. In the 1952 Olympics, like his friend and Oxford colleague Chris Chataway, he had to be content with a fourth place.

1954 was a momentous year. Bannister, now a doctor, had often talked with his friends Chataway and Chris Brasher about the possibility of breaking the four-minute barrier. The three were pioneers of new training methods and of pace judgement of races.

The world mile record had come to a full stop. Like Coe and Ovett, two athletes from the same country had taken large chunks out of the record. In this case the country was Sweden; the athletes were Gundar Haegg and Arne Andersson. In eight years the pair had each broken the record three times and reduced the time by five seconds until Haegg had set the then existing mark at 4:01.4 in 1945. There it stayed for nine years. Until Bannister came along, the pace judged to perfection by Chataway and Brasher.

Like most barriers, once broken the floodgates open. The Australian John Landy, who had also dedicated himself to being the first four-minute miler, set a new mark of 3:57.9 at Turku in Finland on 21 June.

When the two met on 7 August 1954 at the Commonwealth Games in Vancouver, the term 'Mile of the Century' was appropriate. Bannister and Landy were the world's only sub-four-minute milers. In an epic race, Bannister took the lead 50 yards from home, passing Landy on the outside, whilst Landy, glanced inside. Bannister clocked 3:58.8, Landy eight tenths slower.

Bannister returned to Europe. He went to Berne for the European Championships and won another gold medal in the 1500 metres. It was his last race and, until Steve Cram in 1982, no one since had won the European–Commonwealth double in one year, despite Britain's mile tradition.

As a qualified doctor, Bannister could not afford the time for international competition. Chataway in the same summer of 1954 held the world record in the 3 miles and the 5000 metres, and had epic battles with the Russian Vladimir Kuts; and Chris Brasher, fringe international athlete who never won an AAA title, won the greatest prize of all, the gold medal in the steeplechase in the Melbourne Olympics of 1956. Suitable candidates, perhaps, for a *Chariots of Fire II*?

FACTFILE

Born 23 March 1929, Harrow, England

Commonwealth Games
Gold: Mile (1954)

European Championships
Gold: 1500 metres (1954)   Bronze: 800 metres (1950)

World records (indoor)
1500 metres 3:43.0 (1954)   Mile 3:59.4 (1954)

*At 6.03 p.m. the mile race in the annual Oxford University versus AAA meeting was under way. Representing the AAA were Roger Bannister, Chris Chataway, Chris Brasher and W. T. Hulatt, whilst G. F. Dole and A. D. Gordon represented the university side.

Three minutes 59.4 seconds later, Bannister had created history by becoming the first man to break the four-minute barrier for the distance.

The full result of the race was:

First	Bannister	3:59.4
Second	Chataway	4:07.2
Third	W. T. Hulatt	

It is interesting to compare Bannister's split times with those of Seb Coe when he broke the world record for the third time on 28 August 1981:

	Bannister	Coe
440 yards	57.7	55.23
880 yards	1:58.3	1:53.22
1320 yards	3:00.7	2:51.90
Mile	3:59.4	3:47.33

Lap times

Bannister 57.7, 60.6, 62.4, 58.7
Coe 55.23, 57.99, 58.68, 55.43

*At the same meeting Malcolm Pharoah set an Empire, British national and English native record in the discus with a throw of 160 ft 4 in, but never received the recognition the throw deserved as a result of being overshadowed by Bannister's performance
*Bannister's ambition was to row in the Boat Race, but he was too thin. He turned to athletics and was a twenty-five-year-old medical student at St Mary's when he first broke the four-minute mile

Roger Bannister breaks the four-minute-mile barrier at Iffley Road, Oxford, on 6 May 1954. The timekeeper (right) is the first to know

Jonah Barrington

Along with marathon running, jogging and aerobics, the popular fitness sport of the late 1960s and early 1970s was squash. The game mushroomed world wide. Synonymous with this development was the name of Jonah Barrington.

Barrington played squash for Ireland. Although born in Cornwall in the village of Morwenstow, north of Bude, on 29 April 1941, he represented Ireland by virtue of its being his father's birthplace. He was educated at Cheltenham College and Dublin University.

University life was enjoyed to the full. Too full in fact. He left Dublin University 'by mutual consent', after only two years study. Football in the university's League of Ireland team, squash, local black stout and an excess of sociability were blamed.

Barrington came to London in 1964 and took an office job with the Squash Rackets Association, enabling him to have the opportunity to play against top-class opposition.

Before the days of avid sponsorship, the British Open was *the* competition to win – a world championship in all but name. In 1967 Jonah became the first amateur to win the British Open and British Amateur championships in the same year.

After retaining both titles the following year, he lost to Geoff Hunt in the final of the 1969 British Open, after winning the Amateur title again. The solution was to turn professional. Coach Nazrullah Khan, a member of the remarkable squash-playing Khan family, was a guiding influence at this stage.

Professionalism suited Barrington. In the British Open final of 1970 he outlasted Hunt in a match which took over two and a quarter hours to complete. The left-hander's use of the backhand wore away Hunt's resistance. It was the start of four successive wins in the British Open, and a total of six wins in seven attempts.

Barrington continued at the very top. He was ranked sixth in the world at forty, and retired after winning the Canadian Open in 1983. He was then forty-two years old.

During his career he had seen his sport rise beyond the game Rodney, Julian and Nigel used to play in South Kensington. He was the first professional to play exhibition matches throughout the world. The only title to escape him was the World Open; he was too old by the time the competition was initiated. He now endorses rackets, sports equipment and clothes, designs squash and indoor centres. He holds coaching clinics, is the national junior coach, and still has the ability to win major veterans events. He has twice been runner-up (in 1982 and 1983) in the World Veterans Open, losing to Safwat, seven years his junior, on both occasions.

He has made a good living from the game and given much in return. But don't quote Dick Whittington and the gold-paved streets of London to him. To pay his way in the world in order to dedicate himself to squash, he had a variety of jobs – milkman, bowling green keeper and artist's model.

FACTFILE

Born 29 April 1941 Morwenstow, Cornwall

British Open Championship 1967, 1968, 1970, 1971, 1972, 1973
British Amateur Championship 1967, 1968, 1969

British Open – finals scores (winning finals only)
1967 beat A. Jawaid (Pakistan), 9–2, 6–9, 9–2, 9–2
1968 beat A. F. A. Taleb (UAR), 9–6, 9–0, 9–5
1970 beat G. B. Hunt (Australia), 9–7, 3–9, 3–9, 9–4, 9–4
1971 beat A. Jawaid (Pakistan), 9–1, 9–2, 9–6
1972 beat G. B. Hunt (Australia), 0–9, 9–7, 10–8, 6–9, 9–7
1973 beat G. Alauddin (Pakistan), 9–4, 9–3, 9–2

British Amateur — finals scores (winning finals only)
1967 beat R. Carter (Australia), 1–9, 9–6, 7–9, 9–7, 9–6
1968 beat M. W. Corby (GB), 9–3, 9–6, 2–9, 9–5
1969 beat M. W. Corby (GB), 3–9, 9–1, 9–2, 9–3

*Nazrullah Khan, one of the world's greatest coaches, had very little success as a player. In fact, he never appeared in the final of the British Open. He was beaten in the final of the British Isles Professional Championship in 1958 by Azam Khan

Jonah Barrington, six times British Open champion, in play against world finalist Qamar Zaman

Bill Beaumont

Alan Gibson, cricket and rugby writer for *The Times*, wrote a marvellous paragraph describing Bill Beaumont after the England captain had been voted Rothmans Player of the Year in 1980. It read:

His appearance in the television age is familiar: the tubby walrus, one might say. This is not by any means a disparaging remark. Walruses, although undoubtedly well moustached and tubby, are fast movers and capable of withstanding all sorts of weather. If you don't believe me, look up the natural history books and read Compton Mackenzie's novel *The Rival Monsters*. Old Bill is the hero in the end.

Educated at Ellesmere College, Beaumont started his rugby career as the Flyde RFC sixth-team fullback, as a sixteen-year-old in 1968. A sharp increase in height (6 feet 3 inches) and weight (15 st) necessitated a move into the pack, and he made his first-team debut against Waterloo in 1970.

Bill Beaumont made his Lancashire debut in 1972, against Cumberland and Westmorland. Lancashire, with Mike Slemen, Steve Smith, Tony Neary and Fran Cotton, was, with Beaumont, the centre of a revival in English rugby circles. In 1973 Lancashire won the county championship, beating Gloucestershire 17–12 at Bristol, and although they lost 22–12 at Blundellsands in the following season's final, Beaumont's industry was high in national selectorial priorities.

He made his first appearance on 1 January 1975, against Ireland in Dublin. England lost 12–9; Beaumont found himself opposite Willie John McBride, but emerged with credit. He had quietly and unobtrusively accumulated twelve caps by the time that Nigel Horton was injured on the 1977 Lions tour to New Zealand. Beaumont was sent for as a replacement, played three games, and came back to be given the England captaincy over Roger Uttley.

The 1979–80 season was his most successful. He finished on the losing side only three times, twice for Fylde, and once for England against New Zealand. Under his captaincy England won the Grand Slam for the first time since 1957 and, in so doing, won the Triple Crown for the first time since 1960 and the championship for the first time since 1963. Wales were beaten 9–8, Ireland 24–9, France 17–13 and finally Scotland 30–18. Lancashire won the county championship again.

Captaincy of the Lions to tour South Africa was a logical progression. Diplomatically, the tour was a success. The Lions lost the series 3–1, but they could, and should, have won the Third Test at Port Elizabeth, which they lost 12–10. The Lions won the Fourth Test 17–13 at Pretoria, the first Lions team to win the final Test after losing the series. The pack was dominant, but cruel injuries to Holmes and Gareth Davies, Richards, Campbell, Patterson and O'Donnell, to name just a few, upset the threequarters. It was typified by Stuart Lane, the Cardiff flanker, whose tour lasted just 47 seconds of the very first match against Eastern Province. Beaumont chose to praise the South Africans Pienaar, Louw, Germishuys and Mordt.

A series of injuries in the 1981–82 season was beginning to cause concern. Headaches and concussion occurred with alarming frequency. In the 1982 championship final at Moseley, Lancashire beat North Midlands 7–3. Beaumont had to be replaced during the game. Diagnosis revealed a neck injury. He retired immediately.

William Blackledge Beaumont is a director of the family textile mill in Chorley, Lancashire. He is a match summarizer for BBC Television and writes books. He is one of the resident captains on 'A Question of Sport'.

Alan Gibson again:

Nowadays at least at the higher levels, it does not matter much where a captain plays. But it matters who the captain is. However carefully tactical ploys have been worked out, it still needs a captain to guide their application. An inspirational captain on the field counts for so much.

Bill Beaumont played at lock forward thirty-four times for England; on twenty-two occasions he was captain. Both are records. He symbolized the long-awaited revival of English rugby. And, without him, all the old faults seem to have crept back in again.

FACTFILE

Born 9 March 1952, Preston, Lancashire, England

England international career

Debut 1 January 1975, *v.* Ireland
Appearances 34 (England record; won 14, lost 17, drew 3)
Last appearance 16 January 1982, *v.* Scotland

Lions tours

1977 New Zealand (as replacement)
1980 South Africa (captain)

*England, under Beaumont's captaincy, won the Triple Crown, the international championship and the Grand Slam in 1980.
*England had previously won the Triple Crown in 1960, the international championship outright in 1958, and the Grand Slam in 1957
*Beaumont's uncle, Joe Blackledge, played county cricket for Lancashire. In 1962 he played 26 matches, scored 569 runs, with a highest score of 68 and an average of 15.38

Bill Beaumont (centre) prepares to fall on the ball and tidy up England's line-out possession against France at Twickenham in 1981. Beaumont is flanked by Maurice Colclough (left) and Peter Wheeler (right)

Franz Beckenbauer

Inspirational captain of Bayern Munich and West Germany, Franz Beckenbauer was an influential player whose concept of the mobile, attacking role of the sweeper position transformed football. He was a fine passer of the ball, an astute tactician and much quicker than opponents believed him to be.

Born on 11 September 1945 in Munich, Beckenbauer joined Bayern Munich's youth team at the age of thirteen from a local junior team, Munchen 1906. He became a schoolboy and youth international in the old right-half position and was promoted into Bayern's first-team squad in 1964.

He made his debut for the Bayern first team in the newly formed Bundesliga the following year. Immediately catching the attention of Helmut Schoen, the national team manager, he made twenty-seven first-team appearances before gaining his first cap against Sweden. His club played him at outside left; Schoen preferred an attacking midfield role for his new protégé.

Yet it was a tactical decision by Schoen which may have cost West Germany the 1966 World Cup. Now fully established in the national team – he was still only twenty, but already their Footballer of the Year – Beckenbauer's presence in the early rounds was considerable. Two goals against the Swiss and commanding performances against Argentina and Spain had put the Germans into the quarter finals. Another goal in the 4–0 destruction of Uruguay, followed by a lively display against the Soviet Union in the semi-finals, marked him as major discussion point in the England tactical plans for the final. But Schoen withdrew Beckenbauer to a negative marking role on Bobby Charlton for the final; Charlton was rendered less effective, but West Germany lost an attacking option.

On the domestic scene, Bayern were beginning to hum. As yet they were not even the best team in the city, Munich 1860 dominating the Bavarian capital. The Bayern charge began with German FA Cup final wins in 1966 and 1967, and their first European title, the 1967 Cup Winners' Cup, beating Rangers. Beckenbauer, now club captain, led Bayern to the double in 1968–69.

In the 1970 World Cup Beckenbauer was now an able lieutenant to his captain Uwe Seeler. His 25-yard goal under Peter Bonetti's body brought the Germans back into the quarter final against England, before further goals from Seeler and Beckenbauer's Bayern colleague, Gerd Muller, completed Germany's revenge for 1966. In the semifinal Beckenbauer was given wretched protection from the Japanese referee Yamasaki as the cynical Italians imitated the Washington Redskins. He broke his collarbone in one scything tackle, played extra time in a sling; amidst a classic of excitement and a comedy of errors, Italy won 4–3.

With the retirement of Uwe Seeler, Beckenbauer took over the captain's job under Helmut Schoen, and conjured five seasons of total domination at club and national level. Initial success was with the national team. Appointed captain for the 3–0 win against Turkey in 1971, he led the Germans to a win in the 1972 European Championship in Brussels, and picked up the prestigious European Footballer of the Year award from the French magazine *France Football* in December.

FIFA had selected West Germany to stage the finals of the 1974 World Cup. Schoen had based his team around the Bayern side which had, a month earlier, won the European Cup for the first of three successive victories. Schoen picked Beckenbauer, Sepp Maier, Paul Breitner, Gerd Muller, Uli Hoeness and Georg Schwarzenbeck to form the backbone of the team. The side started badly, losing to the East Germans 1–0 in Hamburg, but that meant, luckily, that they qualified for the next stage in an easier group. Team selection caused problems. Beckenbauer and the Bayern mafia won. Muller scored vital goals, Maier made crucial saves and the hosts muddled through to the final. There they beat the talented but fallible Dutch 2–1, and Beckenbauer received the World Cup.

Bayern steam-rolled through Europe for three seasons, the broken-nosed Schwarzenbeck, the squat Muller and Maier of the long shorts as Beckenbauer's cohorts. Footballer of the Year in Europe for the second time in 1976, that season he played his 100th game for the West Germans, in the European Championship final.

The wind of change blew through 1977. After 103 games, and 14 goals in the national team, he retired after the 1–0 loss against France in February. He had missed only ten internationals. Bayern were champions of the world. When Pele retired from the New York Cosmos, Beckenbauer fitted the bill. He could speak the language – the language of money was $2 million.

With Cosmos he won the NASL Championship in both 1977 and 1978. But the Bundesliga beckoned again. Hamburg, who had not successfully replaced Kevin Keegan at the turnstiles, brought him back to Germany, and consequently they won the Bundesliga title in 1982. At thirty-seven it was finally time to retire – at the top.

FACTFILE

Born 11 September 1945, Munich, West Germany

International debut 26 September 1965, *v.* Sweden (won 2–1)
International appearances 103
International goals 14

Honours

West German League Championship 1969, 1972, 1973, 1974
West German Cup 1966, 1967, 1969, 1971
European Cup 1974, 1975, 1976
Cup Winners' Cup 1967
European Super Cup runners-up 1975, 1976

European Championship 1972; runners-up 1976
World Club Championship 1976
World Cup 1974 (captain); runners-up 1966; beaten semifinalists 1970
NASL Champions 1977, 1978 (NY Cosmos)
European Footballer of the Year 1972, 1976

*Beckenbauer's main occupation, other than promotions, is for the German sports firm Adidas
*He took over the post of West German team manager in July 1984, following the resignation of Jupp Derwall

West German captain Franz Beckenbauer controls the ball during the successful 1974 World Cup campaign. No. 12 is Wolfgang Overath

George Best

Few people hold a middle-of-the-road opinion about George Best; they either recall his instinctive genius on the football field, his ability to provide as much entertainment for ninety minutes as anyone in the history of the game, or they recoil in horror at the memory of his childish outbursts, his seeming contempt for authority, his much reported private life.

George Best made his League debut for Manchester United in 1963 as a slim, frail-looking seventeen-year-old, and won his first cap for Northern Ireland seven months later. He came into a United side which relied on the instinctive rapport and stunning individual flair of Denis Law, Pat Crerand and Bobby Charlton, and in under a year he was as popular in Manchester as any of them. Initially he played wide on the left, but as he developed physically he was likely to take on players anywhere, demonstrating perfect close control, a surprising bite in the tackle and a killing change of pace. In short, he dribbled the ball in a way that hardened sportswriters had despaired of ever seeing again.

Despite seldom looking completely at ease in defence, United won the League title in 1965 and 1967 and realized Matt Busby's dream by taking the European Cup in 1968, when Best scored a perfect solo goal against Benfica in the final. He was, quite simply, the most exciting player in Europe and it came as no surprise when he was elected Footballer of the Year both there and at home. Those close to Old Trafford marvelled that Law, Best and Charlton, who had virtually nothing in common outside football and, indeed, saw very little of each other off the pitch, achieved such perfect harmony on it.

By the time the European Cup final came round, Best was already rich beyond the dreams of the shy lad who had been so homesick at Old Trafford in the early days that he had returned to Belfast.

His rise to fame and fortune coincided with the PR men's realization that footballers could be big business. He drove a Jaguar; he was the principal of George Best Enterprises and George Best Associates; he was the personification of the Swinging Sixties; and, of course, he had to feign a sophistication and awareness which were not naturally his.

In the end it sickened him. When the newspapers first wanted to know all about the latest girl, he was flattered, then merely amused, then weary, and finally disgusted. His decline and disenchantment with the game have been charted often enough. No one could condone all his actions – he walked out on United and Matt Busby; he fled to some far-flung beach whenever the pressure was too great; he took refuge in alcohol – but it is worth remembering that the media, so recently sycophantic, had turned increasingly virulent.

On the field, he frequently came in for the most appalling treatment; indeed, there were occasions when not only the opposing player but also his manager and chairman might have been closely questioned. Unlike Pele or Charlton, Best could not handle this abuse. He insulted referees; he became increasingly truculent; he rounded angrily on defenders.

After a period of self-imposed exile, he returned to United but was never the same player. His spells with other clubs, including a longish one with Fulham, occasioned sadness in those who had watched him at the height of his powers. The brain was too quick for those around him; the legs not nearly quick enough.

In all he played 361 League games for the then most famous club side in the world – the equivalent of nine full seasons – and scored 137 goals. In the mid-sixties he offered magnificent entertainment to anyone remotely interested in the game, and will never be forgotten by those who saw him. It is sometimes said of those who struggle for meagre reward that they receive too little, too late; George Best's tragedy was that he never had to struggle for anything – it was simply a case of too much, too soon.

FACTFILE

Born 22 May 1946, Belfast, Northern Ireland

Football League debut 14 September 1963, Manchester United v. West Bromwich Albion
Football League appearances 411
Football League goals 147
F A Cup appearances 41
F A Cup goals 21
League Cup appearances 15
League Cup goals 8
International debut 15 April 1964, Northern Ireland v. Wales
International appearances 37
International goals 9

Honours

Football League Championship 1965, 1967
Top scorer in League 1968 (28, joint)
European Cup 1968
European Footballer of the Year 1968
Footballer of the Year 1968

British League record (to 1 August 1984)

	Appearances	Goals
Manchester United	361	137
Stockport County	3	2
Fulham	42	8
Hibernian	13	3
Bournemouth	5	0

*George Best turned professional with Manchester United in May 1963
*Best's last international appearance was against Holland in 1977
*His last League goal was scored on 5 November 1977 for Fulham against Sunderland
*His last League game was for Bournemouth v. Wigan on 7 May 1983. The game was drawn 2–2; the attendance was 4528

George Best impersonating a rugby league scrum-half! An unusual pose against Nottingham Forest in 1969

Bjorn Borg

At 5.21 p.m. on 31 March 1983, Bjorn Borg mishit a backhand into the tramlines, and his second-round opponent, a nineteen-year-old Frenchman named Henri Leconte, went through to the next round of the Monte Carlo tennis tournament. For Borg, who lives just a mile from the courts, that was the end of his full-time commitment to tennis.

He told Arne Reimer of the Swedish newspaper *Kvallsposten*, 'There is something missing inside me. I had to fight with myself to train four hours every day, which is what I did when I was at the top. I noticed that it was hard to concentrate when I played. I was simply not motivated enough and it didn't matter when I lost.

'It was still fun to play but that is not enough when you play in tournaments. You have to give 100 per cent in every match. I knew I couldn't do that.'

And so, at the age of twenty-six, ended one of the most remarkable sporting stories of modern times – five Wimbledon titles, six French and fifty-one other major events around the world. By means of savings, investments and shrewd business deals, Borg had earned a fortune estimated to be over £20 million.

Born at Sodertalje, near Stockholm, he was always keen on tennis. When his father won a local table tennis title, Bjorn persuaded him to choose a tennis racquet as his prize. His father never saw the racquet again.

At fifteen he was in the Swedish Davis Cup team; he beat Onny Parun of New Zealand in his first tie 4–6, 3–6, 6–3, 6–4, 6–4, on 5 May 1972. He then beat Russell Simpson 9–7, 6–4, 5–7, 6–1. Sweden won the tie. In the next round he didn't win either singles against Jan Kodes or Pala. But he was on his way. That year he won the junior event at Wimbledon, beating Buster Mottram in the final. His association with the world's greatest tournament had begun.

In 1973 he found himself seeded No. 6 in the competition proper at the age of seventeen. Nikki Pilic, the Yugoslavian, had dropped out of a Davis Cup match against New Zealand and had been fined. The other players boycotted Wimbledon as an act of protest. Borg reached the quarter finals, where he was beaten by Roger Taylor.

The following year he won his first major, the French Championships at Roland Garros, beating Manuel Orantes in five sets. In 1975 he helped Sweden win the Davis Cup – the youngest player ever to play in a winning final team. Czechoslovakia were the victims, losing the final rubber. Everywhere he went he was besieged by 'teeny boppers', nowhere more so than at Wimbledon.

For five years the Wimbledon crowd were treated to the annual sign of emotion, the match point, the clenched fist and the fall to his knees. Wimbledon was special; in 1967 he had heard an interview by the then champion John Newcombe saying that he had learned to play the game by following a fifty-year-old instructional book called *Match Play and Spin of the Ball* by the old champion Bill Tilden. Mr Borg Sr had toured Sweden's bookstalls looking for a copy for his boy.

It was Ilie Nastase who summed up those record-breaking years; 'They ought to take him to another planet. We play tennis. He plays something else.'

He was superstitious. He always stopped shaving four days before the championships, always packed his gear the same way, with the tightest of ten racquets at the top. He always stayed in the same Hampstead hotel and took the same route to Wimbledon over Hammersmith Bridge.

Experts say that another reason for his success was his pulse rate. Borg's was no more than 35 beats per minute; most are between 60 and 80. But the experts couldn't work out why he couldn't win the US Open, although he reached the final four

FACTFILE

Born 6 June 1956, Sodertalje, nr Stockholm, Sweden

Wimbledon singles titles
1976 beat Ilie Nastase (Rumania), 6–4, 6–2, 9–7
1977 beat Jimmy Connors (USA), 3–6, 6–2, 6–1, 5–7, 6–4
1978 beat Jimmy Connors (USA), 6–2, 6–2, 6–3
1979 beat Roscoe Tanner (USA), 6–7, 6–1, 3–6, 6–3, 6–4
1980 beat John McEnroe (USA), 1–6, 7–5, 6–3, 6–7, 8–6

French singles titles
1974 beat Manuel Orantes, 2–6, 6–7, 6–0, 6–1, 6–1
1975 beat Guillermo Vilas, 6–2, 6–3, 6–4
1978 beat Guillermo Vilas, 6–3, 6–1, 6–3
1979 beat Victor Pecci, 6–3, 6–1, 6–7, 6–4
1980 beat Vitas Gerulaitis, 6–4, 6–1, 6–2

United States singles titles (Borg lost in the final to Jimmy Connors in 1976 and 1978, and to John McEnroe in 1980 and 1981)

Italian Championships Winner in 1974 and 1978

WCT singles (Dallas) 1976 beat Guillermo Vilas, 1–6, 6–1, 7–5, 6–1
(Borg lost in the final to John Newcombe in 1974, Arthur Ashe in 1975 and John McEnroe in 1980)
Volvo Masters
1979 beat Vitas Gerulaitis, 6–2, 6–2
1980 beat Ivan Lendl, 6–4, 6–2, 6–2
(Borg lost in the final to Arthur Ashe in 1975 and Jimmy Connors in 1977)

*Borg's impressive record in the singles at Wimbledon reads as follows:

    Matches played 55 (won 51, lost 4)
    Sets played 199 (won 157, lost 42)

He has played the following opponents twice in the championships, and with the exception of El Shafei and McEnroe, he has beaten them all twice: M. Riessen (USA), I. Nastase (Rumania), J. Fillol (Chile), T. S. Okker (Netherlands), R. Tanner (USA), I. El Shafei (Egypt), B. Gottfried (USA), V. Gerulaitis (USA), J. P. McEnroe (USA), J. S. Connors (USA – played him four times).

He lost to Roger Taylor (1973), Ismail El Shafei (1974), Arthur Ashe (1975) and John McEnroe (1981)

times. Borg claimed that if he had won it, then he could be called a great player.

The first signs that retirement was in the offing came in 1981. He lost in the Wimbledon final to John McEnroe. No disgrace in that. But when he lost to McEnroe in the US Open final, he uncharacteristically walked off court, ducking the presentation ceremony. He later said that he didn't feel like the gentlemanly loser for failing again to clinch the one title he hadn't won.

Then, in 1982, he said that he wanted to play a reduced schedule – seven Grand Prix events and the French Open, Wimbledon and the US Open. But the Men's International Tennis Council, which governs the Grand Prix circuit, invoked the rule that players must commit themselves to a minimum of ten tournaments, excluding the Grand Slam events, or play through the qualifying rounds of each tournament. The council called his bluff; Borg said he would play in the qualifying rounds. But losses to Yannick Noah and Dick Stockton further discouraged him. The desire had gone.

At his peak Borg's world-wide financial interests were with Scandinavian Airways, Saab, Viking machines, tennis equipment, drinks, food and cereals. Even in his early days he was paid £15,000 for a Tuborg lager logo on his famous headband.

He ruled Wimbledon and Stade Roland Garros. Australia was too far to attempt another Grand Slam event. He would have been the best ever if he had managed just one US Open. Many disregard that and say that he was anyway.

For Christmas 1982 Bjorn Borg gave his wife three presents – a pair of earrings, a porcelain étagère for her collection of perfumes and make-up, and himself. 'The last present was the best he has given me,' says Mariana. For Bjorn, who collects islands as a hobby – he has one near Stockholm and ten in the Baltic – it was time to retire to them.

At the Monte Carlo tennis tournament of 1984, the competitors read the following notice attached to the changing-room door: 'If there are any problems, please contact your liaison officer in Room 7.'

The name on the desk in Room 7 was Bjorn Borg. He doesn't miss playing at all. Yet.

The shot that changed the coaching manuals – Bjorn Borg and the double-fisted backhand

Billy Boston

Shirley Bassey came from Tiger Bay, the dockland area of Cardiff. So too did Billy Boston, the 'Peer of Wigan', the finest winger that British Rugby League has produced.

Boston played his early rugby for Cardiff Internationals, a well-known feeder club for some of the Welsh first-class sides, then moved to Cardiff where he played with Cliff Morgan in the 'Rags'. But northern spies were out, playing on Welsh rugby susceptibility to a chequebook. But Wigan were to be congratulated for their perception and, in 1953, at the age of eighteen, Boston pocketed a £3000 signing-on fee and went to Central Park.

Boston played precisely five first-team games for Wigan before the Great Britain selectors chose him to catch the plane for the Australian tour. The nineteen-year-old Welshman was an overnight sensation. He scored thirty-six tries in eighteen games on the tour. In his first international against Australia he scored twice in a 38–21 win which levelled the series at 1–1. He failed to score in the decider, which went to the Aussies 20–16. On to New Zealand for his third cap and a 27–7 victory for Britain, in which Boston scored four tries; only three players have achieved that feat for Britain to this day.

Wigan took to him immediately. More than 8000 spectators turned up to watch his A-team debut. He went on to score no fewer than 477 tries for Wigan between 1953 and 1968, and kindly captains let him kick four goals from less than impossible positions. In 1956–57 Boston crossed the try line on sixty occasions, just two short of the club record set in 1926–27.

On two occasions Boston scored seven tries in a match; Dewsbury (1955) and Salford (1962) were on the receiving end. Only Australian Brian Bevan, with 796, has more tries in world rugby.

Boston was a fixture at Wembley at the Challenge Cup final. He played there on six occasions and collected three winners' medals.

He was selected for Great Britain on thirty-one occasions, scoring twenty-four international tries. Whilst wearing a Great Britain jersey he reached the try line ninety times. Boston went back to Australasia twice after the 1954 tour. He returned for the 1957 World Cup and, like the rest of the team, suffered disappointments with defeats against Australia and New Zealand. The stocky, balding winger with the deceptive sidestep returned in 1962 and scored twenty-two tries in seventeen matches, though against New South Wales he was one of six to take an early bath after a spectacular brawl.

Boston's last match for Britain was against France on 3 April 1963. The venue: Central Park, Wigan. France were soundly thrashed 42–4 and Boston scored a try. The crowd responded with a standing ovation as he walked back to his wing position.

His retirement at the age of thirty-five was a little premature. He thought he was good for another season or two, but on Easter Monday, 1970, he suffered a severe arm injury which forced him to give up the game.

Boston may not have quite the statistical record of Bevan or Fox or of his old Wigan team-mate Jim Sullivan. But the respect that players carry into retirement never diminishes. The public forget the bad games. Not that the greats play many. And when Rugby League enthusiasts vote in a valued local paper for Billy Boston as the finest ambassador of the last generation, then their opinions are noted. Especially when it's not a Wigan paper.

FACTFILE

Born 1935, Cardiff, Wales

Club Wigan

Challenge Cup

1958	v. Workington Town	won	13–9
1959	v. Hull	won	30–13
1961	v. St Helens	lost	6–12
1963	v. Wakefield Trinity	lost	10–25
1965	v. Hunslet	won	20–16
1966	v. St Helens	lost	2–21

League Championship 1962
Championship play-off 1960, v. Wakefield Trinity, won 27–3

Great Britain honours

Test debut 3 July 1954, v. Australia (Brisbane; scored 2 tries)
Test appearances 31
Test tries 24

Billy Boston, the Wigan and Great Britain winger, bounces off a Hull defender

Ian Botham

If Ian Botham's Test career had only lasted three years, he would still have been worthy of inclusion as one of the all-time great all-rounders. That he then suffered an appalling loss of form coinciding with his being appointed captain of England, only to return to even greater triumphs immediately after resigning the captaincy, makes his story – so far – unique in cricket history.

On the first day of his first Test against Australia at Trent Bridge in 1977 he took 5 wickets for 74, including Greg Chappell bowled for 19. At the tea interval he was presented to Her Majesty the Queen, 1977 was Silver Jubilee Year and the Queen was making a tour of the provinces. Her visit to Nottingham coincided with the first day of the First Test – and the arrival of Botham.

In the next Test at Headingley Botham took 5 for 21, but fractured a bone in his foot and was ruled out for the final match of the series.

Nevertheless, a star had been born, even if the press and the media at the time were slow to spot the quality. There had never been anybody quite like Botham before. He bowled sometimes off a full run, sometimes off a half run, occasionally off two or three paces. Sometimes fast, sometimes slow, sometimes medium off-spinners. Captain Mike Brearley admitted he found it difficult to set a field. Down in Somerset Brian Close had nurtured Botham through his early seasons with a mixture of mateyness and stern discipline which appealed to the youngster, and Tom Cartwright, the coach, had taught him to swing and cut. They could afford to smile at the way his early Test promise had been overlooked by the media in a tidal wave of praise for Brearley's captaincy and the return of the Ashes.

Maybe not all were surprised by the rise of the young Botham. Frank Keating tells the tale of the day he was subediting cricket scores at the *Guardian*. On 12 July 1974, the day of the Benson & Hedges quarter finals, at 5.25 p.m. he read that Hampshire were all out 182, Somerset 113 for 8, and Andy Roberts had just knocked

FACTFILE

Born 24 November 1955, Heswall, Cheshire, England

First-class debut 1974
Total first-class runs 11,676 (average 32.89)
Total first-class wickets 833 (average 25.31)
Highest first-class innings 228, Somerset v. Gloucestershire (1980)
Test debut 1977, v. Australia
Total Test matches 72
Total Test runs 4153 (average 36.75)
Highest Test innings 208, England v. India (1982)
Total Test wickets 305 (average 28.19)
Best bowling 8–34, England v. Pakistan (1978)
(Correct up to 15 August 1984.)

Football League Appearances 9 (from 1979 to 1984, for Scunthorpe United)
Won 1, lost 6, drew 2

*Botham's headmaster described him as 'a waster'
*His first game for Somerset was on 2 September 1973 in the John Player League against Sussex at Hove. He was dismissed off the bowling of Mike Buss for 2. He made his championship debut the following season
*He learned his cricket at two schools in Yeovil, Millfield and Bucklers Mead
*In 1979, in the Sydney Test, the last of the England fast bowlers, Bob Willis, left the field dehydrated. Botham bowled another eighteen overs, then went to see *Midnight Cowboy* for the third time
*After his success in 1981, he was subject of 'This Is Your Life' and was also elected BBC Sports Personality of the Year
*In 1982 he crashed two £12,000 cars practising for a celebrity event at Thruxton
*In December 1983 he resisted instructions from the MCC not to play for Scunthorpe United immediately before the tour to New Zealand and Pakistan

*A comparison of the feats of four current all-rounders, Ian Botham, Kapil Dev, Imran Khan and Richard Hadlee, each of whom has taken over 200 Test wickets and scored over 1500 Test runs, to the end of the 1984 summer series in England:

Batting and fielding

	M	I	NO	Runs	HS	Avge	100s	50s	Catches
Botham	72	116	3	4153	208	36.75	13	18	84
Kapil Dev	62	92	8	2483	126*	29.55	3	13	24
Imran Khan	51	77	12	2023	123	31.12	2	7	17
Hadlee	50	85	11	1820	103	24.59	1	9	28

Bowling

	Wkts	Runs	Avge	Best	5wI	10wM
Botham	305	7987	28.19	8–34	23	4
Kapil Dev	247	6844	27.70	9–83	18	2
Imran Khan	232	5317	22.92	8–58	16	4
Hadlee	235	5626	23.94	7–23	18	4

four teeth out of the mouth of an unknown called 'Bottam'. Keating went to the pub, having earmarked the report to be relegated down page. An hour later he was back to hear from Henry Blofeld at the ground that Somerset had won by 1 wicket and that the unknown had put his teeth in his pocket and, scoring 45 not out, had won the match with an over left. 'We'll hear a lot more about this astonishing young man,' reported Blofeld.

Botham, born in Cheshire but having lived in Yeovil since he was three, spent some time on the Lord's ground staff where 'they thought I was bit of a yokel'. He has taken great delight in proving his ability to them ever since on visits to headquarters. He reached the Test double – 1000 runs and 100 wickets – in a then record time of twenty-one Tests – the record being reached at Lord's, when Mike Brearley caught Sunil Gavaskar off his bowling. The year before, 1978, in his first Test at Lord's, Botham arrived at the wicket conscious that some of his critics and rivals were in various parts of the ground. He took guard, watched the first ball, and imperiously landed the second in the Mound Stand. His third Test century followed. In the same match he also took 8 for 34. Pakistan were the victims.

On the way home from Australia after England had lost the 1979–80 series, Botham and ten others stopped off in Bombay for the Jubilee Test. With England at 4 for 57 when he came in, he hit a responsible 114 and clinched victory by taking 13 wickets in the match. It seemed as though nothing could go wrong for the young giant.

The West Indies were due in England that summer. John Arlott thought it was the strongest side ever to leave the Caribbean. England, having lost Mike Brearley, turned to their all-rounder to produce match-winning skills in every department of the game. The First Test at Trent Bridge was lost narrowly, but England looked a ragged team and Botham himself lost form.

He took the side to the Caribbean the following winter, 1980–81, but a series of disasters including Ken Barrington's death and the Jackman incident affected the whole party. Botham, who had put on weight after giving up smoking, found he had recurring back trouble. There was a court case hanging over him back in England (he was eventually acquitted). His form naturally declined. At the end of the tour John Woodcock said, 'To hang on to the captaincy, Botham will have to overcome strong not to say bitter opposition.'

He remained in charge for two Tests the next season against Australia. But, collecting 'a pair' at Lord's and having to endure the long silent walk back to face members in the pavilion, who looked away, was too much. He resigned the captaincy but was retained in the team for the next Test under Mike Brearley.

In his twelve Tests as captain he had drawn eight and lost the rest. He had scored 276 runs an average of 14 and taken 35 wickets expensively. In his previous twenty-five Tests he had scored 1336 runs averaging over 40 and taken 139 wickets at 18.

Remarkably the magic returned. In 1981 at Leeds, with England 105 for 5 following on in their second innings (still 122 behind Australia), he came to the wicket. Shortly after they were 135 for 7 with Graham Dilley on his way to bat. Dilley had never been on the winning side in twelve Tests. 'I don't fancy hanging around here, do you?' inquired Botham. 'Let's give it some umpety.' Dilley scord 56. Botham was not out 149 and England 356 all out – enough, once Bob Willis had done his work, to win by 18 runs.

In the next Test at Edgbaston Botham took 5 wickets for 11 in Australia's second innings as England won by 29 runs. There was another victory for England at Old Trafford by 103 runs (Botham 118) and in the Sixth Test at the Oval – a drawn match – Botham took 10 wickets.

The remarkable swing in fortune was complete. Since then Botham has not been so consistently explosive but he has been an invaluable all-rounder. Against India in 1982 he scored 208 off 226 deliveries. In 1983 he produced a matching-winning 96 not out for Somerset (again at Lord's) in the NatWest semifinal against Middlesex, and a superb 103 off 99 balls in the Fourth Test against New Zealand at Trent Bridge – his twelfth century in sixty-three Tests and his first for England in twenty-three innings.

By the time Botham ran in to open the bowling for England against the West Indies at the end of the 1984 series, he had scored over 4000 Tests runs and taken 300 Test wickets. Food for thought for Ian Chappell, who, on meeting Botham for the first time in a Melbourne bar in 1976, had been informed by the youngster that he would score more Test runs than his already famous companion. Chappell laughed. And found himself on the bar floor rubbing his chin.

Chappell scored 5345 Test runs. That is the next target for Ian Botham.

Ian Botham hooks an intended bouncer from Malcolm Marshall during the first Test between England and the West Indies at Edgbaston in 1984. Botham ended what was a disastrous series for England with a personal record of over 4000 runs and 300 wickets in Test matches

Sir Donald Bradman

In first-class cricket, Donald Bradman went to the wicket on 338 occasions; 117 times he returned to the pavilion with a century to his name. He went on to a double century on thirty-seven occasions; he reached 300 six times; and once, for New South Wales against Queensland in the 1929–30 season, a halt was called only after he had reached an unbeaten 452.

Bradman was to cricket in between the wars what W. G. Grace had been at the turn of the century, but in a different vein. Grace, with his huge beard and 18-st frame, was the all-rounder – flamboyant batsman and match-winning bowler. Bradman, small and slight, was strangely out of character with his era – a batsman who eliminated mistakes, yet accumulated runs with indecent haste.

He was born on 27 August 1908 at Cootamundra, New South Wales, and spent his childhood at Bowral, a township 80 miles from Sydney. The backyard of the family home was where he practised his shots, using a ball suspended from a tree by string to quicken his reflexes.

The progression to the New South Wales team was relentless. He made his debut against South Australia in Adelaide when just nineteen, and scored 118. The following season when the England team (then MCC) came to Australia, he made an unbeaten 132 for the state team. He was chosen for his country. It was a disaster: England 521 and 342 for 8 declared beat Australia, 122 and 66, by 675 runs. Bradman, at No. 7, made 18 and 1. It was Brisbane's introduction to Test cricket. Bradman was dropped. He returned for the Third Test and made 79 and 112. He followed with 40, 58, 123 and 37 not out. The dye was cast.

In fifty-two Test matches, finishing at the Oval in 1948, he made 6996 runs at an average of 99.94. He made twenty-nine Test centuries, a record not beaten until Indian master Sunil Gavaskar made 236 not out against the West Indies over Christmas 1983. Gavaskar played in ninety-three Test matches.

His contribution to Sheffield Shield cricket was as prolific. From his debut until 1934, he played for New South Wales. Missing the 1934–35 season, he switched allegiance to South Australia until his retirement. In December 1948 he signed off with 123 in his own testimonial match at Melbourne. Bradman had twelve times passed 1000 runs in the Australian summer; the next best is three.

But it was in England that he revelled. Worcester seemed a therapy. In 1930 Bradman began with an innings of 236, en route to 1001 runs at an average of 143 by 31 May. Moving on to the Test matches, he accumulated 974 runs in the series at an average of 139.14,

FACTFILE

Born 27 August 1908, Cootamundra, New South Wales, Australia

Career summary

Season	I	NO	Runs	HS	Avge
1927–28	10	1	416	134*	46.22
1928–29	24	6	1690	340*	93.88
1929–30	16	2	1586	452*	113.28
1930	36	6	2960	334	98.66
1930–31	18	0	1422	258	79.00
1931–32	13	1	1403	299*	116.91
1932–33	21	2	1171	238	61.63
1933–34	11	2	1192	253	132.44
1934	27	3	2020	304	84.16
1934–35	(Did not play)				
1935–36	9	0	1173	369	130.33
1936–37	19	1	1552	270	86.22
1937–38	18	2	1437	246	89.81
1938	26	5	2429	278	115.66
1938–39	7	1	919	225	153.16
1939–40	15	3	1475	267	122.91
1940–41	4	0	18	12	4.50
1945–46	3	1	232	52*	116.00
1946–47	14	1	1032	234	79.38
1947–48	12	2	1296	201	129.60
1948	31	4	2428	187	89.92
1948–49	4	0	216	123	54.00
Totals	338	43	28,067	452*	95.14

Aggregates					
In Australia	216	25	18,147	452*	95.01
In England	122	18	9920	334	95.38
Totals	338	43	28,067	452*	95.14

Test match aggregates	I	NO	Runs	HS	Avge
v. England	63	7	5028	334	89.78
v. India	6	2	715	201	178.75
v. South Africa	5	1	806	299*	201.50
v. West Indies	6	0	447	223	74.50
Totals	80	10	6996	334	99.94

First-class centuries 117

Double centuries in Tests

334   v. England, Headingley (1930)
304   v. England, Headingley (1934)
299* v. South Africa, Adelaide (1931–32)
270   v. England, Melbourne (1936–37)
254   v. England, Lord's (1930)
244   v. England, The Oval (1934)
234   v. England, Sydney (1946–47)
232   v. England, The Oval (1930)
226   v. South Africa, Brisbane (1931–32)
223   v. West Indies, Brisbane (1930–31)
212   v. England, Adelaide (1936–37)
201   v. India, Adelaide (1947–48)

*The only player to have scored over 300 runs in an innings six times, Bradman holds the record for scores over 200 – thirty-seven times

*He is the only Australian to have scored more than 100 centuries – 117 in all, seventy-six in Australia and forty-one in England

*He scored 100 on his first appearance in first-class cricket and in his own testimonial match after announcing his retirement

including 254 at Lord's, 232 at the Oval and 334 at Leeds. The Headingley score was a world record at the time; the 974 runs are still a world record. On the next visit in 1934 he made 206 at Worcester, and in the Test matches returned to Leeds and made 304. At the Oval he took the England attack for 244. His total for the tour was 2020 at 84.16. There were some who said he was human. Three times he was bowled for a duck.

Back in 1938 to feast off the Worcestershire bowling, he gathered 258 off their attack at the start of a twenty-eight-day spell which realized 1056 runs at 150.85 in just nine innings. He made only three single centuries in the Test series, but when the boat sailed Bradman had scored 2429 runs at 115.66. It was, and still is, the best average in the history of English cricket.

1948 was his last year as a cricketer. Aged forty he was fallible. But he was, next to Winston Churchill, the most popular man in England during the summer. He scored just 1 run less than in 1938. Worcestershire were relieved – they dismissed him for 107.

He came to the Fifth and final Test at the Oval needing a boundary for a Test career average of 100. Yardley, the England captain, led a standing ovation to the wicket and called for three cheers. Bradman was bowled second ball by the Warwickshire leg spinner Eric Hollies without bothering the scorers. They said that he never saw the ball. There were tears in his eyes. The applause did not cease until the pavilion door was shut.

Sir Donald Bradman was knighted on his return to Australia, the first playing cricketer to receive the award. He became a selector and chairman of the Australian Board of Control. He had made mistakes, especially as captain, but he was the most successful run scorer the game has known. R. C. Robertson-Glasgow wrote in *Wisden*: 'Two contrary feelings dispute within us: relief that our bowlers will no longer be oppressed by this phenomenon; regret that a miracle has been removed from amongst us. So must Italy have felt when she heard of the death of Hannibal.'

Don Bradman during his innings of 452 for New South Wales against Queensland in 1930. At the time it was the highest score in first-class cricket

---

*He shares with C. B. Fry and Mike Procter the record number of 100s in succession – six

*He has scored the most 100s in a season as an Australian in England – thirteen in 1938

*He has scored the most 100s in an Australian season – eight in 1947–48

*He twice scored over 1000 runs before the end of May. No other Australian has accomplished this, and no Englishman more than once

*He scored the highest aggregate of any Australian in an English season – 2960 runs in 1930

*He scored the highest aggregate in Australia – 1690 in 1928–29

*He has scored over 1000 runs in sixteen seasons, twelve of them in Australia. No other Australian has accomplished this feat more than three times

*He is the only Australian to exceed 2000 runs on four English tours

*He has scored the most 100s in Test matches – twenty-eight; eighteen v. England, four v. India, four v. South Africa, two v. West Indies

*He has scored the most double 100s in Test cricket – twelve, five more than his rival, Wally Hammond

He made the highest score in Test matches in Australia – 299 v. South Africa at Adelaide in 1931–32

*He scored the highest aggregate for one series of Tests – 974 in England in 1930

*He holds the second-wicket world record – 451 with W. H. Ponsford against England at the Oval in 1934

*He holds the fifth-wicket world record – 405 with S. G. Barnes against England at Sydney in 1946–47

*Bradman was always striving to beat Bill Ponsford's record of 437 runs in one innings, and on 4 and 6 January 1930 he reached the milestone, scoring 452 not out against Queensland whilst playing for New South Wales. Ponsford also achieved the feat against Queensland, but two years earlier. On the two days in December 1927 that it took Ponsford to set his record, Bradman was scoring 118 runs in his first-class debut. Bradman reached his total of 452, out of a total of 739, in 415 minutes at an average of 65.34 runs per hour, including forty-nine 4s. The first 100 came in 104 minutes, the second 100 was scored in just eighty-one minutes, the third in 103 minutes, the fourth in eighty-nine minutes, and the final 52 in just thirty-eight minutes. He put on 272 for the third wicket with Kippax in 145 minutes, 156 runs with McCabe for the fourth wicket in eighty-one minutes, and 180 in ninety-three minutes with Allsopp for the sixth wicket

*Apart from Yorkshire players, Bradman was the first cricketer to be given honorary life membership of Yorkshire County Cricket Club

*Bradman's last match in Britain was against Scotland at Aberdeen on 17–18 September 1948 and he scored 123 not out in his last innings

*Bradman was South Australian squash champion

*Bradman took two Test wickets – Barrow (West Indies) in 1930–31 and Hammond (England) in 1932–33

Barry Briggs

Barry Briggs has appeared in a record eighteen World Championship speedway finals. He was world champion four times and runner-up on three occasions, and his total of 201 points amassed in world finals is also a record.

Born in Christchurch, New Zealand, Briggs was an all-round sportsman at school. He played centre forward for the Canterbury Public Schools against the Private Schools in a curtain raiser to an international soccer match between New Zealand and South Africa. He scored a goal.

He also played Rugby League for Canterbury Boys against West Coast Boys in another curtain raiser. Great Britain followed on with an international Rugby League match against New Zealand.

Briggs also excelled at cricket and hockey, and was champion of the province of Canterbury at wrestling!

At the end of the war, his parents split up and he was brought up by his mother. He lived with an uncle at a farm at Haswell, on the outskirts of Christchurch. You need a bike on a farm, and Briggs's first was a Royal Enfield. He went into part-ownership with a friend; they paid just £15 for it.

After leaving school, he worked in an advertising agency, then on a local newspaper. He had a couple of speedway contacts in the UK, so, at the age of eighteen, he jumped on board the SS *Ranchi* and headed for England.

Starting his career with Wimbledon in 1952, Briggs was regarded as a very reckless and careless rider. He soon matured and five years later was world champion, beating the holder Ove Fundin in a thrilling run-off in the 1957 final. He had already helped Wimbledon to a hat trick of British League victories. He was champion again in 1958.

Plough Lane, Wimbledon, was a particularly successful track for Briggs. He had eight seasons with the club and Wimbledon were champions on five of those occasions.

In 1960 he switched clubs from Wimbledon in southwest London to New Cross in the southeast. That move only lasted one season, for he was 'on his bike' again and off to Southampton. The fee was £750, described in those days as 'staggering'. He took Southampton to the League title in 1962.

After two seasons with Southampton, he took the A36 out of town, headed north and finished up at the Abbey Stadium, Swindon. The Wiltshire air suited him and he remained with the Robins for eight years; not only did he win the League title with Swindon in 1967, but was world champion twice more, in 1964 and 1966. He became so British that he represented Great Britain in the World Team Championship in 1968, the first time that Britain had won.

He retired in 1972, but two years later was back in the saddle, riding for Wimbledon. He was now Barry Briggs MBE and his son was at Millfield. After two seasons with Wimbledon, his last year (1976) was spent far from the southern pastures. He rode for Hull.

Involved in promotions in the sport during his later riding days, he now runs a flourishing motorcycle business in Southampton. He was responsible for introducing the Jawa bike into Western Europe, and in 1982 was one of the co-promotors of the World Championship in Los Angeles.

But maybe there's a strange twist developing in the career of Barry Briggs. On 9 January 1984 Briggs got back on his bike. He was in his fiftieth year. He came second in the South Island Championship of New Zealand to world finalist Larry Ross and qualified to ride in the New Zealand final. Eastbourne were interested in signing him, thirty-two years after he had first ridden in England. Hold the front page?

FACTFILE

Born 30 December 1934, Christchurch, New Zealand

British League clubs
1952–59 Wimbledon
1960   New Cross
1961–63 Southampton
1964–72 Swindon
1974–75 Wimbledon
1976   Hull

World Individual Championship
  Winner 1957, 1958, 1964, 1966
  Runner-up 1962, 1968, 1969
World Team Championship 1968 (Great Britain), 1971 (Great Britain)
Embassy Internationale 1964
British League Riders' Championship 1965, 1966, 1967, 1968, 1969, 1970
British League Team Championship 1954 (Wimbledon), 1955 (Wimbledon), 1956 (Wimbledon), 1958 (Wimbledon), 1959 (Wimbledon), 1962 (Southampton), 1967 (Swindon)

Top Ten Leading Scorers in World Individual Finals

		Points	Races	Titles
1	Barry Briggs (New Zealand)	201	87	4
2	Ivan Mauger (New Zealand)	176	70	6
3	Ove Fundin (Sweden)	173	75	5
4	Ronnie Moore (New Zealand)	143	69	2
5	Ole Olsen (Denmark)	109	47	3
6	Peter Craven (England)	96	50	2
7	Anders Michanek (Sweden)	95	51	1
8	Aub Lawson (Australia)	73	44	–
9	Jack Young (Australia)	70	35	2
10	Peter Collins (England)	66	35	1
	Ken McKinlay (Scotland)	66	45	–

*The only person to take a point off Barry Briggs in his four winning years was Jack Geran, who beat him in one heat in 1957

Barry Briggs of Hull on the inside overtakes Richard Greer

Eric Bristow

Eric Bristow is beginning to dominate world darts. Once a sport in which the one-off champion was commonplace, darts, for the first time since the public-bar image was dusted up, computerized and made into a television spectacular, has now a recognized world leader in the 'Crafty Cockney'. World Championship semifinalist Tony Brown summed up the feeling of many of Bristow's fellow professionals when he said, 'I wish his parents had taken him to Sunday School instead of the pub.'

Eric Bristow comes from Stoke Newington, near the Arsenal football ground, and he's one of their most fervent supporters. At fourteen he joined his first darts club, the Arundel Arms at Stoke Newington. He was, he says, the only Coke-drinking member of the team.

He first represented London in 1974, at the age of seventeen. The following year he won his first major event, the Sussex Open.

Bristow was one of a new breed. The ageing, experienced darts players from the working men's clubs were being joined by a younger element, anxious to earn a full-time living from the game. He used to be a furniture salesman, but selling furniture had no chance.

Bristow was just twenty when he first played for England. He won the first ten of his international matches. The 1977 World Masters event was his first big tournament win.

Three years later he was ranked world No. 1 by the British Darts Organization. Hardly a surprise for that year – 1980 – he was world champion for the first time at only twenty-three. He has held the world No. 1 ranking ever since.

Darts and pubs are bound to be great providers of stories, not always particularly funny ones. Bristow has often been accused of being arrogant. The reason is probably that he never shakes hands with strangers. He did once, only to find himself squeezing a hand full of broken glass. Bristow himself is aware of his controversial nature. He plays on it by inviting audiences at his exhibitions to sing 'If you all hate Bristow clap your hands.' He is critical of his fellow professionals. Of Jocky Wilson he said, 'Winning the world title in 1982 was the worst thing that could have happened to the sport', a suggestion that Wilson, who 'enjoyed a refreshment', ought to polish up his image.

Bristow no longer lives in London. Friendly with Maureen Flowers, the best-known British ladies player, and sister-in-law of former England footballer Ron Flowers, Bristow lives near Stoke. He enjoys the atmosphere there. He plays darts for the Talbot Inn, a little back-street pub in the Potteries.

What he likes about darts is that, although he throws for thousands of pounds at televised tournaments and earns up to £1000 a night for exhibitions, he still has to pay his £1 in his local before he can toe the oche. He takes his turn chalking the board. He does serious damage to pints of lager.

Having spent thousands of pounds in pubs, he's come up with a solution. Bristow has bought an old miners' welfare hut, not a mile away from the Talbot and has renovated it at a cost of a quarter of a million pounds. He plans to install thirteen dart boards. And, naturally, it will be called the Crafty Cockney.

FACTFILE

Born 25 April 1957, Stoke Newington, England

World Professional Championship
1980 beat Bobby George (England)
1981 beat John Lowe (England)
1983 lost to Keith Deller (England)
1984 beat Dave Whitcombe (England)

World Masters 1977, 1981
World Cup
  Team 1979, 1981, 1983
  Individual 1983
British Open 1978, 1981, 1983
Nations' Cup 1979, 1980, 1982, 1983

Eric Bristow, who won the first of his world professional darts championships in 1980

David Bryant

The famous cricketer W. G. Grace was the first president of the English Bowls Association in 1903. Grace came from Bristol. Just 13 miles down the B3139 is Clevedon, on the edge of the Bristol Channel, the home of David Bryant. If Grace was the first cricketer, then Bryant is the first bowler.

Born in Bristol on 27 October 1931, he had an immediate start. Father Reg was an international, and before David had even gone to St Nicholas's School, he had been taken to the Princes Road Club.

He owned his first woods at the age of seven. He was on holiday at Exmouth and found an old set behind the clubhouse. His father bought them for five shillings (25p) plus a jack. David took them home to practise.

He joined the Clevedon club at the age of sixteen in 1947. A year later he was in the Somerset Middleton Cup team in the bowls county championship.

It was with Reg that David won his first major title, the English fours in 1957, together with another father and son, the Harrises. Clevedon was on the map.

David and Reg worked on a new theory. Previously the coaching manuals had concentrated on correct arm swing. To this, they added a solid throwing base, from the legs. David was also reminded of the need to keep a good length.

David represented England for the first time in 1958. He was twenty-seven, a remarkably youthful age in a sport which many took up in retirement in those days. He won his first English singles title in 1960, beating Tom Fleming in the final, in those days held at Mortlake, close by the Watneys Brewery and the finish of the Boat Race. In 1962, despite suffering from a duodenal ulcer, he won the Commonwealth title in Perth, and four years later, also in Australia, became the first official world champion. Since then his record is a simple one: he has beaten the best for nearly a generation.

A qualified teacher of handicapped children, his hobbies are gardening and fishing. He is involved in the game as a professional and a businessman. Outside the bowls clubs and the parish, people probably wouldn't recognize him. He prefers it that way.

It is his business interests that have led critics to suggest that he is past his peak. When that happens, he normally goes onto the green and wins another championship. He has an advantage: after an involvement in the game for a generation, he has now reached an age when many people take up the sport.

FACTFILE

Born 27 October 1931, Bristol, England

International debut 1958
World Championship
    Singles 1966, 1980 (third in 1976 and 1984)
    Triples 1980
World Indoor Championship
    Singles 1979, 1980, 1981
Commonwealth Games
    Singles 1962, 1970, 1974, 1978
    Fours 1962
English Bowling Association Championships
    Singles 1960, 1966, 1971, 1972, 1973, 1975
    Pairs 1965, 1969, 1974
    Triples 1966, 1977
    Fours 1957, 1968, 1969, 1971
Middleton Cup 1977 (Somerset)

*Bryant has won national singles title on a record nine occasions: 1960, 1966, 1971, 1972, 1973, 1975, 1978, 1979 and 1983. He has won the world indoor title on each of its first three playings: 1979, 1980 and 1981

*His father, Reg, was born in Minehead on 25 May 1903 and joined the Clevedon club in 1921. He played for Somerset for thirty years and was a member of their Middleton Cup final losing team in 1955. He never played for England in outdoor competition, but was selected in 1958 and 1959 to play for them in indoor competition. He won the EBA fours title in 1957, 1968 and 1969, and the national fours title in 1969 – David was in the same team

*Bryant's pairs partner was Davis Rhys-Jones – born in Gorseinon, Glamorgan, on 28 June 1942. They teamed up together for the first time in 1965 and in that first year they won the EBA pairs title – Jones being the youngest holder of an EBA title at the time. They also won the British Isles pairs title in 1965. And regained the EBA title in 1969 and 1974. Recent successes have been the English pairs title in 1982 and 1983, and the national pairs title in 1983. Rhys-Jones has done little as a singles player but has represented England many times since making his international debut in 1970; he has never competed at the Commonwealth Games. Bryant is now partnered by A. Allcock

David Bryant at the Commonwealth Games. He held the singles title for twenty years

Donald Budge

Donald Budge broke a tennis barrier. Like the four-minute mile and the ascent of Everest, lawn tennis had its unobtainable: the Grand Slam, winning the world's four major tournaments – the Australian, French, US and Wimbledon championships – in the same year. There were difficulties not apparent today: travel to Australia, especially for Europeans, was tedious, and the French, true to tradition, only decided to let overseas players compete in their championships after 1924.

That was until the arrival of John Donald Budge from California. Budge could have been British. He was the son of a former professional footballer in the Scottish League.

He almost shunned tennis in his early days. Brother Lloyd used him as the proverbial cannon fodder for back-garden games; Donald preferred his father's sport, basketball, hockey and cycling. California, with its outdoor facilities, hosted several tennis tournaments for young players, called 'peewees' and Donald, aged fifteen, was chivvied by his parents and brother into entering the California State Championships. He won. It was his first tournament.

Delighted by this unexpected success, Budge devoted more time to tennis and began to discipline himself towards becoming a champion. That aim was accelerated by a growing friendship with Sydney Wood, the 1931 Wimbledon champion. Wood, at 19 years 243 days, had become Wimbledon's second youngest champion in strange circumstances. He won without having to play in the final. Opponent Frank Shields had beaten Jean Borotra in the semi-final, but in the fourth set he had sprained an ankle which had swollen up after the match, causing him to withdraw from the final.

The pair worked hard on Budge's game, instilling a soundness and technique previously missing. Initially shy and a baseline player, Budge developed a backhand which would be copied by teaching professionals down the years.

Wood was a nephew of the president of the USLTA, Julian Myrick, who worked unceasingly to develop the Forest Hills complex, and was a prime mover in the construction of the centre as a national tennis base. Budge moved east in 1933 on elevation to the national squad. He used to relax in the evening 'sitting in' on the drums with Benny Goodman and Tommy Dorsey – shyness very much a thing of the past.

In 1933 Budge made his first trip to Wimbledon. He stunned the British by beating Bunny Austin to reach the semifinals in which he was beaten by Gottfried von Cramm. Doubles partner and close friend Gene Mako helped Budge into the semifinals of the doubles.

Budge made his Davis Cup debut in 1935. The Americans had not won the cup since 1926 and Budge was looked upon as the new patron saint of lost causes. The Americans reached the final, only to lose 5–0 to Britain at Wimbledon, but when Budge beat Gottfried von Cramm, then world No. 2, in an earlier round, it was obvious that the Americans had a new champion in the nineteen-year-old redhead.

In 1936 Budge climbed to No. 3 in the world rankings, courtesy of another semifinal at Wimbledon – he lost to Fred Perry in four sets – and an appearance in the final of the US Open, where Perry beat him 10–8 in the fifth, after Budge had held two match points. But the Budge–Mako combination in the doubles clinched his first major.

Perry, seven years older than Budge, was the accepted master, but the discrepancy between them was fast evaporating. When Perry decided to turn professional, the logical successor was obvious.

So it proved. Budge won all three events at Wimbledon in 1937, dismissing Gottfried von Cramm 6–3, 6–4, 6–2, in the singles final. At Forest Hills von Cramm put up sterner resistance before capitulating 6–1 in the final set, and Budge went on to claim the mixed

FACTFILE

Born 13 June 1915, California, United States

World ranking 1935 sixth, 1936 third, 1937 first, 1938 first

Wimbledon Championships
  Singles 1937 beat G. von Cramm (Germany), 6–3, 6–4, 6–2
      1938 beat H. W. Austin (GB), 6–1, 6–0, 6–3
  Doubles 1937 (with G. Mako, USA) beat Hughes & Tuckey (GB),
      6–0, 6–4, 6–8, 6–1
      1938 (with G. Mako, USA) beat Henkel & von Metaxa
      (Germany),   6–4, 3–6, 6–3, 8–6
  Mixed doubles 1936 (with Mrs M. Fabyan, USA) lost to Perry &
      Round (GB), 9–7, 5–7, 4–6
      1937 (with Miss A. Marble, USA) beat Petra &
      Mathieu (France), 6–4, 6–1
      1938 (with Miss A. Marble, USA) beat Henkel
      (Germany) & Fabyan (USA), 6–1, 6–4

French Championships
  Singles 1938 beat R. Menzel (Czechoslovakia), 6–3, 6–2, 6–4
  Doubles 1938 (with G. Mako, USA), lost to Destremeau & Petra
      (France), 6–3, 3–6, 7–9, 1–6

Australian Championships
  Singles 1938 beat J. E. Bromwich (Australia), 6–4, 6–2, 6–1

United States Championships
  Singles 1936 lost to F. J. Perry (GB), 6–2, 2–6, 6–8, 6–1, 8–10
      1937 beat G. von Cramm (Germany), 6–1, 7–9, 6–1,
      3–6, 6–1
      1938 beat G. Mako (USA), 6–3, 6–8, 6–2, 6–1
  Doubles 1935 (with G. Mako, USA) lost to Allison & Van Ryn
      (USA), 4–6, 2–6, 6–3, 6–2, 1–6
      1936 (with G. Mako, USA) beat Allison & Van Ryn
      (USA), 6–4, 6–2, 6–4
      1937 (with G. Mako, USA) lost to von Cramm & Henkel
      (Germany), 4–6, 5–7, 4–6
      1938 (with G. Mako, USA) beat Bromwich & Quist
      (Australia), 6–3, 6–2, 6–1
  Mixed doubles 1936 (with Mrs M. Fabyan, USA) lost to Mako &
      Marble (USA), 3–6, 2–6
      1937 (with Mrs M. Fabyan, USA) beat Petra &
      Henrotin (France), 6–2, 8–10, 6–0
      1938 (with Miss A. Marble, USA) beat Bromwich &
      Coyne (Australia), 6–1, 6–2

doubles final and reach the final of the men's doubles. America regained the Davis Cup with a 4–1 win at Wimbledon.

'Go for the lot,' suggested Mako as a broad outline for the 1938 campaign. Budge had never attempted the French or Australian championships before.

Wimbledon was an embarrassment. Budge won the singles without dropping a set in the whole fortnight. In the mixed doubles the same statistic prevailed with Alice Marble, the US champion. In a mini Grand Slam, Budge and Mako reached the doubles final also without dropping a set, then slipped up 6–3 in the second set of the final, en route to a four-set win.

In the meantime Budge had quietly collected the French and Australian singles titles. Neither the Australian, John Bromwich, nor the Czech, Menzel, could take a set in the respective finals. History was made – and America retained the Davis Cup.

The 6-foot 3-inch Budge enjoyed the Davis Cup and the theme 'Game to United States' as opposed to 'Game to Budge.' By the end of 1938, Budge had played in eleven Davis Cup ties, winning nineteen out of twenty-one singles and six of eight doubles.

Immediately after the Grand Slam Budge turned professional. He went on a world tour with Ellsworth Vines, the 1932 Wimbledon champion, who had joined the paid ranks four years earlier. Budge won the series 21–18 and refused to practise on indoor courts. 'If I'm the great player everyone says I am, then I can adapt.'

From boyhood shyness to modesty and good naturedness – the players of Budge's era tell a fine tale of his increased confidence. At Wimbledon, after his first win, he met Queen Mary, tennis enthusiast extraordinary. Budge was unused to such protocol. On meeting Her Majesty, he was stuck for a reply. He solved the problem with the immortal phrase, 'Hi, Queen.'

Donald Budge takes the court for his match against Fred Perry in the 1937 Davis Cup at Wimbledon. The USA won 4–1 to regain the Cup

Vera Caslavska

Vera Caslavska, the Prague gymnast, is the most prolific individual gold medallist in the history of women's events at the Olympic Games. Three golds at Tokyo in 1964 and four at Mexico City four years later gave her this record. The 5-foot 2-inch blonde dominated an era in between Larissa Latynina, the first truly great woman gymnast, whom she eventually dethroned, and the Tourisheva–Korbut–Comaneci triumvirate.

The young Miss Caslavska showed possible world class as an ice skater before she had reached her teens. The coach at the local rink was Dagnar Lerchova, the former Czech champion. Caslavska also studied ballet. But a chance appeal on television was to alter her life.

The appeal was made by Eva Bosakova, Czechoslovakia's first outstanding international gymnast. Miss Bosakova had won the combined silver medal at the 1954 World Championships, and a silver medal on the beam at the Melbourne Olympics. She asked for aspiring gymnasts to join in a nationwide talent competition. Vera applied. Within twelve months she was runner-up to Eva in the Czech Championships. Eva was the guiding influence in Vera's early career, and still good enough to win the gold medal on the beam at the 1962 World Championships. She was coach and teammate, winner of eleven major medals before Vera's first, and another five during Vera's career.

Vera, born 3 May 1943, was the youngest competitor at the 1958 World Championships. Her daily routine had undergone a radical change. She was up and training at 5 a.m., then returned to the gym after school for the evening session. Her first major gold medal followed a year later, at the European Championships, on the beam.

Selected for the 1960 Olympics, she came home with a silver in the team competition. Bosakova won gold on the beam. Two years later she won her first major gold medal, at the World Championships, on the vault. She was runner-up to Latynina in the combined exercises.

Latynina was a legend. Winner of more medals than any one else in history, she was the overall Olympic champion in 1956 and 1960. But by the 1964 Olympics she was becoming fallible. Vera won three golds at Tokyo, two in the vault and beam, but, more importantly, had relegated Larissa to second place in the combined exercises.

Domination became complete when Vera won all five gold medals at the 1965 European Championships and repeated the achievement in 1967. By the time of the 1966 World Championships the Soviet Union had unearthed a new find to replace the ageing Latynina. She was Natalya Kuchinskaya and although Vera won the combined exercises, the gold medal count in the five individual events was 3 – 2 to the Russian. By the end of the 1967 European Championships, Caslavska was the master again.

About to defend her titles at the 1968 Mexico Olympics, she had to interrupt her training. The Soviet Union, angered by Dubček's overliberal (in their eyes) regime, invaded Czechoslovakia. Vera had to go into hiding. She humped coal to keep fit. She took a job as a secretary. She had to leave her flat. She had publicly opposed the invasion, but she was too valuable an international figure for the Russians to contemplate harm.

The Auditorio Municipal Arena in Mexico City's Chapultepec Park in the Olympic summer of 1968 was the place to be. The locals cheered for Vera as they would for Pele two years later. She won four golds (equalling the women's record for an Olympic Games) and two silvers. The record was hers. She gave Mexico City her version of the 'Mexican Hat Dance'. They appreciated that.

Immediately after the Games, she married. The bridegroom was Joszef Odlozil, silver medallist behind Peter Snell in the 1500 metres at the Tokyo Olympics. They married in Mexico City's Roman Catholic cathedral in Xocalo Square. The whole town turned out.

When Vera returned home, she gave away her four gold medals. They went, one each, to the four Czechoslovakian leaders: Dubček, Svoboda, Cernik and Smrkorsky.

FACTFILE

Born 3 May 1943, Prague, Czechoslovakia

1959 European Championships (Krakow)
Gold: Beam
Silver: Vault

1960 Olympic Games (Rome)
Silver: Team competition

1961 European Championships (Leipzig)
Bronze: Combined exercises, floor exercises

1962 World Championships (Prague)
Gold: Vault
Silver: Combined exercises
Bronze: Floor exercises

1963 World Championships (Paris)
(The Czechs and the Russians did not compete, due to visa problems)

1964 Olympic Games (Tokyo)
Gold: Combined exercises, vault, beam
Silver: Team competition

1965 European Championships (Sofia)
Gold: Combined exercises, bars, beam, vault, floor exercises

1966 World Championships (Dortmund)
Gold: Combined exercises, vault
Silver: Beam, floor exercises

1967 European Championships (Amsterdam)
Gold: Combined exercises, vault, bars, beam, floor exercises

1968 Olympic Games (Mexico City)
Gold: Combined exercises, vault, bars, floor exercises
Silver: Team competition, beam

*Whilst Vera claimed twenty-one world, European and Olympic titles, her husband, Joszef Odlozil – a middle-distance runner – has two claims to fame: he won the Olympic silver medal in the 1500 metres at the 1964 games and he broke the world 2000-metre record in 1965 with a time of 5 minutes 01.2 seconds, taking the record off Frenchman Michel Jazy

Vera Caslavska balances gracefully on the 4-inch-wide beam. Vera won the Olympic gold medal on the apparatus at Tokyo in 1964

Bobby Charlton

Bobby Charlton is the archetype of a national idol. A prodigy when signed by England's most famous club, he survived the Manchester United air disaster and, together with his manager, Matt Busby, represented the transition between the two marvellous teams that United produced before and after that shattering tragedy. He was a model of sportsmanship and decorum.

Bobby Charlton came from that hotbed of football, the northeast. His uncle was Jackie Milburn, the former Newcastle and England centre forward – 'Wor Jackie' was the hero of the northeast. It seemed natural that Bobby should go to St James Park (it cost 2s 5½d for return travel from his home at Ashington to watch the game and have lunch in the Civic Restaurant). He went to Hurst Park School. His brother Jackie was to follow Bobby into the England team; another brother, Gordon, was a fine amateur; Tommy, the youngest was, like many brothers who don't take up the game, possibly the best of all.

Holidays were all about football. When he was ten Bobby went to his uncle, George Milburn, who was trainer at Chesterfield. Yet Charlton recalls in the book, *There's Only One United*, how he joined Manchester United,

After a youth game between Jarrow and Hebburn, someone said that the United scout had been watching, and later I learned that they had spoken to my mother. It was Joe Armstrong, Manchester's chief scout, and he was first in a queue which grew enormously after a couple of goals for the England Schoolboys at Wembley.

The fact was that Manchester United were prepared to back their judgement before I'd reached the England Schools side. I'd also felt a sympathetic respect for the club when just about everyone else wanted Stanley Matthews and Blackpool to win the 1948 Cup final. And then again, the cream of youth was at United, and I wanted to match myself against them.

He made his League debut against Charlton, ironically, and scored twice in his first game at Old Trafford in 1956, two years after signing for the club. In 1956 – 57, his first season, he scored 10 goals in thirteen matches.

Bobby Charlton was one of nine players who survived the Munich disaster. He went on to play 606 League games for United and score 106 goals. He made a then world record 106 appearances for England and his 49 goals still stand as an English record.

The pinnacles of his career were two Cup finals. Both were at Wembley. Both brought tears. They were the culmination of team endeavours with both club and country.

The 31st of July 1966. Another of those days when everyone remembers what they were doing when England won the World Cup. Brought back to 2 – 2 in the last minute of normal time, Alf Ramsey took Charlton and company to one side: 'You've won it once, now go and do it again.' They did. Charlton didn't score, but such was his reputation that German manager Helmut Schoen detailed Franz Beckenbauer to mark him, a move which cost the Germans their impetus. Charlton, though, had done most to place England in the final, with thunderous goals against Mexico in the group match, and two against Portugal in the semi-final. Converted by Ramsey from an out and out winger into a constructive midfield player, he baled the England attack out of its ineffective ways.

Two years later, and ten years after Munich, United reached the European Cup final, but not via the easy route. Goals by defenders Sadler and Foulkes, that veteran warrior of sixteen years service, taking United to Wembley with two goals in the 3 – 3 draw in the semifinal second leg against the famous Real Madrid side at their Bernabeu Stadium, after United had won the first leg 1 – 0.

Derby Day, 29 May, United faced Benfica at Wembley. Charlton, with a rare glancing header, put United into the lead. Graca equalized, and three minutes from the end of normal time, Alex Stepney earned the freedom of Stretford Road with an enveloping save from Eusebio. Three goals in seven minutes in the first period of extra time, the last from Charlton, and the Cup came to England for the first time. Too weary to carry the Cup around Wembley, Charlton handed it to his team-mates, and trotted round at the rear, doubtless pausing to think of all that had happened in those intervening years.

He continued to give yoeman service to United. He only received a single booking in all the games he played in the United jersey and was never reported to authority. He won a then record 106 caps,

FACTFILE

Born 11 October 1937 Ashington, Northumberland, England
Football League debut October 1956, Manchester United v. Charlton Athletic (scored 2 goals)
Football League Appearances 644 (606 for Manchester United, 38 for Preston North End)
Football League Goals 206 (198 for Manchester United, 38 for Preston North End)
International debut April 1958. v. Scotland, Wembley (scored 1 goal)
International Appearances 106
International Goals 49

Honours

Football League Championship 1965, 1967
F A Cup 1963
World Cup 1966

European Cup 1968
European Footballer of the Year 1966
Football Writers' Player of the Year 1966
Awarded O B E 1969

*In between scoring his first goal for England, against Scotland at Hampden on 19 April 1958, and his last one against Colombia in Bogotá twelve years later, Bobby Charlton scored a record 49 goals for his country in full international matches. The following teams were on the receiving end of his goal-scoring technique: Northern Ireland, Luxembourg, Portugal, Scotland, Wales, Mexico, USA, Switzerland, USSR, Sweden, Argentina, Austria, Columbia, Czechoslovakia, East Germany, Italy, Spain, Yugoslavia.

Twenty-three of the 49 were scored at Wembley, and he scored four hat tricks, against Luxembourg, Mexico, Switzerland and the USA

The lethal left foot of England's record goalscorer Bobby Charlton, seen here in Manchester United's colours in a match against the Scottish champions Celtic

and was wrongly substituted in his final game in the sweltering heat of Leon in the 1970 World Cup quarter final against the Germans. England, 2 – 0 up, lost 3 – 2. People blamed Bonetti, but should have blamed the tactics. Charlton's 49 goals in the national shirt will stand unchallenged for years to come.

Bobby Charlton played his last game for United on 28 April 1973 at Chelsea. Brother Jack retired on the same day. Bobby went to play for and manage Preston North End, and made his last league appearance at Port Vale on 29 March 1975.

Voted both English and European Footballer of the Year in 1966, he won a World Cup winners' medal, European Cup, League championship and FA Cup winners' medals. The most appealing of his qualities was the unaffected modesty with which he wore those honours.

On 28 June 1984, Bobby Charlton, now a successful businessman and TV summarizer, was elected to the board of Manchester United. His high standard of behaviour, his skill, his belief in proper values in a sea of violence will be carried forward and will benefit a club who, in the 1983 – 84 season, managed to exasperate their supporters by finishing fourth in what was meant to be a two-horse race.

Bobby Charlton (left) and brother Jack, who between them amassed 141 appearances in the England jersey. Both played in the 1966 World Cup final

Jim Clark

A man who never intended becoming a racing driver, but developed into the greatest driver of his generation, if not the best of all time, Jim Clark was a quiet, modest person who was transformed when behind the wheel. He was similar in that respect to the great Tazio Nuvolari, the best driver between the wars.

Clark was brought up in the Borders. The son of a wealthy farmer, he began driving at the age of nine in an Austin 7, bought his first car, a Sunbeam Talbot, ten years later, progressed to rallying and club racing, and made his single-seater debut at the age of twenty-three. A natural driver, he was spotted by Colin Chapman, who tried for two years to sign him, eventually succeeding in 1960. The Clark–Chapman partnership at Lotus flourished and dominated motor racing from 1962 until Clark's death at Hockenheim in 1968.

The figures on their own reveal Clark's genius. He raced in seventy-three Grands Prix, won twenty-five times and was in pole position thirty-three times. What the figures do not reveal is Clark's ability to be clear of the field after the first lap, leaving the opposition to settle for the minor placings.

Clark would race 'anywhere in anything'. Barrie Gill wrote that Clark was 'as thrilling to watch in a Lotus Cortina as in a Formula 1 car'. He loved driving. In contrast to the drivers of today who travel everywhere by helicopter, Clark would frequently drive to continental circuits in his own Lotus Elan.

When Stirling Moss retired in 1962, Jim Clark was the natural successor for the British fans. That year he won his first Grand Prix at Spa and finished second in the championship to Graham Hill.

A year later the title was his – he had set a new record of seven wins in the season and, in the Indianapolis 500, amazed the Americans by coming second. He was, at twenty-seven, the youngest world champion ever.

In 1964 the world title went to John Surtees, who took the championship on the last lap of the last race in Mexico. But 1965 was a vintage year for Clark: six Grands Prix wins and the title, and the Indianapolis 500 for the first time. The Americans who had scoffed when Clark first arrived there now had the utmost respect for the Lotus team.

1965 was a difficult year to follow. Many thought that Clark would retire to his farm at Chirtside near Duns in Berwickshire, but he was back in 1966 to win the US Grand Prix; he won four races the next year and the opening Grand Prix of the 1968 season at Kyalami. But on 7 April that year, in a Formula 2 race at Hockenheim, Clark inexplicably ran off the road into some trees at 150 miles an hour. It seemed impossible that driver error could have been the cause. In the event, an investigation revealed a mechanical fault.

Clark, the finest Formula 1 driver of all time, died at the age of thirty-two. In the world of motor racing, where death is all too frequent, he will never be forgotten.

FACTFILE

Born 4 March 1936, Kilmany, Fife, Scotland
Died 7 April 1968, Hockenheim, West Germany

World Drivers Championship
  Winner 1963, 1965
  Runner-up 1962

World Championship Grand Prix wins (25, all for Lotus)
1962 Belgian, British, United States
1963 Belgian, French, British, Dutch, Italian, Mexican,
  South African
1964 Belgian, British, Dutch
1965 Belgian, French, German, British, Dutch, South African
1966 United States
1967 British, Dutch, Mexican, United States
1968 South African

Summary of Grand Prix wins
Belgian 1962, 1963, 1964, 1965
British 1962, 1963, 1964, 1965, 1967
Dutch 1963, 1964, 1965, 1967
French 1963, 1965
German 1965
Italian 1963
Mexican 1963, 1967
South African 1963, 1965, 1968
United States 1962, 1966, 1967

(Clark also won the Pau Grand Prix in 1961.)

*Clark never married. He said, 'I couldn't ask any woman to share this kind of life'

Jim Clark, world motor racing champion in 1963 and 1965

Sebastian Coe

Sometimes one wondered when fortune would smile on Sebastian Coe. He was named after Sebastian in Shakespeare's *The Tempest* and the storm clouds gathered in 1981 with a succession of illnesses constantly hindering the progress of an athlete whose outstanding world records were not backed by the requisite number of major gold medals. With luck, in 1984, the pendulum was beginning to swing again.

Though born in London, where he is now based, Coe's background was of traditional English athletics fare – the Hallamshire Harriers club at his home in Sheffield and the more sophisticated physical education courses at Loughborough Colleges. Initially a sprinter, he moved to 3000 metres and cross-country, before settling for the middle distances. He first met Steve Ovett in the intermediate section of the 1972 English Schools Cross-Country Championships. Coe finished tenth, Ovett second; the winner was a certain Kirk Dumplington, who now contents himself with club athletics in the St Albans area.

The breakthrough year was 1977. After a bronze medal in the 1975 European Championships and his first four-minute mile (3:58.6) in August 1976, Coe won the European indoor 800 metres title in March in a fast 1:46.5 and, in the summer, won the Emsley Carr Mile at the Crystal Palace, beating Filbert Bayi, the world 1500-metre record holder, in a time of 3:57.7. He became the British record holder at 800 metres with a time of 1:45.0.

Coe and Ovett both started as co-favourites when the European Championships 800-metre final took place in Prague on 31 August 1978. A few days earlier Coe had lowered the British record to 1:44.3 in Brussels, but, after he had led the field through the bell in a crazy time of around 50 seconds, both Coe and Ovett were passed by the East German Olaf Beyer, whose 1:43.8 was a world-class time. Seb, with a bronze medal, returned to the Coca-Cola meeting in London and regained his British record, lost in the European Championships to Ovett, with a time of 1:44.0.

In 1979 Seb Coe set the track world back on its heels. Within forty-one days he became the first athlete ever to break the world record for the 800 and the 1500 metres, and the mile. He began at the famous Bislet Stadium in Oslo, taking a second off Alberto Jantuorena's 800-metre time (1:42.33). On 17 July he returned to the cosy little stadium for the Golden Mile, and won that in 3:48.95, nearly half a second inside John Walker's 1975 time. Then, on 15 August, he erased Filbert Bayi's five-year-old 1500-metre mark by one tenth of a second with 3:32.03.

The following year, it was Steve Ovett's turn to enter the record books. Back at the Bislet on 1 July 1980, Ovett ran the mile in 3:48.8 just an hour after Seb had set a new mark in the 1000 metres. Then, just nine days before the Olympic heats, Ovett ran the 1500 metres in 3:32.1 against a field which included many of the athletes who claimed that, but for the American boycott, they would be in the Olympic medals.

At the 1980 Olympics track experts thought that Coe would win the 800, and that the 1500 would be a toss-up. Beyer dropped out early on, and the final on 26 July was a staccato affair. Normally used to positive front running, Coe wandered, tactically unsure, into the outside lanes. He made his move too late; Ovett had shot clear. Coe outsprinted the remainder for the silver but Ovett had his gold.

His summing up was brutally frank. 'Within two laps (the first a turgid 54.3 seconds), I compounded more mistakes, elementary errors, than in the rest of my career put together.' Father Peter, his coach, added, 'Running like a novice is being kind.'

Six days later the pair lined up for the 1500-metre final. Ovett, relaxed and with his gold medal; Coe, conquering his disappointment and basing his confidence on the fact that you don't become a bad athlete overnight. Like all good stories, it had a happy ending: Sebastian Coe won his gold medal.

Looking back over the race, the first lap was a mess, the second little better. Long-distance events in major games were beginning to follow the pattern of cycle races, the dawdle before the sprint. There was one crucial athlete, No. 338, the East German Jurgen Straub. Straub took the lead with 800 metres to go. It played into Coe's hands. He wanted a long run to the line. With 80 metres left he overtook Straub, who took the silver, with Ovett run into third place. Lest anyone doubts the final time, a mediocre 3:38.4, it is worth noting that the last 800 metres was run in 1:46.8 and the last 400 in 52.2. The great Olympic confrontation had finished all square.

His gold safely in his pocket, Coe set about the record books in 1981. He improved his 800-metre time to 1:41.72 in Florence, and he lost and then regained the mile record with 3:47.33 in Brussels. He had broken eight world records. His style was graceful and floating. Then everything started to go wrong.

After winning the 1981 World Cup 800 metres with ridiculous ease, he commented that he had been remarkably lucky with injuries – three seasons with nothing worse than a sore sciatic nerve

FACTFILE

Born 29 September 1956, London, England

Olympic medals
Gold: 1500 metres (1980, 1984)
Silver: 800 metres (1980, 1984)

European Championships
Silver: 800 metres (1982)
Bronze: 800 metres (1978)

World records
800 metres   1:42.33 (1979)
               1:41.72 (1981)
1000 metres 2:13.4 (1980)
               2:12.18 (1981)
Mile 3:49.00 (1979)
       3:48.53 (1981)
       3:47.33 (1981)
1500 metres 3:32.1 (1979)

The second bite of the cherry. Seb Coe wins the Olympic 1500-metre gold medal at Moscow in his 'reserve' event, after Steve Ovett had beaten him over his favourite 800 metres

and a blister. Then, in the winter and spring of 1981–82, he suffered two fractures. The moguls had set up a series of races with Ovett. They were scrapped. He ran in a British team that broke the world record for the 4 × 800 metre relay. He clocked 1:43.9 at the Bislet. In the European Championships in Athens, he ran on what proved to be rubbery and sick legs. Again he took the silver; Hans Peter Ferner, who, a week later, was beaten by three other Britons, took the gold in a moderate time, passing Coe 50 metres out. No 1500 this time for Coe.

A good indoor season, after missing the Commonwealth Games in Brisbane, was a deception. Defeats by international-class – but not world-class – athletes Gonzalez of Spain and Zdravkovic of Yugoslavia over 1500 metres were a prelude to disintegration to Steve Scott over a mile at Crystal Palace, and then to Cram, Wuyke and Elliott over his favourite 800 metres at Gateshead. Scott and Cram were magnanimous in conceding that he was less than fit. He missed the first World Championships.

He was discovered to be suffering from a rare blood disease and also a serious back displacement. Coe based himself in London for treatment. He changed his club and ran for Harringay in a few tentative winter relays.

His motivation was to win gold at Los Angeles. He said, 'To many I'm someone who failed at major championships, though I don't think an Olympic gold, a World Cup and two Europa Cup victories make me a bad runner.'

1984 began slowly. His beloved Chelsea returned to Division One as champions. He trained through the winter with Harringay and also alongside the deer in Richmond Park, stalking the future. Already pre-selected for the Olympic 800 metres, he lost to Peter Elliott in the Olympic 1500-metre trials. The selectors kept faith and selected Coe for both events at the Olympics.

On 12 August he repaid their confidence. Again he had to pick himself up as the Brazilian Joachim Cruz forced him to accept another 800-metre silver medal to join the collection. 'We're too old for these short races,' said Coe to Ovett. His dignity amazed the Americans.

Coe took the gold medal in the 1500 metres in a new Olympic record time of 3:32.53. World champion Steve Cram was second. Steve Ovett sadly had to drop out whilst well placed.

At no time in 1984 had Coe been his old self. He may not be still. No one at the Los Angeles Olympics had struggled through more and succeeded.

Nadia Comaneci

A personification of the modern Communist ideals, Nadia Comaneci had the initial misfortune of inheriting the gymnastics audience developed by Ludmila Tourischeva and Olga Korbut at the 1972 Munich Olympics. Quiet and shy, Nadia's contribution to the 1976 Montreal Olympics was a standard of excellence which enabled her to become the first gymnast to register a maximum 10.00 points at the Olympics. She then notched up a further six such perfect scores.

Born at Gheorghe Dej, 120 kilometres north of Bucharest, on 12 November 1961, Nadia took up gymnastics at the age of seven, her parents suggesting that they were happier with their tomboy daughter falling off bars and beams rather than out of trees. Proximity to Bucharest enabled her schooling to be conducted in the gymnastics training centres, the emphasis being on rigorous, spartan training and intensive coaching, with education fitted in during rest periods. Coming under the influence of Bela Karoli, the Rumanian coach and Svengali, Nadia won her first national title at the age of twelve in 1973.

London was the setting for Nadia's breakthrough to major international status, for it was at Wembley in 1975 where she won the Champions All overall title. Even at this early stage, it represented a comeback, as she had been dropped from the Rumanian team that year for 'a lack of talent'. The result of the competition was as follows:

1	Nadia Comaneci	37.30 pts
2	Ludmila Savina (USSR)	37.10 pts
3	Avril Lennox (GB)	36.55 pts

For the Montreal Olympics Nadia had been entered as the reigning European overall champion. The Soviet Union had arrived with the class of '72, with Olga Korbut and Ludmila Tourischeva, and had added the delightful Nelli Kim to their team. The Soviet interpretation of the floor exercises was superior – but it was on the aerial apparatus that Nadia secured the maximum points. She had the ideal temperament and nerve; her routines wouldn't have been attempted on the floor ten years previously.

At the Montreal Games Nadia won five medals. Three were gold – the overall title, and on the bars and beam. She was part of the Rumanian team which took the silver to the Soviet Union's gold in the team event. And her increasing confidence and interpretation gave her the bronze in the floor exercises.

The years between Montreal and Moscow, venue for the 1980 Olympics, were laced with queries. She won the overall title at both the 1977 and 1979 European Championships, but success in the World Championships was less frequent. In 1978 she took the gold only on her favourite apparatus, the beam, and in 1979 had to retire through injury after being in Rumania's team gold medal quartet. Pictures, articles and allegations about the use of drugs to counter her development from a schoolgirl to a young woman were rife. Rumania, surrounded by other communist regimes, is not the ideal place to seek information. But one thing was increasingly certain, Rumania would be at the Moscow Olympics and Nadia would be the trump card.

FACTFILE

Born 12 November 1961, Gheorghe Dej, Rumania

1971 Friendship Cup (Bulgaria)
Gold: Bars, beam

1973 Friendship Cup (East Germany)
Gold: Combined exercises, bars, vault

1975 Champions All (England)
Overall winner

1975 European Championships (Skien, Norway)
Gold: Combined exercises, bars, beam, vault
Silver: Floor exercises

1975 Pre-Olympics (Montreal)
Overall winner
Gold: Bars
Silver: Vault, floor exercises
Bronze: Beam

1976 American Cup (USA)
Overall winner

1976 Olympic Games (Montreal)
Gold: Combined exercises, bars, beam
Silver: Team competition
Bronze: Floor exercises

1976 Chunichi Cup (Nagoya, Japan)
Overall winner
Gold: Bars, beam, vault, floor exercises

1976 Balkan Championships (Salonika, Greece)
Overall winner
Gold: Bars, beam, vault, floor exercises

1977 European Championships (Prague)
Gold: Combined exercises, bars (joint)
Silver: Vault
(Team withdrawn)

1978 World Championships (Strasbourg)
Gold: Beam
Silver: Vault, team competition

1979 Champions All (England)
Overall winner

1979 European Championships (Copenhagen)
Gold: Combined exercises, vault, floor exercises
Bronze: Beam

1979 World Cup (Tokyo)
Gold: Vault, floor exercises
Silver: Beam

1979 World Championships (Fort Worth, USA)
Gold: Team competition
(Withdrew due to injury)

1980 Olympic Games (Moscow)
Gold: Beam, floor exercises (joint)
Silver: Combined exercises, team competition

Whatever the rumours, the 1980 Olympics were a triumph, with four more medals: two gold and two silver. She retained her beam title and was pleased to win the floor exercises. That gave her parity with Korbut, Kim and Tourischeva. Silver medals in the overall individual event and the team competition gave Nadia an Olympic running total of five golds, three silvers and a bronze.

Controversies Surrounding Comaneci

In the 1977 European Championships in Prague, Comaneci, her coach Bela Karoli and the entire Rumanian team walked out, saying they would not take part in international competitions again until the rules governing the markings were changed (they did not return until the following year).

In the vault, Comaneci had been placed first, but after a Russian protest, she was downgraded and the Russian awarded the gold. The Rumanian coach, Maria Simeonescu, accused the Russian, East German and Czechoslovakian judges of deliberately downgrading, and promptly withdrew her team.

The judges accused were Silvia Hlavicek (East Germany), Isroslava Matischova (Czechoslovakia), and Lidia Ivanova (USSR).

In the 1980 Olympic Games in Moscow, Comaneci was the last to perform her exercise on the beam in the all-round individual competition, knowing she needed a score of 9.95 to win. By her own admission she made two minor mistakes and under normal circumstances would have expected a mark of 9.85. However, all competitors had made mistakes, and, from the way in which the previous marks had gone, a 9.95 was a possibility.

However, when it came to judging, the Bulgarian judge awarded 10.00, the Czech 9.90, and the Russian and Polish judges 9.80 each. After taking off the top and bottom marks, it averaged at 9.85.

Before the mark was announced, the head judge, who happened to be Rumania's Maria Simeonescu, would not enter a score, saying it should be 9.95 in comparison to the other scores. The judges refused to alter the scores and, after twenty-seven minutes of heated argument in public, Russian Yuri Titov, president of the FIG, stepped in and ruled that the original scores should stand. Comaneci was awarded 9.85 and a share of the silver medal; she had been dethroned by Davydova of Russia.

The following day, in the floor exercise, there was a further controversy. The gold was initially awarded to Nellie Kim, but it was then noticed there was an error on Comaneci's score, which was then raised by 0.05 points, bringing her up to share the gold with Kim. The explanation for this was never really known; did a judge genuinely press the wrong button when putting up her mark, or did the Rumanians protest and a judge, in sympathy for the previous day's scoring, make the necessary adjustments in the marking?

After Moscow, Karoli, disillusioned with marking procedures in the sport, remained in the United States. He helped in the coaching of the 1984 Olympic champion Mary Lou Retton. Nadia returned to Bucharest to start life all over again. Still in the sport, she is now an international judge.

Nadia Comaneci, whose tomboy gymnastics superseded those of the Soviet pair Olga Korbut and Ludmila Tourischeva in the late 1970s

Denis Compton

The British sporting hero of the immediate postwar period, Denis Compton was England's finest middle-order batsman and a left winger in Arsenal's FA Cup winning team of 1950.

Neville Cardus wrote:

He counts amongst those cricketers who changed a game of competitive and technical interest into a highly individual art that appealed and fascinated thousands who had no particular regard for the finer points of the game.

In fact whenever Compton was seriously in trouble and under the necessity to work hard, he was an even more arresting spectacle than usual. As we watched him groping and lunging out of his ground before the ball was released, we were more than ever aware that this was no talented cricketer: more a genius solving his own problems.

Once, in Australia, he ran into a new bowler of curious variations of spin – Iverson. Compton was visited by one of his moods of eccentric fallibility: he played forward as though sightless, he played back as though wanting to play forward. At the other end a young novice was accumulating runs steadily, but not quickly enough. He approached Compton for instructions: go on just as you are, you're playing well. I'll get on with the antics!

At his greatest, which was often, he made batting look as easy as the natural way he walked and talked. Versatility of stroke play: swift, yet, paradoxically, leisurely footwork: drives that were given a lovely lightness of wristy flexion at the last second. The word 'Master' couldn't be applied to him – Compton's cricket always looked young, fresh and spontaneous, whilst the word 'Master' often implies age and pompousness.

FACTFILE

Born 23 May 1918, Hendon, London, England

First-class debut 1936, Middlesex v. Sussex
Total first-class runs 38,942 (average 51.85)
First-class centuries 123
Total first-class wickets 622 (average 32.22)
Test debut 1937, MCC v. New Zealand
Total Test runs 5807 (average 50.06)
Test centuries 17
Highest innings 300, MCC v. North East Transvaal, Benoni (1948–49)
Best bowling 7–36, MCC v. Auckland (1946–47)

Football League debut September 1936, v. Derby County
Football League appearances 54
Football League goals 15
FA Cup 1950, Arsenal v. Liverpool

*Here is a breakdown of how Compton scored his record 3816 runs in 1947:

Runs scored in Test matches	753
Runs scored in county games	2033
Runs scored in other games	1030
Total	3816

In addition he took 73 wickets for 2053 runs.

His month by month progression was as follows:

	In month	Running total
May	832	832
June	593	1425
July	646	2071
August	1195	3266
September	550	3816

His runs were scored as follows:

Test matches (v. South Africa)

First (Trent Bridge)	65 & 163	
Second (Lord's)	208	
Third (Old Trafford)	115 &	6
Fourth (Headingley)	30	
Fifth (The Oval)	53 & 113	

Other matches

Players v. Gentlemen (Lord's)	11	
Middlesex v. Rest of England (Oval)	246	
South of England v. Sir Pelham Warner's XI (Hastings)	87* & 86	
MCC v. South Africa (Lord's)	18 & 97	
Middlesex v. South Africa (Lord's)	154 & 34	
South of England v. South Africa (Hastings)	101 & 30	
MCC v. Yorkshire (Lord's)	73 & 7	
MCC v. Surrey (Lord's)	52 & 34	

County Championship matches
At Lord's

v. Somerset	6 & 25	
v. Gloucestershire	22	
v. Worcestershire	88* & 112	
v. Sussex	110	
v. Hampshire	88	
v. Yorkshire	50*	
v. Essex	129 & 48	
v. Kent	16 & 168	
v. Surrey	178 & 19*	
v. Northamptonshire	60 & 85	
v. Lancashire	17 & 139	

Elsewhere

v. Kent (Canterbury)	106 & 4	
v. Leicestershire (Leicester)	151 & 33*	
v. Northamptonshire (Northampton)	110 & 13*	
v. Surrey (Oval)	137*	
v. Sussex (Hove)	100*	
v. Yorkshire (Leeds)	4 & 15	

Six of his eighteen centuries were against South Africa.

Denis Compton drives through mid-wicket, watched admiringly from first slip by Trevor Bailey (centre), one of Compton's England colleagues

Compton made his debut in 1936 at the age of eighteen batting at No. 11 for Middlesex against Sussex in the traditional Whitsun fixture. By the end of the season he had made his first century – 100 not out against Northamptonshire – and had accumulated 1004 runs at an average of 34.62. A year later he made his Test debut against New Zealand and scored 65.

During the Second World War he was posted with the Armed Forces to India and played for Holkar in the final of the Indian Ranji Trophy in 1945, scoring 249 not out. Then, when cricket started up again in England after the war, in a period still sore and shabby and rationed, he spread his ability everywhere. In the first postwar summer he resumed where he had left off six formative years earlier, scoring 2000 runs in the season.

In 1947 he set a record unlikely to be beaten in this one-day age. He went to the wicket on fifty occasions and scored 3816 runs (a record), with eighteen centuries (another record) and twelve half centuries.

In 1948 he played two of his most heroic innings against probably the best of all touring teams, Don Bradman's Australians. He made 184 in dreadful light at Trent Bridge, before slipping onto his wicket. In Manchester, he showed that there was stern stuff about him, the iron breastplate to go with the cavalier plume. He was knocked out by Lindwall. Stitches were sewn into his scalp and he returned to make 145 not out in five hours twenty minutes.

In that winter he made the fastest 300 of all time, in just 181 minutes, against North Eastern Transvaal at Benoni. Typically, he dismissed it, saying that once he had reached his first century he tried to get out to give others practice. He hit five 6s and forty-two 4s, mostly into the delighted Black compound, and slowed only when nearing other century landmarks.

Denis Compton could bowl a bit too. He took 62 wickets in the season in which he scored his 3816 runs. In 1949 he took 73 wickets, and 77 in 1952 at 28.58.

His football suffered from overseas cricket tours. He played eleven wartime games with Matthews, Carter, Lawton and Hagan as fellow members of an Army XI, and appeared in a wartime international against Scotland.

In 1949–50 he played his best football. He was in the team which beat Liverpool 2–0 to win the Cup, and created the second goal from a corner. But it was probably football that was responsible for the need for an operation to remove a fragment from his left knee.

The remainder of his career was a battle to maintain full fitness. In November 1955 he had an even more serious operation to remove a kneecap. A series of minor operations followed to improve the flexion. He returned to first-class cricket in 1956, took a century off Somerset and, a mere seven weeks later, was recalled to play against Australia in the final Test and scored 94. He retired at the end of the 1957 season, to a career in broadcasting and journalism.

Neville Cardus again: 'Nature was generous with him at his cradle: she gave him nearly everything. Then in his prime and in his heyday, she snatched away his mainspring, she crippled him with many summers of his genius still to come.'

Maureen Connolly

Of all postwar Wimbledon lady champions, 'Little Mo' was quite the most outstanding and quite the most tragic. She became the first woman to win tennis's Grand Slam, yet within a year was forced to retire, and, in 1969, she died at the age of thirty-four.

Little Mo began playing tennis at the age of ten, at the public courts in San Diego. Originally a left-hander, she switched to her right as an experiment. She felt more at ease, so right-handed she remained.

At the age of twelve she took up the game seriously. Her first coach was the legendary Eleanor Tennant, who had coached the 1939 Wimbledon champion, Alice Marble. Mrs Tennant was wise enough to recognize a precocious talent and her coaching recipe was original: ballet, tap dancing and skipping to help speed and coordination, whilst working on technical improvement.

Progress was at a phenomenal rate. In 1948 Little Mo won the US Junior Championships at the age of fourteen. Two years later, despite Louise Brough, Shirley Fry and Doris Hart, all Wimbledon champions, she was the US national champion. She played in the Wightman Cup, and worked in a newsagent's shop to make ends meet.

By seventeen Little Mo was Wimbledon champion for the first time. Sadly, she fell out with Eleanor Tennant midway through the championship. 'A one-man task force can only have one commander' was her reply to reporters. The singlemindedness was difficult to control. She insisted on practising for two hours before a match

and, after she had won Wimbledon, she went to an outside court to wind down.

At 5 feet 2 inches and 7 st 8 lb, Little Mo was initially a baseline player, rather like the younger Evert and Austin. Forsaking the baseline for an all-court game, she hit her ground strokes with remorseless accuracy. Her nickname was coined at this stage. Nelson Fisher, a tennis coach whom she remembered from her newspapershop days, guided her fortunes after the break with Tennant. He saw her firing away like a battleship from the baseline, and took the name from a battleship that was then in the news. the *Missouri*.

She practised six hours a day and the result was simplicity itself: she never lost in eighteen matches at Wimbledon. In 1953 her new coach, Harry Hopman, scheduled a programme to include an attempt on the Grand Slam. Little Mo met those requirements without the loss of a set in the four finals. After she had won the 1951 US Championships, Maureen Connolly was beaten on only four occasions, twice by Doris Hart and once each by Beverley Fleitz and Shirley Fry. At Wimbledon only two women ever took a set off her.

1954 began happily enough. She married the Olympic modern pentathlete, Norman Brinker, and won Wimbledon for the third successive year. But shortly after she returned home, tragedy struck. Horse riding was her hobby and while exercising her horse, Colonel Merryboy, one July morning she collided with a cement lorry. Doctors fought to save her right leg, but the main artery and many

FACTFILE

Born 17 September 1934, San Diego, California, USA
Died 21 June 1969, Dallas, Texas, USA

World ranking 1951 third, 1952 first, 1953 first, 1954 first

Wimbledon singles titles
1952 beat Miss A. L. Brough, 7 – 5, 6 – 3
1953 beat Miss D. J. Hart, 8 – 6, 7 – 5
1954 beat Miss A. L. Brough, 6 – 2, 7 – 5

French Championships
  Singles 1953 beat Miss D. J. Hart, 6 – 2, 6 – 4
         1954 beat Mme G. Bucaille, 6 – 4, 6 – 1
  Doubles 1954 (with Mrs H. C. Hopman) beat Mme Galtier and
    Mlle Schmidt, 7 – 5, 4 – 6, 6 – 0
  Mixed doubles 1954 (with Lew Hoad) beat R. N. Hartwig and
    Mme J. Patorni, 6 – 4, 6 – 3

Australian Championships
  Singles 1953 beat Miss J. Sampson, 6 – 3, 6 – 2
  Doubles 1953 (with Miss J. Sampson) beat Mrs N. K. Haughton
    and Miss B. Penrose, 6 – 4, 6 – 2

United States singles titles
1951 beat Miss S. Fry, 6 – 3, 1 – 6, 6 – 4
1952 beat Miss D. J. Hart, 6 – 3, 7 – 5
1953 beat Miss D. J. Hart, 6 – 2, 6 – 4

Wightman Cup appearances 9 (1951 – 54; won all 9 rubbers)

*In the three years she played at Wimbledon, Little Mo never lost in the singles – eighteen successive matches without defeat. Her full list of matches is as follows:

1952
  Second round Mrs C. G. Moeller (GB), 6 – 2, 6 – 0
  Third round Miss A. Mortimer (GB), 6 – 4, 6 – 3
  Fourth round Miss J. S. V. Partridge (GB), 6 – 3, 5 – 7, 7 – 5
  Fifth round Mrs T. D. Long (Australia), 5 – 7, 6 – 2, 6 – 0
  Semifinal Miss S. J. Fry (USA), 6 – 4, 6 – 3
  Final Miss A. L. Brough (USA), 7 – 5, 6 – 3
1953
  Second round Miss D. Killian (South Africa), 6 – 0, 6 – 0
  Third round Miss J. M. Petchell (GB), 6 – 1, 6 – 1
  Fourth round Miss J. A. Shilcock (GB), 6 – 0, 6 – 1
  Fifth round Frau E. Vollmer (W. Germany), 6 – 3, 6 – 0
  Semifinal Miss S. J. Fry (USA), 6 – 1, 6 – 1
  Final Miss D. J. Hart, (USA), 8 – 6, 7 – 5
1954
  Second round Miss J. Scott (South Africa), 6 – 0, 6 – 3
  Third round Frl E. Buding (W. Germany), 6 – 2, 6 – 3
  Fourth round Miss A. Buxton (GB), 6 – 0, 6 – 0
  Fifth round Mrs W. du Pont (USA), 6 – 1, 6 – 1
  Semifinal Mrs C. Pratt (USA), 6 – 1, 6 – 1
  Final Miss A. L. Brough (USA), 6 – 2, 7 – 5

Played 18   *Won* 18   *Lost* 0   *Sets for* 232   *Sets against* 86

'Little Mo' Connolly, who, despite being only 5 feet 2 inches tall, was a commanding overhead player

of the muscles were irreparably severed. The injury was to terminate her competitive career. In December she attempted a comeback, but the blood supply to her right leg was restricted and three times in her first match she collapsed with cramp. She could play no more.

Little Mo pursued a family life. 'I've got to learn to bake apple pie, it's my husband's favourite,' she said. She had two children and took up coaching. The Maureen Connolly Trophy is contested for by under-21 teams; Ann Jones and Virginia Wade, Britain's more recent champions, owe her a debt. Her voice was part of the Wimbledon commentary scene and she became a respected writer.

In 1969 she entered hospital for a series of operations. They failed to halt the growth of cancer. Like those other Wimbledon legends, Suzanne Lenglen and Elizabeth Ryan, Little Mo died on the eve of the championships. Ann Jones, who had listened to and respected Maureen Connolly's advice, won the ladies' singles a fortnight later.

Henry Cooper

Henry Cooper lost his first three amateur fights. When he retired twenty years later, he had, as Reg Gutteridge described, 'stolen the affection of the public for a longer spell than any other sportsman. He had indestructable dignity. Eleven years British champion; the only outright holder of three Lonsdale belts; awarded the OBE. It proves that nice guys don't always finish second.'

Born at Westminster Hospital, Cooper's early days were spent in and around Bellingham, just south of Lewisham. He became ABA light heavyweight champion in 1952. He knocked out Joe MacLean with a left hook. MacLean was not the first to disappear in that way. Henry fought in the 1952 Olympics. He lost on points in the first round to Anatoly Perev of the Soviet Union, the eventual bronze medallist. Lance Corporal Cooper, H., No. 22698686, of the Royal Ordnance Corps, wanted to be a professional fighter when he left the army in 1954. J. T. Hulls, of the old *Evening News*, put him in touch with Jim Wicks, the 'Bishop'. It was a remarkable partnership.

He took into the professional ring two characteristics which would last throughout his career. His left hook, the finishing weapon – 'Enery's 'ammer – was rated as the best of all time. The right-hand was for writing cheques. The other was a tendency to suffer from cut eyes. 'People meant well,' said Henry, 'they would send me pickled onions, vinegar and herbs – shame it didn't work.'

He won his first nine fights, then was cut in the second round by an Italian, Uber Bacilieri, in April 1955. He knocked out Bacilieri five months later in round seven. He was then outpointed by Joe Erskine in a British title eliminator. Four fights later Doncaster's Peter Bates cut him in five rounds. A year later, after successive defeats by Joe Bygraves (a ninth-round knockout for the Empire title), Ingemar Johannsson (a fifth-round knockout for the European title) and Joe Erskine (outpointed again for the British championship), there were many who said that the twenty-four-year-old Cooper ought to pack it in.

Then two fights in the autumn of 1958 changed the whole complexion of his career. He went into a fight with the rising Welsh hope, Dick Richardson, at Porthcawl, with a record of fifteen wins, one draw and seven defeats. He landed the left hook on Richardson in round five. They brought the world-ranked American, Zora Folley, to Wembley. Henry outpointed him confidently. He went on to beat Brian London for the British title. He was to reign for ten years. Imported Americans arrived at Wembley. All except Zora Folley, who returned and knocked out Henry in the second round, went home losers. Then along came a young man named Cassius Clay.

Olympic champion at Rome, Clay had come with the boast that Cooper would fall in five. Apparently coasting to his prediction, Clay walked into the left hook with four seconds of the fourth round left. He stumbled back to his corner. Manager Angelo Dundee claimed that Clay's cut glove would have to be changed. A quick incision in the gash meant the minute's break was doubled. Clay recovered and peppered Cooper's cut eye, to defeat him in the following round. It was, and still is, the most famous punch in British boxing.

When Clay returned to fight Henry for the world title at the Arsenal football ground in 1966, things had changed. He had a new name – Muhammad Ali. And he had respect for Cooper. Ali/Clay was strangely quiet.

Regrettably, the fight was over in six rounds, with Cooper level

FACTFILE

Born 3 May 1934, Westminster, London, England

Total professional fights 55
   Wins 40
   Defeats 14
   Draws 1
Wins inside the distance 29
Defeats inside the distance 9

Title fights

1957	Joe Bygraves (Empire title)	l	ko	9
	Ingemar Johansson (European title)	l	ko	5
	Joe Erskine (British title)	l	pts	15
1959	Brian London (British and Empire titles)	w	pts	15
	Gawie De Klerk (Empire title)	w	rsf	5
	Joe Erskine (British and Empire titles)	w	ko	12
1961	Joe Erskine (British and Empire titles)	w	rtd	5
1963	Dick Richardson (British and Empire titles)	w	ko	5
1964	Brian London	w	pts	15
	(British, Empire and vacant European titles)			
1965	Johnny Prescott (British and Empire titles)	w	rtd	10
1966	Muhammad Ali (World title)	l	rsf	6
1967	Jack Bodell (British and Empire titles)	w	rsf	2
	Billy Walker (British and Empire titles)	w	rsf	6
1968	Karl Mildenberger (European title)	w	dis	8
1969	Piero Tomasini (European title)	w	ko	5
1970	Jack Bodell (British and Commonwealth titles)	w	pts	15
	Jose Urtain (European title)	w	rsf	9
1971	Joe Bugner	l	pts	15
	(British, Commonwealth and European titles)			

(Cooper was unable to defend the European title in 1964 because of injury, and in 1969 gave up the British and Empire titles, and the European title again through injury.)

Other defeats

1955	Uber Bacilieri		rsf	2 (cuts)
	Joe Erskine		pts	10
1956	Peter Bates		rsf	5 (cuts)
1958	Erich Schoppner		dis	6
1961	Zora Folley		ko	2
1963	Cassius Clay		rsf	5 (cuts)
1964	Roger Rischer		pts	10
1965	Amos Johnson		pts	10
1966	Floyd Patterson		ko	4

on points, but cut again. 'Not bad for a bum and a cripple,' claimed
Henry.

Cooper continued to dominate the European scene until 1969.
He had spectacular one-round wins over Americans Chip Johnson –
who had beaten Henry's twin brother George – and Jefferson Davis.
He lost to former world champion Floyd Patterson on a fourth-
round knockout. In 1969 he gave up the British and Empire titles in
protest against the Board's decision not to sanction a fight with
Jimmy Ellis for the WBA world title, and the European championship
because of injury. A year later he had won them back, before losing
a debatable decision to Joe Bugner at the age of thirty-seven. 'That's
me lot,' he said.

A national institution, he became a BBC fight summarizer, a
resident captain on 'A Question of Sport,' a Lloyds underwriter and
an indefatigable fête opener. He said, 'I intend to take it easy, but I
don't intend to become just a name above three greengrocer's
shops.'

*Henry Cooper, the left hook poised for further destruction, beats Karl
Mildenberger to take the European heavyweight title at Wembley on 18 August
1968*

He played the part of John Gully MP in the film *Royal Flash* and
had to fight Oliver Reed. In 1977 he made a record, 'Knock Me
Down with a Feather'. He became a celebrated figure in the Fabergé
Brut 'Splash it on all over' advert – 'They chose me because no one
can call me a poof!'

Now past fifty, Henry's view is 'The public either take to a person
or they don't and, thank God, they took to me. I don't know why,
but if I had a bad fight (Rischer, Amos Johnson) I would admit it.

'If you put on airs and graces, you'll come unstuck. I once saw a
footballer tell a kid to get lost. He lost a fan, but by the time the story
got round, he'd lost a whole neighbourhood of fans.'

Henry Cotton

Henry Cotton won the British Open Championship on three occasions. He was also one of a long line of sportsmen who, throughout their playing days, were outspoken and often misunderstood. 'I was a rebel, but not much of one really,' he said.

It is doubtful whether anyone has done more for the furtherance of the British game after retirement from the playing side as Cotton. His tournaments for aspiring professionals in the sunnier European climes during the long winter months have started many a young player on his career, as well as being the delight of sports editors searching for hard news on a winter weekday.

Cotton was born in London on 26 January 1907. He turned professional in 1924 and, in time-honoured tradition, was appointed assistant at Fulwell, Rye, the medieval, cobblestoned Sussex hilltop town. Soon, though, he was back in Greater London, taking the professional's post at Langley Park, Beckenham, at the tender age of nineteen and a half.

The Ryder Cup selection panel was the first to recognize his ability and included him in the 1929 winning team. The following year he won his first major tournament a long way from home, at Mar del Plata, Argentina; in that country he was to meet his wife, 'Toots'. The same year he won his first Open in Europe – the Belgian. It was his dogged insistence on furthering the game in Europe that sowed the seeds of the European tournament play so popular today. Cotton took a job abroad, at the Waterloo Golf Club (on the site of the 1815 battleground) near Brussels, and was a member of that club when he won his first British Open at Sandwich in 1934. His thirty-six-hole score was a record 132 (67, 65) on a par of 144, the 65 standing as an eighteen-hole record until 1977. A third-round 72 was followed by an awful 79 on the last day, but his 283 was 5 strokes clear of the South African Sid Brews. Ten years of American domination of the Open had ended.

Back home at the Ashridge club, near Berkhamsted, Cotton won his second Open in 1937 at Carnoustie. A steady 74, 72, 73, 71 gave him a four-round total of 290 and a 2-stroke margin over fellow Ryder Cup player Reg Whitcombe.

With the Second World War taking five of his most formative playing years. Cotton was awarded the MBE for his fund-raising services with the Red Cross. Britain chose him as captain of the Ryder Cup team upon resumption of peacetime activities in 1947.

Now based at the Royal Mid-Surrey club, nestling at the back of the Richmond and London Welsh rugby clubs, Cotton became, in 1948, the only golfer to have won the Open both before and after the war. As in 1937, this victory was in Scotland, at Muirfield. A second-round 66 gave him breathing space from the pack, and other rounds of 71, 75 and 72 gave a seventy-two-holes aggregate of 284, 5 strokes clear of the defending champion, Irishman Fred Daly.

Well into his forties, Cotton was still a fine international player – dedicated and, though never a natural player, with the technique to continue when contemporaries had retired to Stableford competitions. As non-playing captain of the 1954 Ryder Cup team, he won final tournament that year, the Penfold 1000 Guineas, and two years later, in his fiftieth year, was sixth in the Open at Hoylake, whilst representing the Temple club, near Henley.

Retirement brought a new challenge. Europe and its winter sunshine were the key, and the young players the raw material. Cotton ran a successful golf school at Monte Carlo, 3000 feet above the harbour. He then moved to Spain and Portugal. He ran rookie tournaments on the courses he designed and taught at. Val de Lobo and the Algarve benefited most. Package holidays caught on. The game blossomed throughout Iberia.

Although recently dogged by illness, his comments on television during the major championships were succinct and valued. And for his services on and off the course, he was one of the few players elected as honorary member of the Royal and Ancient.

FACTFILE

Born 26 January 1907, London, England

'Big Four' wins 3
British Open 1934, 1937, 1948
Belgian Open 1930, 1934, 1938
British Professional Matchplay 1932, 1940, 1946
Italian Open 1936

German Open 1937, 1938, 1939
French Open 1946, 1947
Ryder Cup matches 6 (1929 – 47; Cotton was playing captain in 1947 and non-playing captain in 1953)

*Henry Cotton had a bet with Fred Perry that he would win the Open Golf Championship before Perry won Wimbledon. Cotton won by about six weeks

Henry Cotton drives from the tee at the RAC Club at Epsom during the first full postwar golf season, April 1946

Robin Cousins

One of the truly outstanding free skaters, Robin Cousins's introduction to the sport he was to dominate was unusual. During one of the rare hot British summers of recent years, whilst on holiday in Bournemouth in 1965, Robin and his mother used to visit the ice rink to avoid the sweltering heat.

A year later he took up the sport seriously, coached by Pamela Davis in Bristol, his home town. Robin is the youngest of three brothers and comes from a sporting family: his father played football for Millwall and his mother was a useful club swimmer.

He won the British Junior Championships in 1972 and gained a fine third place in the British Senior Championships the same year. His international debut followed in 1973 at the European Championships in Cologne where he finished fifteenth. His debut in the other annual international skating event, the World Championships, was delayed until 1975, when he finished an improving twelfth. His selection for the World Championships a year earlier had been interrupted by an inflamed ankle.

Now established as Britain's No. 2, Robin found inspiration in the exploits of John Curry, the British No. 1. His programme at Curry's Olympic gold medal triumph at Innsbruck included five triples; he was the only skater to perform the feat. The compulsory exercises, an event in which he often dreaded the judges' marks, had left him trailing the field. His free-skating programme brought him up to tenth place. An admiring television public was treated to a different interpretation of the event from that of the Olympic champion, Cousins's athletic performance contrasting with Curry's balletic grace.

Curry's move to his own professional company was to leave Cousins with a simple target for the next four years: to repeat Curry's 1976 achievement and win a gold medal in the 1980 Winter Olympics at Lake Placid. Cousins's base for the challenge at Lake Placid was four consecutive British titles from 1976 to 1979. He now trained with Carlo Fassi, Curry's trainer, based in Denver and Colorado Springs, who helped him create adequate compulsory exercises. The European Championships of 1977, 1978 and 1979 produced three consecutive bronze medals. The World Championships provided Robin with a bronze in 1978, and when he gained a silver medal the following year, an Olympic medal seemed a certainty and the gold a distinct possibility.

The countdown to Lake Placid began well, with a gold at the European Championships, but, having conquered the Old Continent, Robin was aware of the opposition from the Americans Tickner and Santee. And they were on their own patch.

The three days at Lake Placid mirrored the progression in Robin's skating career. After the compulsories the placings were as follows:

		Points	Placements
1	Hoffmann (GDR)	44.76	11
2	Tickner (USA)	43.76	18
3	Santee (USA)	43.04	27
4	Cousins (GB)	41.44	34

However, things improved after the short programme, with Cousins moving into second place:

FACTFILE

Born 17 August 1957, Bristol, England

British Junior Championships
Gold: 1972

British Senior Championships
Bronze: 1972
Silver: 1973, 1974, 1975
Gold: 1976, 1977, 1978, 1979

European Championships
Bronze: 1977 (Helsinki), 1978 (Strasbourg), 1979 (Zagreb)
Gold: 1980 (Gothenburg)

World Championships
Bronze: 1978 (Ottawa)
Silver: 1979 (Vienna), 1980 (Dortmund)

Olympic Games
Gold: 1980 (Lake Placid)

*The gold medal won by Robin Cousins at the 1980 Winter Olympics took Britain's total number of medals in the Winter Games to twenty – a long way short of Norway's record 155. Below is a list of British gold medallists:

1908	E. Madge Sayers, women's figure skating
1936	Team, ice hockey
1952	Jeanette Altwegg, women's figure skating
1964	Tony Nash/Robin Dixon, two-man bobsleigh
1976	John Curry, men's figure skating
1980	Robin Cousins, men's figure skating

*In his training build-up in the United States in 1979 in readiness for his Olympic assault in 1980, Cousins used the following training schedule: start at 8 a.m. and skate until 1.30 p.m., with a twenty-minute break every hour. In the afternoon either jogging, running, dance routines or stretch exercises. At 6 p.m. return to the rink for more skating, finishing at approximately 8 p.m. (not far short of a twelve-hour day)

*Cousins's coach, Carlo Fassi, is reported to have said of him: 'He's a great skater, but he's chicken and won't win the Olympics.' Later he confessed, 'I only said it to hype him up'

Men's Figure-Skating Champions between 1976 and 1980

	World champion	*European champion*
1976	John Curry (GB)	John Curry (GB)
1977	Vladimir Kovalev (USSR)	Jan Hoffmann (GDR)
1978	Charles Tickner (USA)	Jan Hoffmann (GDR)
1979	Vladimir Kovalev (USSR)	Jan Hoffmann (GDR)
1980	Jan Hoffmann (GDR)	Robin Cousins (GB)

Eight million British TV viewers stayed up half the night to watch Robin Cousins win the gold medal at the 1980 Olympics at Lake Placid

1	Hoffmann (GDR)	85.92	9
2	Cousins (GB)	84.08	26
3	Tickner (USA)	83.96	26
4	Santee (USA)	83.72	29

The gold medal depended on the free-skating marks and, as a result of the following judges' marks, Robin Cousins became the 1980 Olympic champion:

	Technical merit	Artistic impression
Canada	5.9	5.8
East Germany	5.8	5.9
USSR	5.9	5.8
USA	5.7	5.8
France	5.8	5.9
Sweden	5.8	5.9
Great Britain	5.8	5.9
West Germany	5.8	5.9
Japan	5.9	5.9

The final positions were:

1	Cousins (GB)	189.48	13
2	Hoffmann (GDR)	189.72	15
3	Tickner (USA)	187.06	28
4	Santee (USA)	185.52	34

Cousins just missed the Triple Crown – achieved by Curry four years earlier – by losing to Jan Hoffmann at the World Championships in Dortmund, but the loss seemed more of a parting gift to a fine champion twice foiled at Olympic level by Britons.

Robin Cousins, born on 17 August 1957, retired from amateur competition after his Olympic success, but still competes professionally and appears in ice galas and exhibitions, having added the back somersault to his increasing repertoire.

At the end of 1980 there was a welcome surprise for Robin at the BBC Sports Personality of the Year function, when viewers picked him as their favourite Sportsman of the Year. 1980 had shone for Britain: Coe, Ovett, Thompson and Wells had returned from the Moscow Olympics with gold medals; Maurice Hope, Alan Minter and Jim Watt were world boxing champions; there were nine other world and Olympic champions in other major sports. However, the British public voted for Robin Cousins.

Johann Cruyff

The most exciting attacking footballer of the 1970s, Johann Cruyff was the first and, thus far, the only player to win the coveted European Footballer of the Year award three times. Whether in the white shirt with the broad red band of Ajax Amsterdam or the orange of the Dutch national side, the influential Cruyff always wore No. 14. He led Ajax from naivety to the European Cup and his country from a national backwater to the World Cup final.

He first joined Ajax at the age of ten, at the insistence of his mother who was a cleaner at the stadium. Johann worked his way through the myriad of fourteen junior teams at the club and, by nineteen (he was born on 25 April 1947), had made his debut in the Dutch League.

Almost immediately Cruyff made his mark on the European circuit. In December 1966 Ajax drew Liverpool in the Champions' Cup second round. On a pea-souper of a night in Amsterdam, Ajax ran riot in an amazing 5–1 win. Bill Shankly blamed the fog, but, in the mist, it was really Cruyff and his emerging young team-mates who destroyed Liverpool. That season Cruyff was leading scorer in Holland with 33 goals. He was to head the clubs' scorers for the next five seasons and in 1972 was top League scorer again.

Honours came with indecent haste. He was Dutch Footballer of the Year in 1968 and 1969. Now established in the international side, he had built his game around his hero, Faas Wilkes. At 5 feet 11 inches, Cruyff had great speed, was quick to lose his marker and had delicate skills.

Ajax controlled footballing thought in the early 1970s. Fullbacks appeared in No. 10 shirts, goalkeepers took penalties and sweepers scored hat tricks. They had been disappointed when they reached the European Cup final in 1969 and were soundly thrashed 4–1 by AC Milan. They were even more disappointed when their deadly rivals, Feyenoord from Rotterdam, became the first Dutch winners of the European Cup in 1970.

It was at Wembley Stadium that Cruyff and Ajax first became European champions. They beat Panathinaikos, the unfancied Greeks who were trained by Ferenc Puskas, 2–0. Puskas was impressed with Cruyff. Inter Milan were more impressed the following year. Cruyff scored both goals as Ajax retained the trophy. Another Italian side, Juventus, reached the final in 1973; Ajax dismissed them.

By now manager Rinus Michels had left to join Barcelona. Cruyff, too, fancied a change. Barcelona had average gates of 95,000, the best in Europe. They could afford Cruyff's fee. In August 1973 Barcelona signed him for £922,3000 – £400,000 going into his own bank account. Barcelona were immediately rewarded with the Spanish championship. 'El Flaco' – The Thin Man – was a hero.

International appearances were becoming less frequent. Spanish club commitments and financial and tactical arguments with the FA had caused a rift. But for the 1974 World Cup Holland had a chance. Michels was in charge. Cruyff agreed to play again. His old Ajax colleagues – Neeskens, Krol, Rensenbrink, Suurbier and Haan – were there. Holland had devised 'total football' – players running off the ball at full stretch in support of each other – and though 'Puppet on a String', the title of the song which had won the European Song Contest that year, could be applied to any of their three keepers, there was confidence.

Holland skated through the first stage, dropping only one point. The first match in the second stage saw the Dutch at their best. Cruyff scored twice as Holland overwhelmed the Argentinians 4–0. The East Germans were disposed of, then Brazil. Both scores were 2–0 and Cruyff's goal against Brazil was a masterpiece. Top of the group table, they were in the final.

Cruyff led the Dutch team out into the Munich Olympic Stadium. Within 58 seconds he was fouled and Neeskens blasted the penalty past Maier. Even when the Germans scored twice before half time, no one was particularly perturbed.

There was no scoring in the second half. Amazingly, Holland had lost. Poor finishing let them down. It had always seemed a matter of time before the Dutch would score, then there was no time. The final was thrown away.

With that Cruyff also threw away a little time. Squabbles infested the Barcelona team. He had made a few bad business deals; he was again at loggerheads with the FA. When a kidnap threat arrived before the 1978 World Cup, he had had enough – 33 goals in forty-nine international appearances.

Enter again the gentle persuader Rinus Michels. He had moved on to the American scene with the Washington Diplomats. Pele was there; so was Beckenbauer. So why not Cruyff? The crusade finished when Cruyff realized that the Diplomats had no more money than he had.

It was the nondescript Spanish Second Division side Levante which tempted him out of retirement in 1981. There was more. In his mid-thirties, he started playing for Ajax again. The gates shot up from 9000 to 21,000; Cruyff's salary was geared to an increase in attendances. They won the double. Still he hadn't finished. In 1983, with much of the old charisma intact, he once more left Ajax. They wouldn't forgive him this time – he'd joined Feyenoord. And Feyenoord regained the League title from Ajax.

FACTFILE

Born 25 April 1947, Amsterdam, Netherlands

International appearances 48

Honours

Dutch League Championship 1966, 1967, 1968, 1970, 1972, 1973, 1983 (all with Ajax); 1984 (Feyenoord)
Dutch Cup 1967, 1970, 1971, 1972 (all with Ajax)

Spanish League Championship 1974 (Barcelona)
Spanish Cup 1978 (Barcelona)
European Cup 1971, 1972, 1973 (all with Ajax)
European Super Cup 1972, 1973 (both with Ajax)
World Club Championship 1972 (Ajax)
World Cup runners-up 1974
European Footballer of the Year 1971, 1973, 1974

Johann Cruyff, the only player to be elected European Footballer of the Year on three occasions

John Curry

John Curry wanted to be a ballet dancer. However, his father persuaded him away from such notions, so he took up ice skating instead. But it was his desire to maintain his dancing skills in ice skating that gave Curry, world and Olympic champion, a blend of technical expertise, fluency and artistic refinement that brought a new interpretation to the free dance routine.

Living in the Streetly area of Birmingham and educated at Solihull, Curry first donned skates at the age of seven at the nearby Summer Hill ice rink, where Ken Vickers was his first teacher. He also learned to skate out of doors on the frozen East Anglian lakes near Aldeburgh during the Christmas holidays. In 1965 his father died and Curry, aged just sixteen, travelled to London to work as a £50-a-month clerk-receptionist for NCR. In his free time he trained at Richmond ice rink under the tutelage of Arnold Gerschwiler and Alison Smith.

Two years later he was British junior champion and, in 1970, won his first British senior title. He was then twenty-one and was to hold the title until 1975.

During this period his climb through the European and World championships towards the medal positions was positive. In the European Championships he finished twelfth in his first attempt in 1970, and worked his way to the bronze medal in 1974 and the silver a year later. He was fourteenth in his first World Championships in 1971, but, now under the instruction of American Ed Mosler, he climbed no fewer than ten places the following year and by 1975 had secured a bronze medal.

The 1976 season was expected to be dominated by world champion Jan Hoffmann, of East Germany, and the two Soviet skaters, Sergei Volkov and Vladimir Kovalev. But Mosler, industrialist and skating fanatic, offered Curry a chance to train with Carlo Fassi, who was developing a habit of producing champions. Fassi fashioned Curry's balletic and artistic flair, and John outskated the technically skilled but more stereotyped Iron Curtain skaters.

He became only the fourth skater to win all three major titles in one year – European, Olympic and world. Not since 1952, when Jeanette Altwegg won the ladies' crown, had Britain won an ice-skating gold at the Olympics.

He had to overcome an increasing vendetta – which Torvill and Dean were later to experience – on the part of the Eastern European judges, who were perhaps a little more than merely interested in the placings of their own performers. They were critical of his style, but they have a reputation for penalizing inventiveness.

His retirement from amateur competition followed shortly after the Triple Crown. Professional offers flooded in, but John, whose first free-skating programme had been to Strauss's 'The Village Swallows', took up sponsorship offers and founded the John Curry Theatre of Skating. A year later he founded the John Curry School of Skating. His theatre, especially at Christmas, provides spectacular productions throughout the world.

John Curry was awarded the MBE in 1976. And, to crown a memorable year, he became the first ice skater to win the prestigious BBC Sports Personality of the Year award. It was a fitting measure of his popularity.

FACTFILE

Born 9 September 1949, Birmingham, England

British Junior Championships
Gold: 1967

British Senior Championships
Gold: 1970, 1972, 1973, 1974, 1975

European Championships
Bronze: 1974 (Zagreb)
Silver: 1975 (Copenhagen)
Gold: 1976 (Geneva)

World Championships
Bronze: 1975 (Colorado Springs)
Gold: 1976 (Helsinki)

Olympic Games
Gold: 1976 (Innsbruck)

Olympic Games, 1976

		Points	Placements
Positions after compulsory figures			
1	Sergei Volkov	44.76	19.5
2	John Curry	44.96	21.5
Positions after short free programme			
1	John Curry	86.84	13.5
2	Sergei Volkov	85.20	21

	Final positions after free skating		
1	John Curry	192.74	11
2	Vladimir Kovalev	187.64	28
3	Toller Cranston	187.38	30
4	Jan Hoffmann	187.34	34
5	Sergei Volkov	184.08	53
6	David Santee	184.28	49
10	Robin Cousins	178.14	83

*Of the twenty men who took part in the 1976 Olympic figure-skating competition, only two were older than Curry
*The previous best result by a Briton in the men's figure skating at the Olympic Games was fourth by Scotsman John Keiller Greig in 1908
*The marks awarded by the nine judges for Curry's free programme in the 1976 Olympics were:

Technical merit 7×5.9, 2×5.8
Artistic impression 8×5.9, 1×5.8

*Apart from Curry, the other three men to have won world, Olympic and European titles are Ulrich Salchow (Sweden), Karl Schafer (Austria) and Ondrej Nepela (Czechoslovakia)
*Coach Carlo Fassi lives in Colorado Springs, and was himself a proficient skater, winning the Italian Championships every year from 1943 to 1954; he was European champion in 1953 and 1954

The inverted circle, part of the unique repertoire of the 1976 Olympic, world and European champion John Curry

Compulsory figures skated at the 1976 Olympic Games

Right outside rocker   *Left backwards paragraph bracket*   *Right forward paragraph loop*

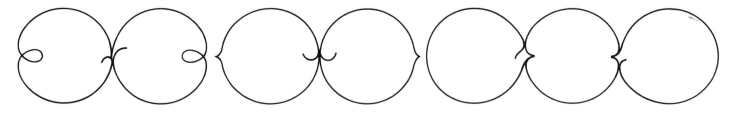

Gerald Davies

There are too many different positions in Rugby Union, each with its own degree of technical skill, seriously to consider choosing the finest all-round player. But the considered view of most rugby writers is that, if they were asked to choose the player whose skill and genius were the most exciting, who epitomized the running game, and who had deadly acceleration and sidesteps, then they would plump for Gerald Davies, the wing with the fine Welsh team of the 1970s. The players' vote was summed up by Willie John McBride, the Lions most successful captain, who said, 'To see Gerald Davies in full flight is like art in motion.'

Davies had a rare ability. He was quick, an even-time 100-yard sprinter, but could sidestep in both directions without any discernible loss of pace. The Welsh flyhalf factory which produced Barry John, Cliff Morgan and Phil Bennett would have been proud to have learned the secret. Gerald Davies could create room where there was a clutter of bodies intent on doing damage and his defensive work was faultless.

Gerald Davies was born at Llansaint, near Kidwelly, in west Wales. He went to that breeding ground of fine players, Queen Elizabeth Grammar School, Carmarthen, and before he left the sixth form he had already played in the scarlet jersey of Llanelli.

Moving on to Loughborough Colleges, he first came to national prominence as a member of the 1966 team which won the Middlesex Sevens, beating Northampton by a record 29–10 in the final.

A teaching post took him to Cardiff and his first selection for Wales, against Australia in 1967. Wales lost 14–11. Davies played in the centre in those days. In his first five internationals, Wales won one, against England, and lost four. In the game against England, he scored two tries, but they were forgotten – Keith Jarrett scored 19 points in that match on his debut.

For Davies, Barry John, Gareth Edwards and the remainder of the fine side in the making of the 1970s, the early international record was poor. John Taylor received a telegram on selection. 'Congratulations,' it said. 'PS. Are they short?'

Davies went to South Africa with the Lions in 1968, but suffered a recurring back injury. The locals at Stellenbosch still recall the try of the tour, Davies's 50-yard effort against Boland.

The Welsh selectors, bowing to increasing pressure, selected Davies on the wing, where there was more space, for the 1969 tour to Australia. Wales were still undergoing difficulties. A supporter on the 'bob bank' suggested that, as he looked so cold on the wing, Davies ought to try sunshine summer holidays in Lapland.

To improve his teaching qualifications, he enrolled at Cambridge where he captained the university in 1970. He didn't receive much ball there either. But Cambridge was reasonably close to London Welsh and, like Cardiff, they were building a good side down at Old Deer Park.

London Welsh were the fulcrum of the Welsh resurgence. Wales won the 1971 Grand Slam and seven London Welshmen went on the all-conquering Lions tour to Australia and New Zealand. Along with Davies were J. P. R. Williams, John Dawes the captain, Mervyn Davies, John Taylor and the locks Geoff Evans and Mike Roberts. The creed was open rugby and, with John Dawes, inside Davies, universally recognized as the finest passer of the ball in the last generation, Davies's career took off again. London Welsh won the Middlesex Sevens – it was impossible to mark him on the vast open space of Twickenham.

He taught at Cranleigh School and played rugby for London Welsh for three years. In 1973 he returned to Cardiff. They too had a good side and tries kept flooding in.

Gerald Davies captained Cardiff. He also had the honour of captaining the Barbarians against the Lions in the 1977 Jubilee match at Twickenham. He was unavailable for the 1974 and 1977 Lions tours. He regretted not being able to go on the South African tour in 1974; he would have gobbled up the spaces at the high altitude. And, after the 1971 success in New Zealand, he would have been welcome back there in 1977. But work took priority; he was now working for the Sports Council of Wales as a development officer.

Gerald Davies retired in 1978 after the summer tour to Australia. He had scored twenty tries in forty-six internationals, a Welsh record shared with Gareth Edwards. He would have scored more but for equally try-conscious team-mates who played inside him. He is now the rugby correspondent in Wales for *The Times*.

One England left winger, who will remain nameless, said that he was the unluckiest man in the world having to mark Davies. On being pressed for the second unluckiest, he said, 'The man who camped at the Little Big Horn, and went over the hill to find out what all the noise was about.'

FACTFILE

Born 7 February 1945, Llansaint, nr Kidwelly, Wales

Wales international career

Debut 1966, *v.* Australia (lost 11–14)
Appearances 46 (won 29, lost 14, drew 3)
Tries 20 (Welsh record)
Tours 1969 Australia, New Zealand and Fiji
    1978 Australia

Grand Slam 1971, 1976, 1978
Triple Crown 1969, 1971, 1976, 1977, 1978
International Championship 1969, 1970 (shared), 1971,
    1972 (shared) 1975, 1976, 1978
Lions tours
1968 South Africa
1971 Australia and New Zealand

Gerald Davies about to sidestep inside the Australian cover during his forty-sixth and final appearance in the red jersey of Wales, in Sydney in 1978. Australia won 19–17

Joe Davis

For twenty years Joe Davis was world snooker champion. Many young would-be professionals had second thoughts about a career in the game, it was so dominated by one man. For variety he played billiards and was world champion at that as well.

Joe Davis was born in Chesterfield in 1901. Billiards and snooker had become a postwar cult and Joe and his younger brother, Fred, were caught in the wave of enthusiasm. Joe used to manage a billiard hall in Chesterfield. By 1927 there was sufficient interest to run a World Professional Snooker Championship. The English Amateur Championship had been running since 1916.

The first world professional snooker champion was Joe Davis. His very first opponent was John Brady, whom he beat by ten frames to five in the second round. In the final he beat Tom Dennis. His prize, including a special award for the highest break, was £6.50. Steve Davis (no relation) took home £30,000 after his 1983 success.

Billiards, though, had been going on for much longer. There had been a World Championship since 1870; organization and administration were much more deeply rooted. Joe reached the World Championship final in 1926 and 1927, only to lose to the world champion Tom Newman. But in 1928 he dethroned Newman and also retained the snooker title.

He was to hold both championships for five years. It was a crucial time and snooker, formerly the poor relation, was to provide the better opportunities.

Three factors brought this about. Billiards suffered a decline in popularity, due chiefly to the dominance of 'close cannon' play, where players attempted to keep the three balls as close together as possible. Joe Davis had researched the untapped possibilities of snooker: he emphasized the vital importance of cue ball control and converted the game into one of genuine skill. Finally, the World Billiards Championship changed hands. Joe lost in 1933 to Walter Lindrum, an Australian. It took Lindrum three weeks to get home and there he stayed. Joe went to Australia in 1934, failed to regain the title, and the world game, as far as England was concerned, went into gradual decline.

Until 1946, it was just a matter of who came second in the World Snooker Championship. Joe beat brother Fred in the final in 1940, the same Fred who is still very much part of the present-day scene. He beat Walter Lindrum's brother Horace in the finals in 1936 and 1937, and again in 1946. He retired from snooker championship play after the 1946 final, and from championship play altogether after retaining the UK billiards title (Walter Lindrum was still Down Under, so the championship had world status).

He was immediately elected chairman of the Professional Billiards Players in 1947 and played countless exhibitions on his retirement. Two performances stand out. In 1955 he made snooker's first official maximum 147 break, against Willie Smith at the Leicester Square Hall in London. On another occasion he made a 639 billiards break, followed by a 106 and a 115 snooker break – all in the same evening.

Joe died in 1978, with the sport, whose basic skills and standing he had helped to create, operating as a major television spectacle. During his career he had always played with the same cue for good luck – he bought it from a friend in Chesterfield for 7s 6d (37½p). He could play with both hands. His wife, singer June Malo, is still a great follower of the game.

He had a secret during his playing days. Not, perhaps, the best-kept secret. Amazingly, for a sport that demanded such precision, he had only one good eye – his right eye was virtually useless.

FACTFILE

Born 15 April 1901, Whitewell, Chesterfield, England
Died 10 July 1978, Hampshire, England

World Professional Championship victories

Snooker (world champion 1927–46 inclusive)

1927	v. T. A. Dennis	20–11
1928	v. F. Lawrence	16–13
1929	v. T. A. Dennis	19–14
1930	v. T. A. Dennis	25–12
1931	v. T. A. Dennis	25–11
1932	v. C. McConachy	30–19
1933	v. W. Smith	25–18
1934	v. T. Newman	25–23
1935	v. W. Smith	25–20
1936	v. H. Lindrum	34–27
1937	v. H. Lindrum	32–29
1938	v. S. Smith	37–24
1939	v. S. Smith	32–29
1940	v. F. Davis	37–36
1946	v. H. Lindrum	78–67

Billiards

1928	v. T. Newman	16,000–14,874
1929	v. T. Newman	18,000–17,219
1930	v. T. Newman	20,198–20,117
1932	v. C. McConachy	25,161–19,259

(Davis lost the finals of 1933 and 1934 to Walter Lindrum.)

Break milestones (snooker)
1928 First century break (v. Fred Pugh at Manchester)
1939 100th century break (v. Alec Brown at London)
1946 200th century break (v. Horace Lindrum in world final)
1953 500th century break (v. Jackie Rea at London)
1955 First maximum 147 break (v. Willie Smith at London)

*Davis's first 147 was against Willie Smith at Leicester Square Hall, London, on 22 January 1955. The two of them were playing a snooker and billiards match concurrently. Davis won the snooker match 23–13 whilst Smith won the billiards match 6988–6036

Joe Davis, undefeated world snooker champion from 1927 until 1946. Note the left-hand grip on the cue

Fred Davis

World professional snooker champion 1948, 1949, 1951
United Kingdom billiards champion 1951
World professional billiards champion 1980

*Younger brother of Joe, born in 1913
*He only beat Joe four times on level terms in competitive play (the first and only man to beat Joe on level terms in tournament play)
*Joe thought that Fred was not dedicated and serious enough to make it to the top
*Fred received £1 for his first exhibition match
*He first appeared the in World Snooker Championship in 1937 and

lost to an unknown Welshman, Bill Withers, 17–14. In the second round Joe beat Withers 30–1 to restore family pride
*Fred first appeared in a world snooker final in 1940, losing to Joe 37–36
*He first won the World Snooker Championship in 1948, beating Walter Donaldson in the final. He and Donaldson met in five consecutive finals between 1947 and 1951
*He suffered two heart attacks, in 1970 and 1974
*He beat Alex Higgins 15–14 in the quarter finals of the 1974 World Championship, winning the last three frames to do so
*He reached the semifinal of the World Championship in 1978, narrowly losing 18–16 to Perri Mans

Steve Davis

Four months younger than another London world champion, Eric Bristow, the career of Steve Davis has followed a remarkably similar pattern. Both play traditional indoor sports which, although they have always had a huge participating body, have mushroomed out of all recognition almost entirely due to television. World professional snooker champion Steve Davis is not only a player who threatens almost total domination of his sport, but is also a fine ambassador. Both requirements are now essential.

Davis learned his trade at the Plumstead Common Working Men's Club where he was taught to play by his father. The influence of Barry Hearn, now his manager, in persuading Davis to his Luciana club in Romford was considerable. Hearn's club attracted the top professionals.

A strange fact of the young Davis's career was that he never won a national junior snooker title, although he won the 1976 British Junior Billiards Championship. His first notable success was as an amateur, when he won the Pontins Open, beating Tony Meo, then also an amateur, in the final. He won the same title the following year – his first as a professional, having abandoned A-level studies – beating amateur Jimmy White 7–3 in the final, despite giving White a 30-point start in each frame.

His first performance to attract public attention came in 1980. Terry Griffiths, a Welshman from Llanelli, caused a sensation by winning the world title in 1979 at his first attempt. Davis caused the sensation of 1980 by eliminating Griffiths. He didn't win the title, but gained consolation by beating Cliff Thorburn, the new

FACTFILE

Born 22 August 1957, Plumstead, London, England

World Professional Championship

1981	v. Doug Mountjoy	won	18–12
1983	v. Cliff Thorburn	won	18–6
1984	v. Jimmy White	won	18–16

World Doubles (with T. Meo)

1982	v. Griffiths/Mountjoy	won	13–2
1983	v. Knowles/White	won	10–2

World Team (with T. Meo and T. Knowles)

1983	v. Wales (Mountjoy/Reardon/Griffiths)	won	4–2

Lada Cars Classic

1983	v. Bill Werbeniuk	won	9–5
1984	v. Tony Meo	won	9–8

Benson & Hedges Masters Tournament

1982	v. Terry Griffiths	won	9–5

Jameson Whiskey International

1981	v. Dennis Taylor	won	9–0
1983	v. Cliff Thorburn	won	9–4

Coral UK Championship

1980	v. Alex Higgins	won	16–6
1981	v. Terry Griffiths	won	16–3

English Professional Championship

1981	v. Tony Meo	won	9–3

Yamaha Organs

1981	v. David Taylor	won	9–6
1982	v. Terry Griffiths	won	9–7
1984	v. John Dunning and Dave Martin	won	(round robin)

Scottish Masters

1982	v. Alex Higgins	won	9–4
1983	v. Tony Knowles	won	9–6

Irish Masters

1983	v. Ray Reardon	won	9–2

Tolly Cobbold Classic

1982	v. Dennis Taylor	won	8–3
1983	v. Terry Griffiths	won	7–5
1984	v. Tony Knowles	won	8–2

Pontins Professional Tournament

1982	v. Ray Reardon	won	9–4

Pontins Open

1979	v. Jimmy White	won	7–3

World Professional Championship matches

1979

First qualifying round	v. Ian Anderson	won	9–1
Second qualifying round	v. Patsy Fagan	won	9–2
First round	v. Dennis Taylor	lost	11–13

1980

Qualifying round	v. Chris Ross	won	9–3
First round	v. Patsy Fagan	won	10–6
Second round	v. Terry Griffiths	won	13–10
Quarter final	v. Alex Higgins	lost	9–13

1981

First round	v. Jimmy White	won	10–8
Second round	v. Alex Higgins	won	13–8
Quarter final	v. Terry Griffiths	won	13–9
Semifinal	v. Cliff Thorburn	won	16–10
Final	v. Doug Mountjoy	won	18–12

1982

First round	v. Tony Knowles	lost	1–10

1983

First round	v. Rex Williams	won	10–4
Second round	v. Dennis Taylor	won	13–11
Quarter final	v. Eddie Charlton	won	13–5
Semifinal	v. Alex Higgins	won	16–5
Final	v. Cliff Thorburn	won	18–6

1984

First round	v. Warren King	won	10–3
Second round	v. John Spencer	won	13–5
Quarter final	v. Terry Griffiths	won	13–10
Semifinal	v. Dennis Taylor	won	16–9
Final	v. Jimmy White	won	18–16

Concentration. Steve Davis becomes, in 1984, the first snooker player to retain the professional world title, at the Crucible Theatre, Sheffield

world champion, to win the UK Championship.

1981 was a momentous year. Making a habit of deposing champions, he eliminated Thorburn in the semifinal of the World Championship and took the title with a win over Doug Mountjoy. Thorburn was reputed to have told Davis, 'You have about as much class as my backside.'

The year's accumulation of titles included the following – UK professional title, the English professional, the Yamaha and the Wilson's Classic. He seemed unbeatable.

Tony Knowles blew that myth in the 1982 World Championships. Knowles beat Davis 10–1 in the very first round and there were the usual moans that off-the-baize activities had taken the place of solid graft. The brewers, John Courage, paid him £220,000 for a three-year contract, during which he had to make forty appearances. The highlight of his year came eleven days into the New Year: playing against John Spencer at the Lada Cars Classic at Oldham, he obtained the first 147 break in front of the cameras, the Granada TV unit recording Davis's maximum, three years earlier the ITV unit had gone to lunch when John Spencer achieved the feat!

He became the sport's first triple world champion in 1983. Together with Tony Meo and Tony Knowles, he helped England to the world team title. With Tony Meo again as his partner, he won the World Doubles and regained the World Professional Championship with a record 18–6 margin over a shattered Cliff Thorburn in the final at the Crucible Theatre, Sheffield. He had also laid the Crucible bogey – no one had won the title there more than once.

He has become a television personality, hosting his own quiz show, and has written a book, *Frame and Fortune*. The fortune bit is apt; he gets £3000 for an exhibition and has another £500,000 contract with Leisure Industries. He reads Tom Sharpe and John Le Carré novels, plays a mean game of space invaders, and whiles away time on motorways playing the harmonica.

In 1984 Steve went to visit his No. 1 fan, Phillis Mould from Eccles, who had been in a coma for two weeks; following the visit she made a complete recovery.

Steve Davis is set to become the first snooker player to earn £1 million in 1984. Whether that happens depended to a large extent on his ability to win the 'big one' – the World Championship. His run-up was spectacular – eight wins in eleven tournaments. The charismatic Jimmy White pushed him to the last but one frame, but Davis's steadiness and nerve held.

Jack Dempsey

'A loser, but still a champion' headlined the *New York Times* the morning after Jack Dempsey had failed to regain the world heavyweight boxing championship from Gene Tunney at the Soldier's Field. The phrase had a double meaning. During the fight there was the 'Long Count', still boxing's most controversial incident. It also epitomized the respect and affection that the world public had for one of its greatest champions.

William Harrison Dempsey was born in the Mormon town of Manassa in Colorado, which supplied his nickname the 'Manassa Mauler'. He was of Irish–Scottish–American descent, and his early stage was the mining and shanty towns of the gold-rush days. Fighting came naturally; penniless and hungry and large, he became the fairground and bar-room champion.

It was pointless fighting as an amateur; cash was the only requirement and Dempsey fought under the name of Kid Blackie. The early record failed to make the annals of *The Ring*, the boxing bible, just as well, for Blackie was under age.

Dempsey's first recorded fight was in 1914 at the age of nineteen, when he beat Fred Woods and earned $3.50. He lost his second fight, to Andy Malloy on points, then knocked out Malloy in round three a couple of days later. The early fights were at places soon to become famous in Westerns – Durango, Goldfield and Cripple Creek.

Disillusioned and disorganized, he packed in boxing for a while and took a job in the Seattle shipyards. His elder brother Jack was a great influence in the early days, and when news filtered through to Seattle of his death, Kid Blackie began to fight again to pay for the funeral costs. Kid Blackie became Jack Dempsey as a mark of respect. Though known as Jack, his brother was christened with another name, but took 'Jack Dempsey' from his boyhood idol, the former world middleweight champion of the same name.

Dempsey suffered four more defeats during those early apprentice days. Jack Downey outpointed him (later reversed in round two), then Fireman Jim Flynn, who had fought for the world title, seriously inconvenienced the twenty-one-year-old on Friday, 13 December 1917, knocking Dempsey out in round one. A year and a day later, the Fireman was extinguished in the first round. Then there was Willie Meehan, an awkward customer, whom Dempsey fought most weekends. The fights were over four rounds and Meehan's back-pedalling tactics gave him a 2–1 lead with two drawn.

Moving amongst the contenders in the latter half of 1918 and early 1919, Dempsey had eleven fights, winning ten on knockouts, and fighting a six-round no decision with Billy Miske. The other ten fights took just thirteen rounds each. He had become a destructive hitter and bathed his hands and face in brine to harden the skin. Managed by Frank Price and increasingly by Jack Kearns, Dempsey was contracted to fight the Pottawatomie Giant, Jess Willard, for the world heavyweight title on 4 July (Independence Day) 1919. The discrepancy in build was considerable: Dempsey weighed in at 189 lb and was 6 feet 1 inch tall; Willard, champion for four years, weighed around 250 lb and was a shade over 6 feet 6 inches. Dempsey's battle plan was simple: 'Tall men come down to my height when I hit them in the body.'

Willard spent most of the first round six feet below Dempsey's cranium. Having floored him seven times in the first round, Dempsey thought that he had beaten the courageous champion at the end of round one. He put on his dressing gown and headed for the showers. Recalled to complete the job, Dempsey left the Toledo ring at the end of the third round as the new heavyweight champion. Willard received $100,000 for the pain, Dempsey $27,000. When asked why he was in such a hurry to finish the fight, Dempsey revealed, 'I bet my purse at 10 to 1 that I would win in the first round.'

A fighting champion to start with, Dempsey began to cash in on his apparent invincibility. His third defence was against the Frenchman Georges Carpentier, the outstanding world light-heavyweight champion. Dempsey won in round four, but that is only part of the story. Promoter Tex Rickard built a huge indoor stadium in New Jersey to house 80,000, and coined the phrase 'Fight of the Century'. Boxing's first million-dollar gate had been achieved.

The next defence but one was equally dramatic. Luis Angel Firpo, the 'Wild Bull of the Pampas', lived up to his name. Dempsey knocked him down seven times in round one but, unlike Willard, Firpo got up and knocked Dempsey out of the ring. Dempsey spared himself further embarrassment in the next round.

For three years Dempsey did not defend. Increasingly involved in exhibitions, he fought twenty-six accredited demonstrations, but was obviously not match fit when he fought and lost his title to

FACTFILE

Born 24 June 1895, Manassa, Colorado, USA
Died 1 June 1983, New York, USA

First professional fight 1914, v. Fred Woods (ko 4)
Total professional fights 84
  Wins 62
  Kos 51
  Defeats 7
Last professional fight 29 July 1940, v. Ellis Bashara (ko 2)

World heavyweight title fights

4. 7.19	Jess Willard	Toledo	w	rtd	3
6. 9.20	Billy Miske	Benton Harbor	w	ko	3
14.12.20	Bill Brennan	New York	w	ko	12
2. 7.21	Georges Carpentier	Jersey City	w	ko	4
4. 7.23	Tom Gibbons	Shelby, Montana	w	pts	15
14. 9.23	Luis Angel Firpo	New York	w	ko	2
23. 9.26	Gene Tunney	Philadelphia	l	pts	10
22. 9.27	Gene Tunney	Chicago	l	pts	10

Defeats

1914	Andy Molloy	pts	10
5. 4.15	Jack Downey	pts	4
13.12.17	Jim Flynn	ko	1
28. 3.17	Willie Meehan	pts	4
13. 9.18	Willie Meehan	pts	4
23. 9.26	Gene Tunney	pts	10
22. 9.27	Gene Tunney	pts	10

Boxing's most famous incident – Jack Dempsey throws a right hook, and Gene Tunney goes down for the famous 'long count' at Chicago in 1927

Gene Tunney, the New York marine, in Philadelphia on points over ten rounds in 1926.

A comeback fight, billed as an eliminator, in 1927, against future champion Jack Sharkey ended successfully in the seventh round and set up the return against Tunney.

They booked the Soldier's Field, Chicago, for the night of 22 September 1927. It was the only place that could hold 104,943. Tunney's shareout was $990,000, Dempsey's $447,500. The kitty was $2,658,660.

The fight went much the same way as the first. Tunney outscoring the heavier puncher until round nine, when a right put Tunney down. In some distress, his legs buckled under him. Referee Dave Barry twice motioned Dempsey to a neutral corner. Twice Dempsey failed to read orders. Only when Dempsey had realized his mistake did Barry start to count. At nine Tunney was on his feet. Some say the knockdown lasted 17 seconds. Tunney claims he would have been ready if the original count had reached eight. Tunney's points advantage enabled him to retain the title. Dempsey retired from the ring and gained even more public adulation by refusing to blame Dave Barry.

His active ring career over, Dempsey turned businessman. He opened a restaurant which has become one of the most famous in New York. He refereed both boxing and wrestling matches. After a four-year lay-off, he milked his popularity and, from 20 August 1931 to the end of the year, engaged in thirty-four exhibition bouts which drew crowds totalling 280,155, who paid nearly half a million dollars for the privilege.

Enthusiasm rekindled, Dempsey had several legitimate bouts, but was always spoonfed and sensibly never stepped out of his league. He had his last fight in 1940, when just over forty-five years old. Refereeing fights of higher quality, he was honoured with the world middleweight fight in 1939 between Cerefino Garcia and Glen Lee in Manila. He reputedly earned 10,000 dollars for his night's work.

In 1942, he enlisted in the US Coastguard and was commissioned as a commander. That healed an old wound: because of financial problems Dempsey had decided to fight for his family instead of enlisting for the First World War.

In his later years Jack Dempsey cut down on his activities. Ill health was a handicap. Jack sadly died in 1983, but his restaurant survives. It's full every day, full of people not only enjoying the cuisine, but reminiscing about the great man himself.

Steve Donoghue

Few jockeys on the British turf have been more popular than Steve Donoghue – and few have started a brilliant career less propitiously.

Donoghue was born in Warrington, Lancashire, in 1884, the son of a steelworker. He always wanted to become a jockey, but his early efforts were doomed to disappointment; indeed, he was never actually apprenticed in England. He worked for John Porter at Kingsclere, but ran away after a thrashing, his mount having bolted on the gallops and upset the brilliant Flying Fox, and then spent short spells at Middleham and Newmarket before applying for a job with the American trainer, Edward Johnson, in France.

These days many English trainers use the little French track of Cagnes-sur-Mer to prepare their horses for a domestic campaign, but in the early part of the century it must have been something of a novelty as Donoghue plied his trade along the Côte d'Azur. He rode his first winner Hanoi, at Hyeres in 1905, and even when he returned to Britain it was not to ride in England, but to partner horses for Michael Dawson and Philip Behan in Ireland.

Once he became established with an English yard, however, it was with a very powerful one. He began his association with the Stockbridge stable of H. S. Persse in 1911 and, only two years later, rode the legendary The Tetrarch. The Tetrarch is still recalled with emotion by all those who saw him run. He had phenomenal speed and was never beaten, even recovering on one occasion when left at the start. More importantly for Donoghue, the 'Spotted Wonder', as The Tetrarch was known, enabled him to capture the public's imagination. By the end of 1914 he had ridden 129 winners and was champion jockey for the first time.

Like Lester Piggott a half a century later, Donoghue cared much more about the quality of races won than the quantity. In this respect the two of them were quite unlike Fred Archer and Gordon Richards. Like Piggott, Donoghue came to view the Classics, and especially the Derby, as all important. During the Great War he won the substitute events for the Derby and St Leger on Pommern and Gay Crusader, but it was when racing resumed at Epsom that his popularity reached its height. The cry 'Come on, Steve!' became a catchphrase of the age, and he was the undisputed master of the tight twists and turns of the Surrey track – no doubt due in no small measure to his salad days in the South of France.

His burning desire to ride the best horses inevitably caused problems when the question of retainers was raised. Like Piggott, he would try everything within his power to be on his first choice on the big day, and it was only his charm and power of persuasion which enabled him to ride Humorist, Jim Joel's Derby winner of 1921; had he respected the system which restricted many less charismatic figures he would have partnered Lord Derby's Glorioso. Lord Derby let Donoghue have his way, but made his displeasure known to Humorist's owner and trainer. The story had an unhappy ending because Humorist died two weeks after the race.

That victory gave the jockey the first of four Derby triumphs in five years; he followed with Captain Cuttle, Papyrus and Manna. He was champion jockey for the tenth and last time in 1923, when he shared the title with Charlie Elliott, and there is no doubt he would have ridden many more winners in the second half of his career but for his single-mindedness, which meant that none of the top trainers wanted to employ him as stable jockey. The public remained totally loyal; it was hard to tell who was more popular in the early thirties, Donoghue or the remarkable stayer Brown Jack, on whom he won the Queen Alexandra Stakes at Royal Ascot six years in a row.

Off the course, Donoghue was a kind, sympathetic man, perhaps naive at times; on it he was a brilliant tactician and absolutely fearless. He knew little about the business side of racing and gave much of his money away to friends both deserving and otherwise. When he went out to ride Manna in the 1925 Derby he was handed a writ by someone in the crowd relating to a sum of £10,000 he owed as guarantor of a loan. Donoghue tucked the writ into his breeches and proceeded to bring Manna home first.

When he retired from the saddle in his fifties he turned his hand to training and breeding but enjoyed little success. It is hard to think he would have made any enemies and everyone was saddened by his death in 1945. He was married twice, to a daughter of Philip Behan and then to Miss Ethel Finn. His son Patrick, from the first marriage, won the Lincoln in 1926, riding King of Clubs.

FACTFILE

Born 1884, Warrington, Cheshire, England
Died March 1945, London, England

First winner Hanoi 1905 (in France)
Champion jockey 1914, 1915, 1916, 1917, 1918, 1919, 1920, 1921, 1922, 1923 (shared with E. C. Elliott)
Most winners in one season 143 (in 1920)

English Classic victories (14)

Derby		1915 Pommern
		1917 Gay Crusader
		1921 Humorist
		1922 Captain Cuttle
		1923 Papyrus
		1925 Manna
St Leger		1915 Pommern
		1917 Gay Crusader
Oaks		1918 My Dear
		1937 Exhibitionist
1000 Guineas		1937 Exhibitionist
2000 Guineas		1915 Pommern
		1917 Gay Crusader
		1925 Manna

Steve Donoghue aboard the legendary stayer Brown Jack in 1928

Duncan Edwards

Bobby Charlton has played with and seen the world's finest players: the Manchester United team before the Munich disaster, their European Cup winning side, fifteen years in the England team, and the side which won the 1966 World Cup. Opponents included Pele, Eusebio, Beckenbauer and the young Cruyff. Of all these, when pressured for the name of the greatest player, his opinion never wavers – Duncan Edwards.

A year older than Charlton, Duncan Edwards lost his life in the Munich tragedy of 1958 when a plane carrying the Manchester United party and members of the local and national press crashed at the end of the runway in blinding snow. They were on their way back to Manchester after a memorable 3–3 draw with Red Star Belgrade in the European Cup which put United into the semifinals. Eight of the United side perished and twenty-three people died in all. Edwards was on an artificial kidney machine and lingered close to death for nearly three weeks. Courage, in the end, could not counteract terrible injuries.

Duncan Edwards came from Dudley, that outcrop of Worcestershire in the Black Country. He appeared in the Dudley Town boys team at the age of eleven (the average age of the team was fifteen). He was first spotted a year later by Jimmy Murphy, the shrewd Welshman who did so much to build the 'Busby Babes'; United wanted to sign him there and then, but they had to be patient.

It wasn't possible then for United to sign Edwards until he was sixteen years old, and then on schoolboy forms. The Midlands' clubs were obviously interested in Edwards, but Matt Busby was the sharpest. There was no better judge of a footballer.

At 2 a.m. on 1 October 1952 – two hours past his sixteenth birthday – Matt Busby knocked on the family front door. Edwards's parents dragged the young Duncan out of bed, and he became a United player.

After just six months progressing through the youth and reserve teams at Old Trafford, Edwards made his first-team debut at Ninian Park against Cardiff City; United won 4–1.

At seventeen, he became an Under-23 international, another honour to set alongside schoolboy and youth international caps. Italy were the opposition in Bologna, England's first Under-23 match ever, the home side winning 3–0.

The youth set-up at Old Trafford was second to none. Manager Matt Busby and Jimmy Murphy had set up a stall for the future with an adventurous youth development policy. With his fine physique, shrewd footballing brain and accurate left foot, Edwards was the jewel in the crown.

Walter Winterbottom, England's team manager, had also seen sufficient skills on United's left flank to be confident that a policy of 'if you're good enough, you're old enough' would suit the national side. Winterbottom selected Edwards to play at left half against Scotland in 1955. At just 18 years 183 days, he was the youngest player ever to wear the white shirt. England beat Scotland by a then record 7–2; Dennis Wilshaw scored four times, Stanley Matthews ran riot down the right wing, and Scotland, as usual, blamed the goalkeeper.

As United's youngsters matured, they won the Football League in 1956 and 1957. Edwards was also a fixture in the England team. United made a serious challenge to Real Madrid for the European Cup.

Then came Munich. Duncan Edwards lay in a coma for sixteen days. He died in the Rechts der Isar Hospital in Munich at the age of twenty-one.

Matt Busby described him as the finest footballer he has seen. He was a player who, at the age of nineteen, was controlling and organizing the England team which beat Brazil 4–2 at Wembley. Virtually the same Brazil team was shortly to win the World Cup. On that day both Matt Busby and Bobby Charlton knew they were right.

FACTFILE

Born 1 October 1936, Dudley, Worcestershire, England
Died 21 February 1958, Munich, West Germany

Football League debut 4 April 1953, *v.* Cardiff City (lost 1–4)
Football League appearances 151
Football League goals 19
Last Football League game 1 February 1958, *v.* Arsenal
  (won 5–4, scored 1)

International debut 2 April 1955, *v.* Scotland (won 7–2)
International appearances 18
International goals 5
Last international match 27 November 1957, *v.* France (won 4–0)

Honours
Football League Championship 1956, 1957
FA Cup 1957

Duncan Edwards, flanked by two famous internationals, Stanley Matthews (left) and Billy Wright, as the England team report for training at Highbury before the 1957 match against Scotland

Gareth Edwards

Gareth Edwards played fifty-three times for Wales. During that time Wales won seven international championships, five Triple Crowns and two Grand Slams. He won his caps in successive games. He also went on three Lions tours; in 1968 to South Africa; in 1971 he was a member of the first Lions team ever to win a Test series in New Zealand; and in 1974 again to South Africa. Under Willie John McBride, the 1974 tourists strode from the High Veld to the Cape of Good Hope unbeaten.

Many careers have a nasty habit of turning sour before the hero retires. Edwards avoided that. A couple of his Welsh team-mates, Barry John and Gerald Davies, did the same. When he retired in 1978, only two players, Clive Shell and Ray Hopkins, had also received a Welsh cap at scrumhalf, and those as substitutes. In the harsh world of international scrumhalf play, his was a miracle of human endurance.

Born on 12 July 1947 in the mining community of Gwaen-cae-Gurwen, Edwards always dreamed of playing for Wales. He recalled to Tony Lewis, the former England cricket captain, on the popular BBC 'Sport on 4' programme how he would return home with grazed knees and elbows after beating England (one weekend Wales won 46–12!). And how he would pop back out after dinner to join the rest of the boys in the street to kick the winning conversion. Max Boyce was to write a song about that.

Two men shaped the course of Gareth's rugby career in his formative schooldays. One was Bill Samuel, head of physical education at Pontardawe Grammar School. He was from the old school of physical education, hard work and discipline; not only rugby, but gymnastics, football and athletics as well. Edwards was a scrumhalf but the school already had one, so he had to play in the centre. The Welsh Schools also picked him to play centre against Yorkshire. It snowed.

It was Bill Samuel who saw the need to broaden Gareth's view beyond the valleys. Writing to R. J. O. Meyer, head of Millfield School, the progressive institution at Street, Somerset, which accommodated both academics and sportsmen, he convinced the headmaster that he had a genius on his hands. 'Boss' Meyer could pick talent. The entire British Davis Cup team came from Millfield, led by Wimbledon

semifinalist Mike Sangster, the first-class cricket counties were swamped with old boys, and Mary Rand, Olympic gold medallist, had been at the school. Jack Meyer, former Somerset cricket captain, who, legend has it, opened a Test trial by bowling an Outspan instead of an outswinger, and Bill Samuel were proved correct. From Millfield, Edwards went on to Cardiff College of Education and joined one of the world's best rugby clubs, Cardiff itself.

At nineteen, in 1967, he was in the Welsh team against France for his first cap; his second was won in the remarkable Keith Jarrett 19-point salvo against England. He was soon to link up with Barry John, then at Llanelli before also joining Cardiff. Together they were the Welsh halfbacks on twenty-three occasions.

Gareth tells a story of virtually their first meeting. Both were chosen at representative level for the first time and Gareth thought he ought to get in touch with Barry John to discuss tactics and a training session. 'Don't worry,' came the answer down the phone, 'you throw it, I'll catch it!'

Edwards and John, and later Edwards and Bennett, were by-words in world rugby during the late 1960s and throughout the 1970s. Realizing that his passing was limited, Edwards learned the spin pass, often at first hand when playing against Chris Laidlaw, the fine All Black scrumhalf.

At the age of twenty years and seven months he was appointed captain of Wales. Hindsight suggests that perhaps the responsibility hampered his play, as it was to do with Ian Botham. But in the record books Edwards is listed as world rugby's youngest captain.

In his fifty-three internationals Edwards scored twenty tries, which, with Gerald Davies's, is a Welsh record which will last for some time. Scotland bore the brunt of the records: they conceded the twentieth, and they conceded the best, an 85-yard kick and chase to finish with red shale covering his face. Yet the best remembered will be his famous 10-yard bursts to the line with the opposition back row festooned on his back.

Edwards was once asked by the chairman of the Welsh selectors, in his early days in the national team, to prove his fitness after missing a few club games with a persistent hamstring injury. Clear-

FACTFILE

Born 12 July 1947, Gwaen-cae-Gurwen, Wales

Wales international career

Debut 1967 v. England
Appearances 53
Tries 20 (Welsh record)
Tours 1969 Australia, New Zealand and Fiji
Grand Slam 1976, 1978
Triple Crown 1969, 1971, 1976, 1977, 1978
International Championship 1969, 1970 (shared), 1971, 1972 (shared), 1975, 1976, 1978

Lions tours
1968 South Africa
1971 New Zealand
1974 South Africa
Test appearances 10

*The Welsh scrumhalf immediately before Edwards was Alun Lewis (Abertillery) in 1967
*The Welsh scrumhalf immediately after Edwards was Brynmor Williams in 1978
*Gareth was twice injured during his fifty-three appearances for Wales. Ray 'Chico' Hopkins played the last twenty-five minutes of the game against England in 1971 (and scored a try), and Clive Shell (Aberavon) played for the last two minutes of the match against Australia in Cardiff in 1973

Gareth Edwards, shielded by the Welsh pack, sets up another threequarter move against England in 1973 when Wales won 25–9

ing a little space in the foyer of the Angel Hotel, he did a back somersault on the spot. His fitness was never questioned again.

Yet, he might well not have been a rugby player at all. Whilst at Millfield he took up athletics. At the All-England Schools Championships he won the 200-yard hurdles in a time which remained a record until the distance was changed. Struggling in 15 yards adrift

was another who was later to make his name in world sport – the champion of Europe and the British Commonwealth at the hurdles, and an Olympic silver medallist, Allan Pascoe.

Edwards retired immediately after the Grand Slam. To the demanding Welsh rugby public he was exciting and never disappointing.

The Day Gareth Was Dropped
Max Boyce

It was the day of the England–Wales rugby international in 1978 at Twickenham. A Welsh supporter who was without a ticket was standing outside the ground in the pouring rain. He called up to some English supporters inside the ground, 'What's happening? What's happening?' and was ungraciously told that all the Welsh team with the exception of Gareth Edwards had been carried off injured.

Some five minutes later there came a great roar from the crowd and the Welsh supporter called out again, 'What happened, what happened, Gareth scored, has he?'

The following poem inspired by the same blinding faith was written at the time when Gareth, seemingly like good wine, was improving with age.

A man came home off afternoons and found his child in woe
And asked him. 'What's the matter bach, pray tell what ails you so?
Your little eyes are swollen red, your hands are white and shaking.'
'Oh! Dad,' he said, 'I've got bad news, my little heart is breaking.
Gareth Edwards has been dropped, 'twas on the news just now.
The Welsh selectors must be mad, there's bound to be a row.'
His father said, 'Now, dry your eyes and don't get in a state.
Let's be fair, mun, after all – the man is seventy-eight!'

Herb Elliott

Herb Elliott retired from athletics in 1960. He was then aged twenty-two and claimed that he had 'nowhere else to go'. In his forty-four races, from 1954 to 1960, over a mile or 1500 metres, he was unbeaten. And that record, in the Blue Riband race of athletics, is unique.

Herbert James Elliott was born on 25 February 1938 in Perth. The family lived at Lesmurdie, 11 miles into the Darling Mountains and 23 miles from his first school at Scarborough, a seaside suburb. He had to travel to school by bus each day and would break the tedium by running some of the way. His father worked in a cycle store, but when he opened a retail furniture business the family moved to Scarborough, five hundred yards from vast expanses of beach and the Indian Ocean.

Perth, in the 1950s, was a sporting backwater. No Test matches, no Davis Cup matches, no cinder tracks. But Elliott's father was a fitness fanatic and the young Elliott, in later years, put his own early fitness down to romping over the sandhills and helping his father construct a three-terraced garden.

His first mile race was at the age of fourteen in the under-17 school championship, which he won in 5 minutes 35 seconds. Now enrolled at the Christian Brothers College, he had only previously raced in the road outside junior school. It was his first organized meeting. Selected for the school to run in the mile in the inter-Christian Brothers College sports, he came up against one Ray Waters, at seventeen three years older than Herb. Waters edged out the young lad by 10 yards. That race was to be significant. It was his last defeat over the distance.

His father's business prospered and Herb was sent to Aquinas College, at Mount Henry, Perth, in 1953. Aquinas was a boarding school with superb facilities, including twenty-four tennis courts and a nine-hole golf course. Selection and a win for the school team over 880 yards in the inter-schools sports at the WACA cricket ground stimulated his interest in athletics; the fixture still is one of the major sports events on the calender, with crowds of over 12,000 attending finals day.

Training began seriously in 1954. Roger Bannister's four-minute mile was all over the papers. Elliott read magazines and books looking for ways to improve his performance.

The first glimpse of national honours came in February 1955. Selected by the state for the Australian Junior Championships, he won the 880 yards in 1:55.7, a national junior record. The temperature that day in Adelaide was 102°. Two days later, in the mile, he won again, in 4:20.8, 20 yards ahead of another athlete who was to become world-famous – Ron Clarke.

Elliott returned to school to a hero's reception and a meeting that was to change his life. Percy Cerutty, innovator of new coaching techniques, was in Perth lecturing to schools. Having watched Elliott win in the school sports, Cerutty pulled him to one side. 'There's not a shadow of doubt,' he declared, 'that within two years you will run a mile in four minutes.'

After leaving school Elliott went to work in the family business. It was not a success, the indoor life didn't suit him. Then, in 1956, the family travelled to Melbourne to watch the Olympic Games. The journey took three days. Leaving Herb with Cerutty, who lived in Melbourne, the family went back to Perth. During the Games, Herb and Cerutty were thrown out of the Olympic village for not having a pass. Four years later Herb was to leave the Olympics with a gold medal.

Percy Wells Cerutty was, so far as athletes were concerned, either a genius or a ratbag. His methods of training, now copied by the rest

FACTFILE

Born 25 February 1938, Subiaco, nr Perth, Australia

Olympic Games
Gold: 1500 metres 3:35.6 (1960)

Commonwealth Games
Gold: 880 yards 1:49.3 (1958)
  Mile 3:59.0 (1958)

World records
 1500 metres 3:36.0 (1958)
      3:35.6 (1960)
 Mile 3:54.5 (1958)
 4 × mile relay 16:25.9 (1959)
 (Australian national team with Wilson, Thomas and Murray)

*Herb Elliott's weekly training routine at Portsea at the age of eighteen was as follows:

Monday 10-mile run (Portsea)
Tuesday 6 or 7 miles in the morning (Portsea); weight training in the evening followed by 10-mile run (Portsea)
Wednesday 10 miles against the clock (local track)
Thursday As Tuesday
Friday Rest
Saturday 'Fun' workout at the local track at lunchtime; 5-mile run in the evening (Portsea)
Sunday 8 to 10 miles in the morning (Portsea); 8 to 10 miles in the evening (Portsea)

The Portsea schedule could be broken up with runs around adjacent golf courses, along the Yarra River and over racecourses and fields. Longer runs at Portsea – marathons, etc. – were substituted at weekends as he got older

*At the age of nineteen Elliott held the world junior record for the mile, the 1500 metres, and the 2 and 3 miles
*When he retired, Elliott had run seventeen sub-four-minute miles; the next best was seven by the Swedish athlete Dan Waern

of the world, were, in those days, considered too severe. His training camp at Portsea, 60 kilometres down the coast from Melbourne, had two tough circuits cut into the sand dunes and an indoor weight-training centre. Elliott ran marathons over the dunes and lifted 200-lb weights. He earned his living by working in a TV store on the way in to Melbourne. It was boring work, but he needed the cash.

The benefits of Cerutty's methods were immediate. In January 1957 Elliott reduced the world junior mile record three times to a best of 4 minutes 4.3 seconds, and the 880 yards to 1 minute 50.7 seconds.

In the Australian winter and spring of 1957 (June to December) Cerutty pushed Elliott through 2500 miles of training. On 25 January 1958, at the Olympic Park in Melbourne, he ran the mile in 3:59.9. He was the first teenager to run a four-minute mile.

1958 was the year in which rumour became fact. Elliott ran two more sub-four-minute miles in Australia, then went to America on his first overseas tour. Three more sub-four-minute miles followed, including the US Championships mile in Bakersfield in 3:57.9. Elliott went on to Britain for the Commonwealth Games in Cardiff. Brian Hewson had beaten him in the half mile at the AAA championships, but Elliott had always claimed that the shorter distance was for speed work. With a gold medal instead of a cup as a prize, he took revenge over Hewson in the half-mile. The last lap was run in 50.5 seconds. The mile was an Australian triumph, Elliott winning from Merv Lincoln, his long-time rival, and Alby Thomas. No one had ever won the 880 yards and the mile at the same Commonwealth Games before.

The 4th of August was a strange day. In the Commonwealth Games finale at the White City (Britain v. The Rest) Elliott won the 880 yards in a time just six tenths of a second outside Tom Courtney's world record of 1:46.8. Cerutty promptly dragged him into a car, took him to Watford and made him run against Gordon Pirie! Elliott won in 1:50.7

Two days later in Dublin, Herb Elliott put Derek Ibbotson's world mile record into the archives. His 3:54.5 mile took 2.7 seconds off the old record. Then, on 28 August in Gothenburg, he broke the 1500-metre world record with a time of 3:36.0 – worth 3:53.7 for the mile.

Returning home, he refused an offer of £89,000 to turn professional; for a little while his dedication vanished. Marriage and a career beckoned. The Shell Company granted him a scholarship to do a three-year science course at Cambridge University. That was to start in November 1960. On 2 May 1959 he married Anne Dudley in Perth and set up home at Clayton, a suburb of Melbourne. Their son, James, was born in February 1960. Life had other priorities. But, as 1959 drew to an end, the prospect of the Rome Olympics revived his interest.

He reported to Cerutty in December. To get rid of the cobwebs, he went with three colleagues on a 100-mile hike through the Australian Alps. Then, on Boxing Day 1959, he went into the Portsea sandhills.

He concentrated on building up his basic fitness early in 1960, running up to 33 miles along the beach. He returned from a trip to the United States in May slightly disappointed with his times, but a week before he was due to fly to Rome he improved his best time on the Portsea circuit by 7.1 seconds, having run 18 miles the previous day.

In Rome the heats were a formality. In the final, Cerutty was to wave a white towel from the crowd if a world record was a possibility. The crowd of 90,000 was busily discussing the 400 metres in which Otis Davis and Carl Kaufmann had each recorded 44.9 seconds – a world record. No one seemed interested in the 1500 metres. Elliott led after 900 metres.

Three minutes 35.6 seconds after the start Elliott had broken his own world record. It was to stand for nine years. Cerutty was evicted from the stadium for dashing into the track waving a towel over his head. He never saw the medal ceremony.

Herb Elliott leads Mike Rawson (No. 35) in the 880 yards at the AAA Championships at the White City. Both were pipped by Brian Hewson who took the title, but Elliott quickly gained his revenge at the Commonwealth Games

Eusebio

The finest footballer produced by the continent of Africa, Eusebio Ferreira da Silva rose from the shanty districts of Lourenço Marques to become European Footballer of the Year and to encourage a multitude of aspiring players from Third World countries.

Born on 25 January 1942, and a shade over 6 feet tall, he was a quick, incisive forward. He was to Europe what Pele was to South America. And wherever he played, there was that permanent smile.

At the age of fifteen Eusebio was signed by his local team, Sporting Club of Lourenço Marques, whose ground overlooked the sprawling, corrugated black African suburban developments. Playing in a league in which the skill factor was high but the discipline woeful, Eusebio eked out 55 League goals in no time.

Brazilian manager, Jose Bauer, who had been imported to bring stability and organization to the side, was the 'plant' for several overseas clubs. Mozambique is a Portuguese colony and, on Bauer's recommendation, Bela Guttman, the shrewd Hungarian manager of Benfica of Lisbon, then the current European champions, persuaded his directors to part with £7500 for Eusebio in the summer of 1961. Eusebio was just nineteen.

An injury to the inside forward Santana gave Eusebio an immediate opportunity to play in the first team. In one of those seemingly endless European tournaments organized mainly to keep the summer pools companies happy, Benfica had been invited to the Tournoi de Paris. They met Santos and Pele. Eusebio scored a hat trick. Before he had even played a League game, the international selectors had noted him and, twenty-five games later, he played for Portugal. Mozambique hadn't bothered to pick him.

In 1962 Benfica retained the European Cup and Eusebio, one of the two changes in the team, was the prime factor. The last two hurdles were particularly difficult. In the semifinal, the English double winners, Tottenham Hotspur, were expected to win. Benfica sneaked through 4–3 on aggregate. In the final they met Real Madrid. The two clubs were the only ones ever to have won the cup – Real five times, Benfica once. If the memorable Real–Eintracht Frankfurt final of 1960 is the best of all finals, with Real triumphing 7–3, then the 1962 final is a close second. Puskas scored a hat trick for Real, but Benfica won 5–3 and Eusebio, the new star, scored twice.

He was on the score sheet again in the 1963 final, but the Eagles of Lisbon, shorn of Germano at centre half, Aguas, the dashing centre forward, and Coluna, the midfield play-maker, were ailing. AC Milan took the trophy with a 2–1 win at Wembley. Eusebio's awards were to come more as a result of his individual performances than through the team's achievements.

Eusebio came to England for the 1966 World Cup finals as the reigning European Footballer of the Year. He had dominated the Portuguese League score charts and the club's successes were beginning to manifest themselves in the national side. He was to leave in tears but, according to Brian Glanville of the *Sunday Times*, he was the outstanding player of the whole tournament.

In the groups the best football was played in the Liverpool and Manchester area. Portugal were there. So were Brazil, the holders, unbeaten in the World Cup since the 1954 final stages.

Portugal's early games were straightforward. They beat Hungary 3–1, thanks to a couple of errors from keeper Szentmihalyi. Then Bulgaria was accounted for. The score was 3–0, a silly back pass, an own goal and a Eusebio special.

Brazil meanwhile had gone down to Bulgaria and Pele, the trump card, had been cruelly cut down by Zetchev. Panicked into nine changes and in rapid decline, Brazil suffered further when Pele was carried off at Goodison after a wretched tackle from the Portuguese fullback Morais. But Eusebio was rampant – a header and a screaming volley, and Portugal won 3–1. Brazil, the holders, had gone.

Most World Cups throw up a carnival match. Portugal's quarter final with the North Koreans was the 1966 fiesta. The Koreans had surprised international football by beating the Italians with Pak Doo Ik's unforgettable goal. Portugal promptly found themselves 3–0 down after nineteen minutes. Then Eusebio took over: he scored four times, made a fifth, and the Koreans subsided quietly away.

England and Portugal staged a memorable game in the semifinals. Two Bobby Charlton specials just beat a Eusebio penalty. Nobby Stiles shackled Eusebio. That was when the tears followed.

For what it mattered, Portugal won the third-place match against the Soviet Union 2–1. Eusebio recorded another goal, his ninth of the tournament, and finished top in the individual honours.

Eusebio had the first of two serious knee operations in 1967 (the other two years later), but recovered with such alacrity that he topped the League scoring lists in 1968. The French magazine *France Football* had instituted a Golden Boot for Europe's top scorer and Eusebio, with 42, was the first winner. Five years later he was to win the award again, one of only three players to date to have done so.

The customary exodus to the North American Soccer League took Eusebio across the Atlantic in 1974. He joined Rhode Island, then moved up the coast to Boston. He left America at the top, taking Toronto Metros to the 1976 championship, with 16 goals.

Returning to Portugal for 1977, he kept little Biera-Mar in the First Division, but his knees were playing up again and, after a season

---

FACTFILE

Born 25 January 1942, Lourenço Marques, Mozambique

International debut 1961
International appearances 77

Honours

Portuguese League Championship 1963, 1964, 1965, 1967, 1968, 1969, 1971, 1972, 1973, 1975

Portuguese Cup 1962, 1964, 1969, 1970, 1972
European Cup 1962; runners-up 1963, 1965, 1968
World Club Championship runners-up 1961, 1962
NASL Championship 1976
European Footballer of the Year 1965; runner-up 1962, 1966
Top scorer in Portuguese League 1963–64 (28), 1964–65 (28), 1965–66 (25), 1966–67 (31), 1967–68 (42; record), 1969–70 (20), 1972–73 (40)

struggling against relegation and a couple of jaunts to America and Mexico, he dropped out of the playing side.

Biera-Mar engaged him as trainer, but it was no time before Benfica recalled him. The fortunes of the national team as a result of Benfica's recovery is encouraging; Eusebio, as Benfica's coach, is now training those to whom he was an idol.

Eusebio heads Portugal's second goal past Brazil's goalkeeper Manga during the group matches in the 1966 World Cup. Portugal beat Brazil, the holders, 3–1 and Eusebio finished as top scorer in the tournament with 9 goals

Juan Manuel Fangio

Fangio was known simply as the 'Maestro' – an appropriate title for the man who, arriving late in European motor racing at the age of thirty-eight, won five world titles in eight years. His reputation was such that Jackie Stewart once said, 'You can be in a room full of racing personalities, world champions and so on, then Fangio comes in. All eyes turn towards him and everyone else is forgotten.'

Fangio arrived in Europe after driving in long-distance races in South America. He won six races with Maserati, joined Alfa Romeo for 1950, and finished runner-up to team-mate Giuseppe Farina, including a remarkable win at Monaco, where he avoided the wreckage of a pile-up to finish a lap clear of Ascari.

He won his first title in 1951 after a fierce battle with the Ferrari of Alberto Ascari. Amazingly, Alfa quit Grand Prix racing after that season. The world champion was left without a regular drive and failed to score a single championship point. Worse was to come – in the Italian Grand Prix he broke his neck, but recovered to race the following year when he won the Italian Grand Prix and finished second in the World Championship to Ascari.

1954 was the year that Fangio's superb driving skills were allied to reliable and mechanically superior cars. He joined Mercedes Benz and won ten out of the next thirteen Grands Prix, but at the end of 1955 he was again without a drive when Mercedes – their objective in promoting their marque achieved – left the sport.

Fangio had an unhappy single year with Ferrari (even though he won the title for the fourth time) and moved to Maserati who had developed the lightweight 250F, tailored to Fangio's style. He dominated the first half of the season and won a remarkable race on the long Nurburgring circuit. Fangio – in the lead – stopped, as planned, for tyres and fuel. The Maserati team thought their tyres would not last the race and, with a pit stop certain, to reduce weight sent Fangio out with half-full tanks. While Fangio refuelled, the Ferraris of Mike Hawthorn and Peter Collins swept through to take the lead; they looked impossible to catch. Fangio set off in pursuit, breaking the lap record time after time, and snatched the lead in the dying seconds. Fangio had broken the lap record in practice. In the event he clipped another 11 seconds off the record. It was his greatest victory, and his last.

Fangio was contracted to race two Grands Prix in 1958 – farewell appearances in Argentina and France. A measure of the esteem in which this 'gracious' man was held was demonstrated at Reims. Mike Hawthorn, on his way to a win and on course to take Fangio's title, had the chance to lap the great man. He eased off so that Fangio would not be lapped in his last race (Fangio finished fourth).

Fangio's record was superb – twenty-four wins in fifty-one races, and he started all but two from the front row. He bridged old-style motor racing and the modern era. Nigel Roebuck says his greatest gift was concentration, and relates the story of the 1950 Monaco Grand Prix when Fangio was away first in his Alfa unaware that behind him there was a massive pile-up and the track was blocked. He came round through the chicane and headed for the scene of the crash at top speed. Suddenly he slowed and was able to thread his way through the tangled wreckage. Observers suggested he had a sixth sense. Fangio quietly pointed out that he was aware of 'a change in colour of the crowd'. They were facing away from him, not watching the leader come into view. 'Obviously,' said Fangio, 'something had happened.'

FACTFILE

Born 11 June 1911, Balcarce, Argentina

World Drivers Championship
 Winner 1951, 1954, 1955, 1956, 1957
 Runner-up 1950, 1953

World Championship Grand Prix wins (24)
1950   Belgian, French, Monaco (all for Alfa Romeo)
1951   French, Spanish, Swiss (all for Alfa Romeo)
1953   Italian (for Maserati)
1954   Argentine, Belgian (both for Maserati); French, German, Italian, Swiss (for Mercedes)
1955   Argentine, Belgian, Dutch, Italian (all for Mercedes)
1956   Argentine, German, British (all for Ferrari)
1957   French, German, Monaco, Argentine (all for Maserati)

Summary of Grand Prix wins
Argentine 1954, 1955, 1956, 1957
Belgian 1950, 1954, 1955
British 1956
Dutch 1955
French 1950, 1951, 1954, 1957
German 1954, 1956, 1957
Italian 1953, 1954, 1955
Monaco 1950, 1957
Spanish 1951
Swiss 1951, 1954

*Fangio's father was an Italian
*Fangio first took an interest in cars at the age of eleven
*His nickname was 'Cheuco', meaning Bandy Legs
*Fangio started racing in 1934, driving a Model A Ford
*On the eve of the 1958 Havana Grand Prix, Fangio was captured by Fidel Castro's revolutionaries. He was later released unharmed

Juan Manuel Fangio, the only driver to have won the World Drivers Championship on five occasions

Tom Finney

For many, Tom Finney was the most complete forward of all time. He was at home on either wing and could play equally skilfully and effectively at centre forward. He is still the only winger to have scored 30 goals for England.

He was a more fluid mover than his wing partner, Stanley Matthews, had the gift of sudden acceleration and, after being coached in his early days, eradicated a seemingly irrepressible urge to dribble and beat players. He became an accurate passer of the ball.

He joined Preston North End, his home town club, in 1937 as an amateur and stayed with them for twenty-three years. It was not until after the war that he made his international debut – against Northern Ireland at Belfast, scoring once in the 7–2 win. It was a controversial selection – he came into the side to replace Matthews and it was not until seven internationals later, in Lisbon in 1947, that the two were paired as wingers. The result was a 10–0 thrashing of Portugal, with Tommy Lawton and Stan Mortensen both scoring four times. The other 2 goals came from Matthews and Finney.

Finney was a favourite both with the crowds and with his teammates. Bill Shankly said of him, 'No back ever stopped him reaching the goal line to make the killing pass back.' Scotland's famous defender, George Young, was another admirer. 'Tom was even better than Matthews, being two-footed and a magnificent header of the ball. He was the complete footballer.'

Finney's best international performance came in May 1950 against Portugal in the unlikely setting of Luton. Finney scored 4 in the 5–3 win, including two penalties, but his third goal, he admits, was the best of his career, although modestly he adds that he thought it a little selfish to beat four men rather than pass to Jackie Milburn, who was in a good position.

Tony Pawson – a great admirer of Finney since playing with him for army sides during the war – summed up Finney's attitude: 'His standards are of a generation when there was pride in performance and great store set on loyalty.'

Loyalty played a major part in Finney's football career. These days he would have been sold to one of the big city clubs for a vast fee with a loud blowing of trumpets and intense investigations into his private life. In 1952 Finney was offered £10,000 to play for Palermo. The offer included a car, a villa and a massive salary. Preston's board asked him not to go and Finney turned it down.

His last cap came against Russia in October 1958. England won at Wembley by 5 goals to 0, with Johnny Haynes scoring a hat trick. He played his last League match for Preston on the 30 April 1960 against Luton. Tommy Docherty, also a one-time team-mate of Finney, says, 'I consider him the greatest British player of all time. He was so versatile that he could play in any forward position and destroy defences with his ball control, speed and body swerve.'

FACTFILE

Born 5 April 1922, Preston, Lancashire, England

Football League debut 31 August 1946, *v.* Leeds United (won 3–2)
Football League appearances 433
Football League goals 187
Last Football League game 30 April 1960, *v.* Luton Town (won 2–0)
International debut 28 September 1946, *v.* Northern Ireland (won 7–2)
International appearances 76
International goals 30

Last international match 22 October 1958, *v.* USSR (won 5–0)
World Cup appearances 7 (1950, 1954, 1958)
World Cup goals 2 (*v.* Uruguay, 1954; *v.* Russia, 1958)

Honours

Footballer of the Year 1954, 1957
F A Cup runners-up 1954

*Finney was known as the Preston plumber – because of his successful trade

Tom Finney aims a shot towards goal during the League match between Arsenal and Preston North End at Highbury in 1959

Dawn Fraser

Inspired by the awarding of the 1956 Olympic Games to Melbourne, Australian sport flourished in that era as if fed on a magic potion. Hoad, Laver, Rosewall, Sedgeman and Neale Fraser were supreme on the tennis courts; Herb Elliott and Betty Cuthbert led an athletics revolution; Richie Benaud brought his cricketers out of the wilderness; Jack Brabham was world motor-racing champion; Peter Thomson was collecting British Open golf titles; Scobie Breasley was champion flat-race jockey. And there were the swimmers – eight gold medals at the 1956 Olympics. Yet in all this extraordinary talent, the best was probably the most reluctant – Dawn Fraser.

History records Dawn as the only swimmer to win the same event – the 100-metre freestyle – at three successive Olympics, spanning eight years.

Dawn began swimming seriously in 1954, when she was seventeen. It took her coach, Harry Gallagher, two years to convince her that motivation was as important as ability. Despite her first major success, the 200-metre freestyle in the 1955 Australian Championships, Dawn lacked the determination to win.

The Melbourne Olympics provided the motivation. She won the 100-metre freestyle gold medal and broke the world record. It was a great achievement for a girl from Sydney to win at Melbourne.

The remainder of her career was spent in reaching peaks for Commonwealth and Olympic gold medals. In 1962 she became the first woman to break one minute for the 100-metres freestyle. All told, she broke twenty-seven world records and won twenty-nine Australian titles, a record six Commonwealth Games titles and a record number of Olympic medals – four gold and four silver. The 'walkabouts', which she may have passed on to Evonne Goolagong, helped to ease the pressure.

By the 1964 Olympics, Dawn was twenty-seven. Although at loggerheads with her own swimming authority, she was selected for Tokyo. Shortly before the Games she was badly injured in a car crash in which her mother died. The mental strength required to continue training was considerable.

The celebration party for her third successive gold medal was spectacular, to say the least. Dawn and her team-mates set out to give Tokyo a night to remember. They copied the locals and staged a kamikaze raid on various buildings. Emperor Hirohito was not amused – he lost the national flag from the palace. There were enough souvenirs to send the Aborigine trinket salesmen on Bondi Beach into permanent liquidation.

Supposing Dawn to be the leader, and taking other breaches of discipline into consideration, the authorities banned her for ten years. The ban was lifted after four years, but any enthusiasm Dawn might have had for coaching youngsters evaporated in loss of respect for the authorities. It was sad; Australia's greatest swimmer had earned a better retirement.

FACTFILE

Born 4 September 1937, Balmain, Sydney, Australia

Olympic Games
Gold: 100-metre freestyle (1956, 1960, 1964)
        4 × 100-metre freestyle relay (1956)
Silver: 400-metre freestyle (1956)
        4 × 100-metre freestyle relay (1960, 1964)
        4 × 100-metre medley relay (1960)

Commonwealth Games
Gold: 110-yard freestyle (1958, 1962)
        4 × 110-yard relay (1958, 1962)
        440-yard freestyle (1962)
        4 × 110-yard medley relay (1962)
Silver: 440-yard freestyle (1958)
        4 × 110-yard medley relay (1958)

Total world records 27
First world record
    100-metre freestyle 1:4.5 (21 February 1956)

*It was in the 100-metre freestyle that Dawn Fraser won gold medals at three successive Olympics. It was also in this event that she set eight of her twenty-seven world records and was the first woman to break the one-minute barrier. Here is her progression in the event:

18 February 1958	1:01.5
21 July 1958	1:01.4
10 August 1958	1:01.2
23 February 1960	1:00.2
23 October 1962	1:00.0
27 October 1962	59.9
24 November 1962	59.5
29 February 1964	58.9

Dawn Fraser, who won the 100-metre freestyle at three successive Olympic Games, led Australian dominance in the sport in the 1950s and 1960s

C. B. Fry

Charles Burgess Fry's achievements could be straight out of *Boy's Own*. In summer, he was to play cricket twenty-six times for England, making 39,886 runs at an average of 50.22, after devoting a short time earlier in his sporting career to breaking the world long-jump record! In the winter months, he played football. He played for Southampton in the 1902 FA Cup final and gained two caps for England, after changing from Rugby Union, at which he played for Blackheath, then the best team in the land, and for the Barbarians.

Academically, he gained first-class honours at Wadham College, Oxford, with a superior grade to two future Lords Chancellor, was president of the Debating Society, stood as an MP on three occasions, served on the League of Nations and was offered the kingdom of Albania. Repton School takes the early credit.

Athletics seemed merely a pleasant intermission in a cricket career which lasted from 1891 to 1921. The long jump was his speciality. In 1892, in his first Varsity match, Fry broke the British record with a leap of 23 feet 5 inches, to add nearly 5 inches to a nine-year-old record. A year later, at Iffley Road – where Roger Bannister was to run his first four-minute mile in 1954 – Fry added $1\frac{1}{2}$ inches to his British record to set a new world record. As a British record, it

FACTFILE

Born 2 April 1872, Croydon, Surrey, England
Died 7 September 1956, Hampstead, London, England

Cricket

First-class debut 1891, Surrey *v.* Warwickshire
Total first-class runs 39,886 (average 50.22)
Highest first-class innings 258*, Hampshire *v.* Gloucestershire, Southampton (1911)
Total first-class wickets 165 (average 28.68)
Test debut 1895–96, *v.* South Africa
Total Test matches 26
Total Test runs 1223 (average 32.18)
Highest Test innings 144 *v.* Australia, The Oval (1905)

Soccer

FA Cup 1902, Southampton *v.* Sheffield United (lost 1–2 after a 1–1 draw)
International appearance 1901, *v.* Northern Ireland (won 3–0) (plus one unofficial cap *v.* Canada, 1891)

Athletics

World record Long jump 23 ft $6\frac{1}{2}$ in (1893)

Rugby Union

Member of Barbarians 1894–95

*Fry's various sporting activities kept him very busy. On Saturday, 26 April 1902, he played in the FA Cup final replay for Southampton against Sheffield United at Crystal Palace, and on the following Tuesday he turned out for London County in a three-day cricket match at the Oval against Surrey. He scored 82 and 49 not out, as well as taking three catches

*Fry's writing was as respected as his sporting ability. In the *Encyclopaedia of Sport and Games* of 1896, he wrote the following article on defensive football:

Sometimes, when a side is a goal or two ahead, and it is thought advisable to play a purely defensive game, a third back is added by diminishing the number of forwards . . . With regard to the shift of withdrawing a forward and putting an extra back, there is this much to be said: that three backs are extremely hard to get through . . . but unless the players thus moved are versatile and capable of performing satisfactorily the duties of their altered positions . . . it is certainly unwise to play a third back, unless the extra man is a capable player in that position.

An insight into the future of the game

*Fry had many ambitions, and one of them was to enter Parliament. As a Liberal candidate he stood three times unsuccessfully, but in the 1923 General Election, standing at Banbury in Oxfordshire, he came close. The full result was:

Major A. J. Edmondson (Unionist)	12,495 votes
Commander C. B. Fry (Liberal)	12,271
Captain E. N. Bennet (Labour)	2500
Unionist majority 224	

His other two election results were:

1922 Brighton (two seats)

Rt Hon. G. C. Tryon (Conservative)	28,549
A. C. Rawson (Conservative)	26,844
C. B. Fry (Liberal)	22,059
H. Wheater (Independent Conservative)	11,913

1924 Oxford

R. C. Bourne (Conservative)	10,079
C. B. Fry (Liberal)	8237
K. M. Linsay (Labour)	2769

The Albanian Affair

There are several different stories as to how Fry was offered the kingdom of Albania, but the following is supposed to be true, and is substantiated by one of his daughters – Faith.

After the First World War, his good friend and international cricketer Ranjitsingjhi, was a member of the Indian delegation to the League of Nations. He appointed Fry as his adviser and, as Ranji was never normally in Geneva long enough for full meetings, Fry became a *de facto* representative of India on the League of Nations.

Because of his linguistic fluency his name was one of several to be put forward for the kingdom of Albania; but the person who accepted had to spend £10,000 per annum in the country. Fry was interested, but would have had to turn to Ranji for the cash. Ranji refused as he needed Fry's services as adviser and personal secretary (this was in 1920). The legendary Zog became king instead.

was to last for forty years until Olympic gold medallist Harold Abrahams added threequarters of an inch to Fry's mark.

If confirmation was needed that athletics was only serious fun, it came in his threatened participation in the 1896 Olympics. He simply forgot they were on until he read about the Games in the morning papers! Fry's world record jump would have won the gold medal by nearly 3 feet!

Cricket was an altogether more serious activity. Fry was born in Croydon, Surrey, on 2 April 1872, though his parents lived in Sussex at the time. He made his first-class debut for Surrey in 1891 (against Warwickshire) – his only game for them.

Up at Wadham, Fry played in the 1892 university match, the first of four successive appearances. He was captain in 1894 and made a century (he was to make ninety-four in his career). Twice against the MCC he took a hat trick, though later he was controversially no-balled for throwing. In the same year – 1894 – he made his debut for his 'native' Sussex. In 1895 he was elected one of *Wisden's* five Cricketers of the Year.

After Oxford, he took a schoolmaster's job at Charterhouse. He had also a more than passing acquaintance with journalism on *Fry's Magazine.*

In 1901, Fry made 3417 runs at 78.67 and recorded thirteen centuries – including six in succession, which only Don Bradman and Mike Procter have since equalled – and in 1903 made 232 in the annual Lord's showpiece for the Gentlemen (the amateurs) against the Players (the professionals). Two years later he scored the first of his Test centuries – 144 against Australia at the Oval.

He gave Sussex fine service. Between 1901 and 1907 he was the leading batsman of the English season on four occasions:

	I	NO	Runs	HS	Avge	100
1901	43	3	3147	244	78.67	13
1903	40	7	2683	234	81.30	9
1905	44	4	2801	233	70.02	10
1907	34	3	1449	187	46.74	4

(Fry was also top of the averages in 1911 – 1728 at 72.00 – and 1912 – 1592 at 56.85 – when with Hampshire.)

He was captain in 1904–5 and 1907–8. Then came another change of county when, already playing football for Southampton, he moved to Hampshire in 1908. Instrumental in this decision was his appointment as commander of the Merchant Navy ship HMS *Mercury*, based at Hamble. He was to command until 1950.

Fry remained a Hampshire man until his retirement in 1921. His highest score – 258 not out against Gloucestershire in 1911 – was made at Southampton. In 1912 he captained England in the triangular series of Tests with Australia and South Africa. Nine years later England required him as captain again. Fry declined, saying he was out of form; he was nearly fifty. He had by then been offered the kingdom of Albania.

Rugby, like athletics, was a pleasant relaxation and the two sports complemented each other. Fry was able to use his speed and acceleration to good effect in rugby. His major season was 1894–95, when he played on the right wing for Blackheath and for the Barbarians. Fry was within eighteen days of gaining a triple blue in 1895, to set alongside his cricket and football honours. Selected for the university rugby match, he had to drop out with a thigh strain. England would have picked him had he played. But Fry was through with rugby after his Wadham days.

His soccer career was typically Corinthian. He played for them too. After four blues – from 1892 to 1895 – he then concentrated on the summer sports. But the Corinthians persuaded him into their side at right back. In those days there was a Sheriff of London Shield, which was contested by the top amateur and professional sides in the country. In the 1900 final, Corinthians beat Aston Villa 2–1. Southampton were impressed with Fry and signed him. A year later he made his international appearance at Southampton when England gained a 3–0 victory over Northern Ireland.

Representing his country in three sports, C. B. Fry captained England at cricket in the 1912 triangular tournament with Australia and South Africa

In 1902 he was in the FA Cup Final. The thirty-year-old Fry played against Sheffield United at Crystal Palace, where the attendance was 110,820. The score was 1–1 and United won the replay 2–1. After that Fry gradually phased himself out of the game.

Having given up cricket at the age of forty-nine, Fry, journalist, teacher and commander, tried to enter politics. He stood as Liberal candidate on three occasions – in 1921 for Brighton, in 1923 for Banbury and in 1924 for Oxford City. The Banbury seat was very close. In 1920 he was 'offered' the kingdom of Albania. King Zog got the job, but there was compensation with a seat on the League of Nations.

The eldest son of Lewis Fry, he was married to Beatrice Holme-Somner; they had two daughters and a son, Stephen, who became a broadcaster with the BBC. C. B. Fry MA, FRGS, died at Hampstead on 7 September 1956 at the age of eighty-four.

In 1939 he wrote his autobiography. It was not difficult to conjure up a title. The book was called *A Life Worth Living.*

W. G. Grace

The inscription on the Grace Gates at Lord's reads: 'The Great Cricketer'. In the golden age he was known as 'The Champion'. Quite simply, he is the most famous cricketer of all time, his bearded features and statuesque bulk known to everyone.

By his own efforts he led cricket out of its formative years. It has been said of him that he invented modern batsmanship, developed bowling from the round-arm style that had been prevalent and, despite his vast size, was a magnificent fielder – especially off his own bowling.

FACTFILE

Born 18 July 1848, Downend, Bristol, England
Died 23 October 1915, Eltham, Kent, England

Total first-class runs 54,896 (average 39.55)
Total first-class wickets 2876 (average 17.99)
Highest first-class innings 344, MCC v. Kent, Canterbury (1876)
Best first-class bowling 10–49, MCC v. Oxford University, Oxford (1886)
Test debut 1880, v. Australia, The Oval (he scored 152)
Total Test matches 22
Total Test runs 1098 (average 32.29)
Total Test wickets 9 (average 26.22)
Highest Test innings 170, v. Australia, The Oval (1886)
Best Test bowling 2–12, v. Australia, Lord's (1890)

*One of the doctor's most famous batting performances was in August 1876, when he scored two triple centuries in four innings. However, the whole month was a profitable one in terms of runs scored, as the following detailed analysis of his matches shows:

3–5   *South of England v. North of England* (at Hull)
      First innings   126 (out of team total of 150)
      Second innings Did not bat
7–9   *Kent & Gloucestershire v. England* (at Canterbury)
      First innings   9
      Second innings 91
10–12   *MCC v. Kent* (at Canterbury)
      First innings   17
      Second innings 344 (in 6¼ hours, average 57 per hour)
14–16   *Gloucestershire v. Nottinghamshire* (at Clifton)
      First innings   177
      Second innings   13 not out
17–20   *Gloucestershire v. Yorkshire* (at Cheltenham)
      First innings   318 not out
      Second innings Did not bat
24–26   *Gloucestershire v. Sussex* (at Bristol)
      First innings   78
      Second innings   7
28–30   *Gloucestershire v. Surrey* (at Clifton)
      First innings   29
      Second innings Did not bat
Total runs in month 1209   *Average* 134.33

*Grace studied medicine at London and at Bristol. In 1879 he became a member of the Royal College of Surgeons and, until 1899, he was a surgeon in Bristol
*He began his career at the age of nine. He scored 3 not out for West Gloucestershire

*His best season was 1871, when he scored 2739 runs and took 78 wickets
*In his first Test he was accompanied by his brothers E. M. and G. F. Grace – the latter died two weeks after the match. W. G. opened the batting with E. M. Grace against Australia and scored 152, the first century by an England batsman in Test cricket
*During a match in 1893, whilst on the way to yet another century, he declared the innings closed with his own score on 93. On being asked why, he replied that it was the only score between 0 and 100 that he had never made
*His keen interest in bowls led him to the form of the English Bowling Association in 1903. He was president until 1905 and continued to play for England until 1908
*After leaving his surgery in Bristol after the disagreements with Gloucestershire, he was appointed manager of cricket and other sports at the old Crystal Palace, during time off from the London County side. He turned the tennis courts into bowling greens and pioneered indoor bowls
*His sons also played cricket. W. G. Grace Jr was a cricket blue at Cambridge in 1895 and 1896. In 1896, with his proud father watching, W.G. Jr was dismissed for 'a pair'. Grace's last surviving son died on 6 June 1938, at the age of fifty-six, whilst playing cricket at Hawkhurst, Sussex
*For the statisticians, Grace's 100th century was made, like Jack Hobbs's, against Somerset. He scored the 100th run of his 100th century off S. M. J. Woods, who played cricket for both England and Australia. The year was 1895, Grace scored 1000 runs in May and 2436 in the season
*W.G. and W.G. Jr played together for the first time for Gloucestershire against Middlesex in 1893
*Grace's mother is the only woman to appear in the list of births and deaths in *Wisden*
*Quotes from the great man: 'When you win the toss, bat. If you're in doubt, consult your team-mates, then bat.' 'They have come to see me bat, not you umpiring'
*W.G.'s brother was a coroner. One day he sent a message to his office in Bristol from the Oval. 'Keep corpse on ice 'til innings closed.' W.G. agreed to declare
*In a match at Hull in 1876 W.G. hit a ball into a railway truck. It's journey's end was at Leeds, 37 miles away
*In a county match W.G. made a towering hit into the outfield. Whilst on his second run, and with the ball still in the air, W.G. declared the innings closed. He managed to convince the umpire that he was not out, the ball having been caught after his declaration

William Gilbert Grace was born in Downend in Bristol in 1848, the fourth of five brothers who were all cricketers. His parents were Dr Henry and Martha Grace. He made his first century at the age of fifteen – 170 for South Wales against the Gentlemen of Sussex. A year later he appeared at Lord's for the first time against the MCC. Aged sixteen he was 'an inch or two' over 6 feet and weighed 14 st 5 lb. And so, in 1864, began an era in which, according to Neville Cardus, 'when Grace was not out at lunch at Lord's the London clubs quickly emptied and the tinkle of hansom cabs along the St John's Wood Road had no end.'

W.G.'s first-class debut came a year later. In all he played forty-four seasons of first-class cricket, from 1865 to 1908, scoring 54,896 runs, including 126 centuries. He took 2876 wickets. Cricket was not his only sport. When he was eighteen he excused himself from playing in a three-day match for England against Surrey at the Oval (he had already scored 224 not out) to win the 440-yard hurdles at Crystal Palace in the first National Olympic Association meeting.

In 1870 it was, appropriately, W.G. who scored the first century ever for Gloucestershire – 143 against Surrey at the Oval. As early as 1899 he was endorsing bats made by L. J. Nicholls of Sussex (Ranjitsingjhi made a similar deal) and it has been estimated that he made the equivalent of £1,000,000 (today's value) from the game as a whole. He was, nominally at least, an amateur.

W.G. would feel quite at home these days with players like Lillee and Botham. Fiercely competitive, on his first Australian tour in 1874 he criticized not only the pitches but the umpires and Australian officials as well. When he returned there in 1891, the pitches still were not to his liking and in one match he led his team from the field in protest.

Grace's gigantic appearance belied his voice. It was high-pitched, even squeaky, but that never prevented him from frequently voicing his opinion. When batsmen, having been given out, stood their ground, W.G. would point, 'Pavilion, you.'

Grace had trouble with Australians, especially in 1878 when a full team toured this country for the first time. A young all-rounder named William Midwinter played for them in the early games. Midwinter, discovered by W.G. playing in Victoria four years earlier, had also appeared for Gloucestershire the previous season. He was possibly the first international cricketing mercenary. On 20 June 1878, just as Midwinter and Charles Bannerman were about to open the innings against Middlesex, W.G. and J. A. Bush burst into the dressing room and persuaded Midwinter to leave with them to play at the Oval. The Australian manager followed them to the Oval only to find the gates slammed in his face as W.G. shouted, 'You're a damned lot of sneaks.' Not surprisingly, the Australians were furious and demanded an apology. Eventually W.G. wrote expressing his extreme regret that in 'the excitement of the moment I should have made use of unparliamentary language'.

Test cricket was in its infancy during Grace's era, so he played only twenty-two Tests and scored only two centuries. He captained England from 1888 until the end of his Test career in 1899, when, leading England against the Australians at Trent Bridge, he was booed from the field. By then he was over fifty, weighed over 18 st and was utterly useless as a fieldsman.

Throughout his first-class career, however, he was supreme. In 1876 he took 318 not out off the Yorkshire bowlers – a remarkable score in any circumstances, but on this occasion, in the previous ten days, he had scored a career best 344 at Canterbury, including fifty-one boundaries, for the MCC against Kent, then 177 for Gloucestershire against Nottinghamshire at Clifton – 839 runs in ten days! Nineteen years later, aged forty-seven, he scored 1000 runs in May.

By 1897 even *Wisden* was prepared to forgive the good doctor his idiosyncracies: 'The work he has done in perpetuating cricket outweighs a hundredfold every other consideration.' By 1899 he had finished his career at Gloucestershire after disagreements with the committee and founded the short-lived London County team. Even

Has technique come full circle? W. G. Grace favouring the style of the 1980s' batsmen by raising his bat before the bowler's delivery. Note also the solid footwear

then he still opened both the batting and the bowling. Once a rather timid request from a fieldsman to change the bowling prompted W.G. to move himself from one end to the other. His last match was on 25 July 1914. Aged sixty-six he scored 69 not out for Eltham against Grove Park. Just over a year later he was dead.

He suffered a stroke while working in his garden at Mottingham and died a few days later, following an air raid on nearby Croydon. The Germans attempted to gain propaganda from his death and announced that he had been killed in the raid.

Neville Cardus said of him, 'Always will cricket hold on to the memory of him as Lord's saw him on countless July days. A blue sky, torrents of sunshine, a match between the Gentlemen and the Players and somebody just out. Grace standing among famous men – Lucas, Steel and Stoddart – his high voice chuckling, "Well bowled, well bowled."'

Lucinda Green

The Badminton Horse Trials, the Derby of the three-day event calendar, was held in the grounds of Badminton House, just off the A46 at the English village of Dunkirk, for the first time in 1949. Formerly a military sport, it is a combination of dressage, 22 miles of cross-country, and show jumping, spread over three days. And it was only in 1954 that women were first allowed into international competition at the European Championships.

From this rugged beginning, the three-day event has undergone an amazing transformation. Through the Pony Club, horse shows, galas and fêtes, have come an armada of skilled, attractive horse-women. And the best of these, by far, is Lucinda Green.

Born on 7 November 1953 in London, Lucinda became the first to win Badminton on five occasions. Twice she has won the European Championships. And in 1982 she became world champion.

She is the daughter of Major General and Lady Prior-Palmer. The general led the amphibian forces up the Normandy Beaches in the Second World War, and earned the Croix de Guerre. During the crucial postwar years, he was British military attaché in Washington, DC.

Lucinda, living just outside Andover, began her career in the Pony Club, but never actually won an event. Mrs Betty Skelton and Mrs Pat Burgess were a great help. She left school, St Mary's, Wantage, just before O-levels.

On her fifteenth birthday she was given a horse called Be Fair (foaled in 1963). The pair were to progress through novice one-day competitions to international three-day events.

Lucinda's first taste of international success was in 1971. As a member of the British junior squad, she was selected for the European Junior Championships. The team came home with a gold medal.

The following year Be Fair and Lucinda were fifth at their first Badminton. Lucinda was short-listed for the Olympics. She didn't go to Munich. Britain came home with the gold medal.

Not yet twenty, Lucinda with Be Fair won Badminton in 1973. Reward was selection for the British team for the first time. Mark Phillips restored honour for the men at Badminton a year later. In 1975 there was no Badminton, but adequate compensation for Lucinda was her first major international title – in the European Championships.

1976 was a tragic year. It began well. On Wideawake, her second horse whom she had patiently schooled and trained, she had received the Winner's Cup from the Queen after her second victory at Badminton. But on the lap of honour the horse collapsed. Ten minutes later Wideawake was dead.

Four months later, at the Montreal Olympics, after going clear in the cross-country to put Britain in the silver medal position, Be Fair was found to have slipped his achilles tendon off his hock. The horse was withdrawn, into retirement.

But waiting in the stables was another horse – George. By Christmas 1977 the pair had won Badminton and retained the individual title at the European Championships. After George, the mould of solid gold produced another winner, Killaire, who won Badminton with Lucinda in 1979.

Marriage to the Australian international three-day eventer, David Green, in December 1981 was a prelude to a marvellous season in 1982. Sensible sponsoring enabled Lucinda to groom new horses and she had another champion – Regal Realm. The pair won both the individual gold medal in the World Championships and anchored the team effort to the gold as well. Almost effortlessly they went on to conquer the Luckington Lane obstacles and win Badminton in 1983.

FACTFILE

Born 7 November 1953, London, England

Olympic Games
Silver: 1984 Team, on Regal Realm

European Championships
1975 Individual, on Be Fair
        (Runner-up in team competition)
1977 Team, on George
        Individual, on George

World Championships
1982 Team, on Regal Realm
        Individual, on Regal Realm

Badminton Horse Trials
1973 on Be Fair
1976 on Wideawake
1977 on George
1979 on Killaire
1983 on Regal Realm
1984 on Beagle Bay

Other placements
Badminton Second 1978, 1980; third 1977
Burghley First 1977, 1981; second 1976, 1982

*Lucinda is the only person to have won Badminton and Burghley in the same season
*She was awarded the MBE in 1978
*Her husband, David, a fashion photographer, is also a horseman. Born in Australia, he is seven years younger than Lucinda. At Badminton in 1982 he finished sixth; Lucinda was seventh. His first major three-day event victory was at Punchestown in 1982 on Botany Bay; Lucinda was again just behind him, in second place
*In January 1984 David Green, who had been selected for the Australian team which did not take part in the 1980 Olympics in Moscow, was given British nationality and included in Britain's Olympic squad

Lucinda Green on the cross-country section of the 1984 Badminton three day event, on the grey Beagle Bay. Lucinda completed her sixth Badminton title on her sixth different horse

Lucinda's preparation of her horses had always been most thorough. The three-day event is the most searching of tests for horse and rider, combining the elegance and discipline of dressage, the stamina and jumping skills of cross-country, and a show-jumping section to test tired limbs and reactions. In a sport where there is a high ratio of one-year wonders, Lucinda has schooled a succession of horses to the highest level. Six wins at Badminton may be equalled, but to win an event of that quality and prestige with six different horses is a record which will, in all probability, survive the twentieth century.

Although Lucinda cheerfully guided the British team to a silver medal in the Los Angeles Olympics three-day event, there were many who said that the reward should have been higher. Savagely marked in the dressage, Lucinda brought Regal Realm through the cross-country and show-jumping sections without loss of further penalties. Had the course been as difficult as Badminton there is little doubt that the quality riders would have prevailed. But typically Lucinda insists that these are not her words.

The Three-Day Event

Major three-day events include individual and team competitions. The first day consists of dressage. The second day tests the horses' and riders' endurance in cross-country. This section is divided into four phases. Phase A, Roads and Tracks, is a warm-up at a trot or a slow canter, normally over country roads or tracks. Phase B is the Steeplechase, in which speed as well as accuracy is important. Over a distance of between 2.4 and 2.6 miles, the competitors have to travel at a speed of 690 metres per minute. They can thus incur time penalties and faults for not negotiating a fence. Time bonuses are also awarded. Phase C, like Phase A, is another Roads and Tracks but over a longer course. The total distance of the two phases is between 9.9 and 12.4 miles. The idea of this phase is to enable the horse to recover before the final phase. Phase D is the Cross-Country. This is the most important part of the event and the one which the majority of spectators see. The riders who survive the first three phases take part in a jumping contest over natural terrain, having to cover the course in 570 metres per minute (20 m.p.h.). Again, there are time penalties and bonuses. The total distance of this section is between 16.9 and 19.9 miles.

The third and final day of the event is the show jumping. Penalties are incurred for knocking down or refusing fences, and there are also time penalties if the desired speed of 400 metres per minute (15 m.p.h.) is not achieved for the 750–900-metre course.

The winner of the competition is the one with the least number of penalty points at the end of the three days. For the team competition, the scores of the three members of the team with the least penalty points decides the winning team.

Mike Hailwood

'Mike the Bike' Hailwood – a man who displayed dedication, skill and daring on the track from an early age – won over a thousand races in his career. He could have been a great golfer, boxer, businessman or musician – he had interest and ability in all those spheres but, encouraged by his father, a millionaire motorcycle dealer, he chose motorcycle racing.

In 1961, aged twenty-one, he won the first of his nine world titles, in the 250-cc class, on a Honda, and the age of Hailwood was established. It was estimated that at the height of his powers two million Hailwood devotees turned up at circuits all over Europe to watch him race. He was a classic rider – he rode a bike as though it was an extension of himself. His cornering skill was exceptional; nobody could match him.

In later years, Hailwood said that 1961 was his best year. He won three Isle of Man TTs in a week – the first man to do so (a feat he equalled in 1967) and only a broken gudgeon pin prevented him winning all four solo classes.

The strain and the adulation took its toll. He himself admitted, 'Racing has made me an old man before my time.' His flirtation with motor racing began early. In 1963 he was eighth in his first Grand Prix – the British – and gained his first championship point a year later, at Monaco, when he was sixth.

In 1966 he rejoined Honda from MV and won nineteen world championship races – a record shared with his great rival, the Italian star, Giacomo Agostini.

After 1967 he concentrated on motor racing, but never really enjoyed the life. 'Formula 1 is too serious,' he told biographer Ted McAuley, who wrote: 'Hailwood was the only livewire among a deadly serious bunch of men.'

Among the brighter aspects of his motor sport career was the clinching of the European Formula 2 title for Surtees in 1972 and the award of the George Medal for outstanding bravery – he pulled Clay Reggazoni from his blazing Ferrari at Kyalami in 1973 when others stood and watched.

A year later Hailwood himself crashed off the track at the Nurburgring, crushing his leg. It was irreparable and spelled the end of his career. It was a sad time for such a great competitor. He had taken part in Formula 1 motor racing in ten different seasons, had forty-eight starts but only won 29 points.

A brief sojourn in New Zealand failed to dampen his appetite for racing and in 1978, to a great reception from his fans, he was back and winning at the Isle of Man TT, setting a new TT record of fourteen wins overall between 1961 and 1979.

He retired for the last time in 1979 and set up in business in Birmingham. But, like Graham Hill, having cheated death on the track, he was killed off it. A car accident near his home in 1981 was responsible for ending the life of one of motorcycle sport's finest ambassadors.

FACTFILE

Born 2 April 1940, Oxford, England
Died 23 March 1981, Birmingham, England

World Championships
1961 250 cc (Honda)
1962 500 cc (MV)
1963 500 cc (MV)
1964 500 cc (MV)
1965 500 cc (MV)
1966 250 cc (Honda), 350 cc (Honda)
1967 250 cc (Honda), 350 cc (Honda)

Isle of Man TT
1961 Senior, lightweight, ultra-lightweight
1962 Junior

1963 Senior
1964 Senior
1965 Senior
1966 Senior, lightweight
1967 Senior, junior, lightweight
1978 Formula 1
1979 Senior

*Hailwood's first win was Ulster Grand Prix in 1959 when he was nineteen
*He was the first man to cover the TT course at an average of 100 m.p.h. on a single-cylinder machine
*At the age of twenty he became the youngest rider to join a works team – Honda

Mike Hailwood gaining a victory behind the Iron Curtain, with his 1963 victory at the East German Grand Prix at Hohenstein

Reg Harris

Reg Harris is one of those sportsmen who was better known outside his own country. He was responsible for putting cycling on the map in Britain, but on the Continent he was a household name. In France and the Benelux countries, he was the superstar, the finest protagonist of their national sport, and the idol of countries recovering from the ravages of war. The quote, when comparisons were needed, of 'it was like a Frenchman scoring a century at Lord's' appeared in all newspapers of the time.

Born in Manchester in 1920, his training ground was the cobbled streets of Mosside and Wythenshawe. He worked in a bakery to supplement his funds. At the age of nineteen he was selected for the British team to take part in the 1939 World Championships, but the imminence of war caused them to be cancelled.

As with Compton, Hutton and Matthews, the war took away five of his formative years. For Harris, who served with the army in the Western Desert, it brought additional problems – he badly injured his back whilst on manoeuvres.

The war over, Harris fought his way back to full fitness, training with the Manchester Velo Club at Belle Vue. The World Championships of 1947 were held in Paris, and Harris, who remained an amateur until after the 1948 Olympics, which were held in London, became the first British world champion since Bill Bailey in the immediate years prior to the First World War.

The Olympics were a little disappointing. Injuries had hindered training again. Harris broke his neck in a car accident, then, on recovery, fractured his arm in a cycling accident. His preference for training in Manchester caused further headaches. Harris was struck off the British team for refusing to train with the national squad. A public outcry led to his reinstatement, but only after a successful run-off against his tandem partner, Alan Bannister.

Herne Hill was the venue for the cycling events at the 1948 Olympics. Harris reached the sprint final, only to be caught cold in the first race by an early break from a twenty-year-old Turin student, Mario Ghella. The second was closer but Ghella, emotionally bouyant after his opening success, held on to win again.

Another opportunity for Harris to win a gold medal came in the 2000-metre tandem with Bannister as his partner. Terruzi and Perona, also Italians, had reached the final. Harris and Bannister won the first race: the Italians drew level by winning the second, then took the gold medal by 6 inches in the decider. The nation was disappointed, but Ghella confirmed his superiority with a win in the World Championships in Amsterdam, Harris taking the bronze.

In 1949 Reginald Hargreaves Harris turned professional and set off for the Continent. Success was immediate. He went to the World Championships and won the professional sprint title, the first cyclist ever to win the title in his debut season. Britain voted him Sportsman of the Year.

Four times Harris was professional sprint champion of the world. His duels with Dutchman Arie Van Vliet were legendary. After Copenhagen in 1949, Harris went on to Liège in 1950 and Milan in 1951 to hear the National Anthem played as he stood on the winners' rostrum. In 1954 Harris won his fourth and last championship and was delighted that Ernie Peacock had made it a double by winning the amateur sprint title.

Perpetual trouble with his back forced Harris to give up after the 1957 season, the injury failing to respond to constant treatment. Harris was now a successful businessman; most cycling equipment bore his name.

Two of Harris's world records, the 1-kilometre unpaced from a standing start – indoors (set in 1952) and outdoors (set in 1957) – remained unchallenged until 1973, although by now cycling's popularity was spreading far beyond the Old Continent. The removal of his name from the record books had an amazing effect on Harris – he decided on a comeback at the age of fifty-four.

Newspaper media and men flocked to Leicester to watch the 1974 British Championships. Their stories went straight onto the front pages when Harris regained his British sprint title, beating Trevor Bull in the final. The following year he was back again to meet Bull, who had doubtless suffered considerable jocularity around the velodromes for twelve months. Bull beat Harris in the final. Yet 'The Lord' was not dismayed. 'When I won the title,' he said, 'it proved that it was possible to make a comeback, even at my age, and to prove that I had once been a fine champion. But when I reached the final again in 1975 and lost, I was almost equally delighted. It meant that the previous year's performance was no fluke.'

FACTFILE

Born 1920, Manchester, England

World Championships
1947 Gold: Amateur sprint
1948 Bronze: Amateur sprint
1949 Gold: Professional sprint
1950 Gold: Professional sprint
1951 Gold: Professional sprint
1953 Bronze: Professional sprint

1954 Gold: Professional sprint
1956 Silver: Professional sprint

European Championships
1955 Gold: Professional sprint

Olympic Games
1948 Silver: 1000-metre sprint; 2000-metre tandem
 (with Alan Bannister)

Reg Harris beats Jan Dirksen in the professional meeting at Herne Hill in 1952

David Hemery

David Hemery won an Olympic gold medal in the 400-metre hurdles at the 1968 Mexico City Games. The margin of victory was the largest since 1924. He broke the world record with a time of 48.12 seconds, and that lasted four years: by 1984 only three men, including two Olympic champions, had beaten Hemery's time.

Born in Cirencester, Hemery spent ten of the first twenty-four years of his life in the United States. He moved across the Atlantic with his parents in 1956 at the age of twelve, graduating from Massachusetts High School. In 1964 he enrolled at Boston University, which had ideal training facilities.

Rumours that there was a world-class British hurdler in the United States filtered back to England by 1966. Hemery won the AAA Championships in the 120-yard hurdles, then won the Commonwealth Games gold medal in Kingston, Jamaica. He needed the speed work to prepare for the longer 400-metre hurdles' distance.

Olympic year began well. Hemery beat the world record holder, Geoff Vanderstock, in the American National Collegiate Championships. A medal looked a possibility.

The final had the makings of a spectacular race. Hemery was in the lead by the third hurdle. He passed halfway in 23.3 seconds, then, round the final turn, cleared daylight between himself and the rest of the field. He wasn't certain that he'd won. He'd looked to the right at the finish but not to the left. Peter Wilson, the *Daily Mirror*'s leading journalist, said in his book, *The Man They Couldn't Gag*:

One of the truly great British Olympics triumphs of my time was that of David Hemery. He not only looked a winner all the way, but he clipped a staggering 0.7 seconds off the world record. This event is one of the 'killers' of the athletics programme; and I have never been sure in my own mind whether altitude was a help, or a handicap that Hemery brilliantly overcame.

Hemery returned to the shorter distance between Olympics. He finished second to the Olympic silver medallist, Eddy Ottoz of Italy, in the 1969 European Championships, and tried his hand at decathlon, registering a best total of 6893. Weakness in the throwing events was a handicap.

At the Commonwealth Games in Edinburgh, he retained his title in the metric distance. He won the title on his twenty-sixth birthday, the band striking up 'Happy Birthday'.

Hemery had two serious candidates for his title at the Munich Olympics. The raw but talented Ugandan, John Akii Bua, had drawn lane one, and the American Ralph Mann, who had clocked world-class times, was in lane six.

In the final, Hemery set off quicker than at Mexico. He passed halfway in 22.8 seconds. Akii Bua shocked him by being there with 100 metres to go and pulled away to win in a new world record time of 47.82, towed through by the old record holder, who lost concentration in the last stride to be pipped by Mann by one hundredth of a second.

With the bronze safely tucked away, Hemery joined the British 4 × 400-metre relay team and, with the Americans in disarray after demonstrations on the medal dais, collected the silver medal after a storming third-leg run.

At the end of 1972 he retired from amateur athletics. He taught at Millfield, went back to the United States, and now does sterling work for the East End youngsters at the Sobell Centre in the London borough of Islington. He keeps fit with annual incursions into the Superstars championship, winning in 1973 and 1976.

His performance at Mexico is still regarded as one of the most outstanding British Olympic performances of all time. Perhaps he took the advice of Brigitte Bardot, who told athletes competing at the 1968 Games: 'Get there early, rest a few days, train carefully, and cut out the romance until you get used to the altitude.'

FACTFILE

Born 18 July 1944, Cirencester, Gloucestershire, England

Olympic Games
Gold: 400-metre hurdles 48.12 (world record) (1968)
Silver: 4 × 400-metre relay (1972)
Bronze: 400-metre hurdles (1972)

Commonwealth Games
Gold: 120-yard hurdles 14.1 (1966)
Gold: 110-metre hurdles 13.8 (1970)

AAA titles
　120-yard hurdles 1966
　440-yard hurdles 1968
　110-metre hurdles 1970
　400-metre hurdles 1972

European Championships
Silver: 110-metre hurdles (1969)

World records
　400-metre hurdles
48.12 (Mexico City, 15 October 1968)

David Hemery clears the final hurdle on his way to a gold medal and a new world record in the 400-metre hurdles at the Mexico Olympics in 1968

Alex Higgins

Alex Higgins is someone who, if his parents had had their way, could have been a well-known sportsman in another field. In 1963, at the age of fourteen, Alex wanted to be a jockey. His parents agreed, and Alex joined the late Eddie Reavey's stable at Wantage, Berkshire. However, the slim 7-st Higgins quickly became a solid 10 st within two years. Reavey's report on him was not complimentary. 'He's a lazy bum,' said Reavey.

Although certain sources claim that Higgins had one ride in public, the late trainer's wife confirms that Alex never rode in public. Higgins's mother pleaded with Reavey to take her son back but, probably unknown to her, a new career was already taking shape.

Since the age of eleven young Alex had been introduced to the vagaries of the Jampot Club back home in Belfast. They had snooker tables there. Teachers thought that Alex was at home – parents thought he was at school. The Jampot saw more of him than either.

The Jampot was where he fashioned his game. He played quickly. He had to, otherwise the light-meter money would run out. He played for stake money. And, by 1968, he became Northern Ireland champion; only months after he was All-Ireland champion.

Turning professional, the 'Hurricane' went about his trade in a different manner from other players. The older generation had been brought up on a diet of exhibition matches. Bowties were the order of the day. Alex was different. He preferred to play in open-necked shirts. He felt that his game would improve if he played impromptu money matches.

By 1972 it seemed that this method of training was working. He had deposed the likable veteran, Jackie Rea, as Irish professional champion that year. Television had made the game more appealing, especially since the advent of colour. And Higgins was to benefit from that.

In 1972 he won the World Championship at his first attempt, beating John Spencer in the final. He was 22 years 345 days old, the youngest ever to win the title, and was also the first champion to win his way through the qualifying tournament. He was television box office, flamboyant, talented and young.

FACTFILE

Born 18 March 1949, Belfast, Northern Ireland

World Professional Championship

1972	v. John Spencer	won	37–32
1976	v. Ray Reardon	lost	16–27
1980	v. Cliff Thorburn	lost	16–18
1982	v. Ray Reardon	won	18–15

Northern Ireland Amateur Championship

1968	v. M. Gill	won	

All-Ireland Amateur Championship

1968	v. G. Hanway (Eire)	won	

Benson & Hedges Masters Tournament

1978	v. Cliff Thorburn	won	7–5
1981	v. Terry Griffiths	won	9–6

Coral UK Championship

1983	v. Steve Davis	won	16–15

World Professional Championship matches

1972

First qualifying round	v. Ron Gross	won	15–6
Second qualifying round	v. Maurice Parkin	won	11–3
First round	v. Jackie Rea	won	19–11
Quarter final	v. John Pulman	won	31–23
Semifinal	v. Rex Williams	won	31–30
Final	v. John Spencer	won	37–32

1973

Second round	v. Pat Houlihan	won	16–3
Quarter final	v. Fred Davis	won	16–14
Semifinal	v. Eddie Charlton	lost	9–23

1974

Second round	v. Bernard Bennett	won	15–4
Quarter final	v. Fred Davis	lost	14–15

1975

Second round	v. David Taylor	won	15–2
Quarter final	v. Rex Williams	won	19–12
Semi final	v. Ray Reardon	lost	14–19

1976

First round	v. Cliff Thorburn	won	15–14
Quarter final	v. John Spencer	won	15–14
Semifinal	v. Eddie Charlton	won	20–18
Final	v. Ray Reardon	lost	16–27

1977

First round	v. Doug Mountjoy	lost	12–13

1978

First round	v. Patsy Fagan	lost	12–13

1979

First round	v. David Taylor	won	13–5
Quarter final	v. Terry Griffiths	lost	12–13

1980

First round	v. Tony Meo	won	10–9
Second round	v. Perri Mans	won	13–6
Quarter final	v. Steve Davis	won	13–9
Semifinal	v. Kirk Stevens	won	16–13
Final	v. Cliff Thorburn	lost	16–18

1981

First round	v. Steve Davis	lost	8–13

1982

First round	v. Jim Meadowcroft	won	10–5
Second round	v. Doug Mountjoy	won	13–12
Quarter final	v. Willie Thorne	won	13–10
Semifinal	v. Jimmy White	won	16–15
Final	v. Ray Reardon	won	18–15

1983

First round	v. Dean Reynolds	won	10–4
Second round	v. Willie Thorne	won	13–8
Quarter final	v. Bill Werbeniuk	won	13–11
Semifinal	v. Steve Davis	lost	5–16

1984

First round	v. Neal Foulds	lost	9–10

Played 38   Won 27   Lost 11

Alex Higgins in play at the Benson and Hedges Tournament, an event in which he was the first to win on two occasions – in 1978 and 1981

Yet it was to be ten years before he won the world title again. In 1976 and 1980 he reached the final, but the more deliberate play of Ray Reardon and Cliff Thorburn triumphed. Brushes with the authorities were frequent. Like George Best, he came from Belfast and settled in the Manchester area; like Best, he was *the* talent of his sport, and, like Best, he had a tempestuous relationship with the media. Ask ten people at random in the Fulham Palace Road in the 1970s to name their favourite snooker player, and eight would say Alex Higgins.

In January 1980 he married Lynn, a former secretary at Manchester Airport, at the United Reform Church in Wilmslow. It was the second time for both. The marriage gave him security. In 1982 he became world champion for the second time, or 'the People's champion', as he called it. There were emotional scenes with his family.

Higgins still practises very little, but increasingly prefers the gamble to the exhibition. He makes the game look relatively simple with his speed of play; he once compiled a century break on television in 3 minutes 57 seconds. He had six maximums to his credit by the start of 1984. Relaxations include golf in Spain. He has a Daimler and a Mercedes, but he cannot drive.

Statistically, Alex Higgins may fall short of other champions so far. But in a decade that has seen snooker rise from a quiet, dignified minority sport to a major professional circus, his portrayal of a Paul Newman 'Hustler' character, with the ability to beat the rest of the world, has made him probably the best-known snooker player of all.

Jack Hobbs
(Sir John Berry Hobbs)

'The Master batsman.' 'Undoubtedly the greatest batsman I ever saw.' Just a couple of the tributes heaped upon Jack Hobbs, a player as highly regarded for his unselfishness, his charm and his humility as for his brilliance as a cricketer. In the years between Grace and Bradman, Hobbs was the world's best batsman. He made 61,237 runs – a world record – at an average of over 50. He scored 197 centuries – ninety-eight of them after he was forty. That, too, is a world record which still stands.

Remarkable though the figures are, they don't begin to tell the story of the man who, in a twenty-nine-year first-class career, won the hearts of the cricketing public, including, it is said, even the most parochial of Yorkshiremen, who doted on great openers produced by their own county, notably Rhodes, Holmes and Sutcliffe.

After a few games for Cambridgeshire, Hobbs offered his services to Essex. They, remarkably, turned him down. Instead, Hobbs went to Surrey, made his debut for them in 1905 against the Gentlemen of England captained by W. G. Grace, and scored 88. In his next match, his championship debut, he demonstrated just how misguided Essex were not to have employed him. He scored 155 against them at the Oval and was immediately awarded his county cap.

Hobbs blossomed rapidly into a fine opening batsman. He played every shot with ease and a natural assurance at the crease that is the hallmark of the truly great cricketer. Opening the innings for Surrey with Tom Hayward in 1907, he shared three century stands in a week. That same year he made his Test debut – the first of sixty-one between then and 1930. For England he partnered Herbert Sutcliffe in fifteen century opening stands in twenty-four Tests, having previously shared eight stands of 100 or more with Wilfred

Rhodes. That included the then world Test record 323 at Melbourne in 1911–12. No wonder Yorkshiremen were impressed.

With his other famous opening partner – Andrew Sandham – he passed 100 sixty-three times for Surrey. In 1926 he reached his career best score – 316 not out. Appropriately it was at Lord's against Middlesex and is still the highest individual score made at Lord's, but some of his most memorable innings were played in tricky conditions, notably at Melbourne in 1929 when, with Sutcliffe, he led England to an unlikely victory on a distinctly difficult wicket.

Hobbs, poised and alert, played his strokes with a power that seemed impossible from his slight frame. Neville Cardus, having watched Hobbs closely in the nets one day, remarked that his footwork was so good 'that it is almost impossible to pitch a length to him when he is at his best.'

A supreme artist at the crease, he was a brilliant cover fielder and – in his early days – an effective swing bowler who opened for England in three Tests in South Africa in 1909–10. Ten years later he topped the national averages with 17 wickets at 11.82.

A further indication of his charm and his ability came in 1934 when, aged fifty-one and about to retire, he turned out for Surrey at Old Trafford against Lancashire to keep a long-standing promise to wicketkeeper George Duckworth whose benefit match it was. Hobbs scored 116 – the only century made against that season's champions on their own ground.

He was knighted in 1953. After retiring from the game, he bought a sports shop in Fleet Street, and every day lunched in the restaurant next door, where, according to many who saw him there, he was 'the most approachable of men'.

FACTFILE

Born 16 December 1882, Cambridge, England
Died 21 December 1963, Hove, Sussex, England

Total first-class runs 61,237 (world record) (average 50.65)
Highest first-class innings 316*, Surrey *v.* Middlesex, Lord's (1926)
First-class centuries 197 (world record)
Test debut 1908 *v.* Australia, Melbourne
Total Test matches 61
Total Test runs 5410 (average 56.94)
Highest Test innings 211, *v.* South Africa, Lord's (1924)
Test centuries 15
Career bowling 113–2709 (average 23.97)
Total catches 317

*Hobbs shared in 166 century stands for the first wicket in 1315 first-class innings
*His 126th and 127th centuries, to beat Grace's record, were both set in the same game against Somerset in 1925. He scored 3024 runs that season and made sixteen centuries
*His 100th century was on 8 May 1923 against Somerset; he scored 116. His last century was on 28 May 1934 against Lancashire; again he scored 116
*In the 1920 season Hobbs topped the bowling averages with 17 wickets at an average of 11.82, although some sources quote Wilf Rhodes as being top, with 161 wickets at 13.18

The most prolific run-scorer in the history of cricket, Sir John Berry Hobbs

Jack Hobbs
John Arlott

There falls across this one December day
The light remembered from those suns of June
That you reflected in the summer play
Of perfect strokes across the afternoon.

No yeoman ever walked his household land
More sure of step or more secure of lease
Than you, accustomed and unhurried, trod
Your small, yet mighty, manor of the crease.

The game the Wealden rustics handed down
Through growing skill became, in you, a part
Of sense; and ripened to a style that showed
Their country sport matured to balanced art.

There was a wisdom so informed your bat
To understanding of the bowler's trade
That each resource of strength or skill he used
Seemed but the context of the stroke you played.

The Master: records prove the title good:
Yet figures fail you, for they cannot say
How many men whose names you never knew
Are proud to tell their sons they saw you play.

They share the sunlight of your summer day
Of thirty years; and they, with you, recall
How, through those well-wrought centuries, your hand
Reshaped the history of bat and ball.

Ben Hogan

Three golfers are guaranteed a place on any all-time list of greats – Nicklaus, Jones and Ben Hogan.

Hogan's record – four US Opens, one British Open (the only one he entered), two US Masters and two US PGAs – is impressive. It is even more remarkable when one realizes that Hogan was unimpressive in his early years as a pro and that many of his major victories came after an appalling car crash had left him in permanent pain.

Hogan began golf life as an eleven-year-old caddie at the golf club where his future great rival, Byron Nelson, worked, in Fort Worth, Texas. Hogan was a natural left-hander but, because of a shortage of left-handers' clubs, he played right-handed.

In 1931 Hogan turned pro. He had little success and decided to return home to practise. He returned to the Tour in 1937 but had little luck and won so little money that he could only afford to eat oranges. His first win came in 1938 in a Hershey fourball but he had no more victories until 1940 when he won five events, the first being the North and South Open, and finished the leading money earner on the Tour with $10,655. The war then intervened. In the meantime Byron Nelson had become known as 'Mr Golf'. Nelson was exempt from war service because of haemophilia and, in Hogan's absence, won everything he entered. Hogan was determined to prove he was the better player. In 1946 he won thirteen times, including his first major championship – the US PGA. He reached a new peak in 1948 with eleven wins, including the US Open at Riviera and the PGA again.

Hogan was the greatest practiser the sport of golf has ever seen and it paid off. Peter Alliss writes: 'He had reached perhaps the nearest any golfer has yet come to mastery over the ball.'

Tragedy struck at 8.30 in the morning on 2 February 1949. Out of the Texas mist loomed a Greyhound bus on the wrong side of the road. Hogan instinctively threw himself in front of his wife Valerie, who was driving. It was an action that probably saved her life. As it was he was left for dead at the side of the road while his wife was attended to. It was five and a half hours before he arrived at El Paso hospital, 120 miles away. There they discovered numerous fractures and it seemed unlikely that he would ever walk again, let alone play golf. But he was determined to continue – even mailing his entry for that year's US Open Championship.

His comeback was not as early as he would have liked, but miraculous for all that. In the Los Angeles Open of January 1950 he lost to Sam Sneed in a play-off. It confirmed his view that he could play top-class competitive golf again, though he understood that his strength would not allow him to play in more than a handful of tournaments a year. He used the lesser events to practise for the majors – the US Open and the Masters. At Merion in the 1950 Open, he tied for the lead with Lloyd Mangrum and George Fazio. Few gave the exhausted Hogan a chance in the play-off, but next day he won the title, beating Mangrum by 4 strokes and Fazio by 6.

The following year he took his first Masters with a final round of 68 in which, so most observers believed, he did not make a single error. In the Open at Oakland Hills on a course he hated he produced a final round of 67 that has been described as his best round ever.

In 1953 he played only five events and won the lot. He won the Masters title at Augusta, then the US Open at Oakmont, in which he led from start to finish and eventually won by 5 strokes. He was persuaded to enter the British Open and prove that he could win on a links course. The 1953 Open was at Carnoustie. Hogan arrived well before the qualifying rounds. He practised religiously over the course and walked Carnoustie every evening, working out the best lines of approach to the greens. The Scots appreciated his respect for their course and nicknamed him the 'Wee Ice Mon'. He qualified easily and produced progressively better scores over the four rounds – 73, 71, 70 and a course record 68 – to win the title. The British press were unanimous. He was the greatest golfer they had ever seen.

Hogan never played the British Open again and his win at Carnoustie in 1953 was his last major. But then he was at the pinnacle of a remarkable career in which he became the only player to win three majors in a single season.

Hogan continued to play – and practise. He appeared in the 1967

FACTFILE

Born 13 August 1912, Dublin, Texas, USA

'Big Four' wins 9
British Open 1953
US Open 1948, 1950, 1951, 1953
US Masters 1951, 1953
US PGA 1946, 1948
Ryder Cup appearances 1947 (playing captain), 1949 (non-playing captain), 1951, 1967 (non-playing captain)
World Cup wins
  Team 1956
  Individual 1956

*Hogan appeared in his first US Open in 1936 but failed to make the cut to play the final 36 holes
*In 1951 Glenn Ford portrayed Hogan in the film *Follow the Sun* – the first full-length feature film about a golfer
*Hogan won the US Open four times – it would have been five but he lost in a play-off to the little-known Jack Fleck in 1955
*In 1956 he won the American Sportsman of the Decade award
*In 1967, at the age of fifty-five, he shot a record tying 30 for the back nine in the Masters
*In the fifteen US Opens he entered between 1940 and 1960, he never finished outside the top twenty
*He won sixty-two tournaments on the US Tour, was top money winner in the USA five times, and had four holes in 1 during his career

Ben Hogan, the 1953 British Open champion at Carnoustie, tackles the famous Burma Road at Wentworth

Masters at the age of fifty-four and produced a third-round 66 that induced speculation that he could win again, but he faded with a last-round 77.

Hogan's record of sixty-two wins on the US Tour is the third best of all time. He never lost a Ryder Cup match. According to Terry Smith, he was 'the finest stroke player golf has ever known'. Like Jack Nicklaus, he was a perfectionist, practising for hour after hour. Peter Alliss relates how, after a round peppered with half a dozen birdies, he joined his friend Jimmy Demaret, the 1950 Masters winner, on the practice ground. Demaret said, 'For Christ's sake, Ben, nobody ever played better than you did today. You can't birdie every hole.' Hogan replied, 'Why not?'

Sir Leonard Hutton

'A master craftsman,' says Trevor Bailey of Len Hutton. Ted Dexter said, 'Hutton was an old master at a very early age.'

There are two great achievements in Hutton's long and distinguished career – his record 364 against Australia at the Oval, and leading England to victory in the Ashes series in the Coronation year of 1953. Hutton was the first professional to captain England. In his typical way, he thought hard about giving up his professional status 'as Wally Hammond had done' but resolved not to. As a result he never captained his county.

A product of the famous Pudsey side, he was coached by George Hirst and Edgar Oldroyd, had a trial for Yorkshire in 1930, made his debut for them against Cambridge University in 1934, and was out for a duck in his very first innings. In his first Test match – against New Zealand at Lord's three years later – he made 0 and 1, but in the next Test at Old Trafford he hit 100 to establish his place in the England team. A year later he won a place in cricket history with an average of over 118 against the Australians, including 364 in the final Test at the Oval. At the age of twenty-two, Hutton had set the record and eclipsed the prolific Bradman, but, according to A. G. Moyes, the innings was 'a model of defensive morality.' As he left the ground after batting thirteen hours and ten minutes a Yorkshire-woman tapped on his car window. 'Congratulations, Len,' she shouted, 'but why didn't you get one more and make it one for every day of the year?'

During the war Hutton broke his left arm in an army gymnasium at York in January 1940. When the arm healed it was 2 inches shorter than the right and he had to adapt his batting technique. He had to eliminate the hook shot which Jim Laker thinks would have made him an even greater player than he actually was. He began to play from the crease, restricting the use of what Neville Cardus called his 'extraordinarily quick feet' and, in the opinion of some, leaving him vulnerable to the off-spinner.

His injury did not prevent Hutton from resuming his career of heavy scoring. In 1949 he made 3429 runs, including 1000 in both June and August – the only player ever to have done so in two separate months of the same season.

Hutton first captained England in 1952 against India. It was his ambition to win back the Ashes from Australia after twenty years and he managed it the following year – Coronation year – captaining a fine side even though it did not include Cyril Washbrook, his regular opening partner, whose omission worried Hutton a great deal.

FACTFILE

Born 23 June 1916, Fulneck, Pudsey, Yorkshire, England

Total first-class runs 40,140 (average 55.51)
Highest first-class innings 364, England v. Australia, The Oval (1938)
First-class centuries 129
Test debut 1937, v. New Zealand, The Oval
Total Test matches 79
Total Test runs 6971 (average 56.67)
Highest Test innings 364, England v. Australia, The Oval (1938)
Test centuries 19

Tours
1935–36 to Jamaica (with Yorkshire)
1938–39 to South Africa (with MCC)
1946–47 to Australia and New Zealand (with MCC)
1947–48 to West Indies (with MCC)
1948–49 to South Africa (with MCC)
1950–51 to Australia and New Zealand (with MCC)
1953–54 to West Indies (with MCC)
1954–55 to Australia and New Zealand (with MCC)

1000 runs in a season 17
2000 runs in a season 8
3000 runs in a season 1

*Hutton's first game for Pudsey St Lawrence was in 1928 when he represented the Second XI in a match against Saltaire
*Another famous Yorkshireman, Herbert Sutcliffe, was also born in Pudsey

*Hutton's first visit to Headingley was as a schoolboy in 1930 to watch the Australians play England in a Test match. That day he watched Don Bradman score 309 runs

Hutton's Record 364 at the Oval in 1938

England (first innings)

L. Hutton	c Hassett b O'Reilly	364
W. J. Edrich	c Hassett b O'Reilly	12
M. Leyland	run out	187
W. R. Hammond	lbw Fleetwood-Smith	59
E. Paynter	lbw O'Reilly	0
D. S. Compton	b Waite	1
J. Hardstaff	not out	169
A. Wood	c & b Barnes	53
H. Verity	not out	8
Extras		50
	Total	903–7 dec

Did not bat: K. Farnes, W. E. Bowes

Dennis Compton recalls that both he and Eddie Paynter, as number five and six batsmen, sat padded up for a day and threequarters whilst Hutton was piling on the runs. Paynter leaned across to Denis and said, 'I bet you a pound we don't make ten between us when we go in.' Welcoming the opportunity to make some easy money, Compton accepted the bet. Paynter went in and was promptly dismissed for 0, and two minutes later Denis was on his way back to the pavilion, with just 1 run to his credit – and minus a pound.

Len Hutton amasses more runs during his innings of 364 against Australia at the Oval in 1938. The wicketkeeper is Ben Barnett

Hutton was the best English batsman of his generation. A stylist with a full repertoire of strokes, he could be very defensive if the occasion warranted. Among his best innings was the superb 145 at Lord's in 1953 – a majestic innings – in a match now remembered chiefly for the rearguard action by Willie Watson and Trevor Bailey that saved the game and England's chances of regaining the Ashes.

Generally a Hutton innings was watchful, put together with fine precision interspersed with classical, effortless cover and straight drives and exquisite late cuts. Ted Dexter wrote: 'His cricket was as thrifty as his speech and humour.' When asked by journalists what had happened when he was once clean bowled by Keith Miller, Hutton replied, 'I missed it.'

Hutton was a great thinker and tactician as a captain. Not content with regaining the Ashes in 1953, he retained them the following year in Australia. He once said that his biggest search when leading England was to find a pair of fast bowlers. He was lucky that Brian Statham and Fred Trueman arrived on the scene, followed by Frank Tyson.

Hutton retired in 1955 and was knighted a year later. He became a successful businessman, saw one of his sons – Richard – follow in his footsteps and play for Yorkshire and England, and remained in close contact with the game.

His record 364 will always be remembered at the expense of other innings which were probably more entertaining. Neville Cardus after watching him in 1938 said that he would 'always satisfy the lover of thoughtful batsmanship'.

He was certainly a hero in Yorkshire. One tale – probably apocryphal – relates how a little boy arrived at Headingley on the first morning of the Test against Australia in 1953 to find his father in the crowd.

'Dad, something terrible's happened. Me mam's ran off wi' milkman and tekken all savings. Grandad's fell in canal, and me sister's set fire to 'ouse.'

'Ay lad,' said his father 'and I've got news for thee. 'Utton's out.'

(Hutton was bowled second ball by Ray Lindwall for a duck.)

111

Tony Jacklin

Tony Jacklin – a Scunthorpe train driver's son – won the British Open in 1969 and the US Open in 1970. His achievement can be measured by the fact that there was an eighteen-year gap since a Briton had last won the Open and it was fifty years since a British success in the US Open.

Jacklin learned the game caddying for his father at Scunthorpe Golf Club. At sixteen he went to work in the Appleby Frodingham steelworks at Scunthorpe, but in November 1962, at the age of seventeen, he turned pro at Potter's Bar club, under the tutelage of Bill Shankland.

In his first full year, 1963, Jacklin was sixtieth in the order of merit, earning £344. He finished thirtieth in the Open and was made Rookie of the Year. After that his progress was rapid. In 1965 he won his first event, the GorRay Assistants Championship at Hartsbourne, and took part in his first American championship – the Carling Open at Arkansas. After four tournament wins in 1967, Jacklin had his first American victory a year later in the Jacksonville Open – the first fully recognized event to be won by a British golfer since Ted Ray's Open victory in 1920.

In 1969 he became the first British golfer to win the Open since Max Faulkner, which set him up for his finest period. He took the 1970 US Open at Hazeltine by 7 strokes, becoming only the second man in history to win the title with all four rounds under par, and the first Briton to hold both the US and the British Open titles at the same time. His stay at the top was brief, however. By 1972 he was disenchanted with the US Tour. He again won the Greater Jacksonville Open, but decided against full-time involvement in the States and headed back to England. His time as a truly competitive world-class player may have been short, but he did enough to ensure a lasting place in the affections of the British sports connoisseur.

At Lytham in the 1969 Open he had gone into the lead on the third day – 2 strokes ahead of Christy O'Connor and Bob Charles – with some impressive bunker play. He was still 2 ahead of Charles when he came to the seventy-second hole. He hit his second to within 3 yards to clinch the title. The following year at St Andrews, he started the defence of his title with an outward 29 in the first round. He completed the round next day, after rain caused an abandonment of play on the first, and returned a 67. He eventually finished fifth. In 1971 at Royal Birkdale, he was third behind Lee Trevino and Mr Lu, though he said he had not played well.

The turning point of Jacklin's career came in 1972 at Muirfield. He started the last round of the Open a stroke behind Trevino. By the seventeenth they were level when Trevino hit a shot through the green and off the back. Jacklin pitched up short of the flag and looked likely to take the lead. Certainly Trevino thought so. As he carelessly selected a club he muttered, 'I've had it.' Thinking he had thrown it all away, he knocked the ball into the hole before an amazed Jacklin. Jacklin was dismayed. He missed the putt and, worse still, the return, and finished third behind Trevino and Nicklaus. Experts have suggested – forcibly – that the seventeenth at Muirfield in 1972 destroyed Jacklin. Certainly between 1967 and 1972 he had always been in contention for the title and although he had only won one championship he had gained a reputation as the best striker of a golf ball in Britain.

He won the 1972 Dunlop Masters at Yarra Yarra in Australia after producing a second round 63 – 9 under par – and went on to win the tournament. He explained afterwards that he had been stung by press criticism alleging that he never tried when in Australia. 'I wouldn't come this far to mess about,' he said.

After 1972 he rarely figured on the leader boards. In 1977 he finished second in the Bing Crosby Pro-Am, but victories were rare – the Venezuela and German Opens of 1979, the Jersey Open of 1981, and the PGA at Hillside in 1982 all promised to be the renaissance of this most popular of sportsmen. Jacklin himself, after the Hillside win, announced, 'Oh, it is good to be back,' with an immense sense of relief.

Even at his best, Jacklin probably was not as good a player as the British press and fans thought he was, but his record is undeniable. For a short time he was the holder of both US and British Open titles and, with three wins in the States and a best finish of twentieth in the money list, he set a standard which no other British golfer has come close to.

Given his world-wide experience, Jacklin was an excellent choice as Ryder Cup captain for Palm Beach in 1983, when the Americans won by just one point and he was immediately chosen to lead the team again at the Belfry in 1985.

The late Henry Longhurst wrote of Jacklin's last hole in his 1969 Open win: 'I saw the shot from just behind him and I shall remember

FACTFILE

Born 7 July 1944, Scunthorpe, England

'Big Four' wins 2
British Open 1969
US Open 1970
Ryder Cup appearances 1967, 1969, 1971, 1973, 1975, 1977, 1979, 1983 (non-playing captain)

*In 1967 Jacklin joined the Mark McCormick organization. That year also saw him make his Ryder Cup debut and win four tournaments, his best total in one year. He won the Forest Products Tournament in New Zealand, the New Zealand PGA, the Pringle Tournament and the Dunlop Masters. His hole in 1 at the 165-yard sixteenth hole in the final round of the Dunlop Masters at St George's, Sandwich, was the first televised hole in 1 in Great Britain; it was also one of those rare occasions when the eventual winner of the tournament had a hole in 1 on his card

*His Open win – his only win of 1969 – earned him £4250. He only won another £1731 on the European Tour a single in year – in 1970.

*He shot his lowest round ever in 1973 – a 62 in the Bogota Open

*He sold his house in Jersey, to live in Spain, where he is attached to the Sotogrande Club

*At the start of the 1984 season, he had twenty-five tournament wins to his credit

it to the end of my days. His swing never left him and this might have been on the practice ground. It might also have been fired from a rifle instead of a golf club – miles down the dead centre, veering neither to right nor left. He tossed the second up to within 10 feet and won with probably the shortest putt that ever won a championship – call it three-eighths of an inch.'

Tony Jacklin tees off at one of the short holes at the 1968 British Open

Bobby Jones

Bobby Jones retired at the peak of his career at the age of twenty-eight – an immortal in the world of golfing greats. As a competitor there was nothing left for him to achieve after 1930 when he had completed the Grand Slam of US Open and Amateur championships and British Amateur and Open titles.

Terry Smith wrote: 'His style was lithe and smooth, with a drowsy, rhythmic grace, as he beat the professionals at their own game while playing on a part-time basis.' Michael Hobbs said his swing had a 'lazy majesty'.

Even at the age of five, when he first began to follow his parents round the course near his home in Atlanta, his promise was obvious. Early photographs of the boy who was too sickly and frail to eat solid food until he was six show that he had a swing which was not much changed by his heyday, 1923 to 1930.

By the time he was fourteen he was hailed as a prodigy. In 1911, at the age of nine, he won the junior championship at his first club, East Lake, Georgia, and at fourteen he won his first Georgia State Championship. In 1919, at the age of seventeen, he was runner-up in the Canadian Open and the US Amateur championships. At twenty he was runner-up in the US Open – a finish which signalled the start of his great years.

A year later, in 1923, he beat Bobby Cruickshank for the title after a play-off at Inwood. In all, between 1922 and 1930 he won the championship four times, was second twice and lost two play-offs, whilst in the Amateur Championship he won the title five times between 1924 and 1930 and was runner-up twice. It is a record that puts him second only to Jack Nicklaus in the all-time major championship winners' list – and Jones's career was compressed into a far shorter period.

Bobby Jones was a true amateur. Throughout his life he pursued either an academic, a business or a legal career. He had degrees in engineering, literature and law, from Atlanta and Harvard universities. He played in only three or four events each year, never played in winter, and practised only a little at the start of the season, preferring during the season to play in a few gentle friendly fourballs.

Temperamentally, he became nervously wound up in competition. He was said to lose about 8 kilos in weight during a particularly tense round and – especially early on – he was renowned for throwing clubs and hitting golf balls in anger at a poor shot. He recalled how, in an exhibition match in 1917, when he was fifteen, he played the national champion, Alexa Stirling. 'Although I should have known that Alexa, and not I, was the main attraction,' he related, 'I behaved very badly when my game went apart. I heaved numerous clubs and once threw the ball away. I read the pity in Alexa's soft brown eyes and finally settled down, but not before I had made a complete fool of myself.'

Jones's days of club throwing may have been over, at least in exhibition matches, but the tension frequently affected him so badly that he could not eat before an important round; in the US Open of 1930 at Interlachan, his tie had to be cut free with a knife, he had sweated so profusely.

In 1921 he appeared in his first Open, at St Andrews. After taking 46 on the outward half in the third round, he tore up his card and hit his ball into the sea in disgust at his performance. In later years he came to love the Old Course.

Jones was back for the 1926 Open at Royal Lytham. He had failed to win the Amateur title earlier and stayed on to see if he could win the Open. He did, defended his title successfully the following year, and won again in 1930 – his greatest year.

In 1930 he set out to win everything – and he did. He thought his trickiest task was to win the British Amateur. The course was St Andrews – the scene of his card-tearing exploit nine years before. He won the final conclusively 7 and 6 after being two down with five to play in his semifinal with George Voight. In the Open at Hoylake he took 7 at the fifth in his last round, played on undaunted and finished with 75 – good enough to win by 2 strokes and sufficient evidence that his temperament was now under control. He returned home to win the US Open at Interlachan and in his last round there had three double bogeys and still clung on to a 2-stroke lead.

His bid for the fourth title in the Grand Slam captured the imagination of America. He needed the protection of the US Marines from his adoring fans; one newspaper alone sent sixteen reporters to cover the event; and five thousand people regularly turned up to watch his practice rounds. He won the title by a convincing 8 and 7

FACTFILE

Born 17 March 1902, Atlanta, Georgia, USA
Died 18 December 1971, Atlanta, Georgia, USA

'Big Four' wins 7
British Open 1926, 1927, 1930
US Open 1923, 1926, 1929, 1930
US Amateur Championship 1924, 1925, 1927, 1928, 1930
British Amateur Championship 1930
Walker Cup appearances 1922, 1924, 1926, 1928 (captain), 1930 (captain)

*Full name: Robert Tyre Jones
*Jones made his first visit to Britain in 1921, when he was eliminated in the fourth round of the Amateur Championship

*In 1926 he won both the British and US Opens, and that year in the Walker Cup he beat Cyril Tolley 12 and 11
*In the Walker Cup in 1928 he went one better by beating T. P. Perkins 13 and 12
*In 1958 he came to Britain to inaugurate the Eisenhower Trophy and, in a highly emotional ceremony, he was awarded the Freedom of the Burgh of St Andrews
*His average winning margin in all Walker Cup matches was 8 and 7
*He served with the US Artillery during the Second World War, rising to the rank of lieutenant colonel
*He played in eleven US Opens, won four, was second on four occasions, and the other three times was fifth, eighth and eleventh
*After retiring, he concentrated on his law business in Atlanta

Bobby Jones, the holder, practises at St Andrews before the start of the 1927 British Open championship

victory in the final at Merion to complete his Grand Slam (as an amateur, he could not enter the US PGA Championship and the Masters was yet to be introduced to the American scene).

Jones himself designed the Augusta course, home for the Masters, initially an event for his old friends and rivals, and played in every Masters from 1934 until 1947, when he retired after the second round, complaining of a sore neck and shoulders. He left the course saying, 'See you on the first tee next year, boys.' But he had played his last competitive round. He was suffering from a rare, inoperable disease called syringomyelia (a congenital disease of the spine). He died in 1971 in Augusta after a long and painful illness. The US Masters course at the Augusta National Golf Club is his memorial.

Jahangir Khan

By the time 1984 dawned, Jahangir Khan had established complete mastery in his sport. He could beat any other squash player, even on a bad day. In 1981 he reached the final of the British Open Championship, only to lose 9–2, 9–7, 5–9, 9–7 to Geoff Hunt, the Australian, who was winning the title for the eighth time. Jahangir was still only seventeen, but that result was significant – up to September 1984 it was the last time he had been beaten.

He was born in Karachi on 10 December 1963, the son of Roshan Khan, who won the British Open title in 1956. Roshan's cousin, Hashim, was the great name of the 1950s, winning the Open every year from 1950 to 1955 and regaining the title in 1957. Hashim was then overtaken by his brother Azam, who had four wins from 1957 to 1961. The Khan family had inherited a love of squash from earlier generations who had all worked as ballboys in the open-air courts of the British service clubs in the North West Frontier.

Jahangir was introduced to squash at the age of ten and by the time he was fourteen had won his country's national junior title. This meant inclusion in the Pakistan team for the 1979 World Amateur Championships in Australia, and Jahangir, aged fifteen, won the title with a four-set win against Phil Kenyon. Ironically, he did not make the Pakistani side for the team event which followed the individual championship. He was too young to be on the national ranking lists. Earlier that same year he lost to Britain's Peter Verow in the second round of the British Amateur Championships.

His father thought that the young Jahangir's development would be better supervised if he were to go to England. He settled in Wembley, a few hundred yards from the courts, immediately after winning the world amateur title. But tragedy was not far away. Brother Torsam, the world No. 6, was to be Jahangir's guide in London, but within a month of Jahangir's arrival Torsam left to play in the Australian Open. He did not return. He collapsed and died whilst playing Neven Barbow of New Zealand. He was just twenty-eight. Cousin Rahmat Khan offered to take on the role of guardian; during those tragic months Jahangir's maturity was astonishing.

In the 1980 British Open, Jonah Barrington had no end of trouble preventing the youngster from reaching the quarter final. Jahangir admired Barrington's training methods and began to practise for six hours a day. Barrington in turn suggested that if Jahangir played for 150 years he would not acquire Hunt's tactical knowledge, but conceded that Jahangir's was much the better all-round game.

Hunt vacated his position as world No. 1 shortly after being defeated by Jahangir in the final of the 1981 British Open. In November 1981 Jahangir won a four-set match with Hunt to win the World Open, then went on to beat Hunt again in April 1982 in the British Open. Though various sponsors had decreed that new events should have 'world' status, the British Open was still the top event.

Statistics are now irrelevant and monotonous. Jahangir's domination is total. He doesn't even allow the other finalist to take a set from him in the British Open. The same can be said for the World Open. Barrington says that he 'has married the talents of Pakistan squash with the Western training methods'.

Jahangir's great-grandfather was a rajah in Peshawar. The name Jahangir, when translated, means 'Emperor of the World', surely a prophetic choice.

FACTFILE

Born 10 December 1963, Karachi, Pakistan

World Open Championships
1981 beat Geoff Hunt (Australia), 7–9, 9–1, 9–2, 9–2
1982 beat Dean Williams (Australia) 9–2, 6–9, 9–1, 9–1
1983 beat Qamar Zaman (Pakistan), 9–0, 9–4, 9–3

World Amateur Championships
1979 beat Phil Kenyon (England), 2–9, 9–3, 9–3, 9–5

World Masters
1981 beat Qamar Zaman (Pakistan), 4–9, 9–5, 9–2, 9–2
1982 beat Gamal Awad (Egypt), 9–0, 9–4, 9–2
1983 beat Qamar Zaman (Pakistan), 9–6, 8–10, 9–0, 9–3

British Open
1981 lost to Geoff Hunt (Australia), 2–9, 7–9, 9–5, 7–9
1982 beat Hiddy Jahan (Pakistan), 9–2, 10–9, 9–3
1983 beat Gamal Awad (Egypt), 9–2, 9–5, 9–1
1984 beat Qamar Zaman (Pakistan), 9–0, 9–3, 9–5

The Rest of the Khan Family at the British Open

1950 Hashim Khan beat M. A. Karim (Egypt), 9–5, 9–0, 9–0
1951 Hashim Khan beat M. A. Karim (Egypt), 9–5, 9–7, 9–0
1952 Hashim Khan beat R. B. R. Wilson (England), 9–2, 8–10, 9–1, 9–0
1953 Hashim Khan beat Azam Khan, 6–9, 9–6, 9–6, 7–9, 9–5
1954 Hashim Khan beat Azam Khan, 9–7, 7–9, 9–7, 5–9, 9–7
1955 Hashim Khan beat Roshan Khan, 9–4, 9–2, 5–9, 9–5
1956 Roshan Khan beat Hashim Khan, 6–9, 9–5, 9–2, 9–1
1957 Hashim Khan beat Azam Khan, 9–7, 6–9, 9–6, 9–7
1958 Azam Khan beat Mohibullah Khan, 9–5, 9–0, 9–1
1959 Azam Khan beat Roshan Khan, 9–1, 9–0, 9–0
1960 Azam Khan beat Mohibullah Khan, 6–9, 9–1, 9–4, 0–9, 9–2
1961 Azam Khan beat Mohibullah Khan, 9–6, 7–9, 10–8, 2–9, 9–4
1962 Mohibullah Khan beat A. A. Taleb (Egypt), 9–4, 5–9, 3–9, 10–8
1975 Geoff Hunt (Australia) beat Mohibullah Khan, 7–9, 9–4, 8–10, 9–2, 9–2

Jahangir Khan takes his first British Open title in 1982 at Bromley

Jean-Claude Killy

The French covet their sporting heroes, but, despite massive government outlay on facilities and coaching, the recent success rate from the other side of La Manche has been as spectacularly poor as their attempts to unblock their own motorways, especially in the field of winter sports, where opportunities are unrivalled. So, when an Olympic champion arrives, he not unnaturally gets star treatment. When he wins three gold medals at a time when the Games are held in France, then there is an instant excuse to send an open motorcade up the Champs-Elysées to the Arc de Triomphe and declare a Bank Holiday. That's what happened to Jean-Claude Killy.

Killy, skier supreme, won three golds at the 1968 Winter Olympics at Grenoble, close to Mont Blanc. He not only won the slalom and the giant slalom – which involves tricky manoeuvring through thirty gates – but also the downhill, the Blue Riband event, in which skiers traverse 3 kilometres straight down the mountainside at speeds of up to 120 kilometres an hour.

Toni Sailer, from Austria, had won the same events in 1956, but skiing had come a long way by 1968. No longer was it a sport for jet setters and aristocrats descending on St Moritz and Klosters. It was now a sport for all, with package holidays, après ski and Gluwein.

Killy was born far from the slopes, at St Cloud by the racecourse in Paris. The Parisians' lifestyle is to have a flat in the city during the week and to move to a country retreat for the weekends. Killy put on skis at Val d'Isère at the age of five. By the time he was nineteen he had battled through the squad system and was chosen for the 1962 World Championships. He did not take part; a broken ankle put paid to his season. He was a reckless skier and always would be.

Two years later, at the 1964 Winter Olympics, Killy finished fifth in the giant slalom. In 1968 he was world champion for the first time. The championships were held at Portillo in Chile, and Killy, who had left school at sixteen to join the French team, won both the downhill and the combined events. General de Gaulle, who had just given Harold Wilson the 'non' for EEC entry, gave Killy the 'oui' and awarded him the National Order of Merit.

Skiing administration was moving quickly as sponsors were attracted to the sport. In 1967 the inaugural World Cup was held.

Killy was the first winner. Such was his dominance that, in the twenty-one days from 9 to 29 January, he won twelve World Cup races. He totalled 225 points for the season; the runner-up collected 114.

Although Killy had a somewhat patchy lead-up to the Olympics, he went to Grenoble as firm favourite. Despite off-the-piste problems with skiing endorsements, he won the downhill, from fourteen on the grid, then the giant slalom, and finally the slalom, in which his great rival, Karl Schranz, was supposedly confronted by a mysterious figure in black near the halfway mark.

Avery Brundage, the president of the IOC, had decreed that sponsorship would not be worn on clothes or equipment. The problem was solved by a friend of Killy, who dashed onto the finishing area festooned in sponsorship logos to embrace the winner. Local police were powerless.

Killy's style did not meet with universal approval. He adopted a wider stance for stability. It did not impress the Americans – 'trying to get into one of Colonel Sanders' lunchboxes' was an unkind comment on a style similar to a flapping chicken.

Much to Brundage's delight, Killy turned professional after Grenoble. He hoped that other skiers would follow suit but, like the Austrian Schranz, they were content to remain £23,000-a-year amateurs. Killy went to the States and endorsed virtually everything that moved in the mountains. Returning to his childhood Val d'Isère, he set up a skiing centre. He became very rich. He was world professional champion, when time permitted, in 1973.

There is a PS for Downhill Racer and James Bond fans. It wasn't Burt Lancaster, Roger Moore or Sean Connery on those skis; it was Jean-Claude Killy. He's a bit old for that now, but rumour has it that he was last seen jumping off a cable car and skiing over crevasses, just to bring someone, somewhere, a box of chocolates. Somehow it sums up his life – that of the fun-loving, danger-seeking extrovert. Mad enough to enter a ski jump competition at Wengen as a youngster and surprise spectators by 'flashing through the air with the greatest of ease' and landing with only longjohns between him and frostbite.

FACTFILE

Born 30 August 1943, St Cloud, nr Paris, France

Olympic Games
Gold: Downhill (1968)
        Slalom (1968)
        Giant slalom (1968)

World Cup
Overall champion: 1967, 1968

World Championships
Gold: Downhill (1966, 1968)
        Combined events (1966, 1968)
        Slalom (1968)
        Giant slalom (1968)

*Of his attitude to skiing Killy said, 'You have to be hungry and draw on your resources of self-pride. That's why I like individual sports, you don't share responsibility for team performances'

'The sensation of the slopes' – Jean-Claude Killy wins a World Cup downhill race in his home village of Val d'Isère

Billie Jean King

FACTFILE

Born 22 November 1943, Long Beach, California, USA

Wimbledon titles (summary)
  Singles 1966, 1967, 1968, 1972, 1973, 1975
  Doubles 1961, 1962, 1965, 1967, 1968, 1970, 1971, 1972,
      1973, 1979
  Mixed doubles 1967, 1971, 1973, 1974
French singles title 1972
Australian singles title 1968
United States singles title 1967, 1971, 1972, 1974

Billie Jean's Wimbledon Championship matches

1961 *Doubles* (with Miss K. Hantze, USA) beat Miss J. Lehane &
  Miss M. Smith (Australia), 6–3, 6–4
1962 *Doubles* (with Mrs J. R. Susman, USA) beat Miss L. E. G. Price
  & Miss R. Schurrmann (SA), 5–7, 6–3, 7–5
1963 *Singles* lost to Miss M. Smith (Australia), 3–6, 4–6
1964 *Doubles* (with Mrs J. R. Susman, USA) lost to Miss M. Smith &
  Miss L. R. Turner (Australia), 5–7, 2–6
1965 *Doubles* (with Miss M. E. Bueno, Brazil) Beat Miss F. Durr &
  Miss J. Lieffrig (France), 6–2, 7–5

From 1966 she competed as Mrs L. W. King

1966 *Singles* Beat Miss M. E. Bueno (Brazil), 6–3, 3–6, 6–1
Mixed doubles (with R. D. Ralston, USA) lost to K. R. Fletcher &
  Miss M. Smith (Australia), 6–4, 3–6, 3–6
1967 *Singles* Beat Mrs P. F. Jones (GB), 6–3, 6–4
Doubles (with Miss R. Casals, USA) beat Miss M. E. Bueno (Brazil) &
  Miss N. Richey (Australia), 9–11, 6–4, 6–2
Mixed doubles (with O. Davidson, Australia) beat K. Fletcher
  (Australia) & Miss M. E. Bueno (Brazil), 7–5, 6–2
1968 *Singles* Beat Miss J. A. M. Tegart (Australia), 9–7, 7–5
Doubles (with Miss R. Casals, USA) beat Miss F. Durr (France) &
  Mrs P. F. Jones (GB), 3–6, 6–4, 7–5
1969 *Singles* Lost to Mrs P. F. Jones (GB), 6–3, 3–6, 2–6
1970 *Singles* Lost to Mrs M. Court (Australia), 12–14, 9–11
Doubles (with Miss R. Casals, USA) beat Miss F. Durr (France) &
  Miss S. V. Wade (GB), 6–2, 6–3
1971 *Doubles* (with Miss R. Casals, USA) beat Mrs B. M. Court &
  Miss E. Goolagong (Australia), 6–3, 6–2
Mixed doubles (with O. Davidson, Australia) beat M. C. Riessen (USA)
  & Mrs B. M. Court (Australia), 3–6, 6–2, 15–13
1972 *Singles* Beat Miss E. Goolagong (Australia), 6–3, 6–3
Doubles (with Miss B. Stove, Netherlands) beat Mrs D. E. Dalton
  (Australia) & Miss F. Durr (France), 6–2, 4–6, 6–3
1973 *Singles* Beat Miss C. Evert (USA), 6–0, 7–5
Doubles (with Miss R. Casals, USA) beat Miss F. Durr (France) &
  Miss B. Stove (Netherlands), 6–1, 4–6, 7–5
Mixed doubles (with O. Davidson, Australia) beat R. Ramirez (Mexico)
  & Miss J. S. Newberry (USA), 6–3, 6–2

1974 *Mixed doubles* (with O. Davidson, Australia) beat M. J. Farrell
  & Miss L. J. Charles (GB), 6–3, 9–7
1975 *Singles* Beat Mrs R. Cawley (Australia), 6–0, 6–1
1976 *Doubles* (with Miss B. Stove, Netherlands) lost to Miss C. Evert
  (USA) & Miss M. Navratilova (Czechoslovakia), 1–6, 6–3, 5–7
1978 *Mixed doubles* (with R. O. Ruffells, Australia) lost to
  F. D. McMillen (SA) & Miss B. Stove (Netherlands), 2–6, 2–6
1979 *Doubles* (with Miss M. Navratilova, Czechoslovakia) beat
  Miss B. Stove (Netherlands) & Miss W. Turnbull (Australia), 5–7,
  6–3, 6–2
1983 *Mixed doubles* (with S. Denton) lost to J.M. Lloyd (GB) &
  Mrs W. Turnbull (Australia), 7–6, 6–7, 5–7

*In all, Billie Jean has played 262 matches, and the breakdown of
them is as follows:

	P	W	L
Singles	105	91	14
Doubles	86	75	11
Mixed doubles	71	57	14
	262	223	39

These figures include matches in which she won outright

*In 1984 Billie Jean said, 'I'll quit when my knees tell me to'
*Of her success at tennis she said, 'The only way I made it was by
chance. I wanted a sport where I could be considered feminine. That
wasn't easy. Hopefully we are no longer regarded as muscle-bound
Amazonian jerks'

On the second day of the 1961 Wimbledon Championships, Billie Jean Moffit lost her first-round singles match against Yola Ramirez of Mexico 11–9, 2–6, 1–6. Twenty-two years and a record twenty Wimbledon titles later, eighteen-year-old Andrea Jaeger beat Billie Jean, in her fortieth year, in the semifinals of the women's singles on the centre court. The result was a disappointment – 6–1, 6–1; in her 110th singles match at Wimbledon she had suffered her worst defeat and, as she walked away, Billie Jean took an obviously emotional glance around the centre court. 'I had a last look over my shoulder,' she said, 'in case it should be the last time. I've never done that before.'

During those twenty-two years she had enjoyed a unique although not always happy relationship with Wimbledon, she had won more major tournaments throughout the world than anyone else, and had seen women's tennis grow from a somewhat static game into a multi-million-pound international circuit. There had been an increase in facilities and organization and, both on and off the court, she perhaps had been the significant factor in the sport's development.

Born in Long Beach, California, into a sporting family, she received the necessary impetus. Her father was a baseball and basketball player, her mother a talented swimmer, and her brother was a pitcher with the San Francisco Giants. She won her first event, the 'D' division of the Long Beach closed tournament, at the age of twelve; her coach, Clyde Walker, was already attempting to convince her that baseball and football, other sports she enjoyed, would have to be abandoned. She won her first major event, the Southern California Tournament, when just sixteen and moved to No. 19 in the US rankings in 1959; the following year, aged seventeen, she was ranked No. 4.

In her first Wimbledon she won the ladies' doubles with Karen Hantze. Karen was to return as Mrs Susman twelve months later and win the women's singles. In 1962 Billie Jean was ranked No. 10 in the world; a promising academic career at California State College was shelved for full-time tennis.

Her first major titles were all gained in doubles events. After her successes with Karen Susman, she teamed with Maria Bueno. Then, with Rosie Casals and Owen Davidson, she rewrote the doubles record books. Singles championships also began to pour in: Wimbledon in 1966, 1967 and 1968, and again in 1972, 1973 and 1975; four wins in the US Championships in 1967, 1971, 1972 and 1974; she completed her Grand Slam successes with a win in the Australian Championships in 1968 and the French title in 1972.

Billie Jean married a Californian lawyer, Larry King, in 1965 and together they began to devote more time to the organization and structuring of the sport. On turning professional after the first open Wimbledon in 1968, after her third successive singles championship, Billie Jean with other leading players saw the possibilities of sponsorship and promotion with cosmetics and fashion firms whose cash injection helped the women's game achieve near parity with the men's circuit.

As the years rolled by the championships rolled in. A series of complicated knee operations failed to dim her enthusiasm. Intrusions on her private life were unfortunate. In 1971 she was the first woman player to win $100,000 in a season. On 20 September 1973 she beat the 1939 triple Wimbledon champion – and male

As permanent as the strawberries and cream, Billie Jean King, who missed the 1984 Wimbledon championships after making her first visit twenty-three years earlier

chauvinist – Bobby Riggs 6–4, 6–3, 6–3, before a crowd of 30,472 at the Houston Astrodrome. There were another fifty million people watching on television. She has been a prominent member of the United States Wightman Cup and Federation Cup teams, and in 1980–81 she was president of the Women's Tennis Association.

On 22 November 1983, still No. 12 in the world, Billie Jean King beat Ann White in the Virginia Slims Tournament at Sydney. Fellow players baked her a cake and decorated it with forty candles.

Olga Korbut

If ever anyone was brought from complete obscurity into the homes of families throughout the world, it was a tiny 4-foot 11-inch gymnast, weighing no more than 85 lb, called Olga Korbut. Television was the culprit, and Olga and her family were among the few who didn't have one at the time!

Olga Korbut was a problem for the Russians. She was the most charismatic, charming, cheeky and original gymnast of all, but she was unpredictable. And she was not as good as Lumila Tourischeva, or Nelli Kim.

The family home was at Grodno, that area of Russia which has experienced both Soviet and Polish rule depending on whichever side won various battles. Her father was a civil engineer, her mother a clerk in the local administration office of Internal Affairs. Olga has three sisters, none of whom are sports minded; two were out of work during the time of Olga's success.

Her first 'coach' was the 1964 Olympic gold medallist, Yelena Voltchetskaya. The solemn Renald Kenysch was her first official mentor; the disagreements between the pair were legendary. The third influence was the former world and Olympic champion, Larissa Latynina, coach to the national team. Gymnastically, Olga's greatest asset was a flexible spine, which allowed her to attempt enterprising movements beyond the scope of most gymnasts.

Though Olga had won her first Soviet title at the age of fifteen in 1970, she was completely unknown outside the USSR before the Munich Olympics of 1972. That was to change overnight. After the team event, won by the Soviet Union, Tourischeva, Korbut and the East German Karin Janz were favourites for the individual title. Coming to the asymmetrical bars, Olga was in third place just 0.65 off the lead. The bars were a disaster from the first run-up step. She received only 7.50 and slipped to seventh overall. Television pictures relayed the crying Korbut and the world joined in.

Two days later, Olga began her quest for the individual medals on the selfsame bars. After being given 9.80 for her programme – leader Janz received 9.90 – the crowd booed and stamped for ten minutes. The situation was saved by the East German Angelika Hellmann, who began her routine whilst the arena was in bedlam, only to overstep drastically on landing and burst into tears.

Olga won two individual gold medals, one on the beam, where her suppleness served her best, and the other in the floor exercises. John Goodbody, in his splendid *Illustrated History of Gymnastics*,* describes how Olga changed her music for the floor exercises five days before the Olympics to the theme from the German war film

*Stanley Paul, 1983.

Woman of My Dreams. She admitted, 'My choreographer taught me to walk, smile and wink.'

Gymnastics became a boom sport after the Munich Olympics. In Britain mothers were taking their toddlers to clubs throughout the country. From half a million members, the figure shot up to over three million. Television companies battled over contract rights for the sport.

Wembley was lucky enough to host the next major event – the 1973 European Championships. There was earnest discussion as to whether Olga's back somersault on the beam was too dangerous; Olga threatened to retire and the publicity outfits received another boost. The championships themselves were an anticlimax. Olga, with a silver in the overall individual competition and a gold in the team event, pulled up on the vault runway and withdrew with a bad ankle.

Ludmila Tourischeva confirmed her superiority at the 1974 World Championships in Varna, winning the overall individual title, with Olga taking the silver. Olga won the vault and gained three more silvers on the individual apparatus, but during the four years between Munich and Montreal the order was: 1 Tourischeva, 2 Korbut. There were also rumblings of another genius on the horizon, a little Rumanian called Nadia Comaneci.

It made no difference. To the public Olga still was Queen. She went on a 'Royal Tour'. President Nixon greeted her with the words, 'I have always been impressed by the way you land on your feet.'

By the time the Montreal Olympics arrived, Olga was no longer a serious threat for gold medals in individual events. She took the gold in the team event and finished fifth overall. A silver medal on the beam, behind Comaneci, was a result of sensible judging rather than hysteria. After Montreal, Olga Korbut retired.

She married Leonid Bortkevich, lead singer of the pop group Pesnyany, in 1978 and lives in Minsk with her family. At the start of 1984 newspapers carried a feature on Mrs Bortkevich taking her first serious steps into the world of equestrianism. In top hat and tails, she was venturing into her new hobby – dressage, a combination of balance and timing on horseback for which her gymnastic career must have helped her develop.

John Goodbody again: 'Olga Korbut succeeded in generating emotions in a widely differing range of people. Soviet soldiers wanted pin-ups, American matrons wanted to mother her, and mothers wanted their daughters to aspire to Olga's charm.'

FACTFILE

Born 16 May 1955, Grodno, USSR

Olympic Games
1972 Gold: Team, beam floor exercises
      Silver: Bars
1976 Gold: Team
      Silver: Beam

World Championships
1974 Gold: Vault
      Silver: Combined exercises, floor exercises, beam, bars

European Championships
1973 Silver: Combined exercises
(Olga missed the 1975 European Championships with an ankle injury.)

How to conquer a universe. Olga Korbut wins the gold medal at the 1972 Munich Olympic Games

Harold Larwood

The former miner from the Nottinghamshire village of Nuncargate who became the fastest bowler on earth, Harold Larwood won the Ashes for England in Australia when Bradman was at his peak, but in doing so provoked a diplomatic incident that almost resulted in relations between the two countries being terminated. All because of one cricketing theory – the leg theory, known ever since as 'Bodyline'.

Larwood was spotted by Joe Hardstaff senior playing on Nuncargate Recreation Ground and was taken down to Trent Bridge for a trial. The committee, seeing the small, slightly built lad, asked Joe what he had brought for them this time. 'A fast bowler,' replied Hardstaff. The committee laughed only as long as it took Larwood to measure out his run and deliver his first ball in the nets. He was taken on to the groundstaff at a salary of 32 shillings a week (£1.60).

The same year while at home at Nuncargate, Larwood received a telegram from the Nottinghamshire captain, A. W. Carr, telling him to report to the ground at Sheffield the next day where he was to play against Yorkshire. It was the first time Larwood had ever been outside Nottinghamshire. He reported to Sheffield in company with his father and mother. He was not yet twenty-one.

Larwood, on his debut, took a handful of wickets and retained his place until the end of the season. Playing in only half Nottinghamshire's matches that season, he finished with 73 wickets.

In 1926 he developed into a fine quick bowler with a natural away-swinger – the product of a classical high action and full follow-through – and he had also developed the off-cutter. It was this ball that accounted for the great Jack Hobbs in the Whitsuntide match at Trent Bridge. Hobbs, when questioned afterwards by the press, remarked casually that the ball must have been a fluke. When he departed the same way in Surrey's second innings he realized the young Larwood's potential. Hobbs was then a Test selector. He reported the news of the Nottinghamshire bowler to his fellow selectors and Larwood was selected for the Second Test against the Australians at Lord's. He was dropped for the next at Leeds but returned at the Oval along with Wilfred Rhodes – recalled at the age of forty-nine. Fleet Street had a field day. 'Rhodes too old, Larwood too young,' they proclaimed. Yet nobody did more than those two to win the match.

In partnership with the left-handed Bill Voce, Larwood contributed to Notts championship win in 1929. Neville Cardus described Larwood at his peak – 'He galloped over the earth like a young horse'.

Then in 1930 at the Oval came an auspicious match. The pitch livened by rain responded to Larwood's pace and caused Bradman, the great master batsman, to duck and weave. Douglas Jardine never forgot seeing the great man look uncomfortable at the wicket, and when he was appointed captain of the MCC for the 1932–33 tour of Australia, he decided on using the leg theory to combat the massive run-scoring ability of the South Australian.

For the First Test of the 1932 tour Bradman was absent after a dispute with the Australian Board. Stan McCabe, though, played one of the great Test innings of all time – 187 not out – proving that the brave could hook the bodyline deliveries. The Australian tail-ender Bill O'Reilly was less confident against the fast straight stuff. He recalled how 'The Little Fella' (his name for Larwood) retreated in the grey-blue distance, and when he arrived at the wicket, O'Reilly never saw the ball leave his hand. England won by 10 wickets. The controversy boiled over after Australia levelled the series at the Melbourne Cricket Ground.

In the Third Test at Adelaide Larwood hit Bill Woodfull over the heart. Then Bertie Oldfield pulled a short ball onto his temple. Before he passed out, Oldfield – according to Larwood – said, 'It wasn't your fault, Harold.' Neither batsmen was hit when bodyline was in operation, but England's 338-run win provoked a cable from the Australian Board to the MCC alleging that the tourists' tactics were 'unsportsmanlike'. After a stormy exchange of views by cable in which Prime Ministers became involved and the MCC even offered to call off the tour, the Australians withdrew their claim. England won the series by four matches to one. Bradman averaged only 56 and Larwood took 33 wickets at 19.51.

That proved to be Larwood's Test swansong. At Sydney in the final Test he splintered a toe bone and never bowled full out again. (Larwood has always said that England never saw him bowl at his fastest – he could only do it in Australia.)

When he returned to Nottingham he was asked by the club president Sir Julian Cahn to sign a letter of apology to the MCC and to the Australian Board. He refused. When he was left out of the First Test against Australia at Trent Bridge in 1934 Larwood swore he would never play against them again – and he never did.

Strangely he chose to emigrate to Australia with his wife and five daughters in 1950. He has lived in Sydney ever since. During the Centenary Test in 1977 at Melbourne, he sat alongside Bill Voce watching Dennis Lillee in action. 'You know, Bill,' said 'Lol', 'this fella's bowled more bouncers in this game than we did in the whole series!'

At his best Larwood was a glorious sight. The smooth run-up gathering pace, the side-on action and the full long sweep of his follow-through. To opposing batsmen, especially tail-enders, he was sometimes to be avoided at all costs. Leicestershire's Haydn Smith, a bowler and no batsman at all, who suffered from a nervous stutter, once arrived at the wicket at Trent Bridge, faced the first ball

FACTFILE

Total first-class runs 7290

Highest first-class innings 102*, Nottinghamshire *v.* Sussex, Trent Bridge (1931)

Total first-class wickets 1427

Best first-class bowling 9–41, Nottinghamshire *v.* Kent, Trent Bridge (1931)

Test debut 1926, *v.* Australia

Total Test appearances 21

Total test runs 485 (average 19.40)

Highest Test innings 98, *v.* Australia, Sydney (1932–33)

Total Test wickets 78 (average 28.35)

Best Test bowling 6–32, *v.* Australia, Brisbane (1928–29)

Total catches 236

from Larwood, which he edged along the ground to Sam Staples at second slip. He promptly departed for the pavilion. 'Come back, Haydn,' shouted Staples. 'I didn't catch it.' 'You b-b-bloody l-l-l-liar,' said Smith over his shoulder. 'You b-b-bloody well did!'

A batsman's view of Harold Larwood, centre of the bodyline controversy in 1932–33 in Australia

Rod Laver

Early in 1983 readers of the world's major sports newspaper, the Paris-based *L'Equipe*, were asked to vote on their choice for the top tennis player of the century. Top of the poll, with twice as many votes as the runner-up, was Rod Laver. Fourteen years earlier he had created tennis history by becoming the first player to win the Grand Slam – Wimbledon, French, Australian and US championships in the same year – for the second time.

Born on 9 August 1938, Laver's first court was an improvised fence on the family farm at Langdale in the outback of Queensland. Rockhampton, 100 miles down the road, was a bigger place, and when the family moved, he took advantage of coaching and facilities. But such was the strength of Australian tennis that, at the age of eighteen, he was no higher than No. 5 on the ranking lists.

But if the ranking was harsh, coach Charlie Hollis had great faith.

FACTFILE

Born 9 August 1938, Langdale, Queensland, Australia

Wimbledon Championships
    Singles 1961 beat Chuck McKinley (USA), 6–3, 6–1, 6–4
             1962 beat Marty Mulligan (Australia), 6–2, 6–2, 6–1
             1968 beat Tony Roche (Australia), 6–3, 6–4, 6–2
             1969 beat John Newcombe (Australia), 6–4, 5–7, 6–4, 6–4
    Doubles 1971 (with Roy Emerson) beat Ashe and Ralston, 4–6, 9–7, 6–8, 6–4, 6–4
    Mixed doubles 1959 (with Darlene Hard) beat Fraser and Bueno, 6–4, 6–3
                  1960 (with Darlene Hard) beat Howe and Bueno, 13–11, 3–6, 8–6

Australian singles
1960 beat Neale Fraser, 5–7, 3–6, 6–3, 8–6, 8–6
1962 beat Roy Emerson, 8–6, 0–6, 6–4, 6–4
1969 beat Andres Gimeno, 6–3, 6–4, 7–5

French singles
1962 beat Roy Emerson, 3–6, 2–6, 6–3, 9–7, 6–2
1969 beat Ken Rosewall, 6–4, 6–3, 6–4

United States single
1962 beat Roy Emerson, 6–2, 6–4, 5–7, 6–4
1969 beat Tony Roche, 7–9, 6–3, 6–1, 6–2

Rod Laver's Grand Slam Opponents

1962
Wimbledon Championships
    Naresh Kumar (India), 7–5, 6–1, 6–2
    Tony Pickard (England), 6–1, 6–2, 6–2
    Whitney Reed (USA), 6–4, 6–1, 6–4
    Pierre Damon (France), 6–3, 6–2, 13–11
    Manolo Santana (Spain), 14–16, 9–7, 6–2, 6–2
    Neale Fraser (Australia), 10–8, 6–1, 7–5
    Marty Mulligan (Australia), 6–2, 6–2, 6–1
French Championships
    Michelle Pirro (Italy), 6–4, 6–0, 6–2
    Tony Pickard (England), 6–2, 9–7, 4–6, 6–1
    Sergio Jacobini (Italy), 4–6, 6–3, 7–5, 6–1
    Marty Mulligan (Australia), 6–4, 3–6, 2–6, 10–8, 6–2
    Neale Fraser (Australia), 3–6, 6–3, 6–2, 3–6, 7–5
    Roy Emerson (Australia), 3–6, 2–6, 6–3, 9–7, 6–2

Australian Championships
    Fred Sherriff (Australia), 8–6, 6–4, 6–2
    Geoff Pares (Australia), 10–8, 18–16, 7–9, 7–5
    Owen Davidson (Australia), 6–4, 9–7, 6–4
    Bob Hewitt (Australia), 6–1, 4–6, 6–4, 7–5
    Roy Emerson (Australia), 8–6, 0–6, 6–4, 6–2
United States Championships
    Eleazer Davidman (Israel), 6–3, 6–2, 6–3
    Eduardo Zuleta (Ecuador), 6–3, 6–3, 6–1
    Bodo Nitsche (Germany), 9–7, 6–1, 6–1
    Tonio Palafox (Mexico), 6–1, 6–2, 6–2
    Frank Froehling III (USA), 6–3, 13–11, 4–6, 6–3
    Rafael Osuna (Mexico), 6–1, 6–3, 6–4
    Roy Emerson (Australia), 6–2, 6–4, 5–7, 6–4

1969
Wimbledon Championships
    Nicola Pietrangeli (Italy), 6–1, 6–2, 6–2
    Premjit Lall (India), 3–6, 4–6, 6–3, 6–0, 6–0
    Jan Leschly (Denmark), 6–3, 6–3, 6–3
    Stan Smith (USA), 6–4, 6–2, 7–9, 3–6, 6–3
    Cliff Drysdale (South Africa), 6–4, 6–2, 6–3
    Arthur Ashe (USA), 2–6, 6–2, 9–7, 6–0
    John Newcombe (Australia), 6–4, 5–7, 6–4, 6–4
French Championships
    Koji Watanabe (Japan), 6–1, 6–1, 6–1
    Dick Crealy (Australia), 3–6, 7–9, 6–2, 6–2, 6–4
    Pietro Marzano (Italy), 6–1, 6–0, 8–6
    Stan Smith (USA), 6–4, 6–2, 6–4
    Andres Gimeno (Spain), 3–6, 6–3, 6–4, 6–3
    Tom Okker (Netherlands), 4–6, 6–0, 6–2, 6–4
    Ken Rosewall (Australia), 6–4, 6–3, 6–4
Australian Championships
    Massimo di Domenico (Italy), 6–2, 6–3, 6–3
    Roy Emerson (Australia), 6–2, 6–3, 3–6, 9–7
    Fred Stolle (Australia), 6–4, 18–16, 6–2
    Tony Roche (Australia), 7–5, 22–20, 9–11, 1–6, 6–3
    Andres Gimeno (Spain), 6–3, 6–4, 7–5
United States Championships
    Luis Garcia (Mexico), 6–2, 6–4, 6–2
    Jaime Pinto-Bravo (Chile), 6–4, 7–5, 6–2
    Jaime Fillol (Chile), 8–6, 6–1, 6–2
    Dennis Ralston (USA), 6–4, 4–6, 4–6, 6–2, 6–3
    Roy Emerson (Australia), 4–6, 8–6, 13–11, 6–4
    Arthur Ashe (USA), 8–6, 6–3, 14–12
    Tony Roche (Australia), 7–9, 6–1, 6–2, 6–2

In 1956 Laver won the junior event at the US Championships and was runner-up in the Wimbledon equivalent. He conceded that he had more problems winning matches at home.

Laver's career was to follow three distinct phases. His early amateur career culminated in the first Grand Slam in 1962. A six-year exile in the National Tennis League and on the professional circuit ended in 1968 with the introduction of open tennis. The return to the major tournaments at the age of thirty gave an impetus to the later stages of his career.

Hollis's belief in his charge brought dividends in 1959. In three years Rod had climbed from a humble junior ranking to No. 9 in the world. He reached all three Wimbledon finals, winning the mixed doubles with Darlene Hard, who also reached three finals. He also had success in the doubles events in the Australian and French championships.

In 1960 he had reached second place in the world rankings. Neale Fraser, his fellow countryman, a left-hander from the Hopman stable, was rated above him. Fraser won the singles title at Wimbledon and Forest Hills; Laver won the Australian title. Each beat the other in the finals.

In 1961, still ranked No. 2, he reached the singles final at Wimbledon for the third time. His opponent in the final was an athletic American college boy, Chuck McKinley. The closest of the three winning sets for Laver was the last at 6–4.

In 1938 Donald Budge had become the first player to win the Grand Slam. Twenty-four years later he was joined in the record books by the 'Rockhampton Rocket'. The championships of Italy and West Germany also fell Laver's way.

Then, with his bag full of cups and medals and his chequebook full of fresh air, he went off to join the professionals. Accurate assessments of their game were difficult, exhibitions and touring circuses being the vogue. Former champions Hoad, Rosewall, Gonzales, Sedgeman were all there, but Laver was the form horse, winning the London tournament from 1964 to 1967, the Wimbledon professional tournament in 1967, and the BBC2 event in 1968. He liked London.

With the final rites of 'shamateurism' blown away, Laver and his colleagues returned to the old scenes. Laver, younger than the others, was to benefit most. In that first open year of 1968 he lost the French final to his closest rival from his professional days, Ken Rosewall, but won Wimbledon after a brief encounter in the final with Tony Roche.

The following year, 1969, he showed such dominance that not only did he become the only player to win the Grand Slam for the second time, but in the four finals he dropped only two sets. Ignoring injuries and choosing tournaments carefully, Laver based his game on discipline; he was light and quick, and had fine control of top spin. He was tennis's first millionaire.

It fell to Britain's Roger Taylor to put an end to Laver's Wimbledon teaparty. Taylor, another left-hander, beat Laver at the 1970 championships – it was the champion's first defeat at Church Road since the 1960 final.

Rod Laver's sturdy left arm directs another backhand return, the outstanding shot in a repertoire which made him the first player to achieve two Grand Slams

Now struggling with tennis elbow and ankle injuries as a new wave of players engulfed the sport, Laver's commitments to the full-time circuit became less. He won the Italian Championships in 1971 and two years later won all three rubbers in the Davis Cup final in Cleveland. He moved quietly into the mushrooming veterans events. He didn't officially announce his retirement.

At Christmas 1983 Australia won the Davis Cup again. Their highest-ranked player was at No. 33 in the world lists. Although team tennis still flourishes, Laver remains, for the moment, the last of the great Australian individual champions. 'And,' wrote Lance Tingay, the distinguished correspondent of the *Daily Telegraph*, 'with their departure much of the fun has gone out of the game.'

Carl Lewis

The best of Carl Lewis is yet to come. He has already won the International Sportsman of the Year award in most major countries – including the Soviet Union. In 1984, he merely improved on the standard of excellence he achieved in 1983.

Lewis's specialities are sprints and long jump. In the latter event he has become the first athlete seriously to threaten the incredible long-jump record set in the rarified atmosphere of Mexico City by another American, Bob Beamon, during the 1968 Olympics. Beamon jumped 29 feet $2\frac{1}{2}$ inches (8.90 metres) and experts predicted that it would be the one world record to last to the year 2000. Until Lewis came along.

Despite not being the world record holder, Lewis is acknowledged even by fellow athletes as the world's fastest human. The 100-metre world record holder, Calvin Smith, set a time of 9.93 seconds at altitude in Colorado Springs in the summer of 1983; Lewis's personal best in that event is 9.97 seconds, at sea level.

The targets for 1984 are four golds in the Los Angeles Olympics, in the 100 and 200 metres, the long jump and the relay. He is also chasing the world records in those events but prefers to attempt them at sea level, rather than set what he considers false records at altitude.

Carl Lewis was born on 1 June 1961. He is 6 feet 3 inches tall. Originally from New Jersey, and now studying telecommunications at Houston, he first started competing as an eighteen-year-old in 1979, with season's bests of 9.5 seconds for the 100 yards and 8.13 metres for the long jump. In 1980 he was selected for the US team for the Olympics after a leap of 8.11 metres; his sister Carol made the women's long jump team. As the world knows, they trained in vain.

1981 was a good year for Carl. He became one of the first athletes to clock exactly 10 seconds for 100 metres at sea level, he was world No. 1 in the long jump with 8.62 metres, and won the World Cup with a leap of 8.15 metres. In 1982 he again clocked 10 seconds for the 100 metres and pushed his long-jump best up to 8.76. After nine attempts he had at last beaten Larry Myricks, his *bête noire*. He was world No. 1 and the World Championships in 1983 confirmed this.

Carl Lewis's achievements in those inaugural World Championships were:

7 August	100 metres: first round	10.37	1
	second round	10.20	1
8 August	100 metres: semifinal	10.28	1
	final	10.07	1
9 August	4 × 100-metre relay: heats	38.75	1
	long jump: qualifyer	8.37	1
10 August	4 × 100-metre relay: semifinal	38.50	1
	long jump: final	8.55	1
	4 × 100-metre relay: final	37.86	1

He won the long-jump qualifying competition with his only jump and in the final had to leave the long jump to run in the relay final, in which the American time was a new world record. His first jump in the final took the gold medal.

On the last afternoon Carol Lewis won the bronze medal in the long jump – her leap of 7.04 metres (23 feet $1\frac{1}{4}$ inches) was wind-assisted, but a personal best.

Two of the more lighthearted moments came after Carl's 100-metre win. A placard with 'Carl Lewis for President' fluttered across the Helsinki stands (1984 was a presidential election year). In the press conference after his 100-metre win, Lewis complained that there was a bumblebee flying around him at the start. There was also a bumblebee encircling him at the finish 10.07 seconds later. 'If that was the case,' said a solemn statistician, 'then that looks like a world record for a bee.'

At the Los Angeles Olympics Lewis set out to emulate his hero Jesse Owens. When Lewis was young and impressionable, Owens had signed his autograph book. At the 1984 Games Lewis, like his idol, won the 100 metres, the 200 metres, the long jump, and ran the anchor leg of the 4 × 100-metre relay for the winning US team.

His schedule for the week was:

3 August
100 metres, round 1 10.32 s
100 metres, round 2 10.04 s

4 August
100 metres, semifinal 10.04 s
100 metres, final 9.99 s

FACTFILE

Born 1 July 1961, New Jersey, USA

Olympic Games
Gold: 100 metres (1984)
     200 metres (1984)
     4 × 100-metre relay (1984)
     Long jump (1984)

World Championships
Gold: 100 metres (1983)
     4 × 100-metre relay (1983)
     Long jump (1983)

World Cup
Gold: Long jump (1981)

World record (outdoor)
     4 × 100-metre relay 37.86 s (Helsinki, August 1983, as member of US team)

Personal bests (to January 1984)
     100 metres 9.97 s (world record 9.93 s)
     200 metres 19.75 s (world record 19.72 s)
     Long jump 8.79 m (world record 8.90 m)
     (All world records set at altitude.)

Mike McFarlane (in white) gazes to his right in admiration of Carl Lewis, during the final few strides of the 1984 Olympic 100-metre final, the first of Lewis's four gold medals

5 August
Long jump, qualifier 8.30 metres

6 August
200 metres, round 1, 21.02 s
200 metres, round 2, 20.48 s
Long jump, final 8.54 m

8 August
200 metres, semifinal 20.27 s
200 metres, final 19.80 s

10 August
4 × 100-metre relay, round 1, 38.89 s

11 August
4 × 100-metre relay, semifinal 38.44 s
4 × 100-metre relay, final 37.83 s (world record)

He was victorious in all his races and won both long-jump competitions with a single jump.

There was an uneasy respect for Lewis in the US camp at the Games. He referred to God as though he were his house guest, and was beginning to generate dislike.

As for the gold medals, it never occurred to him that he would not win them.

Dennis Lillee

Richie Benaud – who should know – labelled him 'the Greatest'. A world record 355 Test wickets and a career lasting almost a decade and a half prove it. Tall, dark, with a drooping moustache, Dennis Lillee is the most attacking and dangerous bowler of his time.

As late as 1982 Michael Holding, who has been described as the 'Rolls-Royce of fast bowlers', declared that Lillee was the better bowler. Arguments will always rage whenever Lillee's name is mentioned, not about the magnificent performances of his career, but about the numerous controversies that littered it. As a result he is probably the most publicized cricketer of all time.

His first season with Western Australia was in 1969–70 and he took 32 wickets. Lillee says that a season in the Lancashire League with Haslingden improved his bowling. He learned to swing and cut in England that season – 1971 – just months after he had made his Test debut against England in the Sixth Test at Adelaide. His first Test wicket was that of John Edrich and he took 5 for 84 against Ray Illingworth's Ashes-winning side; it was almost the first time that season that the Australians had provided an answer to the powerful England team. Prophetically, with his very first ball against England on that tour, Lillee knocked Geoff Boycott's cap off.

Lillee returned to Australia and, as a measure of his growing stature as a quick bowler, took 8 for 29 against the Rest of the World on his home ground, Perth, including one magnificent spell of 6 wickets for no runs. Lillee was close to his first peak. His run-up had developed into a long, flowing, accelerating, smooth approach, before he gathered himself for a leap prior to delivering the ball. He was inspired by Wes Hall. Spectators loved it. Batsmen found him fearsome.

Lillee was back in England for the 1972 tour, taking 31 Test wickets and playing a major part in Bob Massie's 16 for 137 match-winning performance at Lord's. Lillee's ferocious pace at one end left the English batsmen relishing the chance to face Massie's medium-pace swing. They were lured to destruction. Partners for Western Australia, Lillee and Massie, it seemed, would be the Australian opening attack for years to come.

It did not work out. Massie faded from the scene after the 1973 tour of the West Indies. Lillee, on the same tour, suffered four stress fractures in his back. The Warwickshire and Barbados bowler of the sixties, Dr Rudi Webster, advised Lillee on treatment and, against all the odds, after six months in plaster, Lillee returned for the 1974–75 series against Mike Denness's England side.

Lillee had a new opening partner – Jeff Thomson. With an Australian public thirsting for revenge on the Poms after the ignominies inflicted by Illingworth's team, Lillee and Thomson roared into action. Bumpers and bouncers destroyed the morale of the England team. Between them Lillee and Thomson took 58 wickets – Lillee 25 of them. Rigby's famous cartoon pictured the crowd's ominous chant: 'Ashes to ashes, dust to dust, if Thomson don't get ya, Lillee must.'

In his book *Back to the Mark*, published that season, Lillee wrote: 'I try to hit a batsman in the ribcage when I bowl a purposeful bouncer, and I want it to hurt so much that the batsman doesn't want to face me any more.'

Two more great series followed for Lillee. In England in 1975 he took 21 Test wickets. In the 1975–76 season against the West Indies he took 27, including his 100th Test wicket – Viv Richards, caught at slip by Gilmour for a duck at Brisbane. It was his twenty-second Test.

New Zealand were the next Test side to experience Lillee. In the Test at Eden Park in 1977 he found a pitch to his liking and, as Richard Hadlee remembers, he was on the rampage. 'Bearded, mean-looking, strong, athletic, purposeful . . . I managed to hit him back over his head for 6. He applauded the hit. But he came up with his forefinger and made a cross on my forehead. The target. I remember thinking what a stupid young fellow I was to have hit this great fast bowler into the stand.' Lillee took match figures of 11 for 123. Hadlee hit 81. They are now great friends.

It was around that time that Lillee was timed as bowling at 89 miles an hour – slightly slower than Jeff Thomson, who, typically, reported that, on the day, he was not at his fastest. While their speed and athleticism impressed everyone, their attitude to the game – typified by Lillee's remarks in his book – did not meet with universal approval, even in Australia. Journalist H. L. Hendry wrote that during the 1974–75 series against England they bowled to 'intimidate the batsmen with the sole objective of forcing them into errors to avoid physical injury. The methods used are worse than those used in the so-called bodyline series of 1932–33.'

In 1977 came the Centenary Test at Melbourne. England – refreshed with new captain, Tony Greig, and the impish Derek Randall in the middle order – returned to Australia for the match. It was the highlight of Lillee's career with match-winning figures of 11 for 165 (6–26 and 5–139) and a personal duel with Randall, who made 174 as England pressed improbably close to their target of 463. But at the end of the game, with the party to tour England due to be announced, Lillee's career reached yet another crossroads. His back injury returned and he was forced to announce his unavailability for the tour. With Packer's WSC on the horizon, he was absent from the international arena until the 1979–80 season.

In the very first Test at Perth after peace had been declared Lillee was in trouble again. This time for using an aluminium bat that he

FACTFILE

Born 18 July 1949, Perth, Australia

Test record

Debut 29 January 1971, *v.* England, Adelaide
Total matches 70
Total runs 905 (average 13.71)

Total wickets 355 (average 23.92)
Total catches 23
Highest innings 73*, *v.* England, Lord's (1975)
Best bowling 7–83, *v.* West Indies, Melbourne (1981–82)
10 wickets in match 7
5 wickets in innings 22

had patented. England captain Mike Brearley protested that it was damaging the ball. After ten minutes, in which Lillee threw the bat 20 yards and left the field, play resumed with Lillee using a conventional bat. He was severely reprimanded for that transgression.

A year later, on the tour of England in 1981, he admitted backing England to win the Headingley Test when the bookies offered 500 to 1 prior to Botham's magnificent innings. No longer a fast bowler, Lillee was an effective seamer, using guile, strength and variety to prise out batsmen, but whatever he did, controversy was never far away. When the Pakistanis toured Australia in 1982 he was in trouble for kicking Javed Miandad after the Pakistan captain had pushed Lillee off-balance when going for his thirtieth run. Lillee was suspended for two matches and fined $200.

The same season, with the West Indies the visitors for the second half, Lillee took a world record 310th Test wicket on 27 December 1981 when he had Larry Gomes caught at slip by Greg Chappell. Play was again held up – this time while the Melbourne crowd roared their applause in appreciation of their hero. Lillee's 7 for 83 was his best performance in Test cricket (ignoring his 8 for 29 against the Rest of the World in 1972).

The signs that his career was drawing to a close came after yet another operation – this time on an injured knee – which caused him to miss five Tests against England in 1982–83. Although he was back for the World Cup in 1983, he was dropped from the team, which generally performed unimpressively.

For the last time Lillee battled his way back to full fitness and returned to the Test side as third or even sometimes fourth seamer against Pakistan. His last Test came in January 1984 at the Sydney cricket ground. He took 4 for 65 and 4 for 88 against Pakistan to finish with 355 Test wickets, bowing out, along with Greg Chappell and Rod Marsh, on a high – the wicket of Sarfraz, caught at slip off his last ball in Test cricket by Chappell.

Controversy, though, was still to rear its head. Captaining Western Australia in a Sheffield Shield match at Brisbane, he called for a drinks interval against the instructions of the umpires. The Cricket Board fined him $1000 and invoked a suspended two-match ban, imposed after he had been reported for swearing at the crowd a month earlier. Lillee took the board to the High Court, but lost. He then decided to play one last match – for Bishen Bedi's benefit in Calcutta. He hit his old adversary Javed Miandad in the face with a bouncer, which ruled him out of the forthcoming Test series against England.

As Ray Steele of the Australian Board once said: 'Dennis Lillee is the greatest fast bowler the world has seen.' To which should be added 'and the most controversial'. In the Centenary Test he asked the Queen for her autograph. He was politely refused. But the autograph arrived in the post a few days later.

Dennis Lillee in action against Hampshire at Southampton during the 1972 Australian tour to England. The tourists won by 9 wickets

Joe Louis

Joe Louis is still considered by most boxing experts to be the greatest of all modern heavyweight champions. He had seventy-one professional fights, won sixty-eight and lost just three. Fifty-four of those opponents didn't hear the final bell. He was heavyweight champion of the world for twelve years, during a time when there were more registered boxers than ever before. He defended his title on a record twenty-five occasions: only three opponents lasted the course and, of those three, two disappeared in quick time in the return.

So dominant was Louis that his three defeats need explanation. He had won his first twenty-eight fights, twenty-four by knockout, when, on 19 June 1936, aged twenty-two, he was matched with a thirty-one-year-old German, one Maximilian Otto Adolph Siegfried Schmeling. Caught unawares, Louis was knocked down in round four and, never recovering composure, was counted out eight rounds later. Max Schmeling had been heavyweight champion of the world four years earlier.

Fourteen years later Louis was eventually beaten again. On 27 September 1950 he was outpointed by Ezzard Charles over fifteen rounds in an attempt to regain the world title which had been his from 1937 to 1949. His training for the fight had been seventy-five exhibition matches, he had not fought in the professional ring for two years, and would not have contemplated a return but for tax demands.

Louis fought on for another twelve months. At thirty-seven, with eight more wins, he was a contender again. Jersey Joe Walcott, also thirty-seven, was the champion; Louis was pitched in with the new sensation, an unbeaten Italian-American, Rocky Marciano. At twenty-eight Marciano was at his peak: thirty-seven wins, with only four points decisions amongst them. On the canvas in round eight, Louis, as befitted a great champion, was spared the count. The tax man, though, could find other means.

Joseph Louis Barrow, of Cherokee Indian–Negro–white stock, was born in Lexington, Alabama. His family left the cotton fields for

FACTFILE

Born 13 May 1914, Lexington, Alabama, USA
Died 12 April 1981, Las Vegas, Nevada, USA

First professional fight 4 July 1934, *v.* Jack Kraken (ko 1)
Total professional fights 71
  Wins 68
  Kos 54
  Defeats 3
  Draws 0
Last professional fight 26 October 1951, *v.* Rocky Marciano (ko by 5)
World title fights 27
  Wins 26

World heavyweight title fights

1937
22 June	James J. Braddock	Chicago	ko	8
30 August	Tommy Farr	New York City	w	15

1938
23 February	Nathan Mann	New York City	ko	3
1 April	Harry Thomas	Chicago	ko	5
22 June	Max Schmeling	New York City	ko	1

1939
25 January	John Henry Lewis	New York City	ko	1
17 April	Jack Roper	Los Angeles	ko	1
28 June	Tony Galento	New York City	ko	4
20 September	Bob Pastor	Detroit	ko	11

1940
9 February	Arturo Godoy	New York City	w	15
29 March	Johnny Paycheck	New York City	ko	2
20 June	Arturo Godoy	New York City	ko	8
16 December	Al McCoy	Boston	ko	6

1941
31 January	Clarence (Red) Burman	New York City	ko	5
17 February	Gus Dorazio	Philadelphia	ko	2
21 March	Abe Simon	Detroit	ko	13
8 April	Tony Musto	St Louis	ko	9
23 May	Buddy Baer	Washington, DC	w	dis 7
18 June	Billy Conn	New York City	ko	13
29 September	Lou Nova	New York City	ko	6

1942
9 January	Buddy Baer	New York City	ko	1
27 March	Abe Simon	New York City	ko	6

1943–45
Inactive; in US Army

1946
19 June	Billy Conn	New York City	ko	8
18 September	Tarni Maunello	New York City	ko	1

1947
5 December	Jersey Joe Walcott	New York City	w	15

1948
25 June	Jersey Joe Walcott	New York City	ko	11

1949
1 March	Announced retirement	

1950
27 September	Ezzard Charles	New York City	l	15

*After losing his title to Louis, Joe Braddock said, 'The punch was like someone jabbed an electric light in my face and busted it. I thought half my head had caved in'

hard labour in Henry Ford's Detroit car works and young Joe's schooling was typical for a city boy – dodging violin and English lessons and hanging round the downtown boxing gyms. By the time he was twenty he had won the Golden Gloves heavyweight title, America's amateur championship, and, after forty-three knockouts and fifty wins in fifty-four amateur fights, he turned professional under the guidance of Jack Rossborough and Julian Black. Six weeks after his twentieth birthday he demolished Jack Kracken in Chicago in the first round. He was on his way.

The Louis–Schmeling fight was to be an eliminator for the world title held by the 'Cinderella Man' James J. Braddock. Among Louis's twenty-eight straight successes were two – the most recent against former world champions. Louis knocked out Primo Carnera in the sixth round in 1935; Carnera had been champion of the world a year earlier; 62,000 witnessed his defeat. Three months later Max Baer, who had lost his title to Carnera, lasted into round four. After the Schmeling setback, credit must go to the Louis entourage for not hiding their man: his very next fight was against another former world champion, Jack Sharkey. Joe won in three rounds; Sharkey never fought again.

The victory over Sharkey, plus persuasion from Mike Jakobs, promoter and ticket seller, drew Braddock into a defence against Louis. Jakobs secured the fight for 22 June 1937 in Chicago and Joe, after being dropped early in the fight, was heavyweight champion of the world in the eighth round.

Between 1937 and 1942 Louis defended his title on twenty-one occasions. Only two men managed to take him to a points decision: Tommy Farr, the courageous Welshman from Tonypandy, went the full distance in Joe's first and probably closest defence: the other, Arturo Godoy, buckled in eight rounds in a return. The shortest of the twenty-one defences took two minutes and four seconds; the victim – Schmeling.

In 1942 Louis donated the purses from his two fights to the Navy Relief Fund after beating Buddy Baer (brother of Max) and the Army Relief Fund after his defeat of Abe Simon. That same year he enlisted in the US Navy as a physical training instructor; the world was at war and Louis's title went under wraps.

There were, in reality, two Louises – the one before the Second World War, a fighter so complete that his opponents were nicknamed 'The Bum of the Month', and the one who started again after the war. In 1946 nothing was the same: managers Roxborough and Black had been replaced by Marshall Miles. Joe fought four more defences – three knockouts and a win on points over Jersey Joe Walcott. When his army friend Ruby Goldstein, the referee, voted against him, two judges preserved Louis's title. Another lethargic win over Walcott persuaded Joe to retire, at a press conference on 1 March 1949. He was never to be champion again.

He had earned over four and a half million dollars in the ring. He had lived well, had paid much back into war funds, and had been too kind to those who had prospered from him. He owed a quarter of that sum in income tax.

Seventeen months later Louis was back in the ring. His title had gone to a fine boxer, Ezzard Charles, whilst the matchmaker at Madison Square Garden, Mike Jakob's successor, Jim Norris, pulled the strings. Joe's attempt to win back the title was scheduled for the Yankee Stadium on 27 September 1950. After the decision had gone to an unrelenting Charles, a reporter in Joe's changing room wrote: 'He was cut above both eyes, one of which was closed

Joe Louis steps away from the fallen Billy Conn, who failed to beat the count in the eighth round of their world heavyweight title fight in New York in 1946

by swelling. He couldn't see well enough to pull on his trousers.'

Joe shambled on; he wrestled for a living; he even dreamed of another shot at the title until Marciano sent him through the ropes for the last time.

At his peak he weighed 200 lb and was a shade over 6 feet 1 inch tall – the fastest, most accurate and deadliest puncher of his era. Charismatic and polite to the end, despite failing health and mental illness. When Ali and Frazier fought in 1971, the crowd cheered the dignified guest more than the two boxers. Joe died on 12 April 1981, after undergoing heart surgery and a stroke. For solace, he had the affection of the American people, in and out of boxing, to whom he was simply 'The Champ'.

John Lowe

Darts has been played in its modern form since 1896, when a Lancashire carpenter named Brian Gamlin was responsible for devising the present numbering system on the dartboard. But, like snooker, darts has become a winter television sport; the traditional public bar is now a feeder system for the elite few who toe the hockey amidst spotlights and computerized scoring.

Until the mid-1970s the most prestigious title was the *News of the World* Championships, first competed for in 1927 as a London area championship, but open to all since the Second World War. With increased exposure came sponsorship and organization, and four Grand Slam events have been instituted to complement the still excellent *News of the World* Championships. The first to win all five was John Lowe.

He was born at New Tupton, Chesterfield, on 21 July 1945 and is now based at Clay Cross, a few miles to the south. He began to take a more than social interest in darts at the age of twenty-one. In his first competitive match one of his team-mates lent John his darts. John never saw his team-mate again. He is still waiting to return them. A joiner by trade, Lowe progressed through the county championship system: he captained Yorkshire to victory in the 1976 final, even though he was born, and still lives, in Derbyshire.

In 1976 he won his first Grand Slam event, the World Masters, then in its third year. He beat the Welshman from Pencoed, Phil Obbard, in the final. In 1977 he won another major championship, the British Open.

But the yardstick of all darts competitions is the World Professional Championship. In a sport which is notorious for the unpredictability of its results, John Lowe's consistency is remarkable. He reached the first final in 1978, but lost to Leighton Rees. A year later he was back to reverse the result against the burly Welshman. Twice more in the opening five years of the competition he was to reach the final, losing in 1980 to Eric Bristow and the following year to Jocky Wilson from Fife. Until equalled by Bristow in 1984, it was the best individual record in the World Championship.

Despite his individual triumphs, John Lowe's greatest pride is to captain England. He has captained his country to all three wins in the World Cup and also picked up the individual title at the 1981 World Cup. It was Lowe who initiated the defeat of the first officially recognized leading nation, Wales.

1984 began disastrously for John. Over the New Year he caught a severe cold during the World Championship. He struggled through to the semifinals. The cold turned to flu. He lost heavily in the semifinal to Eric Bristow, six legs to nil. But to reach the semifinals of the world's top event with a temperature of 105° shows that, despite winning everything, his competitive instinct remains.

FACTFILE

Born 21 July 1945, New Tupton, Chesterfield, England

World Professional Championship
1978 lost to Leighton Rees (Wales)
1979 beat Leighton Rees (Wales)
1981 lost to Eric Bristow (England)
1982 lost to Jocky Wilson (Scotland)

World Masters
1976 beat Phil Obbard (Pencoed)
1980 beat Rab Smith (Dumfries)
1981 lost to Eric Bristow (London)

World Cup
  Team 1979 (captain), 1981 (captain)
  Individual 1981, 1983

British Open 1977
News of the World *Championships* 1981

John Lowe, perhaps the most consistent of all darts players in the modern game

Willie John McBride

When Willie John McBride began his international career, the Lions were the sort of people who the All Blacks and Springboks would invite to a party – courteous and polite, but never causing any disruption. Talented threequarters would stand like lemons, waiting to produce a rare flash of brilliance, but the forwards as a unit were physically incapable of providing enough opportunities to win a series.

Some twelve years later all that had changed. The Lions for the first time were top of the pile and the strength of the game lay in the northern hemisphere. With Willie John in the van, the forwards were a formidable unit, too good for New Zealand and South Africa.

Willie John McBride is a man of Ballymena. He played all his club rugby for them. He was a bank clerk in the town and still works for the bank. He had his greatest hours during Ireland's darkest times: together with Mary Peters, Johnny Giles and others, he bought sporting peace to a troubled land.

After three caps, McBride went on his first Lions tour, the 1962 visit to South Africa. He played in two of the Tests. South Africa won the series 3–0 with one drawn. In 1966 he played in three of the four Tests against the All Blacks. The series was lost in a whitewash 4–0. Two years later the Springboks won the series by an identical margin to their 1962 efforts. Willie John scored the Lions' only try of the series. He was fed up with going backwards.

At least the Lions enjoyed the 1968 tour. They split into two groups, the 'Wreckers' and the 'Kippers'. Captain of the 'Wreckers' was Willie John, fine tourist and prankster supreme. The source of the problem was that their hosts had given the tourists cigarette lighters. Nowhere was safe – hotels, railway stations or rondavels in the Kruger. The old Union Hotel in Pretoria found its prestigious palm trees alight and the front lawn taking on the appearance of a flaming birthday cake. In Salisbury a bed mysteriously fell seventeen floors out of a hotel window and crashed onto First Avenue. The manager was unamused. It was his bed.

By the time the 1971 tour came round, McBride was one of the senior members of the unit. The backs were tremendous – Edwards and John, Gibson, Dawes, Gerald Davies and Duckham. Coach Carwyn James said that if the forwards could guarantee 40 per cent

of the ball, the Lions would win the series. McBride had useful cohorts: the fine hooker John Pullin and No. 8 Mervyn Davies won their share of ball. The rest of the forwards, based around the Welsh Grand Slam team, were useful. The Lions took the series 2–1 with one drawn, the first Lions to return victorious from New Zealand.

In the meantime, Willie John continued to be the moral authority of the Irish team. It was said, unfairly, that it was more difficult to lose your place in the Irish side than it was to get into the side in the first place. The real truth is that Irish players only play some fifteen to twenty top games a season – unlike Wales, where it is double that number – and can therefore last a couple of seasons longer at the top level. Willie John, despite playing in the second row, played fifty-three games in succession for Ireland.

When the party for the 1974 tour to South Africa was chosen, Willie John was the logical choice. Con Houlihan, of the *Dublin Evening Press*, wrote: 'For Willie John McBride it was the Everest of a Himalayan career. That he unhesitatingly set out on such an unpromising quest is a measure of the man. Ambition was hardly the only spur – he was already a much travelled member of the Lions – so it was likely that he was moved by a sense of duty. McBride is Yeats's "wise and simple man". Wise in that he would not pass judgement on complex issues, simple in that he possesses honesty and responsibility. And unpromising the quest most certainly was.'

The brief facts are that the Lions marched all over South Africa, winning twenty-one and drawing one of twenty-two matches. They scored a record 729 points and were only held in the last match of the tour, 13–13 in the Fourth Test – which, had a try by Fergus Slattery been allowed, would have meant invincibility.

Con Houlihan again:

The Lions returned from South Africa to a home-coming that three months previously had seemed about as likely as Richard Nixon being voted American of the Year. Never did a team set out so threatened with recrimination and so weakened by defections. The recriminations were tinged with self-righteousness, whilst the defections (Gibson, Duckham, Gerald Davies,

---

FACTFILE

Born 6 March 1940, Toomebridge, County Antrim, Eire

Irish international career

Debut 1962, v. England
Appearances 63 (1962–75)
Tours 1967 Australia

Lions tours
1962   South Africa
1966   Australia and New Zealand
1968   South Africa
1971   Australia and New Zealand
1974   South Africa (captain)

Test appearances 17

Tour record					Test record		
	W	D	L	Points	W	D	L
1962	15	4	5	351–208	0	1	3
1966	22	3	8	502–329	2	0	4
1968	15	1	4	377–181	0	1	3
1971	23	1	2	570–231	2	1	1
1974	21	1	0	729–207	3	1	0

*McBride's fifty-three successive appearances for his country is a world record shared with Gareth Edwards

etc.) came mainly as a result of the fact that not everyone could afford an unpaid holiday.

The Lions set out aware that some people were hoping for their failure so that they could be castigated. When they returned victorious, somehow, even to objectors, it made their going seem less reprehensible.

The touring team ventured into the giant's castle praying that they would emerge with some honour. They found that the giant had gone soft through lack of combat and stricken with self-doubt. Yet this did not diminish the magnitude of the Lions' achievement.

In every community there is someone to whom one looks in time of crisis. McBride is such a man.

After sixty-three caps for Ireland and seventeen for the Lions, Willie John McBride called it a day in 1975. Ireland's captain in Ireland's centenary season, he scored a try against France in 1975. There were more people on the pitch than in the stands at that moment. And when, a month later, Ballymena won the Ulster

Willie John McBride leads out the unbeaten 1974 Lions on their tour in South Africa. Gordon Brown (right) follows McBride, whilst Andy Irvine (left) holds the tour mascot

Senior Cup, in their centenary season, that was the cue for retirement.

He is undismayed that, as manager of the 1983 Lions, things went wrong, and that the 1984 Ireland team, under his coaching, took the wooden spoon. His own career started similarly.

Of the game he graced for fifteen years he said: 'Rugby has had a profound influence in moulding my character. It has taught me tolerance and, I hope, the ability to win and lose with dignity – but above all to respect the other fellow.

'In this respect alone sport has a vital role to play in man's relationship with man.'

Rocky Marciano

Two fighters have retired permanently as unbeaten heavyweight champions of the world. One, Gene Tunney, who took the title from Jack Dempsey, had lost a fight earlier in his career, but the other, Rocky Marciano, had the perfect record. Forty-nine wins, and only six men stayed the full course with him. Yet had Marciano been around in the 1980s he wouldn't even have been a heavyweight. At 5 feet 11 inches tall and weighing 184 lb, he would have fitted perfectly into the new cruiserweight division. A boxer of remarkable resilience and stamina, Marciano, born 1 September 1923, won the heavyweight championship in 1952 and announced his retirement on 27 April 1956.

An all-round sportsman at school in Brockton, Massachusetts, a town which was also to produce the world middleweight champion Marvin Hagler. Rocco Francis Marchigiano, of Italian-American stock, initially played baseball and was useful enough to have a trial as pitcher for the Chicago Cubs. But the proverbial destruction of the regimental bully during Second World War service in Manchester – 'some one was ridiculing Francis' – persuaded him that a trial as a boxer would be more appropriate and constructive.

Invited, on the condition that he paid his own fare, to the world's fight centre, Madison Square Garden, Marciano failed initially to impress the Garden's matchmaker, Al Weill, that he had the right

FACTFILE

Born 1 September 1923, Brockton, Massachusetts, USA
Died 31 August 1969, Newton, Iowa, USA

First professional fight 17 March 1947, v. Lee Epperson (won, ko 1)
Total professional fights 49 (won all)
Last professional fight 21 September 1955, v. Archie Moore (won ko 9)

Professional fights

1947
17 March	Lee Epperson	Holyoke	ko	3

1948
12 July	Harry Balzarian	Providence	ko	1
19 July	John Edwards	Providence	ko	1
9 August	Bobby Quinn	Providence	ko	3
23 August	Eddie Ross	Providence	ko	1
30 August	Jimmy Weeks	Providence	ko	1
13 September	Jerry Jackson	Providence	ko	1
20 September	Bill Hardeman	Providence	ko	1
30 September	Gil Cardione	Washington, DC	ko	1
4 October	Bob Jefferson	Providence	ko	2
29 November	Patrick Connolly	Providence	ko	1
4 December	Gilley Ferron	Philadelphia	ko	2

1949
21 March	Johnny Pretzie	Providence	ko	5
28 March	Artie Donator	Providence	ko	1
11 April	James Walls	Providence	ko	3
2 May	Jimmy Evans	Providence	ko	3
23 May	Don Mogard	Providence	pts	10
18 July	Harry Haft	Providence	ko	3
16 August	Pete Louthis	New Bedford	ko	3
26 September	Tommy Di Giorgio	Providence	ko	4
10 October	Ted Lowry	Providence	pts	10
7 November	Joe Dominic	Providence	ko	2
2 December	Pat Richards	New York	ko	2
19 December	Phil Muscato	Providence	ko	5
30 December	Carmine Vingo	New York	ko	6

1950
24 March	Roland La Starza	New York	pts	10
5 June	Eldridge Eatman	Providence	ko	3
10 July	Gino Buonvino	Boston	ko	10
18 September	Johnny Shkor	Providence	ko	6
13 November	Ted Lowry	Providence	pts	10
18 December	Bill Wilson	Providence	ko	1

1951
29 January	Keene Simmons	Providence	ko	8
20 March	Harold Mitchell	Hartford	ko	2
26 March	Art Henry	Providence	ko	9
30 April	Red Applegate	Providence	pts	10
12 July	Rex Layne	New York	ko	6
27 August	Freddie Beshore	Providence	ko	4
26 October	Joe Louis	New York	ko	8

1952
13 February	Lee Savold	Philadelphia	ko	6
21 April	Gino Buonvino	Providence	ko	2
12 May	Bernie Reynolds	Providence	ko	3
28 July	Harry Matthews	New York	ko	2
23 September	Jersey Joe Walcott	Philadelphia	ko	13
(Won world heavyweight title)				

1953
15 May	Jersey Joe Walcott	Chicago	ko	1
(Retained world heavyweight title)				
24 September	Roland La Starza	New York	ko	11
(Retained world heavyweight title)				

1954
17 June	Ezzard Charles	New York	pts	15
(Retained world heavyweight title)				
17 September	Ezzard Charles	New York	ko	8
(Retained world heavyweight title)				

1955
16 May	Don Cockell	San Francisco	ko	9
(Retained world heavyweight title)				
21 September	Archie Moore	New York	ko	9

27 April 1956: announced retirement

credentials, so was taken on by Gene Caggiano. His first professional fight was against Lee Epperson on 17 March 1947 at Holyoke, just outside Boston. Marciano won in three rounds. It then took him until July 1948 to find another opponent and, as if to make up time, he had eleven fights between 12 July and 4 December – none went more than three rounds.

Between 1947 and 1951 Marciano had thirty-six fights, winning thirty-one on knockout. Don Mogard and Ted Lowry (1949), Roland La Starza and Lowry again (1950), and Red Applegate (1951) went into the Hall of Fame for hearing the final ten-round bell. Al Weill had been persuaded that he had made one of the more spectacular errors of judgement and recruited Marciano for a title 'eliminator' against another white hope, Rex Layne. Marciano was the winner in round six. The persuasive Weill was to have to wait a year and give Rocky six more fights before he could offer the world champion, the ageing Jersey Joe Walcott, sufficient incentive to defend. And amongst Rocky's victims during this waiting period was the incomparable Joe Louis, then thirty-seven and impecunious.

Eventually matched with Walcott for the title on 23 September 1952, Marciano soon suffered his first major setback. Early in round one he was put on the canvas for the first time, a short right confusing him, but got up at the count of four. Marciano and Walcott then waged a bitter war in the Philadelphia Stadium until the thirteenth round, when Marciano caught the champion with a tremendous right. Walcott, at thirty-eight, was drained.

If Rocky's success was built around his durability and staying power, it was Weill who refined the bobbing and weaving style with which he was so successful. Marciano's six title defences typified his domination of the heavyweight scene. Walcott lasted just two minutes and twenty-five seconds in the return fight held at the Chicago Stadium six months later and retired to be a parole officer and referee. Roland La Starza's reward for lasting the distance with Rocky was a nomination for a title bout: the college boy from Utah was stopped in eleven rounds.

Ezzard Charles was next in line. Charles, a fine boxer and an underrated former champion, had succeeded Joe Louis as champion and defended successfully on eight occasions. He then got careless against Walcott and was knocked out in the seventh round, and was outpointed in a return. The Walcott–Charles saga had taken four fights. Charles, veteran of ninety-eight fights, frustrated Marciano in the Yankee Stadium, New York, and became the sixth to take Rocky the full distance. But Rocky wore him down in eight rounds exactly two months later.

With the American scene accounted for, Weill looked abroad for Rocky's next opponent. It was to come in the shape of Don Cockell, the British champion from Battersea, a former light-heavyweight champion of Europe, who had moved successfully into the top sphere after weight trouble. Cockell gave an outstanding display of courage and was still on his feet when referee Frankie Brown rescued him in the ninth round.

Marciano's final defence was at the Yankee Stadium against Archie Moore. The same formula applied to the end. Caught (and dropped) early in the fight, Marciano came back to knock out Moore in the ninth round. The last round and a half were fought with Moore, light-heavyweight champion of the world and admitting to thirty-nine years of age, pinned to the ropes, under fire from all angles, before he was counted out. Marciano had run out of opponents.

He was elected to the Hall of Fame in 1959 and became a

Rocky Marciano throws another right to the head of world light-heavyweight champion Archie Moore (left). Marciano backed the wily Moore into the ropes for two rounds before knocking him out in the ninth round in New York, on 21 September 1955, in what was to be Marciano's last fight

successful businessman and speaker. On the way to speak at a convention he lost his life in a plane crash at Newton, Iowa, on 31 August 1969. He would have been forty-six the next day. Marciano made $4 million from the ring and invested wisely. But his wisest decision was not to return to the ring.

Rodney Marsh

A decade and more of Australian bowlers have been encouraged by the sight of the stocky Rodney Marsh crouched behind the stumps, ready to pounce on any edge from a usually nervous batsman.

But it was not always like that. When Marsh was called up for his first Test against England in 1970–71, he was immediately christened 'Iron Gloves' by the crowd at Brisbane's Gabba. Used to seeing specialists like Don Tallon, whose fifty-eight dismissals in twenty-one Tests were no indication of his ability, and Wally Grout, whose 187 victims was a world record, they also rated local keeper John MacLean (who was later to play four undistinguished Tests). But, in the backlash of a horrific Test defeat in South Africa, the selectors had gone for a keeper who could bat. Marsh vindicated that decision by scoring an unbeaten 92 later in the series, deprived of a possible record maiden century for Australian keepers by Bill Lawry's declaration.

Marsh became the most successful wicketkeeper ever – helped, of course, by a series of fine fast bowlers – and also the most capped Australian, despite defection to Packer after the 1977 tour to England.

Marsh's introduction to cricket was in the garden of the family home, with elder brother Graham. Both played schoolboy cricket for Western Australia before Graham sought new fame as one of the world's best golfers. Their school cricket was played at Armadale, 20 miles from Perth. Rod then moved to the West Perth club as an aggressive bat; Graham Becker, the West Perth keeper, was also the Western Australia keeper.

He took over from Becker, who retired in 1968. Under captain Tony Lock, and with Colin Milburn in the team, he made a duck in his first innings of his debut match against the touring West Indians. Charlie Griffiths was too quick. In the second innings he was dismissed by Gary Sobers but not before he'd made 104 in two and a half hours, laying about the bowling in typical left-hander's style, with heavy bottom-hand blows through and over the covers and straight past the bowler.

Marsh was at the forefront of the Australian Test cricket revival along with the Chappells, Lillee, Thomson and Walters. He was also one of the first to sign for Kerry Packer's circus. A renegade to many in cricket's establishment, a figurehead to those Australian cricket supporters, haters of Poms, who have become all too prevalent in recent years, Marsh, apart from being a fine wicketkeeper–batsman, became the archetype Australian cricketer in the mode of 'Slasher' MacKay. Shirt half open, chewing gum, a rugged and belligerent player.

English crowds probably did not see him at his best. Apart from a couple of innings, he only showed glimpses of his most aggressive form and, particularly in 1977, he seemed unable to inspire the team in the field in the way that Alan Knott brought the best out of the England fielders. Christopher Martin Jenkins thought that 'he was more affected by the passions aroused by the Packer crisis than he realized'. Australia in the field on that tour, wrote Martin Jenkins, reflected Marsh's image: 'ragged and messy'.

In Australia, Marsh, after the early barracking in his first Test, settled into the side and headed for 100 Test caps. His wicketkeeping became safer (he passed 350 Test dismissals during the home series against Pakistan in 1983), but his batting became less consistent.

He scored 236 for his state against Pakistan at Perth in 1972–73. He took a 118 not out off the Pakistanis in the Adelaide Test the same season – surprisingly the first Test century ever by an Australian wicketkeeper. In the memorable Centenary Test at Melbourne in 1977 Marsh became the first wicketkeeper to score 100 against England, his 110 not out coming at a vital period – Australia in their second innings were 187 for 5, leading by 230. It was a fine innings, bettered in the match only by Derek Randall's 174. Christopher Martin Jenkins recalled how Marsh 'straight drove anything overpitched with the relish of a forester felling a tree'.

At the end of the 1983 series against Pakistan, Marsh announced that he would not be available to tour the West Indies the following year. With the retirement of Greg Chappell and Dennis Lillee in the previous two days, it seemed that Australia's Test side had lost three of its most famous musketeers. But March is determined to play in 100 Tests and cannot be ruled out of consideration for Tests at home.

In his career, he was a worthy vice-captain, backing up his captain Greg Chappell both volubly and by example on the field. He was less kind to Kim Hughes, saying, 'He's good company but always liable to do something silly, whether he has a bat or a golf club or cards in his hand.' Marsh – along with David Hookes, Jeff Thomson and Dennis Lillee – was critical of Hughes, but for the

---

FACTFILE

Born 4 November 1947, Kalgoorlie, Western Australia

Test record

Debut 27 November 1970, v. England, Brisbane
Total matches 96
Total runs 3633 (average 26.33)
Total catches 343
Total stumpings 12
Highest innings 132, v. New Zealand, Adelaide (1973–74)
Centuries 3
50s 16

*Marsh has taken ninety-four catches off the bowling of Dennis Lillee
*Brother Graham's golfing successes are as follows:

World Matchplay Championship 1977
Swiss Open 1970, 1972
Indian Open 1971, 1973
German Open 1972
Scottish Open 1973
Dunlop Masters 1976
Benson & Hedges Masters 1976, 1980
Lancome Trophy 1977
Dutch Open 1979

Rodney Marsh catches Geoff Boycott off a leg-side deflection during the 1980 Test series between England and Australia

1983 series against Pakistan was named as his vice-captain.

Maybe some of the resentment would have been avoided had Marsh had a chance to captain his country. In state cricket he was good enough to lead Western Australia to the Sheffield Shield in 1976–77, and numerous contemporaries thought that in the absence of the Chappells he was the logical choice.

Sir Stanley Matthews

Stanley Matthews – renowned as the 'Wizard of Dribble' – is England's most famous footballer of all time. The first real football superstar, he made a name for himself outside the game endorsing a variety of products from football boots to milk and, of course, had a career in the top flight that spanned an amazing thirty-three years.

Matthews came from a sporting family in the Potteries. His father was a useful boxer known as the 'Fighting Barber of Hanley'; the family motto was 'Fitness is confidence'. Matthews made his debut for his local club – Stoke City – as a right winger in 1932, the year Stoke finished third in the Second Division. The following year they were champions and Matthews's displays were beginning to attract the attention of the England selectors.

Early the next season – in September 1934 – he made his England debut in the home international against Wales at Cardiff, scoring one of the goals in the 4–0 win.

Matthews's undoubted talent as a winger was geared towards providing chances for other forwards. In his fifty-four internationals he scored 11 goals and in 701 League games only 71. Goals, it has been said, were almost an afterthought for him. 'I aim to dominate defenders,' he stated once, 'to destroy them psychologically so that they are left without confidence or ability.'

There was one occasion, however, when goals flowed for Stanley – in 1937, in an international against Czechoslovakia at Tottenham, after Crayston and Morton had opened the scoring, Matthews suddenly produced a hat trick to win the match 5–4.

The next year he was at Old Trafford for a home international against Ireland. Willie Hall – the Spurs inside forward – was recalled to the side and took full advantage of Matthews in peerless form. England won 7–0 and Hall scored 5, including the fastest hat trick in the history of international football – between the thirty-fourth and the thirty-eighth minute. Matthews, having demoralized the Irish captain, Cook of Everton, with his classic double shuffle, rounded off the scoring himself with a typically sinuous dribble and a shot from an acute angle. The *Daily Telegraph* reported the next morning: 'We have known Matthews as a fine player, sure in his control of the ball and beautifully balanced on his feet. This afternoon he reached the pinnacle and at the close the crowd rose to him as one man to salute the player whose wizardry had them fascinated.'

After the war Stoke sold Matthews to Blackpool for a fee of £11,500. The transfer caused an uproar in the Potteries, but Blackpool saw him as the man to provide the right service for Stan Mortensen, the forward who had scored 28 League goals in the season immediately after the war and who, on his England debut against Portugal in Lisbon – with Matthews as his right-wing partner – scored four times.

It was a fruitful partnership – Mortensen continued to score goals for both England and Blackpool, culminating in the 1953 FA Cup Final at Wembley, when, with the whole nation willing Blackpool and Matthews to win the cup, it was the underdogs Bolton who went ahead in the first minute through Nat Lofthouse. Mortensen equalized, but with twenty minutes to go Bolton were 3–1 ahead. Matthews's third chance of an FA Cup winners' medal had seemingly disappeared. Mortensen made it 3–2 when the Bolton keeper, Hanson, dropped one of Matthews's hanging centres, and he completed his hat trick from a free kick just outside the area. Bolton by that stage had their left half, Eric Bell, injured and playing on the wing, and fullback Ralph Banks, who was suffering from cramp, was left to mark Matthews with no cover at all. Bolton paid the price in the final minute when Matthews supplied the pass for Perry's goal. It was a tense, emotional final, which subsequently became known as 'Matthews's Final', but in fairness Mortensen's contribution was probably the more significant.

For the second year (the first time was in 1948) Matthews was elected Footballer of the Year, one of only four men to win the award twice. In 1956 he was the first European Footballer of the Year. That year he returned to the international side and scored his final goal for England against Northern Ireland at Belfast in the 1–1 draw. He made his last international appearance in May 1957 against Denmark in Copenhagen (a 4–1 win for England); he was then forty-two.

It was a major surprise in the football world when, in October 1961, Stoke agreed to pay Blackpool £2500 for his return to the Victoria Ground. Stoke recouped their investment in his very first appearance: 35,974 turned up to watch the match against Huddersfield Town, 27,500 more than were there at the previous home match. In 1962 Stoke won promotion to the First Division. Matthews was then forty-eight. He stayed in the game for another two years, was knighted in 1965, and played his final match in the First Division for Stoke against Fulham on 6 February 1965 – a 3–1 win. He was just fifty – the only man ever to appear in the First Division at that age.

Typically, he has ploughed back into the game some of his vast knowledge. Youngsters in Malta, Canada and the black townships of Soweto in South Africa have particularly benefited from his coaching. At the age of sixty-five he was still playing 'village football'.

FACTFILE

Born 1 February 1915, Hanley, Stoke on Trent, England

Football League debut March 1932
Football League appearances 701 (322 for Stoke City, 379 for Blackpool; and including 3 in 1939–40 season)
Football League goals 71 (54 for Stoke City, 17 for Blackpool)
International debut September 1934, England v. Wales
International appearances 54

International goals 11

Honours

FA Cup 1953
Footballer of the Year 1948, 1963
European Footballer of the Year 1956

Stanley Matthews, in a Blackpool jersey, showing the remarkable acceleration which so confused defenders, in a League game with Charlton Athletic

Ivan Mauger

Barry Briggs, the rider with the record number of points and appearances in World Speedway Championship finals, comes from Christchurch, New Zealand. By a strange coincidence, Ivan Mauger, winner of a record six World Championships, comes from the same city.

Again, like Briggs, Ivan Mauger was a fine all-round sportsman at school. He played Rugby Union for Canterbury Schools, no mean feat that, and also hockey. He was also a fine sprinter, winning the 220 yards at the Provincial Schools Championships, and eventually became the Christchurch sprint champion.

There is a little British stock in the Mauger family: his ancestors came from the Channel Islands in the nineteenth century and his wife Raye, whom he married at eighteen, comes from Carlisle.

Mauger's first dice with speedway was in one of the by-products of the sport – cycle speedway. Christchurch had a flourishing league, and he rode for Woolston, his local suburb. He first obtained a speedway licence at the age of fifteen and took part in his first meeting on 2 October 1956 at the local Aranui track.

A year later he was on his way to England. His first club was Wimbledon, home of world champion Barry Briggs. He spent two years at Plough Lane, and alongside Briggs was in the team that won the British League in 1958.

But it was to be ten years before that early promise was translated into achievement. He rode for Rye House and Eastbourne, then spent from 1963 to 1968 with Newcastle and was a member of their team that won the Provincial League in 1964.

Mauger's first world final was in 1966. He finished fourth behind Briggs in Gothenburg and was third at Wembley a year later. Back in Gothenburg for the 1968 final, Mauger won the title. In second place was Briggs.

It was the beginning of a run unequalled in World Championship history. Between 1968 and 1974 he was never out of the first two places. He was the first and so far only rider to win the championship three years in succession. In those seven years he was champion on four occasions, and nearly made it five in 1973, losing only on a run-off with Jerzy Szczakiel on the Pole's own Katowice track. Win number five eventually arrived in 1977, and the last in 1979. He had beaten Ove Fundin's five titles.

In 1969 Mauger had moved to Belle Vue. The Manchester-based club, not surprisingly, won the British League from 1970 to 1972. In 1973 Exeter coughed up vast sums for his signature, and he helped them win the League in 1974.

Like Briggs, the Christchurch and Wimbledon connections had other slants. Both Briggs and Mauger rode for Britain when the British team won the world team title in 1968, though Mauger returned to his native country for the 1979 win. Both finished their careers with Hull. By then Mauger was heavily involved in the promotional and managerial side of the sport and, as 1980 approached, he rode less and less.

Involved in controversy on many occasions during his career, he once said that the most unpopular thing to do was to win the World Championship. Mauger was banned in 1983 after comments made after the 1982 World final. The 5-foot 6-inch, 10-st Mauger was involved in bizarre scenes when, as manager of Kenny Carter, the Halifax rider, he stormed the ramparts after Carter was pushed off his bike by Bruce Penhall, the reigning champion. Penhall finished as champion, Carter as runner-up. Mauger disagreed. He was also co-promoter, and the final finished in a shambles.

But there was one incident early in his career which still motivates Mauger. In his early days his boyhood hero was the Australian world champion of 1951 and 1952, Jack Young. Travelling across Australia with Young after Mauger's career had just started, Ivan was horrified to learn that Young was barely scraping a living working in a brickyard. He vowed that it would never happen to him.

FACTFILE

Born 4 October 1939, Christchurch, New Zealand

British League Clubs
1957–58 Wimbledon (also rode for Rye House and Eastbourne)
1963–68 Newcastle
1969–72 Belle Vue
1973–77 Exeter
1978–82 Hull

World Individual Championships
  Winner 1968, 1969, 1970, 1972, 1977, 1979
  Runner-up 1971, 1973, 1974

World Team Championship 1968 (Great Britain), 1971 (Great Britain), 1972 (Great Britain), 1979 (New Zealand)
World Pairs Championships 1970 (New Zealand, with Ronnie Moore)
Embassy Internationale 1970, 1971, 1972
British League Riders Championship 1971, 1973
British League Championship 1958 (Wimbledon), 1964 (Newcastle – Provincial League), 1970 (Belle Vue), 1971 (Belle Vue), 1972 (Belle Vue), 1974 (Exeter)

The New Zealander Ivan Mauger, the only rider to win three consecutive world titles. In this 1979 photo, he becomes world champion for the sixth time, and his country world team champions

Richard Meade

Just across the Severn Bridge on the M4 is the sign 'Croeso Y Cymru' – Welcome to Wales. Past the St Pierre golf course, home of the Masters, the motorway cuts through the fields on the outskirts of Caldicot. To the south is the Meade farm, to the north is the Broome farm – two of the world's best-known equestrian families, separated by four lanes of tarmac.

Richard Meade won three Olympic gold medals, the best of any modern British Olympian and only one short of the record of Paul Ramilovic (water polo) and Henry Taylor (swimming) at the turn of the century. He won the gold medal in the team three-day event in 1968 and the individual and team three-day event gold medal in 1972.

Richard Hannay Meade was born at neighbouring Chepstow on 4 December 1938. His introduction to equestrianism came at home. He was the only son of Mr and Mrs John Meade, the former joint masters of the Curre Hounds in Monmouthshire. His parents bred Connemara ponies.

His education was classically English: Lancing College, a commission in the 11th Hussars, then an engineering degree at Magdalen College, Cambridge. His early practical experience was at point-to-point races, usually under the auspices of the army at Tidworth. It was there that he took part in his first senior combined training event in 1961.

In his early eventing days he was coached by Colonel and Mrs V. D. S. Williams in ground work, and by Richard Stilwell in show-jumping skills. In 1961 he had his first international success when he was in the winning team at the International Students Rally in Amsterdam. It was a pattern that he was to follow throughout his career – an outstanding overseas record with less success in Britain.

Barberry was his first 'name' horse. Taking part in the Olympics for the first time at Tokyo in 1964, he finished eighth. The pair had been runners-up at Badminton a year before and, in Olympic year, had won Burghley (Meade's only success at Burghley thus far).

The quest for Olympic honours in Mexico four years later began in a staccato fashion. He only teamed up with Cornishman V two weeks before the Games. Cornishman and Meade finished fourth in the individual competition, but with Major Derek Allhusen gaining the silver medal and Ben Jones well placed, Britain took their first three-day event gold medal since 1956.

In between Olympics, Meade had a fine horse called The Poacher; they were in the British team that won the 1970 World Championships, and Richard recorded his first win at Badminton the same year.

By the time Munich came round, Meade, as befits a top international rider, had found another horse – Lauriston. The pair won both the individual and team gold medals at Munich and were never seriously threatened.

Now a successful business consultant in London, Meade lives near Chippenham. Ten miles from the Wiltshire market town is Badminton; after a period in the wilderness, Meade won the Badminton three-day event for only the second time on Speculator III in 1982.

1982 was a good year. As reigning European team champion on Kilcashel, Richard added the World Team Championship later in the year. Both Speculator III and Kilcashel were likely to have been selected for the Moscow Olympics and the three-day event probables wasted their preparation time when the team withdrew.

Richard Meade's Olympic triumphs have a common denominator. Mrs Gordon Watson's Cornishman V and Meade won the team gold medal in the Mexico Olympics. Four years later Cornishman V had another gold medal pinned to his bridle. This time, however, alongside Meade on the dais was Cornishman's new rider, Mrs Gordon Watson's daughter, Mary.

FACTFILE

Born 4 December 1938, Chepstow, England

Major wins

Burghley Horse Trials
1964 on Barberry

Olympic Games (took part in 1964, 1968, 1972, 1976)
1968 Team, on Cornishman V
1972 Team, on Lauriston
        Individual on Lauriston

European Championships
1967 Team, on Barberry
1971 Team, on The Poacher
1981 Team, on Kilcashel

World Championships
1970 Team, on The Poacher
1982 Team, on Kilcashel

Badminton Horse Trials
1970 on The Poacher
1982 on Speculator III

*Richard Meade's team-mates in his major championship wins have been:
Olympic Games
1968 Derek Alhusen, Reuben Jones
1972 Mary Gordon Watson, Bridget Parker, Mark Phillips

European Championships
1967 Martin Whiteley, Derek Alhusen
1971 Stewart Stevens, Deborah West, HRH Princess Anne
1981 Virginia Holgate, Sue Benson, Elizabeth Purbick

World Championships
1970 Mary Gordon Watson, Mark Phillips
1982 Rachel Bayliss, Virginia Holgate, Lucinda Green

Richard Meade on Kilcashel during the final show-jumping stage of the 1983 Burghley three-day event

Colin Meads

Colin Meads is the symbol of New Zealand rugby – the large, raw-boned All Black forward, fierce and uncompromising on the field and quiet and courteous away from the rugby arenas.

A farmer from the King Country region of North Island, Meads played 133 times in an All Black jersey, and in fifty-five Test matches from 1957 to 1971. Both are New Zealand records. He was, quite simply, the first player every rugby writer would pencil into his selection for a World XV, and the first to be invited to the plethora of centenary games which coincided with the end of his career.

He is held in no higher esteem than by other members of the lock forwards' union. The mere presence of the man is illustrated by one of the great rugby quotes of all time, from Earle Mitchell, the Scotland second-row forward who played against Meads in the Scotland v. New Zealand Test of December 1967. Meads was seen in distinctly antisocial mood during the first half, grabbing Mitchell's shirt and threatening all kinds of mischief. Suddenly Meads left the scene and rejoined play on the other side of the field. In the dressing room, the conversation later went something like . . .

'What was all that about?' inquired a team-mate.

'Oh, nothing,' said Mitchell. 'I told him to bugger off.'

'You what?' came the reply.

'Yeah,' said the confident Mitchell, 'I told him to bugger off.' Then, after a moment's pause, he admitted, 'Aye, but I didn't say it very loud!'

Meads took up rugby at the age of eight at his prep school. The well-constructed and well-documented provincial system allowed his ability to be noticed, although he was hardly with a major force in the King Country XV.

He made his international debut in 1957 as a flanker in the 25–11 win against Australia. The famous captain, Wilson Whineray, also made his debut in that game. Meads was only the third King Country player to play for New Zealand, and the first from his club, Waitete.

Like many other outstanding players, Meads took some time to settle into the New Zealand side. His problem, possibly, was that he could play either at flanker, No. 8, or in the second row, and his early caps were indicative of his and the selectors' indecision about his best position. In his second game for New Zealand, a week after his first cap, he scored the first of his seven international tries. He was deputizing on the wing!

He was dropped for the opening Test against the Lions in 1959, when Don Clarke's six penalties overruled four tries by the Lions for an 18–17 win in Dunedin. Meads was also left out after the 9–9 draw with Australia in 1962. He was never dropped again, and this coincided with the belief that lock was his best position.

Meads was a fitness fanatic. Building up strength and stamina on the family farm, he used to run with the sheep as unwilling partners to weight-training and running sessions. At 6 feet 4 inches and 16 st, Meads was a formidable opponent.

Against France in 1961 Colin Meads was joined in the New Zealand team by brother Stan. Stan could also play at flanker or lock. Stan was to play fifteen times for New Zealand and when Australia (1964), South Africa (1965) and the Lions (1966) toured the country, the second-row partnership of C. E. and S. J. Meads confronted them. Stan returned to run the family farm after the 4–0 whitewash of the 1966 Lions. Many critics had said that Stan was the finer player.

There were two major disappointments in Meads's career. In 1967 in Mitchell's match against the Scots, Meads was sent off two minutes from the end for 'aiming a kick' at Scots outside half Chisholm. It was later revealed that the Irish referee, Kevin Kelleher, had no choice, having already officially warned Meads. But, despite that, he was never regarded as a foul or dirty player.

The other setback came at the end of his career. Chosen to captain his country against the 1971 Lions, he was unlucky enough to come up against the best British side in living history to tour the Antipodes. John Dawes's Lions won the series for the first time in New Zealand by 2–1, and the Fourth and final Test at Auckland was drawn 14–14. It was Meads's last international. He was thirty-five when he took over the captaincy and, although past his best by his own high standards, he was still a great player.

Andy Haden, his successor in the All Blacks team the next time the Lions toured in 1977, tells another story of Meads's dominance. One of the better locks in Meads's era was Ian Eliason of Taranaki. In a game against King Country, Eliason was so comprehensively outplayed by Meads in the line-out that he decided, literally, to 'take a dive'. The referee fell for the trick. Meads was speechless.

Haden pulled the same stunt at Cardiff against Wales in 1978, remembering Eliason's party trick. Meads wouldn't have approved. He was above that.

FACTFILE

Born 3 June 1936, Cambridge, Waikato, New Zealand

New Zealand international career

Debut 1957, v. Australia (won 25–11)
Appearances 133 (New Zealand record)
Tests 55 (New Zealand record; won 41, lost 10, drew 4)
Tours 1960 South Africa
      1963 British Isles and France
      1967 British Isles
      1970 South Africa (vice-captain)

*Altogether Meads played for New Zealand 133 times: 35 in New Zealand, 34 in South Africa, 28 in Australia, 27 in the British Isles, 6 in France, 2 in Canada and 1 in Fiji

Colin Meads works off jet lag at Richmond at the start of the 1967 All Blacks tour to Britain

Bobby Moore

At his peak, Bobby Moore, England's World Cup winning captain, was the best defensive wing half in the world. His duels with the great Brazilian Pele were a major feature of England's internationals in the sixties and seventies.

Brought up in the East End of London, Moore turned pro for West Ham United in June 1958 and made his debut for them against Manchester United at Upton Park the following September – the first of 668 League appearances for the Hammers. His international debut for England was against Peru in Lima in May 1962 in a 4–0 win marked by a Jimmy Greaves hat trick. Moore retained his place for all four matches during the World Cup in Chile, England going out in a 3–1 defeat by the champions Brazil, in Vina Del Mar, in the quarter final.

That was in the days before Alf Ramsey took over the running of the national side. When he became manager the following year, Ramsey, in an uncharacteristically off-hand moment, suggested that England were good enough to win the World Cup when it was staged in England in 1966. At that point he was not taken seriously.

Bobby Moore was one man Ramsey had in mind when building his World Cup team. Bobby Charlton and Gordon Banks were the others at that time, but it was Moore whom he chose to be captain – in only his twelfth international – against Czechoslovakia in Bratislava in May 1963. It was Ramsey's first win as manager after four matches. Moore's career as England's youngest captain ever began to develop apace. In 1964 he was named Footballer of the Year as he captained West Ham to an FA Cup final victory against Preston. The following year, also at Wembley, West Ham won the Cup Winners' Cup when they beat Munich 1860 by 2–0; and his remarkable hat trick of collecting trophies from Wembley's Royal Box was complete on 30 July 1966 when he lifted the World Cup after England's memorable 4–2 extra-time win over West Germany.

It crowned a notable tournament for Moore. He had forged a formidable partnership with Jackie Charlton and although his defensive gifts were most easily recognizable, he had also turned into an adept prompter of counter-attacks. Tommy Docherty pointed out that England's fourth goal of that match (Hurst's third) demonstrated Moore's quick thinking. 'Most players without Moore's football brain would, at that late stage of the game, have been looking to play it cautiously to ensure the Germans could not regain possession. But Germany watched as Moore struck a lethal 30-yard pass out of defence and into the path of Hurst, who was motoring towards the halfway line.'

Moore – according to Docherty – gave a single-minded concentration to every game. His major strength was to be a thought ahead of his opponents, which belied his seemingly sluggish approach on the ball.

Moore's concentration might well be explained by his own comment during England's best years: 'I and most other players feel that every game for England could be our last. It is one of the constant worries which go with the honour of being an international.'

Moore had little need to worry. He was a permanent fixture in the side and went on to eclipse Bobby Charlton's record when he made his 108th appearance for England in the 1–0 home defeat by Italy in 1973.

Before the 1970 World Cup in Mexico – when England were defending the trophy – Moore was arrested in Bogotá, Colombia, and charged with stealing a gold bracelet worth £600 from a hotel jewellery shop. It transpired that the case was phoney, and aimed at trying to put England and Moore out of sorts before the finals started.

Moore reckoned that England had a better World Cup side in 1970 than in 1966. Lately he has repeated the view that players like Hurst, Peters and Ball were more experienced internationals and better players in 1970. What caused their defeat was that 'the fans were against us, and the altitude and the heat took its toll on the toughest of pros.'

Moore played his final League match for West Ham – his 544th and a record for the club at the time – in 1974, then moved across London to Fulham. It proved to be a remarkable last couple of years. Under his captaincy Second Division Fulham reached the FA Cup final against his old club West Ham. Alas, there was no fairy tale – West Ham won 2–0. In 1977 he played his last League game – his 668th – for Fulham against Blackburn.

Moore will always be remembered for his captaincy of the national side in their finest period and, as Tommy Docherty recalls, for his excellent defensive capabilities. Docherty watched him in the 1970 World Cup, preparing to take on Brazil's Jairzinho, who was racing towards goal. 'Moore bided his time and then suddenly moved for-

---

FACTFILE

Born 12 April 1941, Barking, Essex, England

Football League debut 8 September 1958, *v.* Manchester United (won 3–2)
Football League appearances 668 (544 for West Ham, 124 for Fulham)
Football League goals 25 (24 for West Ham, 1 for Fulham)
Last Football League game 14 May 1977, *v.* Blackburn Rovers (lost 0–1)
International debut 20 May 1962, *v.* Peru (won 4–0)
International appearances 108 (30 in Home International Championship)
International goals 2

Last international match 14 November 1973, *v.* Italy (lost 0–1)
World Cup appearances 14 (1962, 1966, 1970)

Honours

FA Cup 1964 (West Ham); runners-up 1975 (Fulham)
World Cup 1966 (his 47th cap)
Cup Winners' Cup 1965 (West Ham)
Football League Cup runners-up 1966 (West Ham)
American League Championship 1963 (West Ham)
Footballer of the Year 1964

*Moore became manager of Southend United in 1984

Bobby Moore receives the World Cup from Her Majesty the Queen after England's 4–2 extra-time win against West Germany on 30 July 1966. Geoff Hurst (behind Moore) scored 3 of England's goals

ward to meet Jairzinho with an upright determined challenge. He blocked the ball with his right foot and came striding powerfully out of the tackle in possession as Jairzinho tumbled off-balance under the weight of the challenge. It was the perfect block tackle.'

Apart from the World Cup final at Wembley, which he remembers as much for the fact that his two West Ham team-mates, Martin Peters and Geoff Hurst, were on the winning side as for the historic victory, Moore picks the 1964 FA semifinal at Hillsborough when

West Ham beat Manchester United 3–1 as his most memorable game. West Ham, he said, 'were a bunch of lads who'd come up through the ranks together; we faced the mighty Manchester United of Law, Charlton, Crerand and Co., who were red-hot favourites, and we faced them in the Hillsborough mud during a wet period. Our victory set us on the road to bigger things.' Just over two years later Moore was a World Cup winning captain and West Ham supplied three players to the winning team.

151

Ed Moses

Every so often an athlete arrives and refashions people's thinking about an event. Such an athlete is the 400-metre hurdler Edwin Moses. Since 1976 he has dominated the scene to such an extent that some of his rivals contemplate changing to another event. Others wait for a sign of fallibility. It has been a long wait.

Born on 31 August 1955 at Dayton, Ohio, Moses ran his first race over the distance in 1975, when he clocked 52.0 seconds in the 1975 Southern Inter Collegiate Championships.

His progress in the Olympic year of 1976 was astonishing. Starting the season with a best time of 50.1 seconds – the only time he had run the metric distance, Moses came fourth in the AAU Championships. He was developing a thirteen-stride pattern in between hurdles for the entire race (previously athletes had changed to fourteen or fifteen strides for the last few hurdles). Entered for the Olympic trials, he surprised the selectors, and himself, by winning in a time of 48.30 seconds – an American record.

The African boycott spoilt a potentially superb Montreal 400-metre hurdles final. It prevented the Ugandan world record holder and defending champion, John Akii Bua, from attending the Games. Akii Bua, one of forty-three children, had been prevented from participating by Idi Amin, his President, who was upset by atrocities in another African country! Using his thirteen-stride pattern throughout, Moses won the gold medal by a record 8 metres and took Akii Bua's world record with a time of 47.64 seconds. Then the twenty-year-old physics student from Morehouse College, Atlanta, Georgia, returned to his studies and a reprimand from his tutor for allowing his grades to slip.

The next significant date was 26 August 1977. He actually lost a race. Harald Schmid, from Stuttgart, won at a meeting in Berlin. A week later Moses defeated Schmid in the first World Cup in Düsseldorf in the world's second fastest time.

The World Cup was the international highspot for American athletes during the troubled years before and after the Moscow Olympics. Moses became the first to win the same event at three World Cups. When Jimmy Carter pulled Moses and his colleagues out of the Games, his reply was to set a new world record of 47.13 seconds at Milan, just three weeks before the opening ceremony.

The 1983 World Championships were a salvation, the first true 'Olympics' since 1964. Moses v. Schmid, the European champion and the second fastest of all time. Schmid had tried the flat 400 and 800 metres and was a world-class runner in the three events. Moses slaughtered him, winning the gold medal in 47.50 seconds to Schmid's 48.61, with the distraction of a flapping shoelace for almost half the race. A religious man, Moses and his team-mates Andre Phillips and David Lee were seen in a huddle before the start. 'We were praying that we would not get injured. We were thankful that we were all in the final, and we were wishing everyone else in the race the same.'

Moses's plan for 1984 was straightforward – to win a second Olympic gold medal. Settled in Laguna Beach, California, with his German wife Myrella, he was understandably edgy during the early rounds in the Olympic Coliseum. He carried the pressures of a nation's support in a country where second place is a sign of weakness.

He won the Olympic final with his 105th consecutive win.

FACTFILE

Born 31 August 1955, Dayton, Ohio, USA

Olympic Games
Gold: 400-metre hurdles 47.64 (1976), 47.75 (1984)

World Championships
Gold: 400-metre hurdles 47.50 (1983)

World Cup
Gold: 400-metre hurdles 47.58 (1977)
　　　 400-metre hurdles 47.53 (1979)
　　　 400-metre hurdles 47.37 (1981)

World 400-metre hurdles records
47.64 (Montreal, 1976)
47.45 (Westwood, California, 1977)
47.13 (Milan, 1980)
47.02 (Koblenz, 1984)

*The greatest number of consecutive victories by a male athlete is 116 by Parry O'Brien; the all-time record is 140 by Iolanda Balas

Ed Moses, who regained the Olympic 400-metre hurdles title in 1984, bringing his number of consecutive victories to 105

Stirling Moss

Stirling Moss is still the most famous racing driver of all time. His name will live on in the lines of the traffic cop who, having stopped a driver for speeding, is said to have remarked,' 'And who do you think you are – Stirling Moss?' Moss had retired twenty-five years earlier and Britain had had five world champions since then.

Moss was the complete professional in an age when the image of the racing driver was flashy and happy-go-lucky. He is certainly the best driver never to have won the World Championship – though he dominated the sport to such an extent that he was runner-up in 1955, 1956, 1957 and 1958.

FACTFILE

Born 17 December 1929, West Kensington, London, England

World Drivers Championship
  Runner-up 1955, 1956, 1957, 1958

World Championship Grand Prix wins (16)
1955   British (Mercedes)
1956   Italian, Monaco (both for Maserati)
1957   British, Italian, Pescara (all for Vanwall)
1958   Argentine (Cooper), Dutch (Vanwall), Moroccan (Vanwall), Portuguese (Vanwall)
1959   Italian, Portuguese (both for Cooper)
1960   Monaco, United States (both for Lotus)
1961   German, Monaco (both for Lotus)

Summary of Grand Prix wins
Argentine 1958
British 1955, 1957
Dutch 1958
German 1961
Italian 1956, 1957, 1959
Monaco 1956, 1960, 1961
Moroccan 1958
Pescara 1957
Portuguese 1958, 1959
United States 1961

World Championship Positions

		Points	Wins	2nds	3rds
1954	Joint twelfth	4½	–	–	1
1955	1 Fangio (Argentina)	40	4	1	–
	2 Moss	23	1	2	–
	3 Castellotti (Italy)	12	–	1	1
1956	1 Fangio (Argentina)	45	3	2	–
	2 Moss	27	2	1	1
	3 Collins (GB)	24	2	3	–
1957	1 Fangio (Argentina)	40	4	2	–
	2 Moss	25	3	–	–
	3 Musso (Italy)	16	–	2	–
1958	1 Hawthorn (GB)	42	1	5	1
	2 Moss	41	4	1	–
	3 Brooks (GB)	24	3	–	–
1959	1 Brabham (Australia)	31	2	1	2
	2 Brooks (GB)	27	2	1	1
	3 Moss	25½	2	1	–
1960	1 Brabham (Australia)	43	5	–	–
	2 McLaren (New Zealand)	34	1	3	2
	3 Moss	19	2	–	1

1961	1 Hill (USA)	34	2	2	2
	2 von Trips (Germany)	33	2	2	–
	3 Moss	21	2	–	–

Scoring system
1954   Best five results from nine rounds, points 8, 6, 4, 3, 2, and 1 point for driver with fastest lap
1955   Best five from seven, points as 1954
1956   Best five from eight, points as 1954
1957   Best five from eight, points as 1954
1958   Best six from eleven, points as 1954
1959   Best five from nine, points as 1954
1960   Best six from ten rounds. Points changed to read 8, 6, 4, 3, 2, 1 – the 1 point for the fastest lap being abolished
1961   Best five from eight rounds, with the points system being changed to the present-day format of 9, 6, 4, 3, 2, 1

1958 World Championship

In 1958 when he lost the title by a solitary point to Hawthorn, Moss only registered five finishes which counted towards the championship; had he registered just one more – even if it was only a fifth placing – he would have won the title.

However, it is regarded that he lost the title at Oporto in the Portuguese Grand Prix in the August, when he misinterpreted a pit signal and failed to set the fastest lap – Hawthorn went on to do so. Had it not been for that misunderstanding, Moss would have obtained one more point, and Hawthorn one less, and the title would have been Moss's.

1 Mike Hawthorn (GB)   42 points
2 Stirling Moss (GB)   41 points
3 Tony Brooks (GB)   24 points
4 Roy Salvadori (GB)   15 points
5 Peter Collins (GB)   14 points
6 Harry Schell (USA)   14 points
(Stewart Lewis Evans (GB) was ninth, Cliff Allison (GB) joint seventeenth.)

*Moss began his racing career by finishing fourth in a hill climb at Prescott in 1947. He was driving a 500-cc Cooper–JAP
*He also competed in the Mille Miglia in Italy and, with co-driver Ross Jenkinson, was the only Englishman to win the famous event around the roads of Italy (*mille miglia* = 1000 miles)
*According to Moss, 'Nothing is sillier than the notion that drivers have a death wish. Many of them enjoy life infinitely more than the average man, and it's nothing to do with the theory of eat, drink and be merry, for tomorrow we may die'

July 1979, Stirling Moss nostalgically rounds Woodcote Corner at Silverstone. Like Clark and Stewart, he insisted on the lucky number 7

He was British champion at the age of twenty, but his early insistence on driving only British cars undoubtedly restricted his opportunities. It was a mixture of bad manners and bad management by Ferrari that put him off foreign drives. Enzo Ferrari offered the promising Moss a drive at the Balu Grand Prix one year, but on arrival told him that he had found someone else. Ferrari later admitted that that decision 'was my biggest mistake'.

Moss drove only British cars from then on – Jaguar, Frazer Nash and ERA – until he was persuaded to drive a Maserati in the 1954 season. He won at Aintree, Goodwood and Oulton and was persuaded to sign for Mercedes Benz in 1955 to partner his hero and mentor, Fangio. Moss was allowed to win the British Grand Prix at Aintree finishing second behind his team-mate in the championship.

After Mercedes pulled out of racing, Moss joined Maserati for 1956, again finishing as runner-up in the championship. He linked up with the British team Vanwall in 1957 and, at Aintree, became the first British winner of the British Grand Prix in a British car. Moss's car failed early on but he took over Peter Brooks's car and drove it to a memorable victory.

In 1958 Moss won four Grands Prix during the season but failed to win the championship by a point. Mike Hawthorn, who only won one Grand Prix, became champion because of the then unfair points scoring system.

Moss was still a driver to be reckoned with, but driving for Rob Walker's private team at Corsley, Wiltshire, seems to have lost him the chance of the title. In 1960 he brought a Lotus home first in the Monaco Grand Prix, had a horrific accident at Spa, breaking his legs and damaging his back, but was racing again six weeks later. He proved he was as expert as ever by winning for a second time at Monaco and then at Nurburgring in the rain.

Nurburgring proved to be his last win. In 1962 he crashed badly at Goodwood on the Levant straight in the Glover Trophy race and suffered head injuries. While he was in hospital, first, with his life in danger and, later, as he slowly recovered, millions waited for news. Nigel Roebuck believes that at his peak Moss's 'driving was virtually without a flaw' and that it was sad to see him return to saloon-car racing in 1980 – 'just another driver in a sea of anonymous saloon cars'.

Muhammad Ali

It's difficult to know where to begin with Muhammad Ali, boxer and showman supreme, would-be poet and politician, occasional diplomat. A film on his own life, *The Greatest*, was made before he was thirty-five. From the Eskimos to the mud huts of Africa, his was the most recognizable face on earth, and probably still is.

Born Cassius Marcellus Clay, the son of a sign writer, in Louisville Kentucky, he was introduced to boxing at the age of twelve by a local downtown policeman. Seasoned writers began to take notice in 1960 when he won the US National AAU light-heavyweight title, then the Golden Gloves. He was selected for the Rome Olympics and casually outpointed the 213-fight veteran, Zbigniew Pietrzykowski, of Poland, in the final. On the gold medal dais he waved the American flag. He wore the gold medal every day – in the bath, on evenings out, everywhere. He joined the queue of admirers knocking on the front door of triple sprint gold medallist Wilma Rudolph. It was a long queue.

Then there came an incident about which the truths and implications are not properly known even today. Apparently Clay, a couple of friends and the gold medal (then three months old) were crossing the Ohio Bridge. At a café by the bridge, they stopped and entered to buy refreshments, and were immediately accosted by a group of white groupies or bikies, as they were called. They fancied the gold medal. After the inevitable brawl, Clay took the medal onto the bridge and threw it into the Ohio. If that was the American dream, the ideal, then he wanted no part of it. Whether the story is true or not, he turned professional immediately afterwards and his views hardened.

Tunny Hunsaker goes into the record books as Clay's first professional opponent, on 29 October 1960, in Clay's home town; but the eight-round decision was not hometown. Backed by twelve Louisville businessmen, he was fed the run-of-the-mill softees to gain experience. When he fought Kolo Sabedong, his quip was: 'I'm not worried about the fight, more worried about the flight,' a reference to his fear of flying.

He needed an image. Possessed of remarkable reflexes and speed for so large a man, he was already ridiculing the yo-yo champions Patterson and Johansson. Inspiration came from watching Gorgeous George, one of many claimants to the world wrestling crown, but just about America's best. George, a real baddie, had a mane of blond hair, a valet and a receptionist. Clay recalls, 'When he was in the ring, everyone booed. They wanted him beat. I looked round and everyone was mad. But there were 15,000 in there to see him get beat . . . What a good idea, I thought.' So was born the legend, spiced with threats in poem, jibes, tantrums.

The early claims were mainly correct. Doug Jones, who should have gone in five, was still upright at the end of ten rounds – the bubble had burst. Then came Henry Cooper.

'There's two greats,' Clay said, 'Britain and Clay.' He expanded his thoughts. 'He'll fall in five, after I've done my jive.'

Cooper did go in five, but not according to the script. Coasting through to his prediction, Clay was nailed at the end of round four by ''Enry's 'ammer – the left hook. Clambering unsteadily to his feet, Clay wobbled to his corner. Manager Angelo Dundee worsened a gash in Clay's glove and one minute's break became two, enough for a fit man to recover. Clay came out for round five, peppered Cooper's suspect and cut eye, and Tommy Little, the referee, was forced to intervene.

Two fights later Clay was world champion. The holder was the fearsome Sonny Liston. No one knew how old he was. 'Chop his legs off and count the rings,' suggested someone. His two world title fights with Floyd Patterson had lasted a shade under five minutes. Clay entered the ring a 6–1 underdog. It was his twentieth fight, he

FACTFILE

Born 17 January 1942, Louisville, Kentucky, USA

First professional fight 29 October 1960, *v.* Tunny Hunsaker (w pts 8)
Total professional fights 61
  Wins 56
  Kos 11
  Defeats 5
Last professional fight 1982, *v.* Trevor Berbick (l pts)
World title fights 25
  Wins 22

World heavyweight title fights

Date	Opponent	Venue	Result	
25. 2.64	Sonny Liston	Miami	w rtd	6
25. 5.65	Sonny Liston	Lewiston	w ko	1
22.11.65	Floyd Patterson	Las Vegas	w rsf	12
29. 3.66	George Chuvalo	Toronto	w pts	15
21. 5.66	Henry Cooper	London	w rsf	6
6. 8.66	Brian London	London	w ko	3
10. 9.66	Karl Mildenberger	Frankfurt	w rsf	12
14.11.66	Cleveland Williams	Houston	w rsf	3
6. 2.67	Ernie Terrall	Houston	w pts	15
22. 3.67	Zora Folley	New York	w ko	7
8. 3.71	Joe Frazier	New York	l pts	15
30.10.74	George Foreman	Kinshasa	w ko	8
24. 3.75	Chuck Wepner	Cleveland	w rsf	15
6. 5.75	Ron Lyle	Las Vegas	w rsf	11
1. 7.75	Joe Bugner	Kuala Lumpur	w pts	15
1.10.75	Joe Frazier	Manila	w rtd	14
10. 2.76	Jean-Pierre Coopman	San Juan	w ko	5
30. 4.76	Jimmy Young	Landover	w pts	15
25. 5.76	Richard Dunn	Munich	w rsf	5
28. 9.76	Ken Norton	New York	w pts	15
16. 5.77	Alfredo Evangelista	Landover	w pts	15
29. 9.77	Earnie Shavers	New York	w pts	15
15. 2.78	Leon Spinks	Las Vegas	l pts	15
15. 9.78	Leon Spinks	New Orleans	w pts	15
2.10.80	Larry Holmes	Las Vegas	l rtd	10

*Ali on his opponents:
Foreman: 'I've seen him shadow boxing, and the shadow won.'
Liston: 'This is the bear-hunting season – you're a big ugly bear.'
  'You're so ugly, that when you cry, the tears run down the wall.'
Frazier: 'He's easily recognizable, he's the one that leads with his face.'
Louis: 'He was my inspiration, I idolized him. I just give lipservice to being the greatest. He was the greatest.'

Muhammad Ali paws at 'the Bear' – Sonny Liston (right). Ali, then Cassius Clay, was the 7–1 underdog when the pair met for Liston's world title at Miami Beach on 25 February 1964, but Liston failed to answer the bell to start the seventh round

was aged 22 years 39 days. At the end of the seventh round Liston, bemused, quit on his stool, claiming shoulder damage. He called for a rematch, but it was a fiasco, all over inside a round. Jim Murray said of Clay's phantom punch which ended the fight, 'It wouldn't have crushed a grape.'

Another announcement was that he would no longer be Cassius Marcellus Clay, but Muhammad Ali from now on. 'Clay only meant dirt without the ingredients,' he claimed, and followed brother Rudolph Valentino Clay into the Muslim faith.

Clay/Ali marched through three years of increasing invincibility. In 1967 he was stripped of his title for refusing to be conscripted into the US Army. 'No Vietcong ever called me nigger,' he stated. Sentenced, more as an example, to a five-year term which he never served, he was out of the ring from March 1967 until October 1970.

Meanwhile Joe Frazier, the former Philadelphia slaughterhouse worker, had assumed Ali's throne. Frazier, short, squat and with a fine left hook, was another ex-Olympic gold medallist. The WBA/WBC issue had been resolved and Frazier was a fine champion. The pair were to have three of the greatest fights ever seen.

Angelo Dundee and Bundini 'float like a butterfly, sting like a bee' Brown had to get Ali into shape. His first opponent was Jerry Quarry, who, disappointingly, had problems with a cut eye in round three. The Argentinian, Oscar Bonavena, lasted until the final round. They were now ready for Frazier – or they thought they were.

Ali and Frazier beat the publicity drum. They wrestled on the floor in a TV studio showdown, which cost them both £2000. But March 1971 was no gimmick. They fought to exhaustion. Frazier, courtesy of a fifteenth-round knockdown, won the decision. Both went into hospital for a few days.

Frazier then lost his title to George Foreman in Kingston, Jamaica. Ali, at thirty-two, appeared to have missed the boat. Foreman, unbeaten in forty fights with thirty-seven knockouts, could reign as

long as he wished. Ali, beaten by and then the victor against Ken Norton, beat Frazier for the American title and was the logical contender.

Foreman and Ali met in Kinshasa, Zaïre, in October 1974. 'The rumble in the jungle' fitted the prefight ballyhoo. Ali's strategy was perfect. Foreman tired himself out hammering away at Ali's body and arms. Ali struck in round eight.

On then to the 'Thrilla in Manila' and the third encounter with Smokin' Joe. 'He's got two chances, slim and none,' said Ali. 'It's gonna be a chilla and a thrilla when I get the gorilla in Manila,' he added. Ali beat Frazier in round fourteen. Both went back to hospital. 'It was like death, the nearest thing I know to dying,' said the winner.

Even going downhill, Ali picked up the decisions, until he met Leon Spinks, a mismanaged eight-fight novice. Spinks, the best of the US gold medal quintet at the Montreal Olympics, sneaked a points decision. 'I will return, goofy,' said Ali. He did. He had now won the title three times.

He bumbled on, his ego filling a room, until the courts took his title away. Larry Holmes, his former sparring partner, was a deserved champion. Compassionate too. When Ali, nearly forty years old, was thrown in with him and failed, for the only time, to last the course, Holmes said, 'I held back, he was a great man, great athlete and a great friend.' When Ali couldn't beat Trevor Berbick in Nassau, even he saw the light.

Customary words on great champions are commonplace, and Ali is now subject to the same inquisition. He'll always have the last word . . .

'When I die, you won't remember who I was. I'll be just another ex-champ. I woke up this morning, sick of my own voice. I said, if I'm tired of it, so must be everyone else.' And on his career . . . 'It was just a big act, they all fell for it . . . 150 million dollars' worth.'

Alex Murphy

St Helens is known for two major contributions to English society – the best glass and, some would say, the best-known Rugby League team. Fitting, then, that one of Rugby League's most famous sons was born and brought up just a stone's throw from the Knowsley Road ground.

Alex Murphy, impish, dapper and controversial, was a fine half-back and an astute tactician. He may not have been everyone's ideal to represent a sport fast ridding itself of the cloth-cap and smoke-stack image, but he has now taken to management the same respected, forthright views. His playing record is unequalled and it encompassed a period when Britain were the best in the world.

Born on 22 April 1939, Murphy signed for St Helens on his sixteenth birthday and glided straight into the first team. By nineteen he was the youngest player ever to tour Australia. With Murphy playing three Tests at scrumhalf, Britain won the series 2–1.

The following season he scored four tries in a 50–15 thrashing of France at Leigh. It was a boom time. St Helens won the championship, retained it in 1960, and a year later walked down the thirty-nine steps at Wembley with the Challenge Cup.

There was variety in Murphy's game. As a conscript in the RAF, he played Rugby Union, the services being the only arena in which the two codes can mix with the blessing of the RFU. Playing against the top Union clubs, his tactical horizons were broadened.

St Helens continued to dominate in the mid-1960s. Under Murphy's captaincy they won the League championship in 1965, held onto it in 1966, and completed a 1966 double when they beat Wigan 21–2 to win the Challenge Cup at Wembley.

In 1967, though, after a series of disputes and incidents, Murphy left St Helens, and went 10 miles down the East Lancs Road to Leigh, a proud, but slumbering, club. At twenty-seven, he was not only player but coach as well. In four seasons he revamped the playing side, bringing a couple of old team-mates from St Helens to Hilton Park. In 1971 Leigh and Murphy reached the Challenge Cup final against the odds-on favourites Leeds. With a masterly display of tactical acumen, Murphy won the Lance Todd trophy for the Man of the Match although forced onto the bench for the later part of the match after a late tackle, and Leigh won easily by 24–7.

Announcing his International retirement after seventeen tries in twenty-seven appearances for Great Britain from 1958 to 1971, it seemed that Murphy's playing days were numbered. He had moved again, to the 'Wires' at Warrington, who play at the delightfully named Wilderspool. Murphy had made twenty-six appearances for Britain whilst with St Helens; his twenty-seventh was during his early days at Warrington, who, not unnaturally, were next for the treatment. In 1972–73 they won the League Championship. The following year they too reached Wembley, where they beat Featherstone Rovers 24–9. Murphy had become the first to captain three clubs to victory at Wembley. He had played in three positions – centre, stand off and scrumhalf – and had scored in each of the four winning finals, compiling a total of five goals and a try. That season Warrington won four trophies. But, at the age of thirty-five, it was time for Murphy to quit as a player. Warrington were good enough to go back to Wembley in 1975, but they handed the trophy on to Widnes, a few fields down the Mersey. Murphy, the coach, sat frustrated on the bench.

With his reputation for restoration work, Murphy's services were eagerly sought. Town councillors will tell you that, as with football, a major Rugby League team is good publicity for the town. It keeps the place on the map and is good for trade. Salford sought the potion in 1978, but it wasn't a success. A second spell at Leigh brought the reward of the Division One championship in 1981–82. Murphy seemed settled. Leigh also won the Lancashire Cup. However, at the start of the 1982–83 season, the Wigan directors called. There were weeds growing out of the terraces at Central Park. Sure enough, Wigan were revived. They won the John Player Trophy immediately, beating Leeds 15–4.

1983–84 brought further glory. Wigan, who had not been to Wembley for the Challenge Cup final since 1970, were there again, back on Murphy's old stamping ground.

Murphy is now also a respected summarizer for BBC TV. But somewhere in the back of his mind there must be the thought of restoring the national team. Australia have won the last ten successive Tests against Britain. Now that really would be a challenge.

FACTFILE

Born 22 April 1939, St Helens, Lancashire, England

Clubs St Helens, Leigh, Warrington
Challenge Cup 1961 (St Helens), 1966 (St Helens; captain), 1971 (Leigh; captain), 1974 (Warrington; captain)
League Championship 1959 (St Helens), 1960 (St Helens), 1965 (St Helens), 1966 (St Helens), 1973 (Warrington)
Great Britain international appearances 27 (1958–71)
International debut 14 June 1958, v. Australia, Sydney (lost 25–8)
Lance Todd Award 1971, Leigh v. Leeds

*Murphy played in twenty major finals for St Helens
*Murphy has made six Wembley appearances as player and coach, losing twice. His full Wembley record is as follows:

As player		
1961	St Helens *v.* Wigan	won 12–6
1966	St Helens *v.* Wigan	won 21–2
1971	Leigh *v.* Leeds	won 24–7
1974	Warrington *v.* Featherstone	won 24–9
As coach		
1975	Warrington *v.* Widnes	lost 7–14
1984	Wigan *v.* Widnes	lost 6–19

Alex Murphy, who has played in the winning side in the Challenge Cup for four different clubs

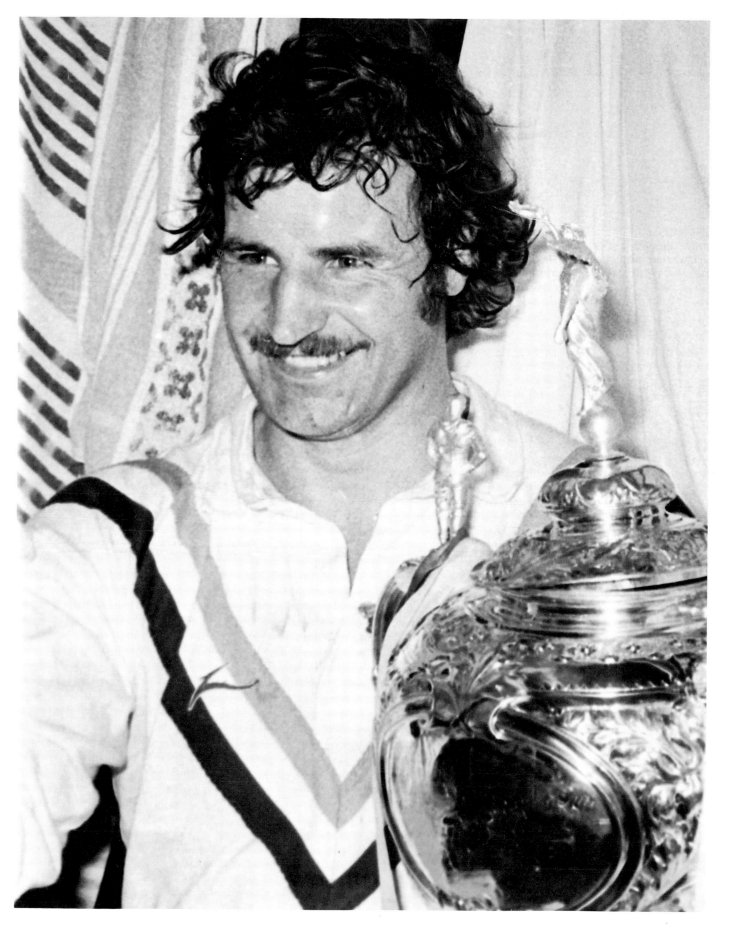

Martina Navratilova

There is a strange dilemma surrounding Martina Navratilova. Many feel that computer-oriented fitness and diet programmes, the build of a middleweight boxer, the accompanying troupe and the verbal outbursts at authority have no place in tennis. Others admire a player who has, in recent years, compiled such an outstanding record that a defeat becomes front-page news.

Her ability is in no doubt. With the exception of Jahangir Khan, she entered 1984 as perhaps the outstanding champion in world sport. But the origin of many of her complexities may lie in her decision in 1975, at barely eighteen years old, to leave her family in Czechoslovakia and settle, alone, in the United States. It was a momentous and courageous decision, and it may account for spells of possible insecurity and its side effects.

Martina tells of her early life in her autobiography:

Tennis was not my first love. My family lived in the Krkonose Mountains in Czechoslovakia. My mother's side of the family was more athletic, and my mother (an official with the Czech Tennis Authority) encouraged me to skate and run. She was a top-class skier, gymnast and tennis player, and my grandmother, Agnes Semanska, was ranked in the Czech tennis top ten for a few years. My favourite sport was ice hockey. It was exciting and the Czechs were good at it. But it wasn't a sport for girls. So I skied a lot and had I stayed in the mountains, that's what I would have liked to be.

When I was five, there were three indoor courts in Prague. My stepfather [her parents had divorced] used to haul clay there, and I used to play tennis against the wall. At seven, the woman who ran the courts encouraged me, and my stepfather taught me after work.

He used to take me round tournaments from the age of nine, on the back of a 175-cc motorbike, until I was fourteen. That year I was national champion for the age group, and at sixteen the Czech Federation allowed me to play tennis in the USA. It was the time of the new Virginia Slims pro tournament,

with Billie Jean King, Rosie Casals and Margaret Court. I wanted to play against them, but my Federation did not recognize them. In 1973 my daily expenses were $11 a day, and $13 in New York.

I used to eat at the courts to save money, and go on spending sprees. I went to a grocer's store in Fort Lauderdale, and bought ham, cheese, milk and orange; the bill came to $5. That was two days' work to my family. I put on 20 lb in three weeks. Every one commented, but I felt more feminine.

In the next two years I became one of the best players in the world. I adopted US slang, music, food and clothes. The American players were my friends. Then my Federation said that I had got lazy. They said I was too Americanized, and they were even going to deny me the chance to enter the US Open in 1975, until Jan Kodes [the 1973 Wimbledon champion] intervened on my behalf.

It was at that US Open that I defected.

What had she achieved up to that point? Martina was world No. 4, having led Czechoslovakia to the Federation Cup. She had reached the final of the 1975 French Open. Her first major title was with Ivan Molina of Colombia in the mixed doubles at Stade Roland Garros. She had certainly come a long way since losing the Wimbledon junior final of 1973 to Ann Kiyomura.

Though Martina won the Wimbledon doubles title in 1976 with Chris Evert, who, at that stage, was undoubtedly the better player, the rehabilitation was uneasy. She slipped to No. 5 in the 1976 world rankings, and was No. 4 in 1977. Her weight shot up to 12 st 5 lb. She had become somewhat rudderless.

Initially she turned for help and advice to top golfer Sandra Haynie. Sandra, used to such matters, became her manager and agent. Martina, slimline and with Tinling clothes, won Wimbledon for the first time in 1978, beating Chris Evert in the final. The 'big two' met again the following year and the result was the same. Not a word

---

FACTFILE

Born 18 October 1956, Prague, Czechoslovakia

World ranking 1975 fourth, 1976 fifth, 1977 fourth, 1978 first, 1979 first, 1980 fourth, 1981 third, 1982 first, 1983 first

Wimbledon Championships
  Singles 1978 beat Chris Evert, 2–6, 6–4, 7–5
           1979 beat Chris Evert-Lloyd, 6–4, 6–4
           1982 beat Chris Evert-Lloyd, 6–1, 3–6, 6–2
           1983 beat Andrea Jaeger, 6–0, 6–3
           1984 beat Chris Evert-Lloyd, 7–6, 6–2
  Doubles 1976 (with Chris Evert)
           1979 (with Billie Jean King)
           1981 (with Pam Shriver)
           1982 (with Pam Shriver)
           1983 (with Pam Shriver)
           1984 (with Pam Shriver)

French Championships
  Singles 1982 beat Andrea Jaeger, 7–6, 6–1
           1984 beat Chris Evert-Lloyd, 6–3, 6–1
  Doubles 1975 (with Christ Evert)
           1982 (with Anne Smith)
           1984 (with Pam Shriver)
  Mixed doubles 1974 (with I. Molina)

160

Australian Championships
  Singles 1981 beat Chris Evert-Lloyd, 6–7, 6–4, 7–5
           1983 beat Kathy Jordan, 6–2, 7–6
  Doubles 1980 (with Betsy Nagelsen)
           1981 (with Pam Shriver)
           1983 (with Pam Shriver)

United States Championships
  Singles 1983 beat Chris Evert-Lloyd, 6–1, 6–3
           1984 beat Chris Evert-Lloyd, 4–6, 6–4, 6–4
  Doubles 1977 (with Betty Stove)
           1978 (with Billie Jean King)
           1980 (with Billie Jean King)
           1983 (with Pam Shriver)
           1984 (with Pam Shriver)

*Martina's earnings and record since the start of 1982 are as follows:

1982: Martina won ninety out of ninety-three singles matches, losing only to Chris Lloyd (Australian Open), Pam Shriver (US Open) and Sylvia Hanika (Avon Championships). She won fifteen of sixteen doubles tournaments, her total earnings for 1982 were $1,475,055.

1983: Martina won eighty-six out of eighty-seven singles matches, losing only to Kathy Horvath at the French Championships. She won thirteen of fourteen doubles tournaments. Her total earnings for 1983 were $1,456,030.

Her career earnings at the end of 1983 were $6,384,089 – a record for any tennis player, male or female.

1984: By 20 August Martina had won sixty-one of sixty-two singles matches, losing only to Hana Mandlikova at the Oakland tournament. Her total earnings for the year were already over $1,500,000.

about it appeared in the Czech papers. Her parents had to travel to stay with friends by the border so that they could watch the final on German television.

But in 1980 Martina was on the edge of a slump. Still the Americans would not grant her citizenship. She slipped from No. 1 to No. 4 in the world rankings. Tales of complacency were rife: writer Rita Mae Brown was her none too successful guide.

The nadir was reached in early 1981. Devoid of ambition and with her career on the start of a helter-skelter to nowhere, she was whitewashed 6–0, 6–0 by Chris Evert-Lloyd at Amelia Island, Florida.

Nancy Lieberman, US basketball star of the Dallas Diamonds, watched the debacle. A month later she happened to watch a similar lifeless practice for the French Open. The two spoke and Nancy became Martina's manager. 'Team Navratilova' was born.

The US citizenship came through in 1981. Renee Richards, the former Richard Raskind, became her coach. Martina closed 1981 with a victory in the Australian Open and opened 1982 with a win in the French Championships. Her mother came from Prague to watch Martina win Wimbledon amidst emotional scenes.

1983 was an awesome year. Only once was she beaten, by the precocious Kathy Horvath in the French Championships. The solution was football style – sack the manager. Out went Richards, in came Mike Estep, former world No. 14, a former doubles partner of Martina, whose full-time playing career was sadly ended by injury but who played with her at Wimbledon in 1984. Martina won Wimbledon again.

Three wins in the summer of 1983 brought special pleasure. Martina won the US Open for the first time, and she helped the USA to win both the Wightman Cup and the Federation Cup. The dog-loving girl who had thrown apples at the Soviet tanks in the streets of Prague, was proud that these team victories had brought success to her new home. And she was, at last, champion of her own country.

'Smartina'

Weekly Diet Chemistry Report for: Martina Navratilova: 1/03/83
(for her eyes only)

Caution: Smartina is a copyrighted and confidential computer program created especially for Martina Navratilova. Unauthorized use of this program and/or the information contained herein is strictly forbidden and unlawful.

Current diet chemistry recommendations for Washington Tournament

Protein	14% of daily calories
Fat	18% of daily calories
Carbohydrate	68% of daily calories
Alcohol	0% of daily calories

Special Haas peak performance nutrient mixes:
1   Formula A–5: breakfast/dinner
2   Formula Q–2: before matches
3   Formula Peak: as needed during matches
4   Formula Maxi: breakfast/lunch/dinner

Specific complex carbohydrates each day:
Code A–1: 2 cups
Code A–2: 4 ounces
Code A–3: 1 cup
Code C–5: $\frac{1}{4}$ cup

Code F–1: as desired

Animal protein sources each day:
Code 1: $\frac{1}{4}$ lb (broiled)
Code 2: $\frac{1}{4}$ lb (steamed)
Code 3: 3 tablespoons (raw)
Code 4: 1 tablespoon
Fresh fruits each day:
Z–2 and Z–8
Z–10: $\frac{1}{2}$ cup
Daily water intake:
Code 4

Eye on the ball, Martina Navratilova prepares to hit a backhand return during her 7–6, 6–2 win against Chris Evert-Lloyd during the final of the 1984 Wimbledon ladies singles championship

Blood chemistry profile analysis
Analysis of most recent blood chemistry profile (12/82) demonstrates sustained blood concentrations within Haas Peak Performance Range. Serum cholesterol ratios currently at Level A; triglycerides at Level A; glucose (fasting) at Level A. All other values are above Peak Performance Range. *Congratulations!*

Warning: Keep you daily caloric expenditure at Level Three during week of 1/3/83 !!!

Training pattern:
Code RH: 30 min./day
Code NL: $1\frac{1}{2}$ hour/day
Code MN: 1 hour/day

This is *Smartina* signing off. May the force be with you.

Team Navratilova at Wimbledon, 1984

Mike Estep, a thirty-three-year-old player and administrator, who has come into the team as coach following the departure of Renee Richards
Robert Haas, a thirty-four-year-old Miami-based PhD and nutritionist, who masterminds the computer program and her diet
Nancy Lieberman, the twenty-four-year-old American basketball star known as 'Lady Magic'. Her gift to Martina is the strange paradox of personal friendship and the ability to hate her opponents: 'The only red meat Martina eats is her opponents'
Rick Elstein, a thirty-two-year-old from the Syosset Tennis Academy, Long Island, New York. His speciality is the dynamics of movement; he is concentrating on Martina's reflexes
Pam Derderian, listed as Lieberman's agent, known to other players as the dog-walker because she looks after Martina's dogs

Jack Nicklaus

From his early days, Jack Nicklaus was determined to become the greatest golfer who ever lived and, having achieved nineteen major tournament victories, it can be firmly argued that he has realized his ambition.

Between 1961 and 1977 he was always in the top three of the US money list, with the exception of 1970 when he was fourth; he was the first golfer to reach $2 million and $3 million career earnings and he will certainly be the first to reach $4 million. The blond, overweight boy with a crewcut who won his first tournament – the Ohio Open – at the age of sixteen as an amateur is now a mature, highly tuned athlete with an aptitude for business.

In 1960, in his very first US Open at Cherry Hills, he was second to Palmer when still an amateur. He turned professional the following year and won the title at Oakmont, beating Palmer in a play-off. He won the PGA and the Masters in the same year – 1963 – then went to Augusta for the 1965 Masters to give possibly his best championship performance. In poor weather he returned 67, 71, 64, 69, for a new Masters record of 271 (since matched by Ray Floyd) and a record-winning margin – 9 strokes. Bobby Jones, who saw Nicklaus that year, described it as the 'greatest performance in golf history'.

In 1966 he joined Sarazen, Hogan and Player as the only men to have won the Masters, the PGA the US Open and the British Open, which he won at Muirfield, a course he came to regard as one of the fairest in the world. Nicklaus even named his own course at Columbus, Ohio, Muirfield Village.

His brilliant 65 in the last round of the 1967 US Open brought him the title at the expense of Arnold Palmer; it was a respected but not a popular win. For a while Nicklaus went into decline until he arrived at St Andrews for the 1970 Open. He won after a play-off with Doug Sanders and it was the start of the most lucrative period of his career.

He changed his image. He slimmed down (no more nicknames like 'Ohio Fats' and the 'Golden Blob'). He lost some length from the tee but remained one of the longest hitters, with an average of around 250 to 260 yards. He won the 1975 Masters after starting the final day 1 shot behind Tom Weiskopf and 3 ahead of Johnny Miller. He beat off the challenge of both with a superb 15-foot putt on the sixteenth.

His duels with Tom Watson in 1977 have been well chronicled. Watson, coming to the fore as a major talent, won at Augusta and then clinched the British Open at Turnberry after a fascinating four rounds in which they had kept pace with each other. The title was decided on the final green, when Nicklaus birdied a long putt, whilst Watson, one up going to the last, holed his from close range to win.

Peter Alliss rates Nicklaus higher than any of his contemporaries for his mental abilities. 'His concentration can seldom be faulted; his nerve has lasted; his thinking about how to play course and shot is incisive; his will to win has kept him going.'

Nicklaus slipped out of the limelight in the 1979 season when he finished seventy-first on the US money list, with no wins on the Tour for the first time ever. The next year he was back. He re-

FACTFILE

Born 21 January 1940, Columbus, Ohio, USA

'Big Four' wins 17
British Open 1966, 1970, 1978
US Open 1962, 1967, 1972, 1980
US Masters 1963, 1965, 1966, 1972, 1975 (record)
US PGA 1963, 1971, 1973, 1975, 1980
Ryder Cup matches 24 (1969–81)
World Cup
  Team 1963, 1964, 1966, 1967, 1971, 1973
  Individual 1963, 1964, 1971

British Open record
1966	Muirfield	282	1st
1967	Hoylake	280	2nd
1968	Carnoustie	291	2nd (joint)
1969	Lytham	285	6th (joint)
1970	St Andrews	283	1st
1971	Birkdale	283	5th (joint)
1972	Muirfield	279	2nd
1973	Troon	280	4th
1974	Lytham	287	3rd
1975	Carnoustie	280	3rd (joint)
1976	Birkdale	285	2nd (joint)
1977	Turnberry	269	2nd
1978	St Andrews	281	1st

(He also finished joint 34th in 1962, 3rd in 1963, 2nd in 1964, joint 12th in 1965, joint 2nd in 1979, joint 4th in 1980, joint 23rd in 1981, joint 10th in 1982, joint 29th in 1983 and joint 31st in 1984.)

*Nicklaus first appeared in the US Amateur Championship at the age of fifteen in 1955
*His first prize money was $33.33 for tying in fiftieth place in the 1962 Los Angeles Open
*His first appearance as a pro in England was at Hillside, Southport, in 1962
*Between 1962 and 1979 he played in seventy-two major championships, only seventeen times finishing out of the first ten, and was in the first three on thirty-nine occasions
*He was non-playing captain of the 1983 Ryder Cup team
*His father was a pharmacist and a keen golfer
*He is the only man to have successfully defended the Masters title
*He is the only man to have won all four major tournaments twice
*He has won more major honours than any other golfer
*His hobbies are fishing and collecting good wines
*He is described as a good winner, but a superb loser
*Nicklaus on his retirement: 'I can say now that I'll know when to get out. But when that time comes I may not know'

Jack Nicklaus at his favourite event, the British Open. Here he drives from the tee at the 1976 championship at Royal Birkdale

emerged to take the US Open and the PGA, though in Britain there was a glimpse of Nicklaus in his 1979 form when he shot an 83 in the first round of the Open at Sandwich. 'All my life,' said one commentator, 'I've wanted to play golf like Jack Nicklaus. Now I find him playing like me.'

It has been estimated that he has an annual gross revenue of $300 million from his various companies. Even so, it was a magnificent gesture, immediately before the 1982 Australian Open, for him to donate his $50,000 appearance money to the prize fund to help golf in that country. His own enterprise is called Golden Bear Inc.

A regular visitor to Australia in the 1970s, he prepared for the 1978 Australian Open by catching a 616-lb black marlin off Cairns in a six-hour battle. Fishing was his major relaxation. He won his sixth title that week.

Tales of Jack Nicklaus's search for perfection are numerous. In 1972, for example, he was practising for the Open at Muirfield when his caddie, Jimmy Dickinson, moved slightly. Halfway through his putting stroke Nicklaus stopped and, without looking up, inquired, 'New shoes, Jim?' Embarrassed, Jimmy said, 'Yes.' 'Better put some oil on them,' said Nicklaus. 'They squeak. I'll be able to hear you moving around when I'm putting.'

Prince Obolensky

Most rugby clubs have an Obolensky. More often than not, he will be the third- or fourth-team winger, well past his prime, comfortably built, marginally quicker than the wife over 100 metres, and scorer of many a 2-yard try. Later in the evening, Obolensky, now a spectacular drinker and soon to become a curry-shop raconteur, has assailed everyone within earshot – the 2-yard try has become a 50-yard sprint with the opposition closing in, but he heroically beats them to the touchdown.

The following morning Obolensky, very frail and fragile, and equally sore, wonders how he got his name and just who was Obolensky? The complete opposite to the person in question is the answer, and it is the biggest compliment anyone can receive.

Prince Alexander Obolensky was England's right wing in rugby internationals just before the Second World War. He did not play on many occasions, but he did enough in one match – against New Zealand in 1936 – to earn a permanent place in the history of the Rugby Football Union.

'Obo' was the son of Prince Alexis Obolensky and was born in Petrograd – now Leningrad – on 17 February 1916. His father was an officer in the Imperial Horse-Guards. During the Russian Revolution, Obolensky came to Britain and went to Oxford University, where, in 1935, he won a blue whilst still a Russian citizen. He also won a blue two years later. Cambridge won both matches easily, and Obolensky thankfully missed the dreadful 0–0 draw in 1936. He attended Kent College and Brasenose College.

Inauspicious as his university match career was – Oxford were going through the same rut as the Cambridge Boat Race crew in the eighties – Obolensky also played with the London club Rosslyn Park. He was selected for the Barbarians in 1936 and 1937, scoring his only try against the East Midlands in a 13–3 defeat.

Very fast and unorthodox, Obolensky was still attracting the selectors' attention, even though representative games found him on the losing side and completely starved of the ball. The England selectors, searching for pace to complement two large centre three-quarters, turned to the Oxford undergraduate for the match against New Zealand on 2 January 1936 at Twickenham. He still had Russian citizenship, but rugby men were not worried about that in those days. England had made a wise choice.

The description of the match is often better chronicled and less biased if viewed from the opposition bench. The New Zealand rugby book, *Men in Black*, describes part of the game:

This game in English circles is still known as Obolensky's match . . .

England was much the better team and deserved to win by a big margin. New Zealand were in the match for the first twenty minutes, but England then opened the scoring. From a scrum the ball went along the chain [three-quarter line] to Obolensky, who rounded his opposite number Ball, then fullback Gilbert, to score a great try after sprinting 30 yards . . .

Two minutes from half time, Cranmer made a break in midfield and passed to fellow centre Candler. Obolensky took Candler's pass on the right wing, close to touch, and, seeing his way blocked, checked and cut infield, wrong-footing the defence. He ran round Gilbert, then evaded Mitchell on a diagonal run to score on the opposite wing to his own, 8 yards in from touch.

England won the match 13–0, the first time they had ever beaten New Zealand. Film coverage and the 72,500 crowd bear witness to the second try as being the finest ever seen at Twickenham.

Obolensky played only four times for England, all in 1936, and in his last three games he didn't touch the ball. On leaving university he began a career in the RAF. Transition to service life initially meant little time for rugby, but he was looking forward to re-establishing himself for the 1939 season once exams and training had been completed.

On 29 March 1940 a Hurricane piloted by Obolensky crashed on landing in Norfolk. He was the first Rugby Union international to lose his life during the war. He was just twenty-four and at a stage when his rugby life was about to begin.

Tom Webster, cartoonist for the *Daily Mail*, commemorates 'Obolensky's Match'

FACTFILE

Born 17 February 1916, Petrograd (now Leningrad), Russia
Died 29 March 1940, East Anglia, England

England international career

Debut 1936, *v.* Ireland
Appearances 4 (1936, *v.* Ireland, New Zealand, Scotland and Wales)
Tries 2
Tour 1936 Argentina

Prince Obolensky, whose two famous tries defeated the 1936 All Blacks

Al Oerter

Al Oerter has the finest record of all Olympians. Four times he competed in the discus, and four times he stood on the highest rostrum of all. To him the Olympics were the 'big one' and what happened during the Olympiad – the term used for the four years in between each Games – was largely incidental.

After finishing second in the 1956 Olympic trials, Oerter, born in Astoria, New York, and living in West Babylon in the same state, travelled to Melbourne with hopes of reaching the final. He unleashed the three best throws of the competition whilst favourites Consolini and Gordien were still eyeing each other, and the twenty-year-old American slipped back to West Babylon with the gold medal. Indeed, the only serious threat came at the medal ceremony when, realizing what he had accomplished, he became 'emotionally unstable'.

In 1957 he won the first of his US discus titles, then was involved in a near fatal car crash. Recovering none too quickly, he used the 1959 Pan-American Games as a platform for Olympic selection, taking the gold medal.

The Olympic season began in similar vein to 1956. For the second time he finished second in the US trials, and for the second time went on to win the gold medal. Rink Babka beat him in the trials; then, in the competition proper, a piece of advice from Babka unearthed a story in the Owens–Long tradition. As Oerter struggled, Babka suggested that the position of his left arm was causing Oerter to throw the discus off-balance. Oerter overtook Babka with his fifth throw, had the courtesy to wish Babka good luck, and silently hoped that Babka's final throw would fall short. It did, by 3 feet 10 inches.

Oerter became the first thrower to pass the magic 200-foot barrier, with 5 inches to spare, in Los Angeles in 1962. It was his first world record. It lasted seventeen days until the Russian Vladimir Trusenyev spoilt the celebrations, but within twenty-seven days Oerter had recovered the record.

Going for the third gold medal in Tokyo in 1964, Oerter followed the predictable pattern with a second place in the US Olympic trials. But neck and back strains had multiplied over the years and Oerter was forced to wear a neck brace. He then received a rib cartilage injury just a week before the Olympic competition. In addition, the genuine threat of the new world record holder, Ludvik Danek, a Czech, unbeaten in forty-five meetings, had to be faced. Conservation of energy was necessary.

Wrapped up like the proverbial Egyptian mummy, Oerter began well, needing just one throw to qualify, an Olympic best of 198 feet 8 inches. In the final he was third as he came up to his fifth throw. Deciding that the pain barrier would have to be well and truly broken, he took the lead and held on in the last round to beat Danek.

Around this time British supporters had a rare opportunity to watch the Olympic legend in action. Competing for New York against London in the Olympic year of 1964, he won the discus in the very first athletics meeting to be staged at London's Crystal Palace, following the permanent move of major events from the White City.

A computer systems analyst, Oerter devoted more time to his career after the Tokyo Games, allowing his various ailments some breathing space. But the fact that no athlete had won the same Olympic title in four Games was a challenge he couldn't ignore. There were more of the familiar struggles to reach Mexico City. For the fourth time Oerter failed to win the US trials and yet again he won the gold medal. The man he beat this time was the thirty-one-year-old world record holder, Jay Silvester, whose best was some 14 feet farther than Oerter had ever thrown.

In the final Silvester, unlike previous champions, opened with a throw which was nearly 2 feet farther than Oerter had ever heaved before. The Oerter response was typical. On his third throw he reached 212 feet 6 inches, 5 feet beyond his previous personal best. Silvester had 'gone home' – three no throws were a weak response to the pressure. The fourth gold was assured. Silvester was heard to mumble, 'You never throw against Oerter and expect to win, you just hope.'

Danek and Silvester were delighted with the news of Oerter's retirement after the 1968 Olympics. Ricky Bruch and others decided that steroids would win medals – the IOC clamped down. Oerter enjoyed retirement.

That was until 1976, when, with the advent of jogging and marathons, Old America woke up and began organizing proper veterans events for those of forty and over. In 1977 Oerter became world veterans champion with a throw of 60.36 metres, 11 metres farther than the previous championship best.

In 1980 America was in turmoil, wondering whether to attend the Moscow Olympics. In the end they didn't go. Politically the world could understand. But the decision may well have spoilt another remarkable chapter in Olympic history. Technically still superb and in fine condition, Oerter threw 69.46 metres in 1980 to rank No. 2 in the world that year. He entered the Olympic trials, a rather low-key affair because the Americans had already decided not to go. Al Oerter, aged forty-three, finished fourth and, had the competition been for real, who is to say that Oerter would not have made the trip? After all, the common denominator throughout all his Olympic trials was not to win, but to take charge of matters from there on. There was also a distinct rumour that Oerter fancied Los Angeles in the summer of 1984. He told reporters, 'I have to think positively, I'm the right side of forty-eight!'

FACTFILE

Born 19 September 1936, Astoria, New York, USA

Olympic Games
Gold: Discus 184 ft 11 in (1956)
      Discus 194 ft 2 in (1960)
      Discus 200 ft 1 in (1964)
      Discus 212 ft 6 in (1968)

Pan-American Games Gold: Discus (1959)

United States discus titles 1957, 1959, 1960, 1962, 1964, 1966

World discus records
61.10 m (Los Angeles, 18 May 1962)
62.44 m (Chicago, 1 July 1962)
62.62 m (Walnut, California, 27 April 1963)
62.94 m (Walnut, California, 25 April 1964)

Best throw 69.46 m (1980)

Four times Olympic champion in the discus, Al Oerter took as much pleasure in being selected as one of the official Olympic flag bearers at the Los Angeles Olympics in 1984

Steve Ovett

'Sit back and enjoy us, we won't be around for ever.' That remark was made by Steve Ovett, world 1500-metre record holder since 1980 and Olympic 800-metre champion. The subject was how Ovett, Coe and Steve Cram – English through and through – had managed to dominate the World Championships, the Olympic Games and the world record charts since 1979.

Somehow Ovett had acquired a 'bad guy' image. Pilloried by the media for refusing to give interviews, his answer was constructive: 'There is, in my opinion, no point in spending an hour explaining how I lost [which he rarely did], when the obvious remedy is to forget it as soon as possible, and try and win next time.' But the *enfant terrible* tag stuck. 'Perhaps,' said Ovett, 'the best thing would be if I ran in all black and my opponents in all white.'

His introduction to 'athletics' was at the age of five. 'Smashed a kid over the head with a milkbottle, had to run like hell to avoid his mother,' said Ovett.

He is Brighton born and bred; his father runs a fruit stall, founded by Steve's grandfather, in the Brighton open market. Ovett ran for Brighton AC and, from 1981, for Brighton Phoenix. In the winter he is a familiar sight pounding the Brighton seafront with the local surfers club, and in summer, not the high-altitude camps, but Stanmer and Preston Parks, altitude 50–200 feet.

Running for Sussex, Ovett won his first major title, the 400 metres, at the All England Schools Championships, that masterpiece of schoolmasterly organization and still the athletics spectacle of the year. He was European junior 800-metre champion in 1972. He ran his first sub-four-minute mile on 17 July 1974 at Harringay, for a UK junior record. At nineteen, he showed promise in the mile, but the two-lap race was where he thought the medals lay. A silver in the 1974 European Championships suggested that his theory was correct.

At the Montreal Olympics, Ovett finished fifth in the 800 metres. For someone developing a keen tactical sense, he found himself hopelessly boxed in at the bell.

After Montreal he decided to move up a distance. In May 1977 he lost an early season excursion against the American Steve Scott.

That was his last defeat over the 1500 metres and the mile for three years – forty-five successive wins.

The honours rolled in. Ovett won the 1977 World Cup – the unofficial world championship – in Düsseldorf. In 1978 he was European champion, and there was another infuriating silver in the 800 metres. Stepping up to the 2 miles, he relieved Brendan Foster of the world's best time. He dodged Coe. Or Coe dodged him.

1980 and the Moscow Olympics. With Coe v. Ovett, both British and the best, it did not matter that there were no Germans or Americans. However, the pair didn't read their scripts. They each won a gold medal, but not the one that the experts had predicted. Coe, 800-metre record holder, was beaten into second place by Ovett, whilst Steve, world record holder at 1500 metres, was beaten into third place by Coe and the East German Jurgen Straub. It was Ovett's first defeat over the distance since Jamaica in 1977. The great Olympic confrontation finished all square.

Four years on, and the Los Angeles Olympics. Ovett was still world record holder for the 1500 metres. Those who said that he could have the finish run out of him, as in the World Championships of 1983 when he finished fourth, should have heeded the case of Sydney Maree. At Cologne on 29 August 1983, Maree broke Ovett's world 1500-metre world record. Maree's tenure lasted precisely one week. Ovett's competitive edge was still there.

Perhaps he was too competitive for his own good. Suffering badly from the heat in the Los Angeles Coliseum, Ovett struggled gamely into the final to defend his Olympic 800-metre title. As Joachim Cruz took the gold medal, Ovett struggled to the finish line 80 metres adrift. He collapsed and was taken to hospital where he was detained for three days.

Courageously he recovered to enter the 1500 metres, his world record distance. Amazingly he qualified for the final through the heat and the heats. In the final, with a medal a distinct possibility, he ducked out towards the high-jump pit on the last lap. He returned to hospital for further painful rehabilitation. 'I just couldn't watch those races on TV,' he said.

He is much more at ease with the media these days. Indeed he is

---

FACTFILE

Born 9 October 1955, Brighton, Sussex, England

Olympic Games
Gold: 800 metres (1980)
Bronze: 1500 metres (1980)

European Championships
Gold: 1500 metres (1978)
Silver: 800 metres (1974, 1978)

World records
  1500 metres   3:32.11 (eq) (1980)
                3:31.4 (1980)
                3:30.77 (1983)
  Mile 3:48.8 (1980)
       3:48.4 (1981)

*Despite all the talk of the rivalry between the two great British athletes, Ovett and Coe, it is perhaps surprising to see that before the 1984 Olympics they had only met each other on six occasions. Ovett was in front of Coe three times:

British Schools cross-country (Intermediate), 25 March 1972
Ovett 2nd, Coe 10th
European Championships (Prague), 31 August 1978
800 metres: Ovett 2nd, Coe 3rd
Olympic Games (Moscow), 26 July 1980
800 metres: Ovett 1st, Coe 2nd
Olympic Games (Moscow), 1 August 1980
1500 metres: Coe 1st, Ovett 3rd
Olympic Games (Los Angeles), 6 August 1984
800 metres: Coe 2nd, Ovett 8th
Olympic Games (Los Angeles), 11 August 1984
1500 metres: Coe 1st, Ovett retired

Steve Ovett beats Seb Coe (254) and the hometown runner Nicolai Kirov (707) to prove his tactical mastery over the 800-metre field at the 1980 Moscow Olympics

almost one of them – he owns sports shops. Of his supposed off-handedness, he says, 'It had got to the stage when I was beginning to sound like a cross between Attila the Hun and Genghis Khan. I wouldn't want kids to think that.'

Steve Ovett, unusually for an Olympic champion, does not have a display cabinet. He gave his gold medals to children in hospital. The other medals he donates to children in need, and as prizes for athletics club competitions.

Jesse Owens

One of sports most quoted phrases is 'Records are made to be broken'. The greatness of James Cleveland Owens was that the records he set took athletes twenty-five years to overcome. And in more than one event too.

Known as Jesse, simply because it sounded like his initials, Owens had the same pedigree as another of his contemporaries, Joe Louis, the world heavyweight boxing champion. He also was the son of an Alabama cotton picker and one of a large family. His basic athletic training was classic – as one of eight, he could use the old cliché 'if you were last in the queue, you got no food.'

Born on 12 September 1913, he was, by the age of eighteen, an outstanding athlete. He had a wind-assisted recording of 10.3 seconds for the 100 metres and had long jumped to within 1 inch of 25 feet. He was now enrolled at Ohio State University, where Jack Nicklaus was later to pursue less frenetic activity, in 1933 Jesse won the American long-jump title with a leap of 24 feet 6¾ inches. He retained his title the following year with an improvement in distance of 6 inches and set a world indoors record for the long jump, but those were the early days of indoor facilities.

Owens's career in 1935 and 1936, when he was to set nine world records, was punctuated by two achievements which were to remain unchallenged until the emergence of Carl Lewis in 1982. On 25 May 1935, representing Ohio State University in the Western Athletic Conference Championships, Owens broke six world records within the space of one hour. The timetable read:

3.15 pm	100 yards: Equalled the world record of 9.4 seconds
3.25 pm	Long jump: Set new world record of 26 feet 8¼ inches with his first and only jump
3.45 pm	220 yards: Set new world record of 20.3 seconds, which also beat the existing time for the 200 metres
4.00 pm	220-yard hurdles: Set new world record of 22.6 seconds, which also beat the existing time for the 220-metre hurdles

The city of Ann Arbor is still grateful for the publicity. As for Owens, he was, he said, suffering from a bad back.

A year later Owens was in Berlin for the Olympic Games. He was in action for six days and won four gold medals. The catalogue was:

2 August	100-metre heat: Won in 10.3 seconds (equalled Olympic record)
	100-metre quarter final: Won in 10.2 seconds (equalled world record, but wind-assisted)
3 August	100-metre semifinal: Won in 10.4 seconds
	100-metre final: Gold medal in 10.3 seconds
4 August	200-metre heat: Won in 21.1 seconds (new Olympic record)
	Long-jump qualifying competition: Won with third and final jump
	Long-jump final: Gold medal with sixth and final jump of 26 feet 5 inches
5 August	200-metre semifinal: Won in 20.7 seconds
	200-metre final: Gold medal in 20.7 seconds
6 August	4 × 100-metre relay: Gold medal in 39.8 seconds

Rumours were, and still are, that Hitler, disgusted with Owens's annihilation of his 'Aryan' race, refused to present the medals. It was stated that Hitler refused to hand medals to black athletes. Two facts, however, are known. Owens was at pains to play down any incident, both during and after the Games. And Hitler's failure to recognize or acknowledge certain winning athletes led the Olympic Committee to write to him. They pointed out that he was their guest of honour, that he should show no partizanship, and acknowledge all winners or none.

Certainly the Nazi government tried to turn the Games into a propaganda vehicle for the glorification of their own ideals. A story has it that Hans Wollke, the shot-put gold medallist, who was a German policeman, came out of his meeting with Hitler three ranks higher than when he had gone in.

Hitler did give medals to his own German victors and the host nation finished ahead of the United States in the medals table, the first time that the United States had failed to hold that position. But scrutiny of the results featuring Owens shows that although a

---

FACTFILE

Born 12 September 1913, Danville, Alabama, USA
Died 31 March 1980, Tucson, Arizona, USA

Olympic Games
Gold: 100 metres (1936)
     200 metres (1936)
     Long jump (1936)
     4 × 100-metre relay (1936)

World records
  100 yards 9.4 s (eq) (1935)
  100 metres 10.2 s (1936)
  220 yards (straight) 20.3 s (1935)
  200 metres (straight) 20.3 s (1935)
  220-yard hurdles (straight) 22.6 s (1935)
  200-metre hurdles (straight) 22.6 s (1935)
  Long jump 26 ft 8¼ in (1935)

*Owens's very last race as an amateur was at the White City, London, on 15 August 1936 (the Olympic Games were still going on in Berlin at the time).

90,000 turned out to watch the United States beat the British Empire 11–3 in a challenge match, in which three world records were broken.

Owens's only event was in the 4 × 100-yard relay, in which he ran third leg in a team that included F. Wykoff, M. I. Glickman and R. H. Metcalfe. Three members of the team were in the US team that won the Olympic title less than a week earlier, in a world record time of 39.8 seconds – a record that stood for twenty years. That day, at the White City, their time for the unconventional event was 37.4 seconds (40.9 equivalent for 4 × 100 metres).

The three world records broken by the US relay team were the 4 × 880 yards (they also claimed the 4 × 800-metre record the same time) and the 4 × one mile.

Jesse Owens, without the benefit of starting blocks, still clocked 20.7 seconds to win the 200-metre gold medal at the 1936 Olympics

German, Luz Long, won a silver in the long jump, there were no German medallists in either the 100 or the 200 metres, and their sprint relay team was beaten into third place. It seems that Hitler's aides, Goering and Goebbels, were more belligerent. In the case of the latter, in his own newspaper, *Der Angriff* (*The Attack*), he described the American black athletes as 'Auxiliaries', and the medals they won were deliberately omitted from the medal charts.

Owens, meanwhile, had formed a lasting friendship with Long. It was Long who advised him to change his run-up markings during the long-jump qualification after Owens had fouled on his first two of three qualifying jumps, and again after he himself had equalled Owens's best of 25 feet 9¾ inches in the final itself.

The old White City was the scene of Owens's last competition just over a week after Berlin. He then turned professional, appearing as a supporting act to the Harlem Globetrotters and, because of his fast start, racing against and beating racehorses over 100 metres. He founded a home for destitute Negroes and made a fine career for himself in radio and television and as a public relations officer in Chicago.

Above all, he believed in the Olympic Creed. It is ironic that all his victories should have been received amidst political traumas. He died, after a long illness, on 31 March 1980 at Tucson, Arizona – Olympic year. His country did not attend the Olympics. He would have understood why, but he would have been disappointed.

Arnold Palmer

Arnold Palmer during his career was the most exciting golfer in the world. He made golf a major television and spectator sport in the States and when he entered the 1960 British Open at St Andrews he revived interest in and the prestige of the tournament.

Club golfers could identify with Palmer. His swing was not classical; he rarely finished two swings in the same way. Henry Cotton said that he finished 'on his knees' and had 'little style'. An American writer compared Palmer's arrival on the tee with that of a boxer climbing into a ring. His game had a powerful, bruising nature. A great putter, depending on confidence rather than the delicate touch like Locke and Jones, Palmer was at his peak in the early 1960s.

After turning pro in 1955, he won his first event, the Canadian Open. Between 1957 and 1972 he was never out of the top ten on the US money list. He won his first major tournament – the Masters at Augusta – in 1958; it was the tournament that always produced the best in him. In 1960 he led until the final two holes when he slipped one behind Ken Venturi. Palmer produced two birdie 3s to win by a stroke. It produced the feeling among his supporters, 'Arnie's Army', that he was a formidable last-round player – 'Arnie's Charge'.

In the 1962 Masters, Palmer was in a play-off against Dow Finsterwald and Gary Player. At the turn Player was 3 up on Palmer with Finsterwald away out of it. In the home nine Palmer shot 31 and won by 3 strokes.

On the last occasion when he won the Masters, in 1964, Palmer produced a memorable and thrilling performance to finish 6 ahead of Jack Nicklaus after rounds of 69, 68, 69 and 70 to become, along with Ballesteros, Nicklaus and Player, the only winner to have broken 70 in three rounds.

His one and only US Open win was another example of his amazing durability and never-say-die spirit. In 1960 at Cherry Hills Mike Souchak was 6 ahead of Palmer at the start of the final round. Palmer reached the turn in 30 with six birdies and parred his way home for a 65 and victory by 2 strokes from Nicklaus.

His exploits in Britain have been equally remarkable. In his first Open at St Andrews in 1960 Palmer finished second to Kel Nagle after a last-round 68, but admitted at the end of the third day that he had been out of contention. A year later at Royal Birkdale he won in poor weather, beating Dai Rees by a stroke. There is a plaque on the course commemorating one of Palmer's shots from the heavy rough on the sixteenth near the foot of a bank which he managed to land on the green.

Arguably Palmer's finest performance came in the 1962 Open at Troon. On the final day he dropped 2 strokes in four holes to allow Nagle to level. He then fired a 67 to lead by 5 shots at lunch. In the afternoon he produced a 69 to set a new Open record of 276 for the four rounds, and won by 6 strokes.

Undoubtedly Palmer's best performances came in the early sixties, but, despite a loss of putting form, he has continued to play simply because of his great love for the game. He was reluctant to join the Seniors Tour in the USA because he felt he still had a win or two left on the main Tour. He did, in fact, win the Canadian PGA in 1980. When he eventually joined the seniors he won their PGA in 1980 and the US PGA in 1981. At the age of fifty-three, his face leathery with so much sun, he led the Los Angeles Open after carding 66, 69, 68, but on the final day fell away with a 72 to finish tenth.

Palmer is a charismatic figure. Peter Alliss said of him, 'He always seemed to be ramming the putts home, driving with violent abandon and sending small bushes flying with recoveries from wild country.''

Bobby Jones – a great admirer of Palmer – said, 'If ever I needed an 8-foot putt and everything I owned depended on it, I would want Arnold Palmer to putt it for me.' Certainly at the peak of his career he seemed capable of willing the ball into the hole.

Michael Hobbs thought that Palmer made 'even the swinging of a golf club a dramatic event'. Palmer himself thought golf should be an exciting and dramatic game. In the 1964 World Matchplay Championship at Wentworth he was two up on Neil Coles with three to play. Palmer approached the sixteenth and took his driver when the situation demanded a 1 iron. He was asked why. 'Because it would have seemed chicken-hearted,' said Palmer, 'to take a 1

FACTFILE

Born 10 September 1929, Latrobe, Pennsylvania, USA

Big Four' wins 7
British Open 1961, 1962
US Open 1960
US Masters 1958, 1960, 1962, 1964
Ryder Cup matches 32 (1961–73; captain in 1963)
World Cup
    Team 1960, 1962, 1963, 1964, 1966, 1967
    Individual 1967
US Tour wins 61 (1955–73)
Overseas Tour wins 19

*Palmer won his first major title, the US Amateur, in 1954
*His first winnings as a pro were in the 1955 Fort Wayne Open. He tied for twenty-fifth place and won $145

*He was the first person to win $100,000 in a season
*In 1968 he became the first golfer to win $1,000,000 when he tied for second place in the PGA
*In 1970 he won the American Athlete of the Decade award
*Up to the end of 1982 Palmer had won over $2 million abroad and just under $2 million in the USA
*He never won the US PGA title, although was runner-up on three occasions
*His father was a steelworker
*He was a personal friend of the late President Eisenhower
*He was the first 'protégé' of the Mark McCormack Empire
*He was reported to be the most popular man on earth at the peak of his success
*He is recognized in the street in virtually every country in the world. There is a tea shop in Japan named after him

Arnold Palmer, who resurrected the British Open and brought the Americans back to Britain. He won the 1961 Open and retained the championship the following year

iron and I wanted to see if I could drive straight in that situation.' He won the match 2 and 1.

On another occasion he once climbed 7 metres up a red gumtree at the Victoria Golf Club in Australia to play a shot.

Australia is just one of the countries that has had the pleasure of entertaining and being entertained by Arnold Palmer. Terry Smith said, 'He has a missionary's zeal, and there isn't a golfing country in the world that hasn't thrilled to the sight of Palmer lashing shots through trees and lacing hooks round corners, with a short fast swing, made workable by very strong hands and arms.'

Pele

Few will doubt that Pele was the finest player of all time. At the age of sixteen he was playing in the Brazilian First Division, and the following year had won a winners' medal in the 1958 World Cup final. Yet he was to maintain this extraordinary level throughout his career with the development of the game in the United States, and was later to act as an ambassador for the sport, with world-wide coaching clinics in Third World countries.

Pele (real name Edson Arantes do Nascimento) was born into an impoverished family in the village of Tres Coracoes, in the state of Minas Gerais, some 150 miles northwest of São Paulo on 23 October 1940. His father had played for the local town team, FC Bauru, but Pele's first club was Noroeste. Their Di Brito, the former international inside forward, was impressed with his extraordinary ball skills, honed in the back streets, and his reading of the game, and took him to Santos, until then probably better known as the port for São Paulo. He was the regular No. 10 for Santos at just sixteen and a year later, in July 1957, played, and scored a goal, in his first game for Brazil against Argentina, who won 2–1

The 1958 World Cup was a fitting stage for his elevation into international class. He had missed the early group matches because of an injured knee, but returned to score the only goal of the game against Wales in the Gothenburg quarter final. In the semifinal he recorded a hat trick against France in Stockholm in a 5–2 win. The final produced an identical score line against Sweden, also in Stockholm. Pele hit the post in the first half, coolly juggled with the ball to score Brazil's third, then added the fifth goal with a brilliant header. Every wealthy club in Europe sought his signature, reigning European Cup holders Real Madrid to the fore, but the Brazilian Congress intervened and, with a novel idea, declared him an 'official treasure' and forbade his sale or trade!

Santos, thanks to Pele, and with a couple of decidedly useful cohorts in the internationals Coutinho and Pepe, plus international keeper Gilmar, dominated the world club scene in the early 1960s. Strangely in Brazil, there was no national League, each state running its own competition. Santos, belonging to the strong São Paulo championship, won the title on eleven occasions in the fourteen seasons from 1956 to 1969. They won the Brazilian Cup, symbol of the country's club strength, in 1962, 1963, 1964 and 1969. And twice Santos won the World Club Championship. In 1962 Benfica, the fine European champions, were overwhelmed by Pele. He scored twice in Santos's 3–2 win in the first leg, then a remarkable hat trick in the second leg in Lisbon's Stadium of Light. Santos won 8–4 on aggregate. Benfica had claimed their outstanding forward Eusebio to be the best in the world: Pele shattered that claim. A year later Santos retained the title with a win in a third match against AC Milan by a solitary goal, after each side had won their home encounters 4–2. Pele scored twice in the first leg, but was a victim of cynical Italian marking and missed the other two games. Coping with defending by inferior opponents was becoming a problem.

Matters came to a head in the 1966 World Cup in England. Brazil had retained the World Cup in Chile four years earlier, but Pele had suffered a severely pulled muscle in Brazil's second-group game in a scoreless draw with the eventual finalists, Czechoslovakia, after having created and scored a goal in the first match, a 2–0 win against Mexico. An older and more cautious Brazil had beaten the Czechs 3–1 in the final, without Pele's flair and influence. When they came to England in 1966 Brazil were clearly in decline and over-reliant on the skills of their No. 10. Pele scored the first goal of the tournament, against Bulgaria, at Goodison Park, but, un-

FACTFILE

Born 23 October 1940, Tres Coracoes, Minas Gerais, Brazil

First-class debut September 1956, Santos v. Corinthians
Total first-class appearances 1363
Total first-class goals 1281
International debut July 1957, v. Argentina
Total International appearances 111
International goals 97
Honours
  São Paulo League Championship: 1956, 1958, 1959, 1960, 1961, 1962, 1964, 1965, 1967, 1968, 1969
  World Cup: 1958, 1962, 1970
  World Club Championship: 1962, 1963
  Brazilian Cup: 1962, 1963, 1964, 1968

*Pele has played for Santos against the following Football League teams:

22.10.62	Sheffield Wednesday	won	4–2 (scored 1)
22. 9.69	Stoke City	won	3–2 (scored 2)
22. 9.70	West Ham United	drew	2–2 (scored 2)
2. 2.71	Chelsea	won	1–0
21. 2.72	Aston Villa	lost	1–2
23. 2.72	Sheffield Wednesday	won	2–0
4. 6.72	Newcastle United	won	4–2 (scored 3)
13. 6.72	Coventry City	drew	2–2 (scored 1)
12. 3.73	Fulham	lost	1–2 (scored 1)
14. 3.73	Plymouth Argyle	lost	2–3 (scored 1)

*The origin of the name Pele is not known – not even by Pele himself. However, one story has it that many Turks lived in the area where he was brought up, and when he played soccer as a young boy he would handle the ball instead of using his feet, and his opponents would cry 'Pé-le.' 'Pé' meaning 'foot' in Portuguese and 'le' meaning 'stupid' in Turkish

World-class Footballers in North America

Pele 31 goals in 56 games, 1975–77; Footballer of the Year, 1976
Beckenbauer 17 goals in 80 games, 1977–80; Footballer of the Year, 1977
Cruyff 25 goals in 53 games, 1979–81; Footballer of the Year, 1979
Eusebio 20 goals in 45 games, 1975–77
Best 54 goals in 139 games, 1976–81

Pele threads a pass through a bemused Czech defence during the 1970 World Cup finals in Mexico. In the same game, Pele almost scored from halfway after spotting Czech keeper Ivo Victor off his line

supported by feeble refereeing, became a victim of brutal tackles from the Bulgarian Zetchev and, in the game against Portugal, by the Portuguese right back Morais. He vowed never to play in the World Cup again.

Four years later, with marriage, a family, and the need for stabilizing finances after disasters with an incompetent business manager, Pele had changed his mind. There were many who thought that his contribution to his fourth World Cup to be his best. He found the net four times, including Brazil's 100th World Cup goal, a header after eighteen minutes in the final against Italy. With Pele in glorious form, Brazil triumphed 4–1, finding the final easier than some of the earlier games. Two other memories from those finals in Mexico were a remarkable attempt from halfway, past the roaming Czech goalkeeper, Ivo Victor, which went a foot past the post, and a bouncing header against England, which produced the save of all World Cups from Gordon Banks. With Pele as inspiration, football triumphed over negativity.

With 111 international appearances and 97 goals, Pele settled for club football with Santos. He had, in 1969, on the 19 November, scored his 1000th goal. Fittingly, it was for Santos and, ironically, from a penalty after being brought down by a Vasco da Gama defender. His final game for Santos was on 2 October 1974 against Ponte Preta. He said that he would play no more.

A year later he had reviewed the situation and decided on a comeback. Not with Santos, but with the North American Football League – razzmatazz, plastic pitches, astrodomes and all. A deal worth $4 million took him to New York Cosmos. In his late thirties, and in a less frenetic atmosphere, he was good for three more seasons. Three years to the day that he left Santos, he played his final game, for Cosmos against Santos. On a cool evening in New Jersey, 75,646 spectators showed their respect.

According to *The Guinness Book of Records*, Pele played in 1363 games. He scored 1281 goals. His career lasted from 7 September 1956 to 2 October 1977. No one has a better documented record.

Fred Perry

Fred Perry was a champion in two sports. He won the World Table Tennis Championship, beating Mihail Szabados of Hungary, in Budapest in 1929. But increasingly preferring lawn tennis, he had entered Wimbledon that year as a qualifier. He lost in the third round to John Olliff. By 1934 he was Wimbledon singles champion.

Born in Stockport, Fred Perry was the son of a Labour MP. S. F. Perry was the member for Kettering, a seat he won in 1923, after failing to win the Stockport constituency in 1922. He lost the seat in 1924, but won it back in 1929. John Profumo later held the constituency.

Table tennis was in the embryo stages of reorganization and Perry was its third world champion. There was no heavy top spin, or Oriental domination, but the sport was well established in Europe and he was a fine champion.

Tennis, though, with its world-wide appeal and greater competitive instinct, proved the greater attraction. Based in London and playing both sports, whilst at the Ealing Lawn Tennis Club, Perry phased himself out of the table tennis scene. He put his head round the entrance of the tennis club and saw smart cars in the drive. That decided him.

He made his debut for Britain's Davis Cup team in 1931. The following year he reached his first Wimbledon final, the men's doubles, with G. P. Hughes. They lost to the French 'Musketeers' Borotra and Brugnon.

The following year Perry was to figure in an amazing double. Ranked as world No. 1, Borotra lost to Perry in the Paris Tennis Tournament. In the evening Perry defeated the reigning world table tennis champion Victor Barna in the final of the Paris Table Tennis Tournament.

His first Grand Slam victory was not long delayed. H. L. Doherty had been the last Briton to win the US Open. That was in 1903. Thirty years later Perry beat Jack Crawford in the fifth set.

Crawford, an Australian, was Perry's opponent in his first Wimbledon final. Crawford, again, was the opponent in Perry's first Australian final. Perry won both. And when Gottfried von Cramm lost to Perry in the 1935 final of the French Championships, Perry became the first player to have won all the Grand Slam events – though not in the same year. He was undisputedly the world's No. 1 player in 1934, 1935 and 1936.

His game was based on modern principles – the complete all-court game but, with it, a fierce determination at crucial match points rather in the mould of Borg and McEnroe.

With Perry as No. 1, and backed by Bunny Austin, Britain achieved a feat thought impossible in these days. They actually won the Davis Cup, not once, but four times in a row, from 1933 to 1936. Austin was an able lieutenant, twice ranked No. 2 in the world, in 1933 and 1938, and a singles finalist at Wimbledon in both 1932 and 1938.

In all Fred Perry played twenty Davis Cup ties, winning forty-five of fifty-two rubbers: thirty-four of thirty-eight singles and eleven of fourteen doubles – the best record of any Briton.

The 1936 US Open saw Perry at his finest. The young American

FACTFILE

Born 18 May 1909, Stockport, Cheshire, England

Lawn tennis

World ranking 1931 fourth, 1932 seventh, 1933 second, 1934 first, 1935 first, 1936 first

Wimbledon Championships
  Singles 1934 beat J. H. Crawford (Australia), 6–3, 6–0, 7–5
    1935 beat G. von Cramm (Germany), 6–2, 6–4, 6–4
    1936 beat G. von Cramm (Germany), 6–1, 6–1, 6–0
  Doubles 1932 (with G. P. Hughes, GB) lost to Borotra & Brugnon (France), 0–6, 6–4, 6–3, 5–7, 5–7
  Mixed doubles 1935 with Miss D. E. Round, GB) beat Hopman & Hopman (Australia), 7–5, 4–6, 6–2
    1936 (with Miss D. E. Round, GB) beat Budge & Fabyan (USA), 7–9, 7–5, 6–4

French Championships
  Singles 1935 beat G. von Cramm (Germany), 6–3, 3–6, 6–1, 6–3
    1936 lost to G. von Cramm (Germany), 0–6, 6–2, 2–6, 6–2, 0–6
  Doubles 1933 (with G. P. Hughes, GB) beat McGrath & Quist (Australia), 6–2, 6–4, 2–6, 7–5

Mixed doubles 1932 (with Miss B. Nuthall, GB) beat Wood & Moody (USA), 6–4, 6–2
    1933 (with Miss B. Nuthall, GB) lost to Borotra & Rosambert (France), 2–6, 4–6

Australian Championships
  Singles 1934 beat J. H. Crawford (Australia), 6–3, 7–5, 6–1
  Doubles 1934 (with G. P. Hughes, GB) beat Quist & Turnbull (Australia)

United States Championships
  Singles 1933 beat J. H. Crawford (Australia), 6–3, 11–13, 4–6, 6–0, 6–1
    1934 beat W. L. Allison (USA), 6–4, 6–3, 3–6, 1–6, 8–6
    1936 beat D. Budge (USA), 2–6, 6–2, 8–6, 1–6, 10–8
  Mixed doubles 1932 (with Miss S. Palfrey, USA) beat Vines & Jacobs (USA), 6–3, 7–5

Table Tennis

World singles title 1929
English doubles titles 1928, 1929, 1930 (all with C. H. Bull, Kent)
English mixed doubles titles 1929 (with Miss W. H. Land, London)

Fred Perry reaches for a low backhand at the Wimbledon Championships

Donald Budge was his opponent. It was a classic game. Perry won 10–8 in the fifth set. His marvellous match temperament and famous running forehand bailed him out of trouble. Budge had noted that Perry's backhand was reputedly suspect, but could not break it down. After that triumph Fred Perry turned professional.

He became a US citizen and fought with the US forces during the war. He is now a writer and broadcaster, and Fred Perry Sportswear, with the distinctive wreath, is one of the leading brands of sports shirts. His business and broadcasting duties were embarked upon with all the determination, forthright views and decisiveness of his playing days.

In 1979 Bjorn Borg beat Roscoe Tanner to win his fourth Wimbledon singles title. Fred Perry was the match summarizer, with Gerald Williams, for BBC Radio. When the match was over, Williams turned to Perry for his comments on the game. Silence. There was an empty chair and a vacant microphone. Perry was at courtside, the first to congratulate Borg on beating his record.

Lester Piggott

Unquestionably the greatest British jockey of modern times, Lester Piggott continues to delight an army of supporters for whom he can do no wrong. In a way, this is a curious state of affairs, for in an age when superstars are brought into the living room merely by the flick of a switch, he remains a remote, introspective figure, not given to making his views public knowledge. It is therefore a tribute to his abiding genius that his devotees are more than happy to let actions speak louder than words.

Lester Keith Piggott was born in Wantage on Guy Fawkes Day,

1935. He was of pure racing stock, his great-grandfather having ridden a Derby winner, and his grandfather three Guineas winners. He became apprenticed to his father, Keith, and indeed enjoyed his first success on one of the stable's horses, The Chase, in a selling handicap at Haydock Park in 1948. He was only twelve years old.

As a child, Lester was partially deaf and suffered from a speech impediment. In later years this often made him seem shy and diffident, especially with strangers, but even as a young boy any trace of nerves disappeared as soon as the race was on. Indeed, there were

FACTFILE

Born 5 November 1935, Wantage, Berkshire, England

Champion jockey 1960, 1964, 1965, 1966, 1967, 1968, 1969, 1970, 1971, 1981, 1982

Most winners in one season 191 (in 1966)

English Classic victories (28)

Derby	1954	Never Say Die
	1957	Crepello
	1960	St Paddy
	1968	Sir Ivor
	1970	Nijinsky
	1972	Roberto
	1976	Emperey
	1977	The Minstrel
	1983	Teenoso
St Leger	1960	St Paddy
	1961	Aurelius
	1967	Ribbocco
	1968	Ribero
	1970	Nijinsky
	1971	Athens Wood
	1972	Boucher
	1984	Commanche Run
Oaks	1957	Carozza
	1959	Petite Etoile
	1966	Valoris
	1975	Juliette Marny
	1981	Blue Wind
	1984	Circus Plume
1000 Guineas	1970	Humble Duty
	1981	Fairy Footsteps
2000 Guineas	1957	Crepello
	1968	Sir Ivor
	1970	Nijinsky

*On 15 September 1984, Piggott won the St Leger, breaking the 19th-century record of Frank Buckle to become the first jockey to win 28 classics

*Piggott will readily admit that Nijinsky was the greatest horse he ever rode. These are the major races in which he rode Nijinsky into first place:

1969   William Hill Dewhurst Stakes (Newmarket)

1970   2000 Guineas (Newmarket), Derby (Epsom), St Leger (Doncaster), King George VI & Queen Elizabeth Stakes (Ascot), Irish Sweeps Derby (The Curragh)

*On the 18 August 1948, the legendary Lester Piggott rode his first winner, only his seventh mount in public. This is how the race card looked in the morning papers that day:

Haydock Park

2.15   *The Wigan Lane Selling Handicap* (one mile; £294)

142	Bang On (M. Everitt)	3-8-12	W. Nevett
200	Prompt Corner (Dennistoun)	4-8-8	W. Rickaby
000	Royal Trail (Owen)	3-7-13	W. M. Evans
204	Kings River (A. Cooper)	3-7-9	J. Sime
033	Cameo Star (Hawtin)	3-7-4	F. Durr
300	Planchard (J. Pearce)	3-7-3	A. Carson
000	The Chase (K. Piggott)	3-7-2	L. Piggott
400	Fair Dell (Dutton)	3-7-2	—
000	Miss Annabel (Binney)	3-7-1	J. Dyson
000	Miss Orient (R. A. Emery)	3-7-1	D. F. Morris
304	Dulcet Call (Storie)	3-7-0	C. Rowley
000	Poiseidonius (W. Stephenson)	4-7-0	J. Walker
000	Colbert (Bullock)	3-7-0	R. Sheather

Of those thirteen, only twelve ran, and D. L. Jones replaced Bill Rickaby on Prompt Corner. The result was:

1st	The Chase	10-1
2nd	Prompt Corner	100-8
3rd	Miss Annabel	100-8

The winning horse, by Foxhunter out of Golconda, was owned by Mrs B. Lavington and was sold after the race for 330 guineas to Mr B. Whitehouse.

Piggott only weighed 5 st at the time and had great difficulty in carrying his saddle and weights – totalling 23 lb – to the weighing-in room. His mother, getting rather fed up with all the telephone calls from wellwishers and reporters after the race, said, 'Don't spoil him. It's not so wonderful, after all, it was only a selling race. I do hope they do not make a hero of him at school.'

*Piggott won his first race, a three-furlong race at Wantage Gymkhana, at the age of six. His father said, 'I meant to make him a jockey. It came off. It doesn't often, but it certainly did with him'

*Piggott's house is called Florizel, after the sire of his first Derby winner

*On Piggott's alleged meanness: After being paid a large sum in cash, he tried to borrow money off a fellow jockey. 'I didn't want to break into it,' he explained

*According to Harry Carr, Piggott 'is the best that got on a horse, anywhere, any time'

Lester Piggott with the Epsom grandstand as a fitting backcloth. In addition to his record nine Derby wins on the course, he equalled the all-time record of Classic winners with his 1984 Oaks triumph on Circus Plume at Epsom

times when he was reckless and he frequently incurred the wrath of the stewards. It was typical of him that, having won his first Derby on Never Say Die in 1954, he was suspended for six months for his riding of the same horse at the Royal Ascot meeting a fortnight later. The stewards ruled that he should spend the time away from his father's stable, and he joined Jack Jarvis.

Like Fred Archer nearly a century before, Piggott is tall for a jockey (5 feet 10 inches) and has problems with his weight. He even turned to riding over hurdles for a spell, but the lucrative world of flat racing proved irresistible, and he imposed upon himself a diet of strong black coffee and large cigars to kill the hunger pangs. The regimen worked, and he has generally been able to ride at 8 st 6 lb.

When Sir Gordon Richards retired in 1954, he took over as first jockey to Noel (later Sir Noel) Murless at Newmarket and rode for him for twelve years. It was a brilliant partnership: a string of Classic successes followed, notably with Crepello (2000 Guineas and Derby, 1957), Carrozza (the Oaks in the same year), Petite Etoile (Oaks, 1959) and St Paddy (Derby and St Leger, 1960 – Lester's first championship year, when he rode 170 winners).

He was also champion for eight seasons from 1964, but the title came to mean less to him than it had to Fred Archer or Gordon Richards. Lester simply wanted to ride the best horses in the best races; that meant the Classics, and it led to an estrangement between him and Murless when he preferred to partner Vincent O'Brien's Valoris in the Oaks of 1966 to Murless's Varinia. Valoris won, and the jockey began 1967 as a freelance.

Many of his Classic successes since then are household names. O'Brien saddled Sir Ivor for the Derby in 1968, and Nijinsky, who took the Triple Crown in 1970. The full brothers Ribbocco and Ribero won the St Leger in 1967 and 1968, and among a host of other prestigious prizes Lester won the Washington International twice on Park Top and Karabas and the Prix de l'Arc de Triomphe twice on Levmoss. He is now stable jockey to Henry Cecil.

In 1960 Lester married Susan Armstrong, daughter of the Newmarket trainer Sam Armstrong, and they have two girls, Maureen and Tracy. Maureen is a top-class three-day eventer and Tracy has worked in Maurice Camacho's stables. He has a small circle of close friends and remains a very private person. Stories about his attitude to authority, his desire to ride big winners and, above all, his legend-ary tightness with money, are legion. Personal favourites include two from fellow jockeys:

Bryn Crossley: 'Lester Piggott goes into the stewards' room like Clint Eastwood and comes out like . . . Clint Eastwood.'

Pat Eddery: 'When he asks me how one of mine has run, I don't tell him. I might not be on it next time.'

Perhaps the best story of all: a long-suffering Fleet Street racing correspondent who, having unfailingly bought dinner for Lester on every occasion they met for the supposedly exclusive interview, one night began to nudge the bill, inch by inch, towards the great man's plate. Finally it came to rest against Lester's cup and saucer, where-upon he picked it up, glanced at it and said, 'That's outrageous. If I were you I'd query it.'

The time cannot be far off when Lester Piggott OBE will retire from the saddle. When that happens he will be remembered as a supreme stylist, a master tactician and probably the best judge of pace the racing world has ever seen. To those who back his mounts as if there is no settling-up day, the sight of the famous posterior still pointing jauntily at the sun with under 2 furlongs to travel is a welcome reminder that God is in his heaven and all is right with the world.

Piggott's Pedigree

Keith Piggott (father) trained Ayala to win the 1963 Grand National
Ernest Piggott (grandfather) rode three Grand National winners: Jerry M (1912), Poethlyn (1918 and 1919). Poethlyn was the only horse to win the race at both Aintree and Gatwick
Tom Cannon (great-grandfather) rode thirteen Classic winners, in-cluding Shotover in the 1882 Derby. He also trained Playfair to win the 1888 Grand National

In addition, Piggott's great uncle, Charles Piggott, trained African Sister to win the 1939 Champion Hurdle – ridden by Lester's father. Lester's mother's great-grandfather was Fred Rickaby, who trained Wild Dayrell to win the 1855 Derby. Both Lester's mother, Margaret, and Lester's wife, Sue, have ridden the winner of the Newmarket Town Plate – at one time the only race open to women jockeys – and Lester's daughter, Tracy, has recently spent twelve months with trainer Maurice Camacho, learning the skills, no doubt to carry on the family tradition.

Gary Player

Gary Player was the first of the modern golfers to present a serious and consistent challenge to the American monopoly of the game. He was the first non-American to win all four of the major tournaments, and his competitive instinct in matchplay won him five World Championships at Wentworth. And, as an indication of his fitness and ability, Player won the majors over three decades.

South Africa is a marvellous place to learn golf, with superb weather and scenery, lush fairways and well-kept greens. There is no need for winter rubber mats on which to tee-off, and one rarely has to queue. Player, born in Johannesburg on the first day of November 1935, had a difficult time as a child: his mother died when he was just eight years old. His first job in golf was as an assistant to the well-known South African professional Jock Verwey – he was to marry Jock's daughter Vivien.

The disciplined practising was ingrained at an early age. He would practise all day and even into the night. He would stand in a practice bunker and not leave until he had holed out five times.

Player turned professional in 1952, but, despite several high placings, it was nearly three years before he gained his first professional victory. That was at the other end of the African continent, at the Geziva Club in Cairo, where he won the Egyptian Matchplay Championship, beating fellow South African Harold Henning in the final. With prize money, the equivalent of $5\frac{1}{2}$ camels, he made his way to Britain.

In 1956 he had his first British success when he won the Dunlop Tournament (not the Dunlop Masters) at Sunningdale. Other than the Open and the World Matchplay Championship, which he won five times, that was to be his only win in Britain.

The following year, after the South African season, he packed his bags and headed for the United States. His first prize money was a total of $16.16 for finishing joint twenty-fifth in the Azalea Open.

1958 was the beginning of the breakthrough. Player finished runner-up in the US Open Championship to Tommy Bolt, won the Kentucky Open and was seventh in the British Open. The following year confirmed his promise, a last-round 68 at Muirfield giving him a 2-shot win against Flory Van Donck in the British Open.

Player, a religious and a family man, did not join the American or European circuit full time. He preferred to remain in South Africa with his growing family and travel to selected events abroad.

The second major was the 1961 US Masters at Augusta National Golf Club. That made history: he was the first non-American to win the event. Arnold Palmer gave Player the green jacket for his 8-under-par score. He handed it back to Palmer the following year when he finished runner-up. In 1962, the third leg of the Grand Slam arrived, the US PGA title at Newton Square.

The final hurdle was completed in 1965 with a victory in the US Open at St Louis. It was achieved the hard way by an eighteen-hole play-off against the Australian Kel Nagle. Player's 71 was enough for him to win by 3 strokes. That took him into the World Matchplay Championship at Wentworth. He won that as well with a 3 and 2 win against Peter Thomson in the final. In an earlier round he had mentally packed his bags, after trailing by seven holes with just seventeen to play, against Tony Lema, the American who had won the 1964 British Open.

The thoroughness of his preparation allowed Player to win a total of nine Grand Slam events. In addition to his record five World Matchplay Championships at Wentworth, he won the World Cup team title with Harold Henning in 1965; he was also the top individual golfer, both then and in 1977. His dedication to the development of domestic tournaments enabled him to win the South African Open twelve times between 1956 and 1979; he also won the Australian Open on seven occasions.

His career has been crystallized in a remark he made at the British Open in 1981. Someone in the crowd shouted, 'You lucky South African' or words to that effect. Player, without breaking stride, replied, 'You know, it's amazing, isn't it – the more I practise, the luckier I seem to get.'

Now in semi-retirement but still accomplished enough to be runner-up in the 1984 US PGA Championship, Player has varied interests. He designs golf courses, the best known of which is at Sun City, a test of skill at golf and snake avoidance, hewn out of the hills and bush at the leisure complex in the black homeland of Bophuthatwana, three hours' drive from Johannesburg. The world's richest tournament was his idea – a better idea was to win the inaugural event!

He has a farm at Colesburg in the Northern Cape, close by the main Cape Town–Johannesburg road. On it he breeds horses and

FACTFILE

Born 1 November 1935, Johannesburg, South Africa

'Big Four' wins 9
British Open 1959, 1968, 1974
US Open 1965 (second 1958, 1979)
US Masters 1961, 1974, 1978 (second 1962, 1965)
US PGA 1962, 1972
World Cup
  Team 1965 (with Harold Henning)
  Individual 1965, 1977
World Matchplay 1965, 1966, 1968, 1971, 1973
South African Open 1956, 1960, 1965, 1966, 1967, 1968, 1969, 1972, 1975, 1976, 1977, 1979
South African Masters wins 11 (1959–79)

South African PGA 1968, 1979
Australian Open 1958, 1962, 1963, 1965, 1969, 1970, 1974

*In the 1974 Brazilian Open at Gavea Golf and Country Club, Rio de Janeiro, second round, on 29 November 1974, Gary Player's card read as follows:

Out:	3	4	3	3	4	2	3	3	4 = 29
In:	2	4	3	4	4	4	2	4	3 = 30
								Total	59

It was the first sub-60 in international competition
*Player, aged forty-two, was the oldest winner of the US Masters in 1978, when his 64 in the last round equalled the course record

has become one of the country's leading breeders. Son Wayne has joined the professional ranks. As Gary says, 'I've six kids and a hundred quarter horses to feed – I don't know who eats the most.'

The shot that won the Open. Gary Player, with his glove protruding from his back pocket, forced to play left-handed from the side of the clubhouse wall at the seventy-second hole of the 1974 Open. He made his par

Graeme Pollock

One of the tragedies of the South African government's policy of apartheid has been that the cricket public have been starved of the opportunity of watching certainly the finest batsman of the 1970s, the elegant left-hander, Graeme Pollock.

He arrived on the world cricket scene, together with the equally youthful and talented Mike Procter and Barry Richards, to spearhead a side which, by 1970, had taken the Springboks to the top of world cricket. There were others to admire: Graeme's brother Peter, who took 116 Test wickets; the former rugby centre Eddie Barlow, who had played in the centre for Transvaal against the 1960 All Blacks; and the wicketkeeper, Dennis Lindsay, who delighted in taking centuries off Australia. Trevor Goddard (2516 runs and 123 wickets in Test cricket) aided Barlow (also 2516 runs, average 44.74, and 40 wickets) in all-round capacities. But above them all was Graeme Pollock. Whatever the ramifications of the disappearance of the Green and Gold from international cricket, the cricket lovers were the sufferers. The Aussies suffered too, in their last nine Tests against South Africa: they won one, drew one and lost seven, mostly by hideous margins.

There is an old cliché that statistics can prove anything. In the case of Graeme Pollock, they matter. By the time South Africa left the international scene in 1970, he had played in twenty-three Test matches, scored seven centuries and eleven half centuries, had amassed 2256 runs – 1453 off the Australians and 750 from England – for a remarkable Test average of 60.97. And he was still only twenty-five.

The scene moves forward another twelve years, when 'international' cricket returned to South Africa. Teams were imported with varying degrees of success from England, the West Indies and Sri Lanka. The 'rebels', as they were called, invited severe bans from their own cricket authorities, but they earned good money and, in the words of South African president Joe Pamensky, 'But for them the game would surely have died out here.' By 1984 only one of the old guard remained – Graeme Pollock, now nearing forty. His 'test' statistics were 886 runs at an average of 63.28, further indication if any were needed of what records would probably have been broken in those twelve missing years.

Pollock was born in Durban on 27 February 1944. His father was a provincial wicketkeeper for Orange Free State and Graeme and Peter grew up in the right cricketing atmosphere. Attending Grey School, when the family moved to the 'Windy City' of Port Elizabeth, Graeme was coached by the old Sussex pro George Cox. There were already stories circulating about some outstanding performances: he made 117 and took 10 for 25 in the same match (he wanted to be a bowler; Peter preferred batting); an innings of 111 out of 120 was also recorded.

Graeme went straight from the examination room at Grey into the Eastern Province first team. In his very first match he was run out for 54 against Border, took 41 off Griqualand West in the next, 60 off Rhodesia, then a half century against Western Province at Newlands. The next stop was the Wanderers ground in Johannesburg, that shrine of Castle Breweries advertising, and against Transvaal 'B' he made 102 – the major provinces field 'A' and 'B' teams in major competitions. Graeme was just 16 years and 355 days old and, until 1983, he was the youngest South African first-class centurion ever. In eight innings that first season he made 384 runs at an average of 48.00

With brother Peter now established in the Test team, Graeme came to England in 1961 to lend family support to Peter, with the touring Fezelas. George Cox, his mentor and guide, enlisted him for six games with Sussex's Second XI. Back home, just twenty days after his nineteenth birthday, he became South Africa's youngest double centurion ever with an unbeaten 209 for Eastern Province against the touring International Cavaliers. That performance earned a Qantas flight to Australia in October 1963 and Test selection.

The series began unhappily with Ian Meckiff being no-balled out of Test cricket. In the Third Test Pollock, two months before his twentieth birthday, made 122 at Sydney, which caused former Australian captains Don Bradman and Lindsay Hassett to stand and applaud the young man back to the pavilion. Top Australian batsman Norman O'Neill was unimpressed. 'Flash in the pan,' he suggested. Fourteen days later, at Melbourne, O'Neill joined in the applause. Pollock made 175, Eddie Barlow 201, and the pair added 341 for the third wicket.

England took a little longer to bring to heel. They won the series with a solitary success on the High Veld, then, in the English summer of 1965 a couple of months later, the Springboks turned the scales with their solitary win at Trent Bridge. Mr and Mrs Pollock's young lads ruined England: Graeme made a quite magnificent 125 on a bad wicket, and 59 in the second innings, whilst Peter took 5 for 53 and 5 for 34.

However, the winds of change were blowing through Africa, mainly out of Pretoria. From that English summer of 1965 until 1970 only nine Tests were played – all at home and all against Australia.

FACTFILE

Born 27 February 1944, Port Elizabeth, South Africa

First class debut 1960–61
Total first-class runs 19,246 (average 55.31)
Total first-class wickets 43 (average 48.02)
Total first-class catches 237
Highest first-class innings 274 South Africa (*v.* Australia) Durban, 1969–70
Best first-class bowling 3–46
Test debut 6 December 1963, *v.* Australia (Brisbane)

Total Test appearances 23
Total Test runs 2256 (average 60.97)
Total Test wickets 4 (average 51.00)
Highest Test innings as above
Best Test bowling 2–50
Total centuries 60
Total half-centuries 89

*For Sussex Second XI in 1961 Pollock's statistics were 112 runs in six innings, highest score 34, average 18.66

Graeme Pollock pierces the offside field during his memorable 125 against England at Trent Bridge in 1965

Bobby Simpson brought his side to South Africa in 1966–67. Pollock hit his first ball of the series, from Tom Veivers, out of the ground on his way to 90 in 114 minutes. In the Newlands Test he made 209. Simpson's team lost the series 3–1.

The other opening batsman, Bill Lawry, brought the next contingent in 1970. If it had been boxing, they would have stopped the fight. South Africa whitewashed the series 4–0 (by 170 runs; an innings and 129; 307 runs; and 323 runs). Up to 1984 it was the most comprehensive thrashing of a touring team in cricketing history. Pollock's major contribution was an innings of 274, including a 5 and forty-three 4s in 417 minutes, the highest by a South African in Test history, at Durban's picturesque Kingsmead. Then, sadly for all save the Aussies, down came the curtain.

During isolation, the seven-days-a-week grind of county cricket was not for Pollock. The tired, drained faces of his pals Richards and Procter were evidence that family life and a flourishing business at Berden's, the factory safety and clothing firm, were preferable. Sir Gary Sobers tried to entice him to Nottinghamshire; he was offered the captaincy of the then erratic, but vastly promising,

Somerset team in 1969, and eleven seasons later Kent offered him a one-year contract.

He was content to clean up domestic records. The Currie Cup (10,642 at 56.30) and Datsun/Nissan Shield (2483 runs at 69.38) records are easily his. His innings of 222 not out for Eastern Province against Border is a one-day world record. A business move in 1977 meant farewell to Eastern Province and a move to Johannesburg and Transvaal, to collect championship honours for the first time. In the week of his fortieth birthday, he helped Transvaal retain the double with an innings of 94 in the 1984 Currie Cup final, and 49 in fifty-one minutes in the Nissan Shield final, both against Western Province.

Cricket Exiles, by Brian Crowley, tells a fine story about the young Pollock. Whilst in England in 1961, he played for Sutton, the Surrey championship club. The seventeen-year-old Pollock was asked if he could bat. 'A bit,' came the polite reply. 'Bat No. 8,' said an unimpressed captain. He did, and Sutton declared before the young master could get a knock.

That would be a scorecard for the historians.

Ferenc Puskas

In the days before televised football became routine, when package holidays were still to come and foreign placenames conjured up romantic images, certain matches lingered in the public memory for years after they were played. Ask those who saw the European Cup final of 1960 about the game and they will instantly brighten, as though recalling an outstanding claret after years of *vin de table*. The occasion was pure theatre: Hampden Park the stage, Real Madrid the virtuoso performers, Eintracht Frankfurt the bit players whose fate was familiar enough – early success swiftly followed by complete bafflement as genius overtook them. Real eventually won 7–3, though the score hardly mattered once they had taken control; easy rhythmic movements in time to names lovingly enunciated by Kenneth Wolstenholme – del Sol, Gento, di Stefano – and Puskas.

By the time he graced Hampden, scoring 4 goals in the process, the legend of Ferenc Puskas was well on the way to being established. A Hungarian, born in Budapest in 1926, he was a vital member of the magnificent side which came to Wembley in 1953 and inflicted upon England their first home defeat, by 6–3. When the old 'Radio Newsreel' film of that match is shown, two things immediately stand out: the sudden realization among the crowd that here was a brand of football they had not witnessed before (they reacted with an awed silence followed by generous applause); and the fact that Puskas would have been the guiding light in any team, in any age. He scored only twice, but his overall contribution was immense. Like all great players, he imposed his own pace – a very gentle one – upon the game, seldom calling upon his right foot but using the left to prompt and cajole the best out of those around him, and then interrupting the pattern with a wickedly placed shot from the most unlikely angle.

He had learned his trade in the streets of Budapest, and joined his first club, Kispest, in 1943. Kispest merged with the army club Honved in 1948, and in that year Puskas scored 50 goals. At both club and international level he enjoyed a perfect understanding with his close friend Joszef Bozsik, and as Hungary basked in the golden years from 1950 onwards, the pair formed the backbone of a team which was unbeaten until the 1954 World Cup final.

The Hungarian uprising of 1956 meant that Puskas's marvellous range of talents was witnessed by many more people than might otherwise have been the case. He was touring South America at the time and decided not to go home, preferring to live in Italy where he spent nearly two years out of competitive football. He was always a most unlikely looking athlete, with plenty of weight around his middle, and such an interruption would probably have meant the end for a less talented performer. In Puskas's case, however, many great years were still to come.

Real Madrid were already a talented side before Puskas arrived in 1958, but when he played alongside di Stefano they looked simply unbeatable. It seemed fitting that they should perform in an all-white strip because there was no discernible flaw in their play, and many experienced watchers fully expected them to remain the top club side for year upon year. These things always end, of course, and across the border in Portugal a young man named Eusebio was beginning to change the order of things. In the European Cup final of 1962 on a balmy night in Amsterdam Puskas scored 3 goals to Eusebio's 2, but Benfica still won the match 5–3 and the golden era of Real Madrid was over.

Puskas played for the Spanish side for eight years and was top scorer in the domestic League on four occasions. When he left, at the age of forty, it was to coach in the United States with San Francisco Eagles, then Vancouver Royals, although his globe-trotting brought him back to Europe as manager of the Greek side Panathinaikos in 1971. It was fitting that they should reach the European Cup final that year and that Wembley, where Puskas had so many devotees, should stage the match. He accepted assignments in Saudi Arabia, Chile (Colo Calo) and Greece (AEK Athens) again; indeed, at times he has resembled the restless nomad, always seeking some new challenge where his immense experience might be of value.

When Puskas walked out for the match against England in 1953 there were those who nudged each other in surprise at his small, dumpy frame. Moments later the whispers were silenced as he walked all the way to the centre spot with the ball balanced on his instep. It wasn't pure showmanship; merely a deep love of the game and its possibilities . . . a love which makes him still potter around football fields with fellow veterans more than thirty years on.

They make other footballers as good as Ferenc Puskas . . . but not more than one or two a generation.

FACTFILE

Born 1926, Budapest, Hungary

First-class debut October 1943, Kispest *v.* Nagyvaved
Total first-class matches 372
Total first-class goals 324
International debut 1945, Hungary *v.* Austria
International appearances 88 (84 for Hungary, 4 for Spain)
International goals 85 (83 for Hungary, 2 for Spain)

Honours

World Cup runners-up 1954
Olympic Games 1952

European Cup 1960 (Real Madrid); runners-up 1962, 1964 (both Real Madrid)
World Club Championship 1960 (Real Madrid)
Hungarian League 1950, 1952, 1954, 1955 (all Honved)
Spanish League 1961, 1962, 1963, 1964, 1965 (all Real Madrid)
Spanish Cup 1962 (Real Madrid)
Top scorer in Hungarian League 1948 (50), 1949 (31), 1950 (25), 1953 (27)
Top scorer in Spanish League 1960 (26), 1961 (27), 1963 (26), 1964 (20)

Ferenc Puskas training anonymously with the Hungarian team at Craven Cottage on 23 November 1953, before the match with England. Two days later he was the most famous player in the world

Ray Reardon

FACTFILE

Born 8 October 1932, Tredegar, Wales

World Professional Championship

1970	v. John Pulman	won	37–33
1973	v. Eddie Charlton	won	38–32
1974	v. Graham Miles	won	22–12
1975	v. Eddie Charlton	won	31–30
1976	v. Alex Higgins	won	27–16
1978	v. Perri Mans	won	25–18

English Amateur Championship

1964	v. John Spencer	won	11–8

Benson & Hedges Masters Tournament

1976	v. Graham Miles	won	7–3

Yamaha Organs Championship

1983	v. Jimmy White	won	9–6

BBC Television 'Pot Black' 1969, 1979

*Since the reorganization of the World Professional Championships in 1969, Ray Reardon's record in the competition is second to none. By the end of the 1984 competition, he had played forty-eight matches, winning thirty-eight, and losing ten. His full record is as follows:

1969

First round	v. Fred Davis	lost	24–25

1970 (April)

Quarter final	v. Fred Davis	won	31–26
Semifinal	v. John Spencer	won	37–33
Final	v. John Pulman	won	37–33

1970 (November)

Group match	v. Perri Mans	won	22–15
Group match	v. Eddie Charlton	won	21–16
Group match	v. John Spencer	won	21–16
Semifinal	v. John Spencer	lost	15–34

1972

Quarter final	v. Rex Williams	lost	23–25

1973

Second round	v. Jim Meadowcroft	won	16–10
Quarter final	v. Garry Owen	won	16–6
Semifinal	v. John Spencer	won	23–22
Final	v. Eddie Charlton	won	38–32

1974

Second round	v. Jim Meadowcroft	won	15–3
Quarter final	v. Marcus Owen	won	15–11
Semifinal	v. Fred Davis	won	15–3
Final	v. Graham Miles	won	22–12

1975

Second round	v. Warren Simpson	won	15–11
Quarter final	v. John Spencer	won	19–17
Semifinal	v. Alex Higgins	won	19–14
Final	v. Eddie Charlton	won	31–30

1976

First round	v. John Dunning	won	15–7
Quarter final	v. Dennis Taylor	won	15–2
Semifinal	v. Perri Mans	won	20–10
Final	v. Alex Higgins	won	27–16

1977

First round	v. Patsy Fagan	won	13–7
Quarter final	v. John Spencer	lost	6–13

1978

First round	v. Doug Mountjoy	won	13–9
Quarter final	v. Bill Werbeniuk	won	13–6
Semifinal	v. Eddie Charlton	won	18–14
Final	v. Perri Mans	won	25–18

1979

First round	v. Graham Miles	won	13–8
Quarter final	v. Denis Taylor	lost	8–13

1980

Second round	v. Bill Werbeniuk	won	13–6
Quarter final	v. David Taylor	lost	11–13

1981

Second round	v. John Spencer	won	13–11
Quarter final	v. Bill Werbeniuk	won	13–10
Semifinal	v. Doug Mountjoy	lost	10–16

1982

First round	v. Jim Donnelly	won	10–5
Second round	v. John Virgo	won	13–8
Quarter final	v. Silvino Francisco	won	13–8
Semifinal	v. Eddie Charlton	won	16–11
Final	v. Alex Higgins	lost	15–18

1983

First round	v. Eugene Hughes	won	10–7
Second round	v. Tony Knowles	lost	12–13

1984

First round	v. Jim Wych	won	10–7
Second round	v. Silvino Francisco	won	13–8
Quarter final	v. Kirk Stevens	lost	2–13

*When he worked down the mine, Reardon wore white gloves to keep his hands clean
*He used to train by potting marbles
*Reardon has played his old friend and rival, John Spencer, on seven occasions in the World Professional Championship, winning five, and losing two
*His other rival, Eddie Charlton, has played Reardon on five occasions in the World Championship, and is still looking for his first win over him

Ray Reardon, six times world snooker champion in the 1970s, at the table

What have a coalminer, PC184 and Dracula in common? They are all focal points in the life of Ray Reardon, world professional snooker champion, with an outstanding record in a sport which has become one of the major British growth industries of recent times.

Born in Tredegar, Wales, in 1932, Ray Reardon's introduction to the game he was to dominate came from his father, still his greatest admirer. At the age of seventeen, Ray had compiled his first century break.

He first went down a mine at the age of fourteen. In 1955 the family moved from Tredegar to Stoke on Trent. Ray worked in the mines at Florence Colliery, in the north Staffordshire coalfield. Involved in an accident in which he was buried for three hours in a roof fall, Ray decided on a life in the open air. He joined the Stoke on Trent Constabulary.

PC184 received two commendations whilst in the police force, one for bravery whilst disarming a man with a shotgun. He met his wife Sue in 1957. Snooker, in those days, was a relaxation. But he was pleased to win the English amateur title in 1964, and the victory completed an international double: in his mining days in Tredegar he had won the Welsh amateur title six years in succession, from 1950 to 1955.

In 1967 Ray took a major decision. He left the security of the police force for a career in professional snooker. He signed at the same time as Gary Owen, the 1963 and 1966 world amateur champion, and John Spencer. But it was a risk – there had been no new professionals since 1951.

1967 was the year in which colour television became available. TV sport was looking for new outlets. Snooker, with its green baize and brightly coloured balls, was an obvious choice for the programme planners. And with football fast falling foul of the hooligan, snooker's image was acceptable. Though it had slumped a little in popularity, it had a dignity which appealed.

BBC2 began their first snooker television series in 1969. The programme was called 'Pot Black'. The first winner was Ray Reardon. The following year Ray Reardon won the World Professional Championship, beating John Pulman in the final. Only a year earlier he had made his first appearance in the event, losing in the very first round, by 25 frames to 24, to Fred Davis.

Between 1970 and 1978 Reardon was to win the world title on six occasions. He became a television personality, calm and at ease in front of the cameras. He was the subject of 'This Is Your Life' and appeared on 'Desert Island Discs'. He was nicknamed 'Dracula' on 'The Paul Daniels Show'. It stuck.

In 1978 the town of Tredegar proudly claimed the world professional and amateur champions in Reardon and Cliff Wilson. The two had been brought up together, and matches in their early days attracted much local attention. For Wilson it marked the end of fifteen years of frustration: in 1963 he too had tried to gain entry to the professional ranks, but his amateur record was not considered good enough.

A year later there seemed to appear the first chinks in the Reardon game. An ash cue which had been given to him in 1949 by the legendary Joe Davis after Ray had won the *News of the World* Amateur Championship, fell apart. It was thirty years old. Ray took eighteen months to find a suitable replacement, but, once one was found, his game began to improve again. He became a threat to those younger elements who had joined the professional ranks, those who had initially been encouraged by Reardon's example and were now ready to dethrone him.

Quite how long it takes for a snooker player to lose his edge is uncertain. Ray Reardon won the last of his world titles in 1978. There was comparison of Reardon's broken cue with Arnold Palmer's broken putter. But, in 1982, he was back to reach the final of the World Championship, losing to Alex Higgins at Sheffield's new home of snooker, the Crucible Theatre. Snooker is a game in which there is now pressure from opponents and from a television audience, watching not only the play, but also the player's characters. In this era, the record of Ray Reardon is easily the most outstanding.

Sir Gordon Richards

As long as people discuss horse racing there will be those who put forward the name of Gordon Richards as the best jockey of all time. Some will support him because they were his contemporaries; others will regard his record as sufficient proof. Between 1920 and 1954 he rode 4870 winners from 21,843 mounts, was champion jockey on no fewer than twenty-six occasions and won fourteen Classics.

There is little point in comparing great jockeys of different generations; for example, no one can say what targets the legendary Fred Archer might have set had personal tragedy not caused him to take his own life. Two points are worth making, however: Gordon Richards could ride comfortably at 8 st 2 lb in his fiftieth year – unlike Archer and Lester Piggott, he had no worries in this respect;

and whereas Piggott made the prestigious races, both in Britain and abroad, his top priority, Archer and Richards were concerned with riding as many winners as possible.

Gordon Richards was born on 5 May 1904 at Oakengates in Shropshire, one of twelve children; his father, Nathan, was a miner. He was apprenticed to Martin Hartigan and rode his first winner on Gay Lord at Leicester in 1921. Perhaps the answer he gave in the paddock that day offered a clue to his unflappability (as well as revealing his keen sense of humour): when asked why he had taken Gay Lord all the way around on the outside, he replied innocently, 'I was told he needed a longer trip.'

Even in the early days there was no question of his having to fight

FACTFILE

Born 5 May 1904, Oakengates (now Telford), Shropshire, England

Champion jockey 1925, 1927, 1928, 1929, 1931, 1932, 1933, 1934, 1935, 1936, 1937, 1938, 1939, 1941, 1942, 1943, 1944, 1945, 1946, 1947, 1948, 1949, 1950, 1951, 1952, 1953

Most winners in one season 269 (in 1947)

English Classic victories (14)

Derby	1953	Pinza
St Leger	1930	Singapore
	1937	Chumleigh
	1940	Turkhan
	1942	Sun Chariot
	1944	Tehran
Oaks	1930	Rose of England
	1942	Sun Chariot
1000 Guineas	1942	Sun Chariot
	1948	Queenpot
	1951	Belle of All
2000 Guineas	1938	Pasch
	1942	Big Game
	1947	Tudor Minstrel

*On Tuesday, 3 October 1933, Gordon Richards passed the winning post in the 4 p.m. at Nottingham in first place. His next ride, the following day at Chepstow, saw him come home first again, as he did in all six races that day. The following day, he rode the first five winners, again at Chepstow, making an amazing run of twelve successive winners, and in so doing, be became the first man since Fred Archer (on 5 August 1882, at Lewes) to ride all six winners at one meeting.

This is how those amazing three days went:

Tuesday, 3 October 1933 – Nottingham

4.00 p.m.	Barnby	1st

Wednesday, 4 October 1933 – Chepstow

2.00 p.m.	Manner	1st
2.30 p.m.	Brush Past	1st
3.00 p.m.	Miss B	1st
3.30 p.m.	Arcona	1st

4.00 p.m.	Red Horizon	1st
4.30 p.m.	Delicia	1st

Thursday, 5 October 1933 – Chepstow

2.00 p.m.	Covanenter	1st
2.30 p.m.	Kirrimuir	1st
2.55 p.m.	June Rose	1st
3.30 p.m.	Montrose	1st
4.00 p.m.	Lady Swift	1st

This run came to an end in the 4.30 when he was beaten into third place on Eagle Ray by just a head and a neck

*Of his trainer, Fred Darling, Richards said, 'He was a genius. He'd walk down the yard at night with his stick under his arm, and all the horses would stand to attention'

*In 1942 Richards won four of the five English classics on horses owned by King George V

*In the 1953 Derby he beat the Queen's horse Auriole into second place, shortly after she had announced his knighthood. However, the fairytale had a twist of irony for the following season, when he was well ahead in the jockeys' table, one of his mounts reared and fell, fracturing and dislocating Richards's pelvis and putting an end to his riding career. The irony was that the horse was one of the Queen's fillies

*Richards retired from training in 1970 after some success. He continued as racing manager to Lady Beaverbrook and Michael Sobell

*In 1970 he was made an honorary member of the Jockey Club – the first professional jockey to be elected

Leading Ten Jockeys of All Time in Great Britain

			No. of winners
1	Gordon Richards	1921–54	4870
2	Lester Piggott	1948–	4219
3	Doug Smith	1931–67	3111
4	Fred Archer	1870–86	2748
5	Joe Mercer	1950–	2718
6	George Fordham	1850–84	2587
7	Eddie Hide	1951–	2555
8	Eph Smith	1930–65	2313
9	Scobie Breasley	1950–68	2161
10	Bill Nevett	1924–56	2067

(Correct up to end of 1983 season.)

Sir Gordon Richards, twenty-six times champion jockey in the twenty-nine seasons from 1923 to 1953

for recognition. He was acknowledged by the best judges as a future champion and, in his very first season as a fully fledged jockey in 1925, took the title with 118 winners. The next year, however, brought a setback; he missed the summer because of a tubercular patch on one lung, and although he returned to the saddle and regained the championship in 1927, this piece of medical history led to his being turned down when he volunteered for both the Army and the Air Force in 1939.

The queue for his riding services grew ever longer. Fred Darling took third claim on him in 1928, the year he married, and from then until his retirement in 1954 he was champion jockey every year except 1930, when Freddy Fox rode the fourth and fifth winners on the last day at Manchester to pip him 129–128, and 1941, when he was out of action with a broken leg.

There were times when he looked invincible. Like Archer, he rode every race as if it were his last, leaving nothing to chance. In 1933 he broke Fred's record, riding 259 winners in the season, including a run of eleven straight victories at Chepstow. Having gone through the card on the opening day and ridden the first five winners on the second, he was beaten a neck and a head on Eagle Ray. (A cautionary note for backers – Gordon believed this to be the best bet of all twelve).

The public idolized him. Millions backed him blindly in threepenny doubles and trebles; his daily strike rate was as important to them as the Test score to the two train travellers in Hitchcock's *The Lady Vanishes*.

Yet, with all this, one very important prize eluded him – the Derby. Often he rode indifferent horses; sometimes he rode brilliant ones which failed to stay the distance, like Tudor Minstrel, who started at 7 to 4 on in 1947. It was hardly compensation that he broke his own record with 269 winners.

However, in Coronation year, 1953, everything came right as if preordained. The Queen conferred a knighthood on Gordon shortly before the start of the Epsom meeting; in Pinza he partnered a horse ideally equipped for the job; and in the famous year when Stanley Matthews claimed his FA Cup medal, the Hungarians silenced Wembley and the Ashes were regained, the pair of them stormed clear to beat (of all rivals) Her Majesty's Aureole by four lengths. It was his twenty-eighth and final attempt and the crowd was ecstatic.

Gordon Richards retired after a fall the following year and set up as a trainer. A quiet, private man, he remained intensely loyal throughout his professional and personal life and never once reneged on an agreement. It mattered little to an adoring public that his vigorous, unorthodox style in a tight finish was hardly classical; to them the only thing that counted was: 'Gordon always tries.'

Sugar Ray Robinson

Sugar Ray Robinson sounds better than Sugar Walker Smith. The best-known boxer outside the heavyweight division of world boxing, he was christened Walker Smith in Detroit in 1920.

Inspiration came easily. The young Walker Smith hung around the boxing gyms of Detroit, the 1930s American boom city with the Henry Ford car plant in full swing, and a Mecca for thousands of Negro families. The most famous person in Detroit in those days was Joe Louis, heavyweight champion of the world. Walker Smith, fanatic and promising amateur, was his bagman.

His amateur record was perfect. He won the Golden Gloves featherweight title in 1939 and the lightweight crown in 1940. He turned professional in 1940 after a record eighty-five fights (or contests as they are referred to in the amateur ring), eighty-five wins, with sixty-nine knockouts, forty in the first round.

Already he was acquiring the skills which were to become his trademark. An excellent puncher with both hands, he had an equally good defence. The nickname 'Sugar' was obvious, and Walker Smith became Ray Robinson when, in his first year as a professional, he stood in for a boxer of that name.

Shrewdly managed by the 'Emperor', George Gainford, Robinson's 100 per cent professional record lasted until fight number forty, when he lost on points in 1943 to Jake La Motta, whom Robinson had earlier beaten and was to beat again two fights later. Former champions Sammy Angott and Fritzie Zivic were part of the tuition. Now boxing as a welterweight, he was matched for the vacant world title in December 1945. His credentials were impressive – seventy-five fights, seventy-three wins (forty-nine knockouts), one draw (against one Jose Basora) and the loss to La Motta. The opponent was Tommy Bell, whom Robinson had outpointed in a ten-round contest in his fifty-third fight. After fifteen rounds Robinson was world welterweight champion.

The first defence was a sad one. Jimmy Doyle, knocked out in the eighth round, died later from his injuries. Robinson defended his title on five occasions and in between won forty-three non-title fights. But, with increasing weight difficulties, he campaigned in the middleweight division and won the Pennsylvania middleweight championship. That gave him a shot at the world title, held by none other than Jake La Motta.

La Motta, the 'Bronx Bull', had picked up the world title from the Frenchman Marcel Cerdan, who had died in a plane crash in the Azores on the way to a return fight. Robinson relieved La Motta of his crown with a thirteenth-round stoppage. Newspapers ran the cliché about the 1951 St Valentine's Day massacre.

Six months later Robinson was matched with Britain's Randolph Alphonsus Turpin for his first defence. Like his boyhood idol Louis, Robinson had embarked on a 'Bum of the Month' tour and had already met eight non-title opponents since annexing the crown, six in Europe.

The fight took place at Earl's Court. Robinson's record was 132 fights, 129 wins, two draws and a loss; Turpin had forty-one wins, a draw and a loss to his credit, and was the European champion. Robinson was a 7 to 2 on favourite, Turpin 3 to 1, and you could get 20 to 1 that Turpin would win on points. The 20 to 1 shot won; Robinson needed fourteen stitches over his left eye.

Two months later the pair met again in Madison Square Garden. Turpin was stopped in the tenth round, in one of the all-time great fights. Referee Ruby Goldstein, wrongly in many people's eyes, called a halt with just a couple of seconds of the round to go, but he may have been influenced by the death of George Flores in the same city a week earlier.

After a couple more successful defences, Robinson fancied a chance at the light heavyweight championship. The fight against Joey Maxim was arranged for New York City on 25 June 1952. It was hot that day, too hot to fight. At the end of the thirteenth round Robinson,

FACTFILE

Born 3 May 1920, Detroit, Michigan, USA

First professional fight 4 October 1940, *v.* Joe Escgeverria (won ko 2)
Total professional fights 201
   Wins 174
   Kos 109
   Defeats 19
Last professional fight 10 November 1965, *v.* Joey Archer (lost pts 10)
World title fights 22
   Wins 15

Defeats

Year	Opponent	Result	Rounds
1943	Jake La Motta	pts	10
1951	Randolph Turpin (World middleweight title fight)	pts	15
1952	Joey Maxim (World light-heavyweight title fight)	ko	14
1955	Ralph Jones	pts	10
1957	Gene Fullmer (World middleweight title fight)	pts	15
	Carmen Basilio (World middleweight title fight)	pts	15
1960	Paul Pender (World middleweight title fight)	pts	15
	Paul Pender (World middleweight title fight)	pts	15
1961	Gene Fullmer (NBA middleweight title fight)	pts	15
1962	Denny Moyer	pts	10
	Phil Moyer	pts	10
	Terry Downes	pts	10
1963	Joey Giardello	pts	10
1964	Mick Leahy	pts	10
1965	Memo Ayon	pts	10
	Stan Harrington	pts	10
	Fred Hernandez	pts	10
	Stan Harrington	pts	10
	Joey Archer	pts	10

Sugar Ray Robinson catches Carmen Basilio with a hard right during their world middleweight title fight on 26 March 1958. Robinson won the title for a record fifth time with a split points decision

exhausted, was retired by his corner. In all his 201 fights this was the only time he did not hear the final bell. He was miles ahead on points and it was no consolation that he lasted longer than referee Ruby Goldstein who had collapsed in the tenth round. Robinson announced his retirement.

He was out of the ring for two and a half years. Five days into the New Year of 1955 he made his comeback. Six fights later, and now thirty-five years of age, he attempted to win the world middleweight championship for the third time. After La Motta and Turpin, Carl Bobo Olsen now had the title. Robinson took five minutes to regain it.

Twice more he lost the title, and twice more he won it back. He 'lent' it to Carmen Basilio and Gene Fullmer. Then he lost the title again to the 'Boston Fireman', Paul Pender. This time there was no comeback. In the return, Pender won again on points. Robinson was forty years and thirty-four days old.

Amazingly he carried on for another forty-seven fights. His defence was so good that no one stopped him; he was virtually unmarked when he retired. On 10 November 1965 he was outpointed by Joey Archer. One month later – 10 December – he held a party to announce his retirement. When he fought Archer he was forty-five and a half years old. He didn't bow out quietly; it was his fifteenth fight of 1965, and Archer was to go on to be the victim of a split decision when he fought Emile Griffith for the world title just seven months later.

At his peak, Robinson was a charismatic showman. When he fought Turpin in London, he had an entourage of fourteen. He turned skipping into a show-business number and he had a 17-foot-long purple Cadillac with the word 'Sugar' written in his own handwriting on the driver's door.

Three years after retirement he tried to break into Hollywood. The move petered out. Like his hero Louis before him, he struck hard times. When he retired, the officials at Madison Square Garden presented him with a gold trophy. On it was the inscription: 'The World's Greatest Fighter'.

But when he returned home he placed it on the bare floor. There was nothing in the house except a flimsy card table and a bed.

Irina Rodnina

A shy, quiet lady, Irina Rodnina's record in ice pairs competition is unrivalled. She also had the dignity to remain cool and composed during emotional times both on and off the ice – none of the difficulties she encountered being of her own volition.

Irina was born in Moscow on 12 September 1949. With the average winter temperature −3°C during the intolerable winter months, it seemed natural that she would drift down to the ice rinks to while away the long winter evenings. Her father, an army officer, was often away on duty, and her mother worked in the local government office.

Ice pairs skating differs from ice dance in that the gymnastic-type movements encouraged in figure skating are allowed. The ice dance sequences of Torvill and Dean, which the Communist Bloc countries queried, are more artistic, ice pairs more flamboyant. Ice dancing, as its name implies, has more contact with the ice. So, for ice pairs, it is natural for the girl to be smaller and lighter. Irina, at 4 feet 11 inches and weighing 7 st, fitted the requirements perfectly.

She began competitive skating at the age of fourteen. Her first coach was also her last, the abrasive Stanislav Zhuk. Irina didn't care for his ruthless approach, but Zhuk was the significant influence throughout her career.

Internationally, Irina's first success was not universally well received. With her partner Alexei Ulanov, she won the 1969 European Championships. But they had dethroned the Protopopovs, then well into their thirties but still the most elegant and creative of all skaters. Ulanov, born in 1947, and Rodnina had developed a busy and lively programme, full of new leaps and jumps. The older pair went into retirement.

Ulanov and Rodnina retained their world titles in 1970 and again in 1971. By the time the Sapporo Olympics of 1972 approached a problem had arisen. In ice pairs, it was of the worst kind. Ulanov, complaining that Irina had ridiculed him, had formed a distinctly more than 'just friends' relationship with Lyudmila Smirnova, from the second-ranked Russian international pair. Rodnina and Ulanov were professional enough to win their Olympic gold medal, Irina showing her emotions in tears at the rostrum, but the damage was irreparable.

A competition to find a succesor to Ulanov was launched. The winner was a young skater from Leningrad called Alexsander Zaitzev.

The partnership flourished on the ice. From 1973 to 1978 they won the World Championship on each occasion, and at the Montreal Olympics Irina retained her title. It is doubtful that it would have given Irina much pleasure, other than professionally, to know that in those first two years – 1973 and 1974 – Ulanov and Smirnova were runners-up.

Americans Tai Babalonia and Randy Gardner won the world title in 1979, but the expected confrontation between the Soviets and Americans at the Lake Placid Olympics did not take place. Gardner suffered an injury and Irina's path to her third gold medal was relatively uncluttered.

Off the ice, the partners went to the altar. They married in 1975, and Irina's pregnancy was the reason the pair did not defend their world title in 1979. The Olympic gold followed less than a year after the birth of their son.

Rodnina and Zaitzev were to their discipline what Torvill and Dean were to ice dancing. At the 1978 European Championships the pair received a record twelve maximums, and at both the 1976 and 1980 Olympics they received a unanimous number-one score from all nine judges.

Irina Rodnina won ten world titles (four with Ulanov and six with Zaitzev) and three Olympic gold medals. The only other skater to equal that performance was Sonia Henje.

Irina's hobbies are now dancing and ballet. She and Alexsander live in Leningrad, and in the last few months Irina has taken on a job which could lead her back into prominence. She's training to be an astronaut.

FACTFILE

Born 12 September 1949, Moscow, USSR

Olympic Games
Gold: 1972 (with Alexei Ulanov)
  1976 (with Alexsander Zaitzev)
  1980 (with Alexsander Zaitzev)

World Championships
Gold: 1969–72 (with Alexei Ulanov)
  1973–78 (with Alexsander Zaitzev)

European Championships
Gold: 1969–72 (with Alexei Ulanov)
  1973–78 (with Alexsander Zaitzev)

Irina Rodnina takes perhaps the first steps towards her new occupation as a trainee astronaut. Husband and partner Alexsander Zaitzev supervises lift-off

Sir Garfield Sobers

'Suddenly it's summer' – that was how one local newspaper journalist began his report on a day's play at Trent Bridge in May 1966. Along with a smattering of spectators, he had watched the greatest cricketer in the world score 153 out of 221 for the West Indies against Nottinghamshire with five 6s and twenty 4s. In those days, whenever Sobers played, it seemed that the sun shone. Before the mass media coverage of today, the arrival of Sobers in a city (especially for a Test match) was an event. He drew crowds to watch him practise – in those days he still went for the odd net. There was pleasure in watching the great man rehearse his repertoire of strokes, with his high back-lift and quicksilver movement of feet. His light-hearted approach belied his concentration as he frequently broke into his characteristic wide grin. Sobers was a happy genius, probably the greatest all-rounder of all time.

As a batsman, he had grace and power in abundance; he played every shot in the book and a few more of spectacular Caribbean improvisation. He bowled left arm quick, slow orthodox and slow chinamen, and, as a fielder, especially close in and particularly at short leg, to Lance Gibbs's off-spin he was superb.

Sobers was seventeen when he made his debut for the West Indies against England at Sabina Park in 1954. He took 4 wickets for 75, as replacement for Alf Valentine, bowling left arm slow on a plumb wicket in an innings which included a double century by Len Hutton and an England total of 414 – a not inauspicious start, but one which went largely unnoticed.

For the next nineteen years Sobers was a fixture in the Test side – from his debut in 1954 he did not miss another Test until the home series in 1973 against Australia.

The Australians became aware of his potential when they toured the Caribbean the following year – 1955. Promoted to open the innings with J. K. Holt, Sobers hit Miller and Lindwall for 43 runs in only a quarter of an hour. Recalling that innings in *A World of Cricket*, C. L. R. James wrote: 'With all his varied experience, that spirit is never far from the surface; it can be seen in the very way he walks to the wicket.'

At the age of twenty-one, Garfield Sobers achieved his first record, typically, for the highest individual score in Test cricket. His 365 not out against Pakistan at Kingston eclipsed Len Hutton's 364 made against Australia at the Oval twenty years earlier. It was his first Test century and made as an opener. In his next Test, he scored 125 and 109 not out and made a total of 824 runs in the series; in his career he made over 500 runs in a series six times!

Sobers's rise to fame was briefly threatened when, in 1959, a car he was driving on the way to London crashed, killing the Jamaican and West Indies batsman Collie Smith. Sobers lost his best friend

and, as a result, decided to adopt an even more happy-go-lucky approach to life. It transmitted itself to his cricket, and from the middle to the spectators who flocked to grounds all over the world to see evidence of his vast talent.

Sobers regarded himself as an entertainer. Along with Frank Worrell, he was primarily responsible for the resurgence of interest in Test cricket in Australia in 1960. He played what he now regards as his best innings – 132 in 123 minutes – at Brisbane in the famous tied Test when he had previously been thought to be out of touch in the state games.

Under Worrell, Sobers learned the art of captaincy and, after another thrilling series in England in 1963, he took over as skipper in 1965 against the visiting Australians, who were captained by Bobby Simpson. Sobers placed himself at six in the batting order (too low, said the critics, forgetting that he had to bowl too), scored only 352 runs with a top score of 69, but led the West Indies to a 2–1 series win. It was the first time the West Indies had beaten the Australians in a series.

In 1966 he brought to England the strongest touring side since Bradman's Australians in 1948. He played a crucial role in the 3–1 series victory. scoring 722 runs at an average of 103.14 and taking 20 wickets and 10 catches. His innings of 161 at Old Trafford and 174 at Leeds won matches. His 163 not out at Lord's saved one. With the West Indies 95 for 5 in their second innings just 9 runs ahead, he added 274, unbeaten, with his cousin, David Holford, who made 105 not out. Less than two years later on a bad wicket at Sabina Park his 113 not out demoralized England – they collapsed to 68 for 8 as Sobers, bowling spinners, gave expert support to Lance Gibbs.

Sobers's deeds in the middle sixties prompted Sir Neville Cardus to write in *Wisden* that Sobers was 'the most renowned name of any cricketer since Bradman's High Noon . . . Power, relaxation, and the gift of holding himself in reserve . . . the sure sign of mastery, of genius of any order, is absence of strain, natural freedom of rhythm . . .'

Whilst his batting always attracted attention – and he will always be remembered for those six 6s in one over off Malcolm Nash for Nottinghamshire against Glamorgan at Swansea – Sobers's bowling was an immense resource available to his team. Frequently, he would act as the support bowler to Hall, Griffith and Gibbs. Often he would take the new ball and, with all the craft learned during his spell in the Lancashire League, spear the ball into or away from the batsman at will, using that classical body action with the full-flowing follow-through. He himself thought he bowled on occasions as fast as either Hall or Griffith. Geoff Boycott was one opener who

FACTFILE

Born 18 July 1936, Barbados, West Indies

Total first-class runs 28,315 (average 54.87)
Highest first-class innings 365*, West Indies *v*. Pakistan (1957–58)
Total first-class wickets 1043 (average 27.74)
Best first-class bowling 9–49, West Indies *v*. Kent (1966)
Test debut 1953–54, *v*. England

Total Test appearances 93
Total Test runs 8032 (average 57.78)
Total Test wickets 235 (average 34.03)
Best Test bowling 6–73, *v*. Australia (1968–69)
Total catches 407

Garfield Sobers, smiling his way to an unbeaten 163 in the second Test at Lord's against England in 1966

found him awkward to play. There were others who found him impossible.

Whilst his bowling and fielding were Test class, Sobers's batting made him a legend. In his day he was the hardest hitter of a cricket ball – the man who could hit a golf ball farther than most professionals demonstrated similar skills in the middle. He never wore a thigh pad, was quick enough to be hit only once by a pace bowler (Richard Jeffersen, bowling for Cambridge University against the MCC at Lord's in 1961) and could adapt his game to any conditions.

After his 254 for the World XI against Australia at Melbourne in 1971 Sir Donald Bradman said it was 'probably the best ever seen in Australia. The people who saw Sobers have enjoyed one of the historic events of cricket. They were privileged to have such an experience.'

The keyword is 'enjoyed'. Spectators enjoyed watching Sobers. He enjoyed the game, rarely nervous even on the final afternoon of the momentous tied Test. Richie Benaud recalled that Sobers was bowling left arm medium to him and Alan Davidson. His bowling was tight and led to the run-out of Davidson by Joe Solomon. But he bowled both round and over the wicket to left- and right-handers and the sight screen at the Stanley Street end was moved each time. After three singles and three sight screen shiftings, he changed his mind in mid-stride as the attendant was halfway through his next moving exercise, and the crowd really gave him 'the razz'. 'Go on,' said Benaud over the tumult, 'I bet you are not game to have it moved back again.' He just grinned. 'How much?' he said. 'Forget it, they'll be over the fence,' said Benaud hastily.

Sobers never refused a bet.

Mark Spitz

At the 1968 Olympic Games in Mexico City, Mark Spitz predicted that he would win six gold medals. He was multiple world record holder. As a sprint swimmer, he would not be affected by the altitude. He won only two golds, those his team-mates helped provide in the relays.

In the 1972 Olympics at Munich, Mark Spitz was expected, despite those earlier failures, to win seven gold medals. Temperamentally better suited, he won seven gold medals, and each was in a world record time.

Born on the 10 February 1950, Mark Andrew Spitz was brought up in Modesto, California, with its advantages of sun and college education. He burst onto the international scene in spectacular style at the 1967 Pan-American Games. He won five gold medals in freestyle, butterfly and relay events and, in the 100- and 200-metre butterfly, broke the existing world records.

With that background, and spurred by the old cliché that it was more difficult to get into the US Olympic team than win a gold medal, Spitz went to Mexico City confident of erasing Don Schollander's four golds at Tokyo from the record books.

Not that two gold medals can be called a disaster, but the dream came hopelessly unstuck. His colleagues baled him out with two golds in the freestyle relays. True, he won a silver in the 100-metre butterfly, and a bronze in the 100-metre freestyle, but he was, after all, the world record holder going into the Games. Confidence shattered and nerve broken, he trailed in a sad last in the 200-metre butterfly.

Persuaded by his father to carry on with a sport that he had threatened to leave, Spitz had further disappointments in the 1970 US Championships. He set a new world record in the heats of the 100-metre freestyle, but was beaten in the final by one hundredth of a second. In the 200-metre butterfly he again broke the world record in a heat, but could only finish fourth in the final.

At this stage there were serious doubts whether Spitz would continue in what was, even at that stage, a long swimming career. Thoughts of those Olympic disasters were the ultimate challenge, boosted by his father's quote: 'Swimming isn't everything, winning is.' And he was still, on the clock, the leading swimmer in the world and was still the favourite, if he could maintain the right attitude.

He was training to be a dentist. With one term to go before being fully qualified, and with a dentist agency set up, he dropped out.

In Munich the 200-metre freestyle was the first event. In Mexico, ironically, it had been the last. Clearly nervous, Spitz ploughed through the water as though chased by piranha fish, and was 2.16 seconds clear of Gary Hall at the finish. The clenched-fist salute and the punching of the water were as much relief as delight at gaining his first individual gold.

The shackles broken, the records tumbled. The 100- and 200-metre races in both freestyle and butterfly produced four individual gold medals, and he joined in with his team-mates to clinch all three relay titles. And on each of those seven occasions the world record books had to be changed.

No one had ever won more than five gold medals at one Olympics before. The grand total was nine gold, one silver and one bronze; only Ray Ewry at the turn of the century with fourteen in standing jumping events, long since discontinued, could claim more. Spitz set twenty-six world records between 1967 and 1972.

He left the amateur ranks in a blaze of publicity. Turning professional for a fee of $5 million, he signed a vast contract with a sports goods firm and made films, two of which were candidates for Channel 4's 'Worst of Hollywood'. Somehow he never really fulfilled the promoters' dream, and the rumour was that he had applied to become a dentist.

FACTFILE

Born 10 February 1950, Modesto, California, USA

Olympic Games
Gold: 4 × 100-metre freestyle relay (1968, 1972)
    4 × 200-metre freestyle relay (1968, 1972)
    100-metre freestyle 51.22 (1972)
    200-metre freestyle 1:52.78 (1972)
    100-metre butterfly 54.27 (1972)
    200-metre butterfly 2:00.72 (1972)
    4 × 100-metre medley race relay (1972)

Silver: 100-metre butterfly (1968)
Bronze: 100-metre freestyle (1968)

Total world records 26
First world record
    400-metre freestyle 4:10.6 (25 June 1967)

*On his promotions career, Spitz said, 'I was ridiculed, exploited and eaten alive. But don't count me out yet. I was once tagged as a failure as a swimmer'

The 100-metre butterfly, one of seven gold medals for Mark Spitz at the 1972 Olympics, and won in a time which remained an Olympic record until the 1984 Los Angeles Olympics

Jackie Stewart

The most statistically successful of all drivers and certainly the best of his era, Stewart assumed the mantle of the great Jim Clark after the latter's death at Hockenheim in 1968.

Stewart demonstrated the ultra-professional approach throughout his career. He reached the top rapidly after winning seven races in a Cooper–BMC in Formula 3 with Ken Tyrell's team in 1964, and a year later he was third in the Formula 2 championship with BRM, having won his first race in his eighth Grand Prix start at Monza. He was co-driver with Graham Hill for BRM, replacing Ritchie Ginther.

British drivers, it seemed, would dominate motor racing for years to come – Jim Clark was at his peak and Graham Hill and John Surtees were also winning titles. But 1966 was a bad year for Stewart. He nearly won his first attempt at Indianapolis but at Spa was trapped in his cockpit after a bad crash, with the danger of the car bursting into flames at any second. Not surprisingly, Stewart lost his edge for a while but the experience made safety at circuits and in cars a prime concern.

Three wins for Matra in 1968 at Zandvoort, Nurburgring and Watkins Glen lifted him into second place in the championship behind Hill; the following year he won six races and took the title for the first time. Two years later he won six times again and announced that any driver can win the title once but it takes real talent to win twice. By the end of 1973 his superiority was complete. A third title in the bag and, after ninety-nine Grands Prix and a record twenty-seven wins, he retired. His 100th Grand Prix was to be the Watkins Glen race at the end of 1973, but team-mate François Cevert was killed in practice. Stewart withdrew and never raced again.

Stewart became a media personality. He was always aware that as world motor racing champion he was a marketable commodity and he made a fortune. His dealings in the commercial world rewarded him for his massive driving skill and compensated for the risks he faced on the circuits of the world. Astute but always polite, Stewart retained his deep interest in the sport, despite being something of an anti-establishment figure. He was a leader in the campaign for greater safety at a time when many of the sport's officials still regarded motor racing as a game where risks were part and parcel of the pleasure.

FACTFILE

Born 11 June 1939, Dumbarton, Scotland

World Drivers Championship
    Winner 1969, 1971, 1973
    Runner-up 1968

World Championship Grand Prix wins (27)
1965   Italian (BRM)
1966   Monaco (BRM)
1968   German, Dutch, United States (all for Matra)
1969   French, British, Dutch, Italian, South African, Spanish
        (all for Matra)
1970   Spanish (March)
1971   Canadian, French, German, British, Monaco, Spanish
        (all for Tyrrell-Ford)
1972   Argentine, Canadian, French, United States
        (all for Tyrrell-Ford)
1973   Belgian, German, Dutch, Monaco, South African
        (all for Tyrrell-Ford)

Summary of Grand Prix wins
Argentina 1972
Belgian 1973
British 1969, 1971
Canadian 1971, 1972
Dutch 1968, 1969, 1973
French 1969, 1971, 1972
German 1968, 1971, 1973
Italian 1965, 1969
Monaco 1966, 1971, 1973
South African 1969, 1973
Spanish 1969, 1970, 1971
United States 1968, 1972

*Stewart had his first race in Marcos in 1961
*His helmet was very distinguishable – he always wore the Stewart tartan
*As a clay-pigeon shooter, Stewart nearly made the British Olympic team
*Stewart's family ran a prosperous Jaguar dealership in Dumbeck, overlooking the Firth of Clyde
*His last race was the 1973 Canadian Grand Prix. He finished fifth
*Turning down a £1 million offer for a comeback in 1979, Stewart said, 'Retirement comes on as a giggle, irrepressible, like champagne bubbles in the back of your nose. I lie in my big bed in the Ritz, the Plaza or the Georges V, and laugh and laugh'
*On motor racing: 'In my sport the quick are only listed among the dead'

The 1973 world champion Jackie Stewart in his Tyrrell Elf during that year's British Grand Prix at Silverstone

John Surtees

The Italians christened him 'Il Grande John'; to the British he was simply 'Big John', the only man ever to win world titles at both motor racing and motorcycling.

Surtees was a fiercely determined young man when he arrived on the motorcycling scene in 1951. He had his first World Championship ride in the Ulster Grand Prix the following year and rode for the British Norton team in 1955 before starting his most impressive years, with MV, in 1956.

As team leader he won the World 500-cc Championship for the first time in 1956 and in two outstanding years, 1958 and 1959, won all twenty-seven World Championship races he entered, clinching both the 350-cc and 500-cc titles both years. He repeated the feat in 1960, the year he made his debut in motor racing, in a Formula Junior Cooper for Ken Tyrrell. In his second Formula 1 race – the British Grand Prix – he came second in a works Lotus, and then won the Isle of Man senior TT for MV within the month.

By 1961, however, he had decided to concentrate on cars and two years later won the German Grand Prix in a Ferrari – his first Formula 1 win. The next year he repeated the win, added a victory at Monza, and completed a late charge to the title, with second place in Mexico, to pip Graham Hill and Jim Clark.

In 1965 he became owner of the Lola team which won the CanAm Championship, but a crash in Canada seemed to have ended his career. However, he came back to win the 1000 kilometres at Monza, and a year later won at Spa in the rain. It looked as though he had done enough to prove his fitness, but he had not convinced Ferrari who said he was not fit for Le Mans – the twenty-four hour race. Surtees always defended his principles fiercely and the issue was settled when he walked out of the Ferrari camp. In a Cooper, he again proved his point by winning in Mexico and then taking the CanAm Championship for the second year running.

1967 saw Surtees with the Honda team; he won a memorable race at Monza in a lengthy battle with Jack Brabham, but his best days as a competitor were over. A disappointing season with BRM followed. In 1969 he founded the Surtees team which made its Formula 1 debut in 1970. It won minor races, notably the Oulton Park Gold Cup race in 1970 and 1971 – but never a Formula 1 Grand Prix, although Mike Hailwood came close at the Italian Grand Prix in 1972.

In 1978 Surtees wound up his team, the general feeling being that he could not find a driver he could respect. Surtees was tough, determined and honest, but never a diplomat.

He now lives in Edenbridge in Kent, where he owns a small investment company connected with motor machines and the restoration of antique furniture and period houses. He owns a collection of old cars and bikes, but presently drives a modest estate car.

As one of the all-time greats – a world champion on two and four wheels – he is unique.

FACTFILE

Born 11 February 1934, Westerham, Kent, England

Motor cycling

World Championships (all for MV)
1956 500 cc
1958 350 cc, 500 cc
1959 350 cc, 500 cc
1960 350 cc, 500 cc

Isle of Man TT
1956 Senior
1958 Senior, junior
1959 Senior, junior
1960 Senior

Motor racing

World Drivers Championship
  Winner 1964
  Runner-up 1966

World Championship Grand Prix wins
1963 German (Ferrari)
1964 German, Italian (both for Ferrari)
1966 Belgian, Mexican (both for Ferrari)
1967 Italian (Honda)

An early photograph of John Surtees on a 500-cc works Norton at the 1954 Scarborough International

Irena Szewinska

Irena Szewinska, in a fifteen-year career, won more major titles than any other female athlete. Tall (5 feet 11 inch), graceful and a superb ambassadress for her sport and her troubled nation, Irena competed in five Olympic Games and won seven medals in five different events. She found her niche, the 400 metres, late in life, but set new standards in an event many thought too severe a few years earlier.

Born Irena Kirzenstein, on 24 May 1946, Irena developed through the tried Polish athletics system and made the first of a record forty-eight appearances in 1963. She came to the notice of the British public in 1964 when, at the age of eighteen, she collected the silver medal behind Mary Rand in the Olympic long-jump final at Tokyo, with a leap of 21 feet 8 inches (6.60 metres). She set a European record in the 200 metres in 23.1 seconds to claim another silver medal, then struck gold and a new world record in the 4 × 100-metre relay. The IAAF took the world record away when Ewa Klobukowska, the 100-metre winner and a member of the relay team, failed a sex test. Klobukowska retired to start a family.

Irena's progression was maintained in 1965. The highlight was her first world record, the 100 metres in 11.1 seconds. Irena won the sprint double in the World Student Games, set five junior world records and won her first national title, in the long jump. It was the first of nineteen national titles – the other domestic statistics being a final total of thirty-eight national records.

The 1966 European Championships were a triumph. Three gold medals, in the sprint relay, long jump and 200 metres, and a silver in the 100 metres. The following year she married her coach Janusz Szewinsk on Christmas Day, after a five-year courtship.

The Mexico Olympics were a little disappointing. As world record holder, she had hoped for gold in the 100 metres but could 'only' manage the bronze. The long jump was a disaster; after the promise of Tokyo, Irena failed to qualify. But the rarified atmosphere suited her in the 200 metres – she won the gold medal and set a new world record of 22.5 seconds.

Her first baby, son Andrzej, was born in 1970, and Irena had problems fitting in training with running a family. A bronze medal in the 200 metres at the 1972 Olympics was more a reward for keeping fit than for disciplined training. She felt that she was losing her edge in the explosive events.

The 400 metres appealed, and Irena ran her first race over the distance in 1973 at Warsaw, running for her club side Gwardia Warsaw. The time was a promising 52.0 seconds. The next time she ran the distance, the world knew about it. The magic landmark of a sub-50-second 400 metres had been broken, by a tenth of a second.

Irena dominated the one-lap race for five years. She ran a winning streak of thirty-five races. After opting for and winning the sprint double in the 1974 European Championships in Rome, Irena concentrated on the 400 metres for the Montreal Olympics. The East German machine was catching up fast, and the thirty-year-old Szewinska was confronted by an eighteen-year-old East German, Christina Brehmer, who had taken her world record earlier in the year. It was no contest, as Muhammad Ali used to say. Irena won by 10 metres and reclaimed her world record.

Invincibility lasted until the European Championships in Prague in 1978, where Irena had to settle for bronze behind the new queen, Marita Koch, a dental nurse from Rostock, East Germany. It was Irena's tenth medal in the Europeans, six of them gold – a record; in the Europa Cup, no one matched Irena's 73 points for her country.

At thirty-four, she surprisingly announced that she would defend her Olympic title at the 1980 Moscow Olympics. In the semifinal, the world saw the sad sight of Irena limping over the line with a pulled muscle. The incident allowed sixteen-year-old Linsey McDonald a passage into the final.

But there may have been a reason behind her decision to compete. Perhaps she felt that she could sign off with a medal in the country of her birth. Irena was born in Leningrad.

FACTFILE

Born 24 May 1946, Leningrad, USSR

Olympic Games
Gold: 4 × 100-metre relay (1964)
    200 metres (1968)
    400 metres (1976)
Silver: 200 metres (1964)
    Long jump (1964)
Bronze: 100 metres (1968)
    200 metres (1972)

European Championships
Gold: Long jump (1966)
    200 metres (1966, 1974)
    4 × 100-metre relay (1966)
    100 metres (1974)

Silver: 100 metres (1966)
Bronze: 200 metres (1971)
    4 × 100-metre relay (1974)
    4 × 400-metre relay (1978)
    400 metres (1978)

World records
100 metres 11.1 (1965)
            11.1 (1968)
200 metres 22.7 (1965)
            22.7 (1967, unratified)
            22.58 (1968)
            22.21 (1974)
400 metres 49.9 (1974)
            49.75 (1976)
            49.29 (1976)

Irena Szewinska sets a trend which Ed Moses was to follow by winning a major event with shoelaces undone. Irena is seen here breaking the 400-metre world record at the Montreal Olympics

Daley Thompson

Francis Morgan Thompson, better known as Daley, won every major decathlon title in the world in a four-year spell from 1980 to 1984. His record includes one peculiar statistic – he's never competed in a major decathlon in England!

Born in Kensington, London, on 30 July 1958, Daley had ambitions as a footballer. That was until Fulham turned him down. Son of a Nigerian father and a Scottish mother, who split up when he was eight, his father dying five years later, Daley was brought up near Crawley, which boasted another 1980's world champion in middle-weight boxer Alan Minter.

Extrovert even at school, Daley's first incursion into serious athletics began when he was only sixteen, winning the Welsh AAA decathlon championship at Cwmbran with 6685 points. His individualistic nature was suited to athletics. Two months later he went back to the same stadium to win the AAA junior title, with 7008 points.

The following season – Montreal Olympic year – he won the AAA Senior Championships at Cwmbran and was selected for the Games. The youngest member of the British party, Daley finished eighteenth at Montreal. Winner Bruce Jenner, on his way to a career in films, pointed at Daley and said, 'There's your next Olympic champion.' Daley was eighteen on the final day of competition. Six weeks later Jenner's words gained some credence – Daley broke the world junior record at Talence in France with 7905 points.

Early in 1977, in a four-cornered match between England, Spain, Denmark and Italy in Madrid, Daley broke the 8000-point barrier by 190, a fine warm-up for the European Junior Championships in Donetsk, which he won with some ease.

In 1978, aged twenty, Daley won his first major title, the Commonwealth gold medal at Edmonton. Wind assistance in the first two events – the 100 metres in 10.50 s, and a huge long jump, way over 26 feet – ruined any attempt on Jenner's world record of 8617 points which had been set in Montreal, but 8467 points constituted a genuine threat. Three weeks later, the favourite but still tired from the Edmonton trip, Daley had to settle for silver in the European Championships, losing to the Russian Grebenyuk, whose total of 8340 points was 55 more than Daley's.

Injuries curtailed his build-up in 1979. His training for the ten events was to enter three or four good-class events with his club, the often threatened Essex Beagles. He won the UK long-jump title in 1979 and, in a British League match, scored a record 54 points in an afternoon. In winter he travelled to sunnier climes to perfect a series of disciplines. He did not bother with the American universities, turning down the offers of twenty US scholarships. 'I hear they do a course on comics,' was his retort.

Early in 1980, after training at Wimbledon, Crawley and Crystal Palace, he chose his warm-up competition. The venue was Götzis, a little Austrian town of 1500 souls, which swells to 15,000 at the end of each May, when the best decathlon outside the majors is held. Daley, threatened by the immediate presence of Guido Kratschmer, and the growing threat of Jürgen Hingsen, both West Germans, struck a psychological blow by breaking Jenner's world record with 8622 points. Kratschmer finished second, well adrift, and although Kratschmer went on to beat Daley's record a few weeks later in Bernhausen, the Germans knew that Daley was the better all-round athlete. They declined to go to Moscow.

Daley won the gold medal at Moscow with ease, a couple of eminently forgettable Russians trailing in over 100 points behind. Thompson, cheerful and outgoing, ambled through the last event of the Games, the 1500 metres, the medal securely his.

1982, the year of double championships – European and Commonwealth – began in fine style at Götzis. A points haul of 8704 erased Kratschmer's name from the record books. Then Hingsen added 10 more points in August at Ulm. In June, however, Daley was injured when his pole broke in the pole vault and the jagged end dug deep into his arm, which needed extensive stitching. In the European Championship at Athens, Daley toyed with Hingsen, first ensuring gold, then with a careering run over the last

---

FACTFILE

Born 30 July 1958, London, England

Olympic Games
Gold: Decathlon 8495 pts (1980); 8797 pts (1984)

World Championships
Gold: Decathlon 8666 pts (1983)

European Championships
Gold: Decathlon 8743 pts (1982)
Silver: Decathlon 8289 pts (1978)

Commonwealth Games
Gold: Decathlon 8467 pts (1978)
         Decathlon 8410 pts (1982)

World decathlon records
8622 pts (1980)
8704 pts (1982)
8743 pts (1982)

Daley Thompson's best performances
   100 metres   10.28 s (w); 10.36 s (1984)
   Long jump   8.11 m (w) (1978); 8.01 m (1980)
   Shot   16.10 m (1983)
   High jump   2.14 m (i) (1982); 2.11 m (1982)
   400 metres   46.86 s (1982)
   110-metre hurdles   14.26 s (1983)
   Discus   47.44 m (1981)
   Pole vault   5.20 m (1981)
   Javelin   65.38 m (1980)
   1500 metres   4:20.3 (1976)

Decathlon: Order of Events

Day One	Day Two
1 100 metres	6 110-metre hurdles
2 Long jump	7 Discus
3 Shot	8 Pole vault
4 High jump	9 Javelin
5 400 metres	10 1500 metres

A familiar scene. Daley Thompson stands amongst an assorted collection of fallen Germans and Russians at the 1982 European Championships at Athens

200 of the 1500 metres, retaking the world record by a margin of 20 points. The Commonwealth Championships were like a package holiday to Brisbane with a bit of hard work thrown in.

So to Helsinki for the inaugural World Championships. Hingsen had again stolen Daley's world record, and again Daley beat the German. The pair buried the hatchet in Lanzarote when they found themselves sharing the same training facilities.

Tactically, Thompson is sound. His strong events, the 100 and 400 metres, are on the first day. The long jump is probably his best event. He has also learned to put pressure on rivals by recording good heights at both the high jump and pole vault, also strong events, and building from there. He's spent endless hours improving his technique in the throwing events, in which again he builds from a sound first throw. It has meant that he has never really been seriously pressured in the killing 1500 metres, preferring to jog in, eye on the clock.

Daley went into Olympic year as one of the hottest favourites for a gold medal at Los Angeles. He did his winter training in San Diego. He began the defence of his Olympic title with fine performances in three of the five first-day events, the 100 and 400 metres, and a personal best in the long jump. When Jürgen Hingsen was expected to issue his normal second-day challenge, Daley exerted pressure on him in the pole vault and the West German lost his grip on the pole. The points margin was such that Daley needed only a 4-minute 35 second jog in the final event, the 1500 metres, to reclaim the world record.

In the end he failed by one point to add the world record to his second Olympic title. At Los Angeles 1984, the jokes may have fallen flat, but the performance was quite outstanding. And, who knows, one day he might even be tempted to compete in a decathlon in England. His is a story which is far from over.

Jayne Torvill and Christopher Dean

If the world ice dance champions, Jayne Torvill and Christopher Dean, have a problem, it is probably more from the calendar than from the opposition on the ice. Despite European and world titles, their ultimate objective has always been an Olympic gold medal. Jayne and Chris became the best in the world in 1981 and have had to wait an entire Olympic cycle, staving off challenges, changing sequences and setting new standards, to aim for their goal at the Yugoslav provincial town of Sarajevo.

Their first trainer was Janet Sawbridge in 1975. Both Jayne and Chris were training at the Nottingham rink and both needed a partner. They agreed on a one-month then a two-month trial. Skating, however, had already entered their lives.

Jayne Torvill was born in Nottingham on 7 October 1957, the daughter of a newsagent. She was educated at Clifton Hall Grammar School and worked as an insurance clerk before taking up the sport full time. Her teacher in junior school took her down to the rink when she was barely ten years old. A fine individual skater, she first made her mark on the British scene in the pairs championship. Her partner was Michael Hutchinson and together they won the British junior title in 1970 and were runners-up in the senior event. Next year they were British senior champions.

Christopher Dean was also born in Nottingham, on 27 July 1958; he is the son of an electrician. He also started skating at the age of ten. His mother wanted him to do something after school, so he tried skating and was encouraged to continue after receiving a pair of skates for Christmas. Shortly after, he broke his leg, but couldn't wait to return to the Nottingham ice rink. Unlike Jayne, who was involved in ice pairs, Chris was always an ice dance specialist. In 1974 he won the British Junior Ice Dance Championship with Sandra Elson. Now Sandra Horvath, she is married to a Hungarian businessman and spends most of her time abroad.

No one really remembers what happened to that one-month agreement. In their first competition at Bristol, Torvill and Dean were second; their first victory was the Sheffield Trophy, followed by the Northern Championship and the St Gervais title, all in 1976. Two years later they were British champions for the first time.

They were now under the increasing influence of Betty Calloway, who had the future world champions Hungarians Rogoczy and Sallay under her command. In 1978 Jayne and Chris finished ninth in their first European Championships and eleventh in the World Championships. By 1980 they had improved to fifth place in the Olympics, and fourth at the World Championships.

For the first time they had sponsors. The Sports Aid Foundation donated £8000, and the Nottingham City Council £42,000 over a three-year period. Up to then they had had to struggle by fitting in sessions early in the morning or late at night. Chris had been a policeman with the Nottingham force working shifts, whilst Jayne had been so tired after training that she had often fallen asleep at her desk.

The grant meant the opportunity to take up the kind offer to use the West German training centre, a superb rink at Oberstorf. The results were immediate. Jayne and Chris won the world title at Hartford, Connecticut, in 1981. They were also European champions. Had it been too soon though?

Whilst preparing for Sarajevo, Jayne and Chris had a virtually unchallenged run of success: British champions every year from

---

FACTFILE

Jayne Torvill born 7 October 1957, Nottingham, England
Chris Dean born 27 July 1958, Nottingham, England

World Champions 1981, 1982, 1983, 1984
European Champions 1981, 1982, 1984
Olympic Champions 1984

Maximums
  1981 British Championships (Nottingham) 7 out of a possible 9
  1982 European Championships (Lyon) a total of 11 for their free
    routine. 8 for presentation
  1982 World Championships (Copenhagen) 5 maximums for
    artistic impression in final routine
  1983 World Championships (Helsinki) An unprecedented 9 out
    of 9 for presentation of 'Barnham' routine
  1984 European Championships (Budapest) 3 for technical merit
    and 8 for presentation of the 'Bolero' routine
  1984 Olympic Games (Sarajevo) A total of 19 maximums gained
    for the three routines
  1984 World Championships (Ottawa) An unprecedented
    29 maximums scored

*In 1981, Torvill and Dean's free programme consisted of a routine made up of four different pieces of music as follows:
  (a) a quick-step called 'Hot Lunch Jam' from the musical *Fame*
  (b) a speciality dance to 'Caravan'
  (c) a slow, romantic rumba to 'Red Sails in the Sunset'
  (d) a pulsating finale to 'Swing, Swing, Swing'
*Ravel's 'Bolero' is estimated to have earned over £2 million in royalties. Olympic gold medals for Torvill and Dean might well enable them to earn the same sort of money after turning professional
*Betty Calloway, Jayne and Chris's coach, left St Vincent's Convent in London to join the Blackpool Ice Follies. With her first husband, Roy, she taught at Richmond ice rink for eighteen years. She was appointed West German national coach in 1968. On her own she trained Erich and Angelika Buck, the 1972 European champions and runners-up in the World Championships, and the Hungarians, Sallay and Rogoczy, the 1980 World champions. On 6 April 1978 she travelled to Nottingham to meet Jayne and Chris for the first time.

She now lives in Beaconsfield with her second husband, Bill Frittall, a retired British Airways training captain

Bolero at Sarajevo. The culmination of three years at the peak of world sport, Jayne and Chris literally skate to Olympic gold, in February 1984

1978 to 1984, European champions in 1981–82 and 1984, and world champions from 1981 to 1984. The missing European Championship in 1983 has a story. Whilst practising Chris fell, causing Jayne to fall and injure her shoulder. They did not compete.

Jayne and Chris prefer not to employ their own choreographer, though there was an exception when Michael Crawford taught them the 'Barnum' routine. Extroverts on stage, they are quiet and shy away from the ice.

The concept that they have brought to skating is best summed up by two British world champions, John Curry and Courtney Jones. Curry: 'They are fine skaters in their own right. Their subtleties are lost on those who don't know.' Courtney Jones: 'They have pushed out the frontiers farther and farther. They have opened up a new era, if only the rest of the world can grasp what they do.'

The rest of the world is beginning to learn. Or at least the judges are. In the World Championships in 1982 at Copenhagen, they gave a superb rendering of 'Summertime' in the set pattern. Then, in the free dance section, five judges awarded the maximum 6 marks for the interpretation of 'Mack and Mabel'.

In 1983 the pair had been to London to see Michael Crawford in *Barnum* at the Palladium. Choosing the show's music for the free dance, Jayne and Chris produced the skating performance of all time at the World Championships at Helsinki. All nine judges gave them the maximum 6 points for artistic impression, an unprecedented event in the sport's history.

In Olympic year the horizons changed again. The free dance was Ravel's 'Bolero', and the set pattern rendition of the 'Paso Doble' is rated even better. The costumes for 'Bolero' took six months to design. They cruised to the Olympic, world and European titles. The only thing that never changed was the marks.

Ludmila Tourischeva

If Ludmila Tourischeva had a problem during her gymnastics career, it was that she was a team-mate and contemporary of Olga Korbut. Technically she was a far superior gymnast: she was more consistent and, to her eternal credit, she was completely unconcerned with the adulation and hero worship that Olga received. She was the gymnasts' champion.

Ludmila was born on 7 October 1952 in the village of Grozny, near the industrial and river port of Rostov on Don, the traditional Soviet gateway to the Caucasus mountains, a hundred miles to the south.

The product of the Soviet 'security in numbers' programme, she was one of 700,000 gymnasts enrolled at schools and clubs. Her father was a chauffeur, driving a 'Harry Lime' black sedan, and her mother was a housewife; Ludmila has an elder sister.

Her coach was Vladislav Rastorotsky. She trained from six until eight o'clock in the morning, studied during the day, and returned to the gym for a two-hour session in the evening.

At sixteen, she was in the team which won the gold medal at the 1968 Olympics in the team competition, but initially Ludmila was pushed through more quickly than was perhaps desirable. Vera Caslavska from Czechoslovakia was the queen. Larissa Latynina had retired and the Soviet champion, Natalia Kuchinskaya, was in the early throes of a glandular disease which was to end her career. The East Germans were threatening.

Ludmila had also developed a habit of falling off the beam. The affliction began in the 1968 Olympics and continued through domestic events for another two years.

By the 1970 World Championships in Ljubljana, Yugoslavia, she was world champion in the combined exercises and team competition. Coached by Latynina, she also won gold in the floor exercises. At the European Championships at Minsk the following year she was equal first with Tamara Lazakovitch, her team-mate, in the combined exercises – they each won two of the four individual disciplines.

So to Munich and the 1972 Olympics, where Olga Korbut took the publicity and three gold medals whilst Ludmila took two. She was combined Olympic champion and team champion. But in the individual events, though never out of the top five, her best was a silver in the floor exercises.

Wembley was the scene of the long-awaited rematch. The 1973 European Championships were scheduled for the famous pool. The English crowd had caught gymnastics fever and they preferred the flamboyance of Olga to the shapely, attractive Ludmila, who seemed 'too Russian'. The team and combined competitions came first, with the top thirty-six moving on to the individual disciplines later. After the first part, the Soviet Union had obviously won the team title. Again, though, it was Ludmila, the better gymnast, who won the combined gold medal, with Olga, slowed by an injured ankle, second. Ludmila was better at the floor exercises and now had confidence on the beam. Plagued by her ankle, Olga withdrew from the competition after coming to a shuddering halt on the vault runway, and Ludmila took all four individual golds.

FACTFILE

Born 7 October 1952, Grozny, nr Rostov, USSR

1968 Olympic Games (Mexico)
Gold: Team competition

1969 European Championships (Landskrona)
Bronze: Combined exercises, floor exercises, bars

1970 World Championships (Ljubljana)
Gold: Combined exercises, team competition, floor exercises
Silver: Bars
Bronze: Vault

1971 European Championships (Minsk)
Gold: Combined exercises, vault, floor exercises
Silver: Beam, bars

1972 Olympic Games (Munich)
Gold: Combined exercises, team competition
Silver: Floor exercises
Bronze: Vault

1973 European Championships (London)
Gold: Combined exercises, vault, beam, floor exercises, bars
(Winning all five golds equalled the record of Vera Caslavska in 1965 and 1967)

1974 World Championships (Varna)
Gold: Combined exercises, team competition, beam, floor exercises
Silver: Vault
Bronze: Bars

1975 European Championships (Skein)
Bronze: Floor exercises

1976 Olympic Games (Montreal)
Gold: Team competition
Silver: Vault, floor exercises
Bronze: Combined exercises

*Caslavska, Tourischeva and Comaneci have dominated women's gymnastics since the early 1960s. Between them they have a total of eighty-seven world, Olympic and European medals. The following table compares how the three girls have fared:

Vera Caslavska	Gold	Silver	Bronze
Olympic Games	7	4	0
World Championships	3	3	1
European Championships	11	1	2
Total	21	8	3 = 32
Ludmila Tourischeva			
Olympic Games	4	3	2
World Championships	7	2	2
European Championships	8	2	4
Total	19	7	8 = 34
Nadia Comaneci			
Olympic Games	5	3	1
World Championships	1	1	0
European Championships	9	3	0
Total	15	7	1 = 23

Major gymnastics events arrive with indecent haste. The following year the World Championships were held in Varna, the Bulgarian Benidorm. Again Ludmila was first and Olga second in the combined exercises. Olga lasted the course in the individual exercises, winning the vault and taking the silver in the other three disciplines, Ludmila won two golds (beam and floor) and a silver and bronze.

With the Korbut threat dispelled, Ludmila looked to the Montreal Olympics with confidence. But at the 1975 European Championships in the little Norwegian port of Skein came disaster. She came only fourth in the combined exercises after a nightmare on the bars; the winner was to prove a growing threat – Nadia Comaneci.

Winning the new World Cup in London in 1975 boosted Ludmila's confidence, although she finished her routine on the bar only a split second before the bars themselves clattered to the floor. The supports had given way.

But the Montreal Olympics merely confirmed what everyone knew: Ludmilla had abdicated the combined title to Nadia; Nelli Kim finished second. Ludmila, Nelli and Olga were supreme in the team event. For all her titles, Ludmila had never won an individual title at the Olympics. The nearest she came to a gold medal was in the very last exercise that she undertook in international competition, the floor exercises, her favourite. This time she beat Nadia, but, in the final routine of all, was pipped by Nelli Kim.

After Montreal Ludmila married another gold medallist from the Munich Olympics, the sprinter Valeriy Borzov. Now a Kiev housewife and mother, Ludmila is a respected national coach.

Valeriy Borzov

*Ludmila's husband is also a Russian Olympic champion. Although he cannot match his wife's record, but he still has quite a few titles of his own to his credit, namely:

1968	European junior 100- and 200-metre champion
1969	European 100-metre champion
1970	European indoor 60-metre champion
1971	European indoor 60-metre champion
	European 100- and 200-metre champion
1972	European indoor 60-metre champion
	Olympic 100- and 200-metre champion
1974	European indoor 60-metre champion
1975	European 100-metre champion
	European indoor 60-metre champion
1976	European indoor 60-metre champion

*He was the first European to win the men's Olympic sprint double
*At the 1976 Olympics, he was third in the 100 metres, the first time the reigning men's 100-metre champion had won a medal at the following Games
*He never set an outdoor world record, but shared the 60-metre indoor world record in 1968

Ludmila Tourischeva waiting for the music to open her floor exercises at the 1972 Munich Olympics. She took the silver medal in the discipline, but won the overall Olympic title

Freddie Trueman

A 100 per cent Yorkshire character, Fred Trueman was possibly the most famous British sportsman in the early 1960s. Fiery Fred had a peculiar talent for arriving impressively. When he was born in 1931 he weighed over 14 lb. Before he played in one, he had never seen a Test match. In his debut series, in 1952 against India, he took 29 wickets, terrifying the Indian batsmen, who were totally unused to such pace. At Old Trafford they were 4 wickets down without a run on the board and were all out for 58 in eighty minutes, with Trueman taking 8 for 31 and loving every minute.

Trueman's stubborn Yorkshire character was always likely to bring him into conflict with the game's authorities. Early in his career with Yorkshire he had experienced the fickle nature of officials and selectors when, after taking 31 wickets in eight games in his 1949 debut season, the county decided to pick schoolmaster Bill Foord, who was thought to be a better prospect, instead of him even though Foord could only play during the holidays.

Trueman's pride was injured. After his career had been interrupted by National Service (he was given leave of absence to play for England, but rarely for Yorkshire), he went on the 1953–54 tour to the West Indies. Trouble followed him wherever he went – he was accused of abusing umpires and batsmen. Officials at Lord's believed the allegations and Trueman's career came to a temporary halt.

FACTFILE

Born 6 February 1931, Stainton, West Yorkshire

First-class debut 1949, Yorkshire v. Cambridge University
Total first-class wickets 2304 (average 18.29)
Best first-class bowling 8–28, Yorkshire v. Kent, Dover (1954)
Highest first-class innings 104, Yorkshire v. Northamptonshire Northampton (1963)
Test debut 5 June 1952, v. India, Headingley
Total Test appearances 67
Total Test wickets 307 (average 21.57)
Best Test bowling 8–41, v. India, Old Trafford (1952)
Total Test runs 981
Highest Test innings 39*, v. New Zealand, The Oval (1958)

First-class wickets taken by Trueman in England

Year	Runs	Wickets	Average
1949	719	31	23.19
1950	876	31	28.25
1951	1852	90	20.57
1952	841	61	13.78
1953	1411	44	32.06
1954	2085	134	15.55
1955	2454	153	16.03
1956	1383	59	23.44
1957	2303	135	17.05
1958	1414	106	13.33
1959	2730	140	19.50
1960	2447	175	13.98
1961	3000	155	19.35
1962	2717	153	17.75
1963	1955	129	15.15
1964	2194	100	21.94
1965	1811	127	14.25
1966	2040	111	18.37
1967	1610	75	21.46
1968	1375	66	20.83
1969	93	2	46.50

*Fred took just four first-class hat tricks – three of them against Nottinghamshire: 1951 Yorkshire v. Nottinghamshire (Nottingham); 1955 Yorkshire v. Nottinghamshire (Scarborough); 1958 Yorkshire v. MCC (Lord's); 1963 Yorkshire v. Nottinghamshire (Bradford)

*He took 8 wickets in an innings ten times – again, three of them were against Nottinghamshire

*Trueman's National Service commenced in 1951 when he joined the RAF. After initial training he was posted to Hemswell in Lincolnshire, first as an AC2, rising later to an AC1. His duties included looking after the sports equipment and the football and cricket pitches. Whilst there, he played as a centre forward with the Lincoln City junior team.

*Stories of Fred's tour to Australia in 1958–59 continue to be legendary in after-dinner speeches . . .

At a stop-over in the Middle East, the tour manager, anxious to gain Fred's confidence, is reported to have said, 'Fred, I hear that the sheikh over there has 198 wives.' 'Two more, and he can qualify for a new ball,' was the reply.

England were taking a hammering on a hot afternoon during the Test series. At the end of a tiring and wearing day, the England captain summoned Fred for one more spell. Our hero was not keen. 'Come on,' said the captain, 'England is expecting.' 'So that's why it's called the mother country,' said Fred.

The newly ordained Rev. David Sheppard, a fine batsman but a suspect fielder, spent the tour being hidden in the slips. He dropped much off Fred's bowling. After yet another spilling, Fred was quoted as saying, 'Vicar, thee might keep thy eyes shut whilst praying, but keep 'em bloody open when I'm bowling!'

*Fred's father, a keen local cricketer, gave Fred, one of a family of eight, every encouragement

*Fred was the first bowler to take 300 Test wickets

*He is now a respected summarizer for the BBC and overseas networks

*When asked for a title for his autobiography, Fred replied, 'The Definitive Volume on the Finest Bloody Fast Bowler that Ever Drew Breath'

*In one game, when he was chasing 100 wickets in a season, Fred said, 'I need 9 wickets from this match. You'd better start drawing straws to see who I get'

Fred Trueman in action against Australia in 1964. During the series he became the first bowler to take 300 Test wickets

England may not have wanted him, but Yorkshire certainly did. Just one of his remarkable analyses was returned in 1954 when playing against Kent at Dover. Trueman took 8 wickets for 28 – all before lunch on the first day. In the ten seasons between 1957 and 1966 he took 100 wickets a season for Yorkshire, forced his way back into the England side and became a national hero. In 1964 he became the first bowler to take 300 Test wickets and appropriately it was against Australia – always the country most likely to bring out the real competitive streak in Fred.

Trueman's powers had shown signs of wear in that series. In fact, he had been dropped for the Fourth Test at Old Trafford, but his replacements had made no impression on a Manchester featherbed wicket and he was recalled for the Fifth and final Test at the Oval.

Just before lunch on the Saturday the England skipper, Ted Dexter, was still thinking about who should bowl from the pavilion end, when the ball was snatched from his hand by Trueman, who had been unimpressive in an earlier spell. He then proceeded to bowl Ian Redpath and have Graham McKenzie caught by Colin Cowdrey at slip in successive balls. With his total at 299 Test wickets and no time for another batsman to come in before lunch, the crowd were on tenterhooks for forty minutes. Could the magic 300th be achieved with a hat trick?

It wasn't, but just when Dexter was thinking of taking Trueman off, Neil Hawke edged to Cowdrey at slip. The catch was safely pocketed and the first man to congratulate Trueman was the batsman on his way back to the pavilion.

Later, when asked the time-honoured question, 'Well, Fred how do you feel?' he gave the simple but honest reply – 'Knackered.'

It was a typical comment from a forthright, whole-hearted character. On his first tour of Australia in 1958–59, playing against one of the country elevens, he had three successive appeals – two lbws, one catch – against one batsman turned down by a stone-faced Australian umpire. Fuming, Trueman rolled back to his mark, flicked back his thick mane of dark hair, slipped into his rhythmical run-up and classical sideways-on action, and let go a screaming yorker that uprooted the batsman's middle stump. Turning to the umpire, who was gaping in awe, Trueman snatched his sweater and growled, 'Nearly had 'im there.'

Trueman was perfectly built for a fast bowler; in his day he was as fast as anybody – his own tribute to himself was 'The best bloody fast bowler that ever drew breath' – but he is the first to acknowledge the debt he owes to his England bowling partner, Brian Statham. Statham's relentless accuracy was the perfect foil for Trueman's fiery unpredictability.

When the West Indies arrived in England in 1963 with Wes Hall and Charlie Griffith, Trueman was determined not to be overshadowed. He took 34 wickets in the series, including 11 for 152 at Lord's and 12 for 119 at Edgbaston, against a side that included Hunte, Kanhai, Sobers and Butcher at their peak.

According to Trevor Bailey, Trueman's most useful trait was that he was supremely confident. He genuinely believed that every ball he bowled was liable to take a wicket. He was a fine ambidextrous fielder – especially close in on the leg side – and as a batsman he scored three centuries which probably gave him as much pleasure as anything – except perhaps captaining Yorkshire to victory over the 1968 Australians at Headingley.

Tom Watson

Two months in 1982 established Tom Watson as one of golf's all-time greats. In June, at Pebble Beach, he reached the seventeenth hole in the last round of the US Open, wanting two pars to force a play-off with Jack Nicklaus. Five yards away, but in grass 5 inches deep, he birdied the hole with what will undoubtedly become one of golf's legendary shots, then birdied the last to win by 2 strokes. It was his first US Open title. In July, at Troon, he took the British Open, his nerve lasting when those of Clampett, Price and others failed. Watson's opinion is that he won the US title fair and square, but the British was given to him. The truth is that his last-round 70, including an eagle at the eleventh, was good enough deservedly to earn the title.

Watson began as a professional after only a moderate amateur career. He lost tournaments he should have won until 1974, when he won the Western Open, after coming from 6 back, returning a last-round 69. In 1975 he went to Carnoustie for a look at the British Open and, after a play-off with Jack Newton, became only the fourth man ever to win the event at his first attempt (Hogan, Lema and Rogers being the others).

In 1977 Watson had a superb year, winning four US events including the Masters after a fascinating duel with Nicklaus. They were level until the seventeenth on the final round. Again he birdied and eventually won by 2 strokes.

The Masters, however, was merely an appetizer for the British Open that year at Turnberry. Watson and Nicklaus began identically – 68, 70, 65 – then, still level in the final round, Watson birdied the seventeenth and Nicklaus parred. On the last Nicklaus pushed his drive out to the right; Watson hit his approach shot to within 2 feet of the pin. Somehow Nicklaus came back with a massive putt across the green. Watson, now facing a test of nerve, calmly slotted his putt to win by 1 stroke with a new record aggregate of 268.

There was yet another Open win in Scotland – his third – in 1980 at Muirfield, when his third-round 64 enabled him to overtake Lee Trevino, who was ahead by 3 shots at the start of the day.

According to Peter Alliss, Watson's greatest quality is nerve. 'The quality which the early Watson seemed to lack, but which is now fully present, is in a close-fought finale, whether he is coming from behind or in the equally testing position of having to conquer the fear of surrendering a commanding lead.'

1982 was the year when Watson began to lose the 'automaton' tag which had not endeared him to the fans. His dance of glee after holing his shot from the grass at the seventeenth at Pebble Beach proved that he did have feelings. The story of his schoolboy-like prank after winning the 1980 championship at Muirfield brought a smile to faces of golf followers, who previously had thought of Watson as an excellent golfer, but a trifle humourless, a serious man going about his serious business. After his win at Muirfield, Watson, with Ben Crenshaw, sneaked back onto the course and played with hickory-shafted antique clubs, only to be chased off by an irate Muirfield secretary!

In 1983 he won his first Open title outside Scotland when he lifted his fifth championship at Royal Birkdale. Earlier in the year at the US Open in Oakmont, Pennsylvania, he finished second to Larry Nelson. Nelson put together the lowest two final rounds in US Open history – 65, 67 – to pip Watson after an uncharacteristic lapse on the seventeenth. Watson found a greenside bunker, then missed a 4-foot putt for par which would have tied for the lead. Watson's 1983 in America was poor by his standards – without a win and finishing twelfth on the money list, but his fifth win in nine attempts in the British Open was some consolation.

Watson's praise of golf in Britain is glowing. 'It's exciting to play here, and the galleries understand the game and are very respectful. In my opinion, it's the last civilized country left in the world.'

FACTFILE

Born 4 September 1949, Kansas City, Missouri, USA

'Big Four' wins 8
US Open 1982
British Open 1975, 1977, 1980, 1982, 1983
US Masters 1977, 1981
Ryder Cup appearances 1977, 1981, 1983
US PGA Player of the Year 1977, 1978, 1979, 1980, 1983
Leading money winner in USA 1978, 1979, 1980

*Watson turned pro in 1971. His first winnings were on 24 October 1971, when he won $1065 for equal twenty-eighth place in the Kaiser Open
*He won three consecutive American tournaments in 1980
*He has a degree in psychology from Stanford University
*He met his wife Linda when they were both thirteen. They were both appearing in a local production of *The Pirates of Penzance*
*By the start of 1984 US PGA Tour he had won $3,103,903 – second only to Nicklaus
*In his bid for a hat trick of British Open wins Watson was beaten by 2 strokes in the 1984 championship by Severiano Ballesteros

Tom Watson, five times British Open champion, and runner-up to Severiano Ballesteros at St Andrews in 1984

Johnny Weissmuller

The first and most famous of the screen Tarzan's, Johnny Weissmuller won five Olympic gold medals in freestyle swimming events and set twenty-four world swimming records before leaving for Hollywood. When he died in 1984, the Tarzan jungle call was echoed as part of the funeral.

Johnny Weissmuller was born near Vienna and moved to the Appalachian coalfield when he was just four. His father, a miner, contracted tuberculosis after the family had moved to Chicago, and died, unaware of his son's prowess, whilst Johnny was still a schoolboy.

On 9 July 1922, when only eighteen years old, Weissmuller created swimming history by becoming the first to swim the 100-metre freestyle in under one minute. Two years later he lowered his time to 57.4 seconds – a record that would last for ten years.

The 1924 Paris Olympics were the first international platform for Weissmuller's talent. Favourite for the 100-metre freestyle, his confidence received an enormous boost when he won the gold medal in the 400-metre freestyle from the world record holder, Arne Borg of Sweden. Arne and his twin brother Ake were on either side of Weissmuller. The same curious family arrangement applied to the 100-metre freestyle. Weissmuller was flanked by the 1912 and 1920 champion, Duke Kahanamouku, then aged thirty-four and soon to pursue a lucrative career as the statutory Hawaiian king in films, and Duke's brother Sam. Before the start, Duke hoped that, whoever won, the American flag would fly for all three medal places. Weissmuller won by 1.4 second from Duke, who beat Sam by a touch. Duke went on to earn another fortune patenting surfboards.

The same day, Weissmuller led the US team to the gold, swimming the final leg of the 4 × 200-metre freestyle. That night he collected the bronze medal as part of the water polo team.

Paris warms to showmen. Weissmuller performed not only as a distance swimmer, sprinter and water-polo player for medals, but provided a comedy diving act as a bonus for the crowd. It was rumoured that several Parisians came just for the act.

Four years later, at the Amsterdam Olympics, Weissmuller's world record for the 100-metre freestyle still hadn't been seriously threatened. The defence of his title was a formality, though he recalled that he'd almost choked with water at the turn. Weissmuller completed his Olympic career with his fifth gold medal in the 4 × 200-metre relay.

He was set on a third Olympic Games to round off his career. The 1932 Games were to be held in Los Angeles, and he would be 'only' twenty-eight – swimmers in those days were more mature. However, two years before the Games, Weissmuller received a $2000 per month offer to advertise and model underwear and swimwear for the BVD company. The film moguls in Hollywood spotted the photo, and Weissmuller was asked to apply for the part of Tarzan. In 1932, Olympic year, Weissmuller made his screen debut in *Tarzan and the Ape Man*. He appeared in twelve Tarzan movies over the next sixteen years. The Olympic title went to a fifteen-year-old Japanese schoolboy who brought his schoolbooks with him and recorded a time still eight-tenths of a second behind Tarzan's best.

David Wallenchinsky's *Complete Book of the Olympics* records Weissmuller's world-wide popularity. He was taking part in a celebrity golf tournament in 1959 in Cuba at the time when Castro's rebels were involved in frequent skirmishes with those loyal to the Batista government. Weissmuller was on his way to the course when he and his friends were surrounded by a bunch of Castro's supporters. Guns were pointed in all the wrong directions. Weissmuller, rising to his full height, beat his chest with his fists. After a moment's stunned silence, the revolutionaries realized who they were pointing their guns at. Down went the rifles, out came the autograph books, and Weissmuller and his friends proceeded to the course, courtesy of a rebel escort.

Weissmuller enjoyed the taste of wedding cake – he married five times. In 1950 he was voted the greatest swimmer of the first half of the twentieth century by 250 sports writers. He died in early 1984 at the age of eighty.

On retirement, Tarzan offered the following: 'I swim, I play golf. I have my business interests. I have seventy-five health food stores. I do nothing. I don't exert myself any more. I'm not interested in politics, but President Nixon is a good friend of mine. I used to play golf with him, but I haven't seen him for a little while. I lost touch with him when he went to Washington. I guess he doesn't have time for fun any more. I do.'

FACTFILE

Born 2 June 1904, nr Vienna, Austria
Died January 1984

Olympic Games
Gold: 100-metre freestyle (1924, 1928)
     400-metre freestyle (1924)
     4 × 200-metre freestyle relay (1924, 1928)
Bronze: Water polo US national team (1928)

Total world records 24
First record
    300-yard (and 300-metre) freestyle 3:16.6 (3:35.2)
     (25 March 1922)
Last record
    440-yard freestyle 4:52.0 (25 August 1927)

*Weissmuller was one of four Olympic medallists to play the role of Tarzan. The others were Buster Crabbe (bronze, 1928, 1500-metre freestyle), Herman Brix (silver, 1928, shot), Glen Morris (gold, 1936, decathlon)

Future Hollywood stars. Johnny Weissmuller (right) and Duke Kahomatu shaking hands before the start of the 100-metre freestyle at the 1924 Paris Olympic Games

Jimmy Wilde

Most sportsmen assume nicknames. Jimmy Wilde had three – the Mighty Atom, the Tylorstown Terror, and the Ghost with a Hammer in his Hands. All three were a mark of respect and endearment.

Jimmy Wilde was born in Quakers Yard, near Tylorstown, just a couple of miles from the Rhondda, the most famous of all Welsh industrial valleys. He was the first, and best, of a cluster of world champions from the area.

Boxing and the fight against poverty are synonymous with the Rhondda, and Wilde, no bigger than Olga Korbut, was, from schooldays, fighting for his life. He learned his trade in the fairground booths.

Many world champions these days have thirty or forty fights in a career. Some, like Leon Spinks and Davey Moore, become world champions before their career has totalled ten fights. Yet Wilde fought eighty-three times in four years – and probably as many again unrecorded – before being able to fight for even a British title.

For such a slight man, Wilde built a reputation as a fearsome hitter with both hands; he had a particularly destructive left hook. He was a freak, with long arms, and fought like an enraged octopus. He was capable of a clean knockout, but his victims were mainly the results of perfect timing and correct leverage in his punching. Never weighing much more than 7 st 10 lb, he often had to fight challengers up to 9 st.

Before his first British title fight, the previous two opponents had both been claimants to the world title – Sid Smith, who lost to Wilde in nine rounds, and Joe Symonds, who lasted the full distance. Certainly he fought no-hopers – one of his opponents was one Matt Wells 'Nipper' – but how many boxers have to beat two world champions before fighting for a domestic title?

Early in 1915, climbing off his sick bed with a grotesque swelling on his ear, Wilde challenged Tancy Lee for his British and European title. Wilde's corner (not Wilde) threw in the towel in the seventeenth round.

It was a year before Wilde could challenge again. Lee had lost his title to Symonds in sixteen rounds at the end of 1915, and then Symonds immediately lost to Wilde on St Valentine's Day, 1916. In April of that year Wilde became a claimant to the world title when he beat Jonny Rosner, defended all three titles successfully against Lee, whom he stopped in eleven rounds, and on 18 December 1916 became undisputed world champion when he beat Young Zulu Kid of the United States at the Central Hall, Holborn, with an eleventh-round count-out.

After beating George Clarke at the National Sporting Club for the British, Empire and World titles early in 1917, Wilde had established such a mastery over the rest of the world's flyweights that not even the Americans bothered to challenge him. After winning a twenty-round fight with Pal Moore in July 1919, Wilde packed his bags and went to the States. It was Moore who had handed Wilde his second defeat, albeit over three rounds, in an Imperial Services tournament at the Albert Hall. Wilde was a company sergeant major at the time.

Wilde had eleven fights in the United States, one in 1919 and the remainder in 1920. He was unbeaten, again bowling over men up to 2 st heavier than himself. His world title was never seriously threatened, certainly never challenged.

A new house in Cardiff beckoned, and Wilde, sick of waiting for a fight against the world bantamweight champion, Pete Herman, for which he was offered a then staggering £8000, returned to Wales. When, at last, Herman agreed to come to London – the cash was inviting – the build-up was reduced to a Keystone Cops farce.

For a start, Herman arrived in London minus his title – mysteriously outpointed by a certain Joe Lynch. It meant that another title would not stay in Britain if Wilde won. Jimmy at first refused to fight, but, after requests from the highest ranks (i.e. royalty), he agreed to meet Herman. Then there was another catch – Wilde thought that the weigh-in would be at ringside just before the fight, but was informed that the weigh-in would be in the afternoon. Herman scaled 8 st 6 lb, went away for a 'bulking-up'

FACTFILE

Born 15 May 1892, Quakers Yard, Tylorstown, Rhondda, Wales
Died 10 March 1969, Whitchurch, Cardiff, Wales

First professional fight 1911, *v.* Lewis Williams (won ko 3)
Total professional fights 140
   Wins 126
   Kos 77
   Defeats 4
Last professional fight 18 June 1923, *v.* Pancho Villa (lost ko 7)

World flyweight title fights

14 February 1916	Joe Symonds	w	rtd	12
24 April 1916	Johnny Rosner	w	rtd	11
26 June 1916	Tancy Lee	w	rsf	11
31 July 1916	Johnny Hughes	w	ko	10
18 December 1916	Young Zulu Kid	w	ko	11
12 March 1917	George Clark	w	rtd	4
30 May 1924	Pancho Villa	l	ko	7

Other defeats

25 January 1915	Tancy Lee	ko	17
12 December 1918	Pal Moore	pts	3
13 January 1921	Pete Herman	ko	17
18 June 1923	Pancho Villa	ko	7

Elected to Hall of Fame 1959

Jimmy Wilde (left) looks for an opening for a left hook in his contest against Pal Moore in 1919. Wilde won on points over twenty rounds

meal, and was considerably heavier than that when he climbed into the ring. Wilde weighed 7 st 1 lb. Herman won the fight at the Albert Hall in seventeen rounds, and Wilde, still on his feet, was rescued by referee Jack Smith with the words, 'I'm sorry, I have to pick you up, because you don't know how to lie down.' Five months later Herman easily beat Lynch, who had not defended his title, and Jimmy Wilde had seen enough. He retired.

Two years later, Wilde came back. At last someone had been found to challenge for his world title – the Filipino Pancho Villa, who was based in New York. Wilde had not fought since the Herman fight. He travelled to New York and lost in seven rounds. He had fought 140 times, lost just four, numbers 88, 117, 139 and 140. Wilde retired to write columns for the *News of the World*.

Reg Gutteridge, the excellent British boxing writer, describes his last meeting with Jimmy Wilde in his book *The Big Punchers*.* It was in February 1969, at the Tegfen Ward, Whitchurch Hospital, where Wilde had been a patient for four years. a broken man, unaware that his wife had died two years earlier.

His blue eyes glowed and he smiled at everyone. The nurses adored him. His body still had the sheen of a newborn baby. I sat and wondered how many times those knuckles had crashed into a rival's face. How much they had earned. He could not converse.

Jimmy had looked after his money, but his health had deteriorated after being beaten up by teenage thugs on a lonely Welsh railway station. (PS. If the culprits are ever found – take it for granted – retribution will occur long before the case ever gets to court.) He had never really recovered from a serious car crash near Cardiff.

He died, aged seventy-six, on 10 March 1969.

It was an honour to have known him.

*Stanley Paul, 1983.

Fred Winter

Fred Winter is the only person to have not only ridden, but later trained, the winners of all the major National Hunt races. Yet he started in racing wanting to be a flat-race jockey, idolizing Richards and Donoghue.

Fred was first apprenticed to his father, Fred Sr, and Mr Jellis as a flat-race jockey. At the age of thirteen and weighing 5 st 12 lb, he had his first ride in public on 15 May 1939 and rode his first winner at a wartime meeting at Salisbury shortly afterwards. However, during the war, Fred put on weight and, in 1947, switched to National Hunt. His first winner was for his father on a horse called Carton at Kempton Park in December 1947. Soon he was to ride for Ryan Price, a combination that was to dominate racing for sixteen years.

Five years later he became champion jockey for the first time. In doing so, he rode 121 winners in the 1952–53 season to set a new record that was to last until Josh Gifford overtook it in 1966–67. He was the first jockey since Fred Rees in 1924 to ride over 100 National Hunt winners.

From triumph to disaster – the first fence in the very first race of the following season at Newton Abbot on Cent Francs proved the stumbling block. Winter broke his leg and missed the entire season. It took him time to recover nerve and confidence, but from 1955 to 1958 he was crowned champion jockey four times in succession. The elusive Grand National became his when he steered the big, clumsy Sundew to triumph in 1957. It was not an easy journey: Sundew took the lead at the end of the first circuit – Aintree is a lonely place for leaders.

In the later years of Fred's jockeyship, the consistent day-by-day accumulation of winners was replaced by successes in the big races. In 1959 Fair Time gave Fred his second Champion Hurdle (Clair Soleil in 1955 was the first) and two years later Eborneezer gave him his third.

Eborneezer's win in 1961 marked a fine Cheltenham Festival for Fred; two days later Saffron Tartan won the Gold Cup, the one major race to elude him. Top jockey Dave Dick said that Fred was the best he ever saw in that race. He retained the Gold Cup the following year with his favourite horse, the faithful Mandarin.

A month later Kilmore gave Winter a perfect ride and a perfect end to his serious riding career when he cantered home in the 1962 Grand National 10 lengths clear.

There was one further indication of Winter's superb technique and understanding as a jockey. He rode Mandarin to victory in the Grand Steeplechase de Paris at Auteuil. There was nothing particularly remarkable in that – the French National Hunt expertise lags behind that of the flat – but Fred had to steer the horse around the 4-mile circuit for the majority of the way without a bit. It had snapped at the fourth fence. Mandarin won by a head and, typically, a shattered Winter remarked, 'The horse gave me a great ride.'

In 1964 Fred retired from the saddle, a decision accelerated by a punctured lung the previous season, with the respect and the confidence that the racing public had reserved for Gordon Richards. Tim Fitzgeorge Parker wrote a book about the leading National Hunt jockeys, and listed their names as chapter headings. All except one: his chapter on Fred Winter was headed 'The Greatest of Them All'.

Training was not initially the prime thought when Fred, complete with CBE – the first National Hunt jockey to receive the award – hung up his breeches. He wanted to become an assistant starter, but it was felt that he was too close to the other jockeys and would not command enough respect. He turned to training. It was a silly decision, but National Hunt benefited.

Training at Uplands near Lambourn, in a profession in which his father and brother were so much admired. Fred began systematically to duplicate all he earlier triumphs as a jockey. He had the best possible start. In his first season. Jay Trump, with American amateur C. Smith on board, won the 1965 National and, the following year, Anglo, a 50 to 1 shot, won by 20 lengths.

Many of his horses became household names – Pendil, Bula and

FACTFILE

Born 20 September 1926, Andover, Hampshire, England

As a Jockey

Champion jockey 1952–53 (121 wins), 1955–56 (74 wins), 1956–57 (80 wins), 1957–58 (82 wins)

Grand National 1957 Sundew
1962 Kilmore
Cheltenham Gold Cup 1961 Saffron Tartan
1962 Mandarin
Champion Hurdle 1955 Clair Soleil
1959 Fare Time
1961 Eborneezer
King George VI Chase 1952 Halloween
1954 Halloween
1960 Saffron Tartan

As a trainer

Champion trainer 1970–71 (73 wins – £60,739), 1971–72 (71 wins – £62,396), 1972–73 (85 wins – £79,066), 1973–74 (89 wins – £101,782), 1974–75 (81 wins – £74,205), 1976–77 (75 wins – £85,202), 1977–78 (90 wins – £145,915)

Grand National 1965 Jay Trump
1966 Anglo
Cheltenham Gold Cup 1978 Midnight Court
Champion Hurdle 1971 Bula
1972 Bula
1974 Lanzarote
King George VI Chase 1972 Pendil
1973 Pendil

Fred Winter (right) on Kilmore clears another obstacle on his way to victory in the 1962 Grand National at Aintree

Lanzarote. Yet training horses is far more personal than riding them. They live in the yard near the house and you see them every day. And although Fred was turning out winners, there were times when he returned home, his face etched in disappointment. In the National of 1973 the hopelessly overladen Crisp, conceding 23 lb, was narrowly beaten by Red Rum, after dying in the last few yards – slowing to almost a rocking horse action. 1977 was a particularly sad year. Bula and Lanzarote, his favourites, were both put down after accidents. Racing missed them both.

National Hunt racing is a tough game. For Fred Winter the moment of truth came very early on in his career. In his fifth ride he dislocated his shoulder and in his seventh he broke his back. His army training as a parachutist seemed to have served no purpose at all. How one overcomes that sort of crisis is a matter of character. That is why so many recruits from the flat never rise to the top in National Hunt. And it is why those who do exhibit a brand of physical bravery and moral courage rarely found in any other walk of life.

Emil Zatopek

At the age of eighteen, Emil Zatopek knew nothing about athletics. Neither did he care. Born at Koprivnice, Czechoslovakia, on 19 September 1922, he was quite happy working in a shoe factory. But factories in Czechoslovakia during the war years had a habit of organizing mass sporting affairs. They forced Emil to run round the block. He finished second.

Four years later he had set Czech records at three distances up to and including 5000 metres. Bereft of natural ability, he had embarked on lengthy and strenuous training sessions.

The London Olympics of 1948 were the first internationally to witness the curious gait of the Czech champion. His country had undergone political turmoil. Nothing was known of their postwar athletes. When the Czechs claimed great feats for their man, the world laughed. Zatopek's style was flailing arms, head rolling and tongue out. His red vest was three sizes too large, his face a crimson mask, and the next step seemed to be his last.

In the 10,000 metres Zatopek set off at his own pace, ducked under 30 minutes and won the gold medal by a staggering 48 seconds. He had not had time to learn race tactics – he had run his first race over the distance just two months earlier.

With a lap to go in the 5000 metres final, Zatopek was hopelessly off the medals pace. But, with either a remarkable reserve of energy or, more likely, a dreadful lack of race judgement, he ploughed his way through the pack to the silver medal. Winner Gaston Rieff of Belgium finished two tenths of a second ahead at the finish and would have been caught if the race had been over 5001 metres.

A year later Zatopek set his first world record. Fittingly it was in Czechoslovakia, at Ostrava, where he became the first to take the 10,000-metre time under $29\frac{1}{2}$ minutes. Europe was the stronghold of world middle-distance running, but the margin that Zatopek had over his rivals was almost embarrassing.

In the 1950 European Championships those embarrassments were complete. Emil won the 10,000 metres by 69 seconds – he lapped the entire field. Slackening off in the 5000 metres, he won that by a mere 23 seconds.

Helsinki has a tradition for world-class distance runners; the Flying Finns had created an aura and a tradition. Finland was looking forward to their Olympics of 1952. Whether they were prepared for Zatopek is questionable.

Between 20 and 27 July 1952 he won gold medals in the 5000 metres, the 10,000 metres and the marathon – a unique treble; he began with victory in the 10,000 metres and a winning margin of 120 yards. A heat of the 5000 metres was routine. In the final four athletes went into the last bend with a gold medal chance – Zatopek, Mimoun of France, the German Schade and Britain's Chris Chataway. Chataway stumbled and fell on the curve; Zatopek, head down, ground his way down the home straight to win by 5 yards. He said that he had only entered to fill in time before the marathon.

Rumour had it that he had only entered the marathon to take his mind away from watching his wife in the javelin. Dana Zatopekova, born on the same day as Emil, was her country's champion. Emil set off into the lakes and forests of suburban Helsinki and arrived back in the stadium in a shade over 2 hours 23 minutes. He had beaten the rest of the field by over two and a half minutes. He then revealed that this was the first time he had ever run the marathon. An hour later Dana had won the gold medal, to make them the only married couple ever to win Olympic track and field golds at the same Olympics (others have performed the feat, but not at the same Games).

Between 1952 and 1955, Zatopek held all eight IAAF world records between 5000 and 30,000 metres. He broke the 29-minute barrier for the 10,000 metres in 1954 in Brussels. That year Emil and Dana repeated their gold medal feat of two years earlier in the European Championships. On the same day, Emil won the 10,000 metres and Dana won the javelin.

By now, however, injuries were beginning to plague his career. The awkward style was causing knee and ankle strains. Zatopek competed in his last Olympics in 1956, just two weeks after a hernia

FACTFILE

Born 19 September 1922, Koprivnice, Czechoslovakia

Olympic Games
Gold: 10,000 metres (1948, 1952)
    5000 metres (1952)
    Marathon (1952)
Silver: 5000 metres (1948)

European Championships
Gold: 5000 metres (1950)
    10,000 metres (1950, 1954)
Bronze: 5000 metres (1954)

World records
    5000 metres 13:57.2 (Paris, 30 May 1954)
    6 miles 28:08.4 (Stara Boleslav, 1 November 1953)
        27:59.2 (Brussels, 1 June 1954)

10,000 metres 29:28.2 (Ostrava, 11 June 1949)
        29:21.2 (Ostrava, 22 October 1949)
        29:02.6 (Turku, Finland, 4 August 1950)
        29:01.6 (Stara Boleslav, 1 November 1953)
        28:54.2 (Brussels, 1 June 1954)
10 miles 48:12.0 (Stara Boleslav, 29 September 1951)
One-hour run 12 miles 268 yards (Prague, 15 September 1951)
        12 miles 809 yards (Stara Boleslav, 29 September 1951)
20,000 metres 61:16.0 (Prague, 15 September 1951)
        59:51.8 (Stara Boleslav, 29 September 1951)
15 miles 76:26.4 (Stara Boleslav, 26 October 1952)
        74:01.0 (Celakovice, 29 October 1955)
25,000 metres 79:11.8 (Stara Boleslav, 26 October 1952)
        76:36.4 (Celakovice, 29 October 1955)
30,000 metres 95:23.8 (Stara Boleslav, 26 October 1952)

operation; he carried his wife on his shoulders whilst training. He finished sixth in the marathon, his first marathon since Helsinki.

He retired in 1957, winning his last race over 5000 metres on 28 October in his capital city of Prague. He had won 115 of 134 races over 5000 metres and had lost just eight of sixty-one races over 10,000 metres. In the longer distance, five of those eight defeats came in his final year; he was unbeaten over the distance from 1948 until 1954, when Olympic silver medallist Joszef Kovacs of Hungary beat him. With his retirement announced, he took pleasure in being best man at the wedding of Hal Connelly and Olga Fikotova, athletics' 'cold war' romance. He took great pride in Dana's achievement of breaking the world javelin record, albeit for just fifty-three days, in 1958.

Zatopek devoted himself to his country and his sport. When the Russians marched into Prague in 1968 to crush Dubček's liberal socialism, he was an obvious target. They stripped him of his colonel's rank, his position of coach, his job in the Ministry of Defence and his membership of the Communist party. They had taken his self-respect. He was an example.

In the mid-1970s reporters found him doing cleansing jobs in the streets. Sports officials threw an embarrassed cloak over his whereabouts. He was eventually given a clerk's job in the Bureau of Sports Information. He doesn't leave Czechoslovakia any more. But, as Dana said, 'Emil always spoke his mind.'

Dana Zatopekova

Born 19 September 1922, Tryskat, Czechoslovakia
Maiden name: Dana Ingrova

Olympic Games
Gold: Javelin (1952)
Silver: Javelin (1960)
Fourth: Javelin (1956)
Seventh: Javelin (1948)

European Championships
Gold: Javelin (1954, 1958)

Czechoslovakian national titles 13 (1946–60)
International appearances 41 (1946–64)
World record
    Javelin 182 ft 10 in (1 June 1958)

*Dana was the first female Czech athlete to win a gold medal in Olympic track and field events – in 1952
*In 1958, at the age of thirty-five, she became the oldest female European champion
*She held the world javelin record for only fifty-three days, but, in breaking it, she was, at the age of 35 years 255 days, the oldest woman to break a world record – and still is
*In 1960, at the age of 37 years 248 days, she became the oldest female Olympic athletics medallist
*She holds the record number of Czech national titles for a single event and has made a record number of international appearances for a Czech female athlete

Emil Zatopek, with the familiar grimace, leads Gordon Pirie and Ken Norris in the 1955 London v. Prague match at the White City